CHRIST AND THE JUST SOCIETY IN THE THOUGHT OF AUGUSTINE

Christ and the Just Society in the Thought of Augustine is a fresh study of Augustine's political thought and ethics in relation to his theology. The book examines fundamental issues in Augustine's theological and political ethics in relation to the question 'How did Augustine conceive the just society?' At the heart of the book's approach is the relationship that Augustine outlines in his *City of God* and other writings between Christ and those believers who acknowledge him to be the only source of the soul's virtue. The book demonstrates how Augustine sees Christ's grace and the scriptures contributing to the soul's growth in virtue, especially as these issues are framed by the Pelagian controversy. Finally, the implications which Augustine sees for Christ's mediation of virtue are examined in relation to his revision of the ancient concepts of heroism and the statesman.

ROBERT DODARO is Professor of Patristic Theology in the Patristic Institute, the Augustinianum, Rome.

CHRIST AND THE JUST SOCIETY IN THE THOUGHT OF AUGUSTINE

ROBERT DODARO

CAMBRIDGE
UNIVERSITY PRESS

PUBLISHED BY THE PRESS SYNDICATE OF THE UNIVERSITY OF CAMBRIDGE
The Pitt Building, Trumpington Street, Cambridge, United Kingdom

CAMBRIDGE UNIVERSITY PRESS
The Edinburgh Building, Cambridge, CB2 2RU, UK
40 West 20th Street, New York, NY 10011–4211, USA
477 Williamstown Road, Port Melbourne, VIC 3207, Australia
Ruiz de Alarcón 13, 28014 Madrid, Spain
Dock House, The Waterfront, Cape Town 8001, South Africa

http://www.cambridge.org

First published 2004

Printed in the United Kingdom at the University Press, Cambridge

Typeface Adobe Garamond 11/12.5 pt.   *System* LATEX 2$_\varepsilon$ [TB]

A catalogue record for this book is available from the British Library

Library of Congress Cataloguing in Publication data
Dodaro, Robert, 1955–
Christ and the just society in the thought of Augustine / Robert Dodaro.
p.   cm.
Includes bibliographical references and indexes.
ISBN 0 521 84162 3
1. Augustine, Saint, Bishop of Hippo.   2. Christian sociology – History – Early church, ca. 30–600.
3. Christianity and justice – History of doctrines – Early church, ca. 30–600.   I. Title.
BR65.A9D63   2004
261.7′092 – dc22   2004045826

ISBN 0 521 84162 3 hardback

Contents

Acknowledgements

I am deeply indebted to the Most Reverend and Right Honourable Rowan Williams, Archbishop of Canterbury, who many years ago as the Lady Margaret Professor of Divinity in the University of Oxford directed the doctoral dissertation which led me into the questions at the heart of this book. Rowan and his wife, Jane, welcomed me into their home during my years at Christ Church, Oxford, and from that time have offered me their counsel and friendship. Other friends and colleagues have helped to shape my work on this book, both in its earlier form as a dissertation and later at Rome. I am particularly grateful to Lewis Ayres for many forms of advice and assistance, as well as to Basil Studer, whose own penetrating work on Augustine has deeply influenced me from the time of my initial studies in Rome. Robert Markus took an early and encouraging interest in the core arguments of this book, which no expression of gratitude on my part can match. Conversations about Augustine and shared academic work with Eric Rebillard, George Lawless, Hubertus Drobner, Margaret Atkins, Wayne Hankey, Oliver O'Donovan, Robert Crouse, John Rist, Robert Wilken, Peter Garnsey, and Peter Kaufmann have broadened my thinking about the central questions of this book beyond where it would be without them. I am grateful as well for invitations to discuss aspects of my work at seminars and conferences organized over the last ten years by Elena Calvalcanti at the University of Rome III, Luigi Alici at the University of Perugia, Mark Vessey at the University of British Columbia, Eric Rebillard and Claire Sotinel at the Ecole française de Rome, Susanna Elm at the University of California at Berkeley, Peter Kaufmann at the University of North Carolina at Chapel Hill, Elizabeth Clark at Duke University, Wayne Hankey at the University of Dalhousie, John Rotelle and Thomas Martin at Villanova University, and Giovanni Catapano at the University of Padua. I also wish to thank the members of the Augustinian Order, in particular the members of the Chicago Province, whose prayer, work, and sacrifice supported my study over many years. Among Augustinian friends, John

Szura has offered invaluable encouragement and insight, which contributed greatly to this book. I am deeply indebted to my colleagues and confrères at the Patristic Institute, the Augustinianum, at Rome, who have sustained an academic environment supportive of research and writing. I am grateful as well to my editor, Katharina Brett, at Cambridge University Press, whose skill and enthusiasm brought this project to completion. I also wish to thank Eugenio Hasler for important technical assistance. Finally, I cannot adequately express my appreciation for Tom Mueller, who painstakingly worked over every page of my manuscript for clarity of expression.

I lovingly dedicate this book and all it represents to my parents, William and Margaret Dodaro.

Rome,
28 August 2004

Abbreviations

CCL	Corpus Christianorum, Series latina. Turnhout, 1959–
CPL	Clavis Patrum Latinorum, 3rd edn. ed. E. Dekkers. Turnhout, 1995.
CSEL	Corpus Scriptorum Ecclesiasticorum Latinorum. Vienna, 1866–
C. Th.	Codex Theodosianus. ed. T. Mommsen. Berlin, 1904–5.
D	Augustin d'Hippone, *Vingt-six sermons au peuple d'Afrique.* ed. F. Dolbeau. Paris, 1996.
MA	Miscellanea Agostiniana, vol. 1: Sancti Augustini Sermones post Maurinos Reperti. Rome, 1930.
PL	Patrologia Latina, ed. J.-P. Migne. Paris, 1844–64.
PLS	Patrologiae Latinae Supplementum. 3 vols. ed. A. Hamman. Paris, 1958–63.
SC	Sources chrétiennes. Paris, 1915–
SPM	Stromata Patristica et Medievalia. ed. C. Mohrmann and J. Quasten. Utrecht, 1950–

Introduction

In this book, I have tried to answer the question 'How did Augustine conceive the just society?', a question which I first addressed in my 1992 doctoral dissertation at the University of Oxford, 'Language and Justice in Augustine's *City of God*'. The question refers not to the communion of saints in the heavenly city, which is the ideal 'just society', but to the city of God in its earthly pilgrimage. I noted that there were sufficient scholarly studies available which treated various aspects of Augustine's social and political thought, as well as a good number of studies concerned with particular aspects of his *City of God*. Robert Markus's *Saeculum: History and Society in the Theology of St Augustine* (Cambridge, 1970, 1989) in many respects represents the best of both sets of studies. However, I thought that there was room and, indeed, need for a study which attempted to bring together various areas of Augustine's thought which are too often studied in isolation from each other. This is a defect that I find generally present in Augustinian studies, and in my view it hinders deeper understanding of his thought. It is clear to me, for example, that studies concerned with Augustine's political thought invariably pay little attention to his thinking about Christ and scriptural interpretation, and make almost no effort to ask what role these and other areas in his thought contribute to his political ethics. Anyone familiar with Augustine's thinking in general knows how alien it is to our modern, compartmentalized approach to issues in philosophy or theology. For example, Augustine cannot think about 'Christ' without simultaneously thinking about 'the church', and vice versa. Thus, for me, the question 'How did Augustine conceive the just society?' involves aspects of his thinking about Christ, human knowledge, the church, and scriptural hermeneutics, as well as political thought and ethics. Doubtless, even I have failed to take the considerable breadth of Augustine's thought sufficiently into account in attempting this synthesis. But I hope that what I have done will provide a map for others who will follow.

The question in Augustine's mind about the 'just society' specifically arises in conjunction with his objection to Cicero's claim in *De re publica* that Rome had ceased to be a commonwealth when it abandoned justice. In Chapter 1, I suggest that Augustine's initial retort to Cicero (in Book 2 of the *City of God*) that Rome had never been a *res publica*, because it always lacked true justice, provides him with a way into the question of the history and true nature of civic virtues, such as justice. In exploring the relationship between true justice and the commonweath, however, Augustine contrasts Cicero's ideal statesman in *De re publica* with Christ, the founder and ruler of the city of God. Augustine consciously alludes to Cicero's description of the ideal statesman, whose function is to promote justice within the community by his example of just conduct and his eloquence. It seemed reasonable to assume that Augustine would demonstrate the superiority of Christ's example and eloquence to those examples of Rome's 'best citizens' (*optimi uiri*) highlighed in *De re publica* and in other Roman literature. At the same time, it became clear that Augustine followed Cicero's lead in focusing the concept of the just society on the role of its leaders in establishing justice.

However, in Augustinian terms, the question concerning how virtue is learned also raises the issue of original sin and its twin consequences in the soul, ignorance and weakness. These become the central topics of Chapter 2, in which I examine the extent to which Augustine attributes the failure of Rome to achieve true justice to the failure of its people, misguided by their leaders, to overcome these permanent defects. In arguing this case, I bear in mind that Augustine wrote the *City of God* during the period of his dispute with the Pelagians over the necessity of grace for virtue. During the controversy, which begins c. AD 411, Augustine deepens his analysis of ignorance and weakness, and this analysis forms the base of his objections to Roman pagan virtues, as discussed in Books 1–10 of the *City of God*.

In view of the pervasive nature of original sin from Augustine's perspective, Christ is able to establish a just society only because, as the God-man, he alone is able to heal human beings of the ignorance and weakness which prevent them both from understanding the obligations of justice and from fulfilling them. In Chapter 3, I examine the connection in Augustine's thought between Christ's role in mediating virtue to the soul and his role in establishing the just society. Only by comparing this discussion of Christ in the *City of God*, in particular in Book 10, with what Augustine says about Christ in other writings does the centrality of his role in establishing a just social order become clear in Augustine's thought.

The question of the function of the scriptures in instructing believers to live justly becomes the focus of Chapters 4 and 5. Questions concerning the correct interpretation of the Bible's ethical teachings emerge as an issue in Augustine's correspondence with public officials, notably with Rufius Volusianus, the pagan proconsul of Africa c. AD 411/12. Volusianus had objected that the non-violence preached by Christ (for example in the Sermon on the Mount, Mt 5:39–41) diminishes Christianity's capacity to defend the Roman Empire. Volusianus had also objected to the variance in the ethical teachings between the Old and New Testaments. In responding to Volusianus, Augustine touches on a principle which he explains in greater detail in other writings, namely that the scriptures of both testaments represent a single, harmonious divine discourse. In Chapter 4 the implications of this principle for interpreting the ethical content of the scriptures are examined together with other principles employed by Augustine for interpreting the Bible. I argue in this chapter that in the *City of God*, Augustine parallels the scriptures as God's 'oratory' to the role that Cicero assigns to the statesman's oratory in promoting justice in the commonwealth. Christians who seek to know how to live justly discover in the scriptures divine teachings which reveal the nature of true virtue. However, Augustine insists, the true meaning of the scriptural word is often hidden from the surface of the text. In Chapter 4, I examine the reasons Augustine gives for the techniques which he believes God, as the author of the scriptures, uses in communicating the essential truths which they contain in a hidden fashion.

My discussion in Chapter 5 follows directly from this treatment of scriptural interpretation in Chapter 4, but it examines this question in the light of Augustine's explanation in *De trinitate* of the divine transformation of the knowledge about virtue which believers acquire from reading the scriptures. This is perhaps the most demanding chapter in the book, for it uncovers the relationship in Augustine's thought between human knowledge and divine wisdom, on the one hand, and the union of Christ's human and divine natures, on the other. In this chapter I also return to the Pelagian controversy as the backdrop for Augustine's renewed insistence that virtues have an intellectual content, that they first have to be understood in order to be practised, and that human beings are prevented by ignorance and weakness from understanding the deepest meanings of virtues. Chapter 5 should be read in close proximity to Chapter 3, because both chapters discuss from complementary viewpoints Augustine's insistence that Christ alone among human beings achieves perfect virtue and that all 'true virtue' in human beings depends upon his mediation of virtue to the soul.

Finally, in Chapter 6 I return to the contrast which Augustine draws in the *City of God* between Cicero's examples of Rome's 'best citizens' and those examples of Christ and the saints. I argue that Christ's unique status as a fully just human being means that he cannot serve as an example of repentance and dependence upon divine grace, which, Augustine concludes, believers require in order to live justly. The city of God on pilgrimage through the earthly city therefore requires as its 'heroes' saints such as King David and the apostles Peter and Paul, whose public acts of penance make them suitable models for members of the just commonwealth ruled by Christ. This society, in Augustine's view, is largely penitential while it is confined to the earthly city. Augustine concludes that its capacity to achieve true justice depends on the extent to which it follows the example of Christ and the saints in praying, 'Forgive us our sins as we forgive those who sin against us' (Mt 6:12).

JUSTICE

The reader of this book should bear in mind that Augustine's use of the term *iustitia* involves the conflation of three general meanings; the first comes from Greek and then Roman philosophy generally and regards justice as 'the habit of the soul or the virtue whereby one gives to each individual his due';[1] the second comes to Augustine from the New Testament and Latin patristic writers and equates the virtue with the love which is due to God and to one's neighbour;[2] the third sense follows logically from the second and is sometimes translated 'righteousness'. It describes the Pauline notion of *dikaiosune*, the condition of the soul whereby it stands in a 'right', because properly ordered, relationship with God, its Creator.

Augustine discusses the shift in usage between the first and second meanings of the term in Book 8 of *De trinitate*, in conjunction with Rom 13:8, 'owe no one anything except to love one another'. As he interprets this verse, the classical philosophical sense of justice as 'giving to each person his due' is translated into giving to God and to one's neighbour the love which is their due by virtue of the double commandment of love (Mt 22:40). Thus,

---

[1] See *ord.* 1.19, 2.22, *diu. qu.* 31.1, *lib. arb.* 1.27, *en. Ps.* 83.11, *ciu.* 19.4, 19.21. For the philosophical and juridical background of this usage, see, for example, Aristotle, *Nicomachean Ethics* 1129A, 1130A, *Rhetoric* 1366B9, Cicero, *De inuentione* 2.160, *De finibus* 5.65, *Digesta* 1.1 [Ulpian] = Justinian, *Institutiones* 1.1.

[2] See, for example, *diu. qu.* 61.4. This use of the term *iustitia* is found generally in Latin patristic writers such as Cyprian, *De opere et eleemoysinis*, Lactantius, *Institutiones diuinae* 5, *Epitome* 54–5, and Ambrose, *De officiis ministrorum* 1.20–3, 1.252, 1.130–6, 1.142, 1.188, 2.49, *Expositio Psalmi CXVIII* 35.7, *De Nabuthe historia* 47–8.

living justly (*iuste uiuere*) means loving one's neighbours in a way that aids them in living justly by enabling them to love themselves, their neighbours, and God in the manner prescribed by divine law and by the example of Christ. Justice is thus understood in conjunction with Augustine's concept of order, in particular with the 'order of love' (*ordo amoris*), which imparts a hierarchy of goods established by God as objects of love and desire.[3] Justice conceived according to this proper ordering of love harmonizes the volitional aspect of love with the created order of nature.[4] Viewed in this way, justice expresses a series of right relationships which escalate in value in proportion to the order willed by God. In this context, Augustine defines justice as 'love serving God alone and thus ruling well those things subject to human beings'.[5]

---

[3] See *diu. qu.* 36.1–3, *lib. arb.* 1.11–15, *c. Faust* 22.27, *cat. rud.* 14.1–2, *ep.* 140.4, *trin.* 9.14, *ciu.* 11.17, 15.22.

[4] See *conf.* 13.10, *s. Lambot* 2.13.

[5] See *mor.* 1.25. Platonic and Neoplatonic influences can be detected behind this link between justice and an ordered concept of the universe. See Plato, *Timaeus* 29E–30B, Plotinus, *Enneads* 3.2.13–14, Porphyry, *De abstinentia* 2.45, *Ad Marcellam* 21.

CHAPTER I

Eloquence and virtue in Cicero's statesman

What is a just society? How is it structured and how does it function? In approaching these questions, Augustine turns to Cicero's writings, principally to *De re publica*, both in his *City of God* and in his correspondence with public officials.[1] His references to Cicero's work and thought in these letters suggest two significant points of divergence between their respective conceptions of a just society: the nature and aim of civic virtues and the crucial role of the statesman in fostering them within society. In these discussions, Augustine uses Cicero's text as a foil to argue the moral superiority of his own, alternative concepts of virtue and political leadership. Attention to these themes helps to explain why Cicero's discussion of justice in *De re publica* is important to the *City of God*, and ultimately how that discussion relates to Augustine's concept of a just society.

When in June 408 a mob stormed the Catholic church at Calama, 65 km. south-west of Hippo Regius, looted it, and set it ablaze, killing a Christian

---

[1] There is but scant scholarly discussion of the philosophical influence of *De re publica* during the fifth century. However, see C. Becker, 'Cicero', *Reallexikon für Antike und Christentum*, vol. 3, ed. T. Klauser et al. (Stuttgart, 1957), 86–127, at 102–4. Noteworthy is Macrobius' *Commentarii in somnium Scipionis*, especially in terms of its discussion of political virtues and the value of their possession by statesmen (1.8.1–13). See W. H. Stahl, *Macrobius: Commentary on the Dream of Scipio* (New York, 1952), 14, 120–4. Following P. Labriolle, *La Réaction païenne. Etude sur la polémique antichrétienne du Ie au VIe siècle* (Paris, 1948), 355, scholars have also commented upon the extent to which Cicero's text can be detected behind Macrobius' *Saturnalia*. See, for example, H. Bloch, 'The Pagan Revival in the West at the End of the Fourth Century', *The Conflict between Paganism and Christianity in the Fourth Century*, ed. A. Momigliano (Oxford, 1963), 193–218, at 208–9: 'that the connection of the *Saturnalia* with *De re publica* is a deliberate one can be easily proved'. See also E. Heck, *Die Bezeugung von Ciceros Schrift De re publica* (Hildesheim/New York, 1966), 43–68, for citations of *De re publica* in Ammianus Marcellinus, *Res gestae* 15.5.23, 22.16.16, 30.4.7, Favonius Eulogius, *Disputatio super somnium Scipionis*, and Boethius, *De institutione musicae* 1.27. See Heck, *Die Bezeugung*, 105–53, for a listing of the citations in Ambrose, Augustine, and Jerome. However, A. Cameron, 'Paganism and Literature in Late Fourth Century Rome', *Christianisme et formes littéraires de l'antiquité tardive en occident* (Geneva, 1977), 1–30, at 25, suggests that by late antiquity only Christians read the *De re publica* for its content. Following Cameron, E. M. Atkins, 'Old Philosophy and New Power: Cicero in Fifth-Century North Africa', *Philosophy and Power in the Graeco-Roman World: Essays in Honour of Miriam Griffin*, ed. G. Clark and T. Rajak (Oxford, 2002), 251–69, argues that 'by the early fifth century, the *De Republica* has long ceased to be popular as a political text'.

in the process, Nectarius, a former public official, wrote to Augustine on behalf of the municipal council and pleaded for his intercession with imperial officials to show clemency toward those non-Christians who would inevitably be accused, interrogated, tried, and punished for participation in the violence.[2] In his response, Augustine observed that Nectarius had borrowed his praise of patriotism from Cicero's *De re publica*,[3] and briefly discussed the character of civic virtue as described in that text. In the second exchange of letters, Nectarius and Augustine debated further the respective strengths of Roman and Christian civic virtue, with *De re publica* as their common point of departure.[4]

Between the autumn of AD 411 and the spring of AD 412, just before beginning work on the *City of God*, Augustine corresponded with the proconsul of Africa at Carthage, Rufius Volusianus, and with a Catholic notary and tribune, Flavius Marcellinus, concerning the former's hesitations in converting to Christianity.[5] Marcellinus had reported that Volusianus, along with many others at Carthage, seemed convinced that the non-violence

---

[2] See *ep.* 90 (Nectarius to Augustine). Nectarius had been an imperial official; it is not known what rank or position he held. H. Huisman, *Augustinus Briefwisseling met Nectarius. Inleiding, tekst, vertalung, commentar* (Amsterdam, 1956), believes that he served outside Calama. C. Lepelley, *Les Cités de l'Afrique romaine au Bas-Empire*, vol. 1: *La Permanence d'une civilisation municipale*, vol. 2: *Notices d'histoire municipale* (Paris, 1979, 1981), 1:291, regards him as a member of the municipal council (*curia*) at Calama at the time of the civil disturbance, and maintains that he was a 'païen convaincu' (2:102). J. Martindale, *A Prosopography of the Later Roman Empire*, vol. 2: *A.D. 395–527* (Cambridge, 1980), 774, s. v. Nectarius 1, suggests that he may have been the 'defensor ciuitatis' for Calama and that he was a pagan. For further discussion, see *Prosopographie chrétienne du Bas-Empire. 1. Prosopographie de l'Afrique chrétienne (303–533)*, ed. A. Mandouze (Paris, 1982), 776–9, s. v. Nectarius. However, Atkins, 'Old Philosophy', holds that, though he may not have been baptized, he leans toward the Christian faith.

[3] See *ep.* 90 (Nectarius to Augustine). This is a commonplace theme in ancient literature, but see Cicero, *De re publica* 6.1, *De officiis* 1.57, *De partitione oratoriae* 25.8. Augustine certainly believed that Nectarius had *De re publica* in mind. See *ep.* 91.3 (CSEL 34/2.429): 'intuere paululum ipsos de re publica libros, unde illum affectum amantissimi ciuis ebibisti . . .'.

[4] See *ep.* 103–4. For analysis of these arguments, see R. Dodaro, 'Augustine's Secular City', *Augustine and his Critics*, ed. R. Dodaro and G. Lawless (London, 2000), 231–59. See also Atkins, 'Old Philosophy'. I also discuss these arguments below, pp. 9–10, 196–200.

[5] Augustine and Volusianus: *ep.* 132, 135, 137; Augustine and Marcellinus: *ep.* 136, 138. The entire correspondence was composed between September 411 and the end of February 412. For background to the correspondence, see the pertinent observations by M. Moreau, 'Le Dossier Marcellinus dans la correspondance d'Augustin', *Recherches augustiniennes* 9 (1973), 5–181, P. Martain, 'Une conversion au Ve s.: Volusien', *Revue augustinienne* 10 (1907), 145–72, A. Chastagnol, 'Le Sénateur Volusien et la conversion d'une famille de l'aristocratie romaine au Bas-Empire', *Revue des études anciennes* 58 (1956), 241–53, Mandouze (ed.), *Prosopographie*, 671–88, s. v. Marcellinus, E. Rebillard, 'Augustin et le rituel épistolaire de l'élite sociale et culturelle de son temps', *L'Evêque dans la cité du IVe au Ve siècle. Image et autorité*, ed. E. Rebillard and C. Sotinel (Rome, 1998), 127–52, and N. McLynn, 'Augustine's Roman Empire', *History, Apocalypse and the Secular Imagination: New Essays on Augustine's City of God*, ed. M. Vessey et al. (Bowling Green, 1999) = *Augustinian Studies* 30:2 (1999), 29–44, at 40–4. J. van Oort, *Jerusalem and Babylon: A Study into Augustine's City of God and the Sources of his Doctrine*

preached by Christ diminishes the capacity of the Christian religion to support the just defence of the Empire,[6] an urgent matter at a time when its security was threatened by migrating tribes of Goths and Vandals.[7] Marcellinus stressed that Volusianus, though careful not to say this openly, was ultimately distressed over the harm to the Empire caused by Christian emperors.[8] Once again, Augustine is conscious that he was addressing men who had received a liberal education,[9] and he frames his response in terms of Cicero's discussion of political themes in *De re publica*. If Christian ethical precepts as outlined in the scriptures were adhered to, he argues, the commonwealth (*res publica*)[10] would fare better than it had under Romulus, Numa, Brutus, and other outstanding Roman statesmen (*uiri praeclari*).[11] Augustine decried the harmful effects of multiple, idolatrous cults on the peace of the city, for only Christianity provides a concept of God which exhibits the fullness of virtue that human beings require as a standard. The advent of true religion, culminating in Christ, alone produced true civic virtue. Volusianus can look to history for proof that the decline of Rome's fortunes was caused by the decline of virtue in its leading citizens, a moral failing which is an inevitable byproduct of traditional, Roman polytheistic

of the Two Cities (Leiden, 1991), 62 n. 273, argues that Augustine began work on the *City of God* in AD 412, and that Books 1–3 were completed by the end of AD 413. Letter 138 was therefore composed close to the time that Augustine was also treating Cicero's *De re publica* at *ciu.* 2.21.

[6] See *ep.* 136.2 (Marcellinus to Augustine) (CSEL 44.95): 'tum deinde quod eius praedicatio atque doctrina, reipublicae moribus nulla ex parte conueniat; utpote, sicut a multis dicitur . . . quae omnia reipublicae moribus asserit esse contraria', citing Rom 12:17, 1 Thes 5:15, Mt 5:39–41. See my discussion of this question below, pp. 135–9.

[7] A thorough, readable account is offered by P. Heather, *Goths and Romans 332–489* (Oxford, 1991).

[8] See *ep.* 136.2: Marcellinus to Augustine (CSEL 44.95): 'haec ergo omnia ipsi posse iungi aestimat quaestioni in tantum, ut per christianos principes christianam religionem maxima ex parte seruantes tanta, etiam si ipse de hac parte taceat, rei publicae mala euenisse manifestum sit'.

[9] See *ep.* 138.9 (CSEL 44.134): '. . . cum uiris liberaliter institutis'.

[10] I translate *res publica* freely as 'commonwealth', a term which, for moderns, unfortunately suggests 'state'. M. Schofield, 'Cicero's Definition of *res publica*', *Cicero the Philosopher*, ed. J. G. F. Powell (Oxford, 1995), 63–83, at 66–9, argues persuasively that despite the expression's 'notoriously elastic range of uses' in Latin authors before and after Cicero, it will not bear that connotation. Nor should it be translated 'republic' because in Cicero's thought it does not necessarily refer to a republican form of government. Schofield suggests as possibilities, depending upon the context, 'public [-spirited] activity', 'public affairs/business', 'the public interest', and 'the country'. See also R. Stark, 'Ciceros Staatsdefinition', *Das Staatsdenken der Römer*, ed. R. Klein (Darmstadt, 1980), and N. Rudd, *Cicero: The Republic and The Laws* (Oxford, 1998), xxxv. With C. N. Cochrane, *Christianity and Classical Culture. A Study of Thought and Action from Augustus to Augustine*, rev. edn (London, 1944), 46, we should keep in mind that 'the term *res publica* could hardly be used without an implied reference to its counterpart, the *res priuata*'. Augustine marks the distinction at *ep.* 140.63. He uses the term *res publica* even when speaking about the Roman Empire contemporary with his times. See, for example, *ep.* 138.10 (CSEL 44.135), where he complains that the Christian religion is often criticized as 'inimica reipublicae'.

[11] See *ep.* 138.10.

religion.[12] This argument, constructed against the backdrop of Cicero's discussion in *De re publica* of the best citizens (*uiri optimi, optimates*), parallels that found in Augustine's earlier letters to Nectarius.[13]

Circa AD 413, as part of an exchange of letters with the imperial vicar of Africa, Macedonius, concerning the bishop's role in seeking clemency on behalf of condemned criminals, Augustine sent the vicar a copy of the first three books of the *City of God.*[14] Following Macedonius' reply, Augustine wrote to him again and discussed the vicar's strongly positive reaction to the work.[15] Although the only direct reference to *De re publica* in this letter concerns Cicero's definition of the commonwealth,[16] Augustine's discussion focuses once again on the nature of civic virtue, its sources and aims.[17] Christ has shown in his death and resurrection the future happiness for which we ought to strive, and his grace alone, not our effort, assures us of attaining it.[18] Human reason, because of the power of sin, is not capable alone of attaining the wisdom and other virtues necessary for living happily, either in this life or in the life to come. Virtue cannot be possessed unless it is received as grace from God.[19] The reader already sees in this letter hints of Augustine's future debates with Pelagius and his associates over the role of Christ's grace in perfecting virtue.[20]

It is, therefore, a history of civic virtue and a philosophical discussion of its true nature that form the foundation of Augustine's arguments to public officials such as Nectarius, Volusianus, Marcellinus, and Macedonius.[21]

---

[12] See *ep.* 138.16–18. Augustine discusses polytheism in relation to civic virtue at *ciu.* 3.12–14, 3.18, 4.8, 4.10–11, and 4.13–14. See my discussion below, pp. 48–53.

[13] Note the comparison of Roman and Christian virtues, their sources and effects, that is common to Augustine's correspondence with Marcellinus (*ep.* 138.16–17) and Nectarius (*ep.* 91.2–4, *ep.* 104.6, 11–12, 15–16). For an interpretation of the latter passages, see Dodaro, 'Secular City', 243–8. See also Augustine's discussion at *ciu.* 2.21 of Cicero's perspectives (*De re publica* 5.1) on the decline in the morals of Rome's best citizens.

[14] See *ep.* 153, a reply to a letter from Macedonius (*ep.* 152), which was an answer to the initial letter from Augustine, no longer extant.

[15] See *ep.* 155, written in response to Macedonius (*ep.* 154). See the texts and notes in E. M. Atkins and R. Dodaro, *Augustine: Political Writings* (Cambridge, 2001), 70–99, 267–71. The entire correspondence takes place between AD 413 and AD 414, the dates of Macedonius' tenure as vicar of Africa. See F. Morgenstern, *Die Briefpartner des Augustinus von Hippo. Prosopographische, sozial- und ideologiegeschichtliche Untersuchungen* (Bochum, 1993), 107–8.

[16] See *ep.* 155.9, citing Cicero, *De re publica* 1.25.39.

[17] Note the four virtues listed at *ep.* 155.10 (CSEL 44.440), which Augustine says Macedonius must exercise in the public sphere: good sense (*prudentia*), courage (*fortitudo*), moderation (*temperantia*), justice (*iustitia*).

[18] See *ep.* 155.4–5, 16.

[19] See *ep.* 155.6 (CSEL 44.437): 'quia nec uirtus nobis erit, nisi adsit ipse, quo iuuemur'.

[20] See, for example, *ep.* 155.13.

[21] Civic virtues are also known as 'political' or 'cardinal' virtues: prudence, fortitude, temperance, and justice. Their treatment is commonplace in ancient philosophical ethics. See, for example, Plato,

Augustine's decision to dedicate his *City of God* to Marcellinus, his ally in the conversion of Volusianus,[22] attests to the importance which the discussion of these matters receives in his *opus magnum et arduum*.[23] His correspondence with these officials also explains his choice of *De re publica* as the organizing framework for much of the *City of God*: by providing a widely esteemed account of civic virtue, one grounded in a conventionally accepted political vocabulary, along with a critical, historical perspective on Rome's failure to live up to its social ethical ideals,[24] Cicero's work offered a secure philosophical foundation for a debate between Christians and non-Christians over the sources and goals of rival Roman and Christian theories of civic virtue. Augustine's discussion of these virtues as exemplified by Rome's 'best citizens' enables him to construct an effective contrast between Roman statesmen and Christ, the 'founder and ruler of the city of God'.[25]

JUSTICE AND TRUE JUSTICE

De re publica first appears in Book 2 of the *City of God*, where Augustine takes up Cicero's argument that no commonwealth could exist without 'common agreement about what is right' (*consensus iuris*), and therefore without justice (*iustitia*).[26] Even Cicero had concluded that Rome had ceased to exist as

---

Republic 427E. See also *Stoicorum veterum fragmenta*, ed. H. von Arnim (Stuttgart, 1968), 1:49–50 (nn. 200–1), 3:63–72 (nn. 262–94), Cicero, *De inuentione* 2.159–67, *De officiis*, Book 1, Macrobius, *Commentarii in somnium Scipionis* 1.8.3. Scholarly discussion of these virtues constitutes a vast literature. Still useful as a guide is H. North, 'Canons and Hierarchies of the Cardinal Virtues in Greek and Latin Literature', *The Classical Tradition: Literary and Historical Studies in Honor of Harry Caplan*, ed. L. Wallach (Ithaca, 1966), 165–83.

[22] See *ciu.* 1, praef. See also *ciu.* 2.1. On the strategy behind Augustine's dedication, see McLynn, 'Augustine's', 41–2.

[23] See *ciu.* 1, praef.

[24] On Augustine's use in the correspondence with Nectarius of Cicero's historical perspective in *De re publica*, see G. P. O'Daly, 'Thinking through History: Augustine's Method in the *City of God* and its Ciceronian Dimension', *History, Apocalypse and the Secular Imagination: New Essays on Augustine's* City of God, ed. M. Vessey et al. (Bowling Green, 1999) = *Augustinian Studies* 30:2 (1999), 45–57.

[25] See *ciu.* 2.21, below, n. 28.

[26] See *ciu.* 2.21. In constructing his argument, Augustine draws from two different passages of *De re publica*: 1.25.39, where Cicero gives the definition of *res publica*, and 2.44.70, where he states that no *res publica* can exist without justice. See also *ciu.* 19.21, where Augustine repeats his argument. I discuss the fragmentary nature of the extant text of *De re publica* below, p. 21 n. 73. For studies of *De re publica* published in the twentieth century see P. Schmidt, 'Cicero *De re publica*: Die Forschung der letzten fünf Dezennien', *Aufstieg und Niedergang der römischen Welt*, vol. 1:4, ed. H. Temporini (Berlin, 1973), 262–333, W. Suerbaum, 'Studienbibliographie zu Ciceros De re publica: *Gymnasium* 85 (1978), 59–88, along with the studies cited by P. MacKendrick, *The Philosophical Books of Cicero* (London, 1989), 45–65, and J. E. G. Zetzel, *Cicero. De re publica: Selections* (Cambridge, 1995), 254–61.

a commonwealth, he claims.[27] With characteristic irony, Augustine insists that Cicero's definition of commonwealth, properly understood, means that Rome had never been a true commonwealth at all, since it had always lacked true justice, which exists alone in that city 'whose founder and ruler is Christ'.[28] Augustine's decision to abandon the question at this juncture and to return to it later in the work has always puzzled his readers.[29] He offers little explanation either for this abrupt departure or for the long hiatus before he returns to the argument toward the end of Book 19. There he repeats Cicero-Scipio's definition of commonwealth, this time adding the brief but crucial explanation that Rome was guilty of a double injustice: by promoting an idolatrous cult it both denied its people worship of the true God and denied God the undivided allegiance which every individual owes to him.[30]

Augustine's preoccupation with this argument should be understood in relation to his observation in Book 2 that it is Christ alone who founds and rules the just commonwealth.[31] Later, in Book 19, Augustine states that true justice implies the correct knowledge and worship of the true God.[32] If these two passages mark the boundaries of the argument that Rome was never a true *res publica*, they also help to explain why Augustine waited sixteen books before returning to the question. His argument for transforming Cicero's notion of right (*ius*) into true justice (*uera iustitia*) – a move that distinguishes their interpretations of *consensus iuris* and, thereby, disqualifies Rome as a commonwealth – becomes clear only in Book 19, by which point Augustine has contrasted Christ with Cicero's ideal statesman, as ruler of the city of God.

Augustine locates in Cicero's concept *consensus iuris* the basis for the Roman philosopher's affirmation that without true justice no commonwealth is possible.[33] Volkmar Hand suggests that Augustine also finds in the concept of *consensus iuris* reason for equating his own concept of true justice (*uera iustitia*) with Cicero's concept of justice (*iustitia*).[34] Hand supports

---

[27] See *ciu.* 2.21. Cf. Cicero, *De re publica* 5.1.

[28] See *ciu.* 2.21 (CCL 47.55): 'uera autem iustitia non est nisi in ea re publica, cuius conditor rectorque Christus est'. Augustine employs a similar expression for Christ in a letter to Macedonius. See *ep.* 155.1 (CSEL 44.430): 'diuinae illi caelestique rei publicae, cuius regnator est Christus'.

[29] See *ciu.* 2.21 (CCL 47.55): 'sed alias, si deus uoluerit, hoc uidebimus'.

[30] See *ciu.* 19.21.   [31] See *ciu.* 2.21 (above, n. 28).   [32] See *ciu.* 19.21.

[33] Compare *ciu.* 19.21 (CCL 48.688): 'quid autem dicat iuris consensum, disputando explicat, per hoc ostendens geri sine iustitia non posse rem publicam' with Cicero, *De re publica* 2.44.70: 'sed hoc verissimum esse, sine summa iustitia rem publicam geri nullo modo posse'. Augustine also argues this point at *ciu.* 2.21, drawing upon the discussion at *De re publica* 3 surrounding Philus' argument that every commonwealth involves the practice of some injustice (3.8.12–20.31).

[34] V. Hand, *Augustin und das klassisch-römische Selbstverständnis. Eine Untersuchung über die Begriffe gloria, virtus, iustitia und res publica in De civitate dei* (Hamburg, 1970), 43–5. Hand draws this

his interpretation by observing that Augustine's conclusion, 'where true justice (*iustitia uera*) does not exist, there can be no right (*ius*)',[35] follows logically from two propositions: (1) that nothing can be said to be done 'by right' or 'lawfully' (*iure*) which is not done 'justly' (*iuste*);[36] and (2) that right (*ius*) has its origin at the source of justice (*fons iustitiae*).[37] According to Hand, Augustine bolsters his argument by citing Cicero's opposition to Philus' contention that justice is defined by the 'interest of the stronger', and that no successful commonwealth can exist without some injustice.[38] Hand's conclusion of a continuity between Augustine's Christian concept of justice and Cicero's classical, Roman concept seems flawed, however, inasmuch as the precise meaning of *consensus iuris* in *De re publica* and the extent to which the expression can be identified in Cicero's text with justice is not easy to ascertain, given the condition in which *De re publica* survives today. Moreover, although Cicero rejects Philus' position and holds that justice is requisite for any true commonwealth, his argument does not assume, as Augustine's does, that *consensus iuris* is closely linked with justice (*iustitia*) in its ideal form.[39] Cicero intends that property and

conclusion from a comparison of *ciu.* 19.21 and Cicero, *De re publica* 2.44.70 (as above, n. 33). Cicero's concept of *iustitia* is grounded in the concept of *aequitas*, as expressed in the classical definition of the former: 'suum cuique reddere'/'suum cuique distribuere'. See, for example, Aristotle, *Nicomachean Ethics* 1129A–1130A, *Rhetoric* 1366B, Cicero, *De inuentione* 2.160, *De finibus bonorum et malorum* 5.65, Plotinus, *Enneads* 2.3.8, 3.2.13, 4.23.13. The classical concept of *iustitia* as *aequitas* was also fundamental to Roman law. See Justinian, *Institutiones* 1.1 = *Digesta* 1.1 (Ulpian). See also G. Donatuti, 'Iustus, iuste, iustitia nel linguaggio dei giuristi classici', *Annali della facoltà di giurisprudenza dell'Università di Perugia* 33 (1922), 377–436, A. Carcaterra, *Iustitia nelle fonti e nella storia del diritto romano* (Bari, 1949), A. Dihle, 'Gerechtigkeit', *Reallexikon für Antike und Christentum*, vol. 10, ed. T. Klauser et al. (Stuttgart, 1978), 233–360, at 280–9.

[35] Hand, *Augustin*, 43–4, referring to *ciu.* 19.21 (CCL 48.688): 'ubi ergo iustitia uera non est, nec ius potest esse'.

[36] See *ciu.* 19.21 (CCL 48.688): 'quod enim iure fit, profecto iuste fit; quod enim fit iniuste, nec iure fieri potest'.

[37] See *ciu.* 19.21 (CCL 48.688): 'non enim iura dicenda sunt uel putanda iniqua hominum constituta, cum illud etiam ipsi ius esse dicant, quod de iustitiae fonte manauerit'. 'Ipsi' refers here to the positions of Scipio, Laelius, and, therefore, of Cicero in *De re publica*. Hand cites Cicero, *De re publica* 3.22.33, 3.24.36, 5.5, *De officiis* 3.72, *De legibus* 1.16 on the relation between *ius* and *fons iustitiae*.

[38] See *ciu.* 19.21. See also Hand, *Augustin*, 44. For Philus' argument, see Cicero, *De re publica* 3.8.12–20.31. See also Plato, *Republic* 339A–341A, for a parallel argument by Thrasymachus. Cicero-Laelius' position is given at *De re publica* 3.22.33–29.41.

[39] F. Cancelli, '*Iuris consensu* nella definizione ciceroniana di *res publica*', *Rivista di cultura classica e medioevale* 14 (1972), 247–67, at 254, takes *iuris* as a subjective genitive in the key phrase and translates *consensus iuris* as an 'armonia o consonanza di diritti'. He thus argues against K. Büchner, *Ciceros Bestand und Wandel seiner geistigen Welt* (Heidelberg, 1964), 217–18, that *consensus iuris* has to do with establishing a harmony of rights and interests between citizens, and not with an idealized justice. In this connection, see also K. Büchner, 'Die beste Verfassung. Eine philologische Untersuchung zu den ersten drei Büchern von Ciceros Staat', *Studi italiani di filologia classica* 26 (1952), 37–140, especially at 98. H. Kohns, 'Consensus iuris – communio utilitatis (zu Cic. De re publica I 39)', *Gymnasium* 81

material goods be distributed in a manner that acknowledges individual rights (*iura*), but he also conserves a public sphere of activity (*res publica*) in the city. In this way, *consensus iuris* is held in tension with that other value which Cicero draws into his definition of a commonwealth, shared utility (*utilitas communis*).[40]

However, Hand oversteps other, more crucial, theological boundaries when he attempts to draw a parallel between Augustine's and Cicero's understandings of the relationship between right (*ius*) and God. To believe, with Hand, that the two ancient philosophers intend the same thing in claiming that 'all that is right (*Recht*) flows from the fount of justice (*fons iustitiae*), that is, from God himself' is not only to confuse right (*ius*) with justice (*iustitia*), but also to conflate the vastly different conceptions of God which Augustine and Cicero hold.[41] Although Cicero's Stoic concept of divinity can certainly be termed theological, it is far removed from Augustine's concept of the true God (*uerus deus*).[42]

In order to understand more clearly the differences between Augustine and Cicero where the concept of true justice is concerned, it is useful to turn to Lactantius' treatment of the same question. Giulia Piccaluga has recently examined the role which Lactantius' *Diuinae institutiones* plays in

---

(1974), 485–98, agrees with Büchner and with W. Suerbaum, *Vom antiken zum frühmittelalterlichen Staatsbegriff. Über Verwendung und Bedeutung von res publica, regnum, imperium und status von Cicero bis Jordanis* (Münster, 1961), 24–37, that *consensus iuris* depends upon a correlation between law and justice, but, like Cancelli, Kohns rejects the identification between *consensus iuris* and *iustitia* argued by Büchner and Suerbaum.

[40] See also Cicero, *Pro Sestio* 91 and *De finibus bonorum et malorum* 3.64. Kohns, 'Consensus', 495, suggests that Cicero makes a parallel point at *De officiis* 1.17. Support for Kohns's observation of parallels between Cicero's concepts *consensus iuris* and *communio utilitatis* as discussed in *De re publica* and *De officiis* is provided indirectly by A. A. Long, 'Cicero's Politics in *De officiis*', *Justice and Generosity: Studies in Hellenistic Social and Political Philosophy. Proceedings of the Sixth Symposium Hellenisticum*, ed. A. Laks and M. Schofield (Cambridge, 1995), 213–40, who draws out the implications for Cicero's theory of justice as found in *De officiis*, and concludes (240) that 'the *De officiis*, not the *De re publica*, is Cicero's Republic'. See also E. M. Atkins, '"Domina et regina virtutum": Justice and *Societas* in *De officiis*', *Phronesis* 35 (1990), 258–89. Zetzel, *Cicero*, 128–9, notes a 'deliberate ambiguity' behind Cicero's concept of *consensus iuris*. He rejects those interpretations that see within the concept some commonly held idea of justice or even of 'juridical equality', and suggests instead that it be understood as referring to 'an acceptance of shared laws'.

[41] See Hand, *Augustin*, 45, in conjunction with *ciu.* 19.21. A similar view to his is offered by M. Colish, *The Stoic Tradition from Antiquity to the Early Middle Ages*, vol. 1, *Stoicism in Classical Latin Literature*, vol. 2, *Stoicism in Christian Latin Thought through the Sixth Century* (Leiden, 1985), 1:93–101, who argues that *De re publica* 3.22.33 expresses 'for the first time in the Latin language the Stoic conception of a universal and eternal law of nature, identified with God and right reason and superimposed on the laws and institutions of Rome'.

[42] See, for example, *ciu.* 4.30, where Augustine scorns Cicero's involvement with false gods. At *ciu.* 19.22, immediately following *ciu.* 19.21, in which he discusses *fons iustitiae*, Augustine offers yet another refutation of the Roman concept of divinity. On Augustine's concept of *fons iustitiae*, see also *Io. eu. tr.* 5.1, *en. Ps.* 61.21, *pecc. mer.* 2.6, *spir. et litt.* 11, *gr. et lib. arb.* 45.

the transformation of *ius* into *uera iustitia*, by demonstrating his attention in Books 5 and 6 to the religious foundation upon which the juridical, political, philosophical, and social aspects of *ius* depended in Roman culture.[43] Among Latin Christian writers, it is Lactantius, not Augustine, who first denies that Romans ever knew true justice because they had failed to know and worship the true God. He charges that this ignorance led the Romans to torture and exterminate those (Christians) who knew and worshipped God, the source of justice.[44] Lactantius' argument thus depends upon a confrontation between *uera iustitia*, which comes from God, and the Roman philosophical and juridical conception of *ius* as the principle which defines the religious obligations of Rome to its deities, among whom are Faith and Justice.[45] His discussion of justice incorporates the Roman myth of the Golden Age during the reign of the god Saturn, a 'pre-cultural' time when Justice (*iustitia*) dwelt among the peoples of the earth, when all forms of selfishness and strife were absent and when Saturn alone was worshipped.[46] For reasons closely linked with his apologetic, Lactantius accepts mythical accounts of the subsequent flight of Justice into the heavens once Jupiter displaced Saturn, along with the consequent invention of a false justice (*ius*, *iustitia*), a principle guaranteeing the maintenance of proper relationships between human beings and the multiple deities which then ruled the universe.[47] According to this myth, which Lactantius reports,

[43] See G. Piccaluga, '*Ius e uera iustitia* (Lact. div. inst. VI 9, 7). Rielaborazione cristiana di un valore assoluto della religione romana arcaica', *L'etica cristiana nei secoli III e IV: Eredità e confronti. Atti del XXIV Incontro di studiosi dell'antichità cristiana, Roma, 4–6 maggio 1995* (Rome, 1996), 257–69.

[44] See Lactantius, *Diuinae institutiones* 5.1.6, 5.14.9–12, 6.12.1, cited by Piccaluga, '*Ius*', 259.

[45] Piccaluga, '*Ius*', 259–60, citing Lactantius, *Diuinae institutiones* 6.9.7 (CSEL 19.511): 'aliut est igitur ciuile ius, quod pro moribus ubique uariatur, aliut uera iustitia, quam uniformem ac simplicem proposuit omnibus deus'. Piccaluga cites Cicero, *De officiis* 3.29.104, who aligns *ius iurandum* (a sworn oath) with the cult of Fides. See G. Piccaluga, 'Fides nella religione romana di età imperiale', *Aufstieg und Niedergang der römischen Welt*, vol. 2.17.2, ed. W. Haase (Berlin, 1981), 703–35. See also J. Fears, 'The Cult of Virtues and Roman Imperial Ideology', *Aufstieg und Niedergang der römischen Welt*, vol. 2.17.2, ed. W. Haase (Berlin, 1981), 827–948. On Lactantius' concept of justice, see V. Loi, 'I valori etici e politici della romanità negli scritti di Lattanzio. Opposti atteggiamenti di polemica e di adesione', *Salesianum* 27 (1965), 65–133, V. Loi, 'Il concetto di "iustitia" e i fattori culturali dell'etica di Lattanzio', *Salesianum* 28 (1966), 583–625, E. Heck, 'Iustitia civilis – iustitia naturalis', *Lactance et son temps. Recherches actuelles. Actes du IVe colloque d'études historiques et patristiques, Chantilly, 21–23 septembre 1976*, ed. J. Fontaine and M. Perrin (Paris, 1978), 171–84, V. Buchheit, 'Die Definition der Gerechtigkeit bei Laktanz und seinen Vorgängern', *Vigiliae christianae* 33 (1979), 356–74, V. Loi, 'La funzione sociale della iustitia nella polemica anti-pagana di Lattanzio', *Letterature comparate. Problemi e metodo. Studi in onore di E. Paratore* (Bologna, 1981), 843–52.

[46] See L. Swift, 'Lactantius and the Golden Age', *American Journal of Philology* 89 (1968), 144–56, and V. Buchheit, 'Goldene Zeit und Paradies auf Erden (Lakt., inst. 5, 5–8)', *Würzburger Jahrbücher für die Altertumswissenschaft* 4 (1978), 161–85.

[47] Lactantius, *Diuinae institutiones* 5.5.2. At *Diuinae institutiones* 5.5.4–12, Lactantius cites, among others, the following passages from Latin poets who evoke the myth of the reign of Saturn: Germanicus,

this counterfeit justice imperfectly fills the void created by the departure of Justice from the earth. For Lactantius, it is this ersatz justice which is the object of philosophers' speculations; the poets, on the other hand, knew of a primordial, pure justice no longer available to human reason. During the reign of Saturn, all relationships between human beings, and between them and the one god, were in perfect accord with this 'true justice', without the need for codification or enforcement through juridical and political institutions. The advent of such institutions in human society thus paradoxically represents the rise of social *injustice*, symbolized by the invention of rights such as those of political masters (*ius dominorum*), who long for honours and the trappings of power, and who rule by the sword.[48] Lactantius is also aware, however, that the Romans look forward to a return of Justice to the world, to a return of the paradisiacal religious and social conditions which were enjoyed in the Golden Age. He seizes upon these religious aspirations and announces their fulfilment in Christian monotheism, accompanied by the advent of *uera iustitia*.[49]

In discussing Cicero's conception of justice as found in *De re publica*, Lactantius follows the line of reasoning which he had developed earlier when he opposed the idea that philosophers could ever understand the nature of true justice. They are thus incapable of demonstrating the proposition that it is a necessity for the commonwealth.[50] Justice has piety (*pietas*) as its source, Lactantius explains, and therefore cannot be known unless one knows God. He acknowledges that Plato wrote much about the one God, but nothing about true religion. 'Plato dreamed of God, but did not know God.' True knowledge of God and, hence, the proper understanding

---

Aratus 112, 113, 137, Vergil, *Georgics* 1.126–7, *Aeneid* 8.320, Ovid, *Metamorphoses* 1.111. See A. Goulon, 'Les Citations des poètes latines dans l'œuvre de Lactance', *Lactance et son temps. Recherches actuelles. Actes du IVe colloque d'études historiques et patristiques, Chantilly, 21–23 septembre 1976*, ed. J. Fontaine and M. Perrin (Paris, 1978), 107–56, V. Buchheit, 'Der Zeitbezug in der Weltalterlehre des Laktanz (Inst. 5, 5–6)', *Historia* 28 (1979), 472–86, V. Buchheit, 'Juppiter als Gewalttäter (Inst. 5, 6, 6)', *Rheinisches Museum* 125 (1982), 338–42.

48 See Lactantius, *Diuinae institutiones* 5.6.5 (CSEL 19.417): 'hinc honores sibi et purpuras et fasces inuenerunt, ut securium gladoriumque terrore subnixi quasi iure dominorum perculsis ac pauentibus imperarent', in the context of the entire chapter.

49 See Lactantius, *Diuinae institutiones* 5.15.1–2 (CSEL 19.447): 'Duobus igitur illis iustitiae fontibus immutatis omnis uirtus et omnis ueritas tollitur et ipsa iustitia remigrat in caelum. ideo non est uerum illut bonum a philosophis repertum, quia ignorabant uel unde oreretur uel quid efficeret: quod nullis aliis praeterquam nostro populo reuelatum est. dicet aliquis: nonne sunt aput uos alii pauperes, alii diuites, alii serui, alii domini? nonne aliquid inter singulos interest? nihil nec alia causa est cur nobis inuicem fratrum, nomen inpertiamus, nisi quia pares esse nos credimus'.

50 See Lactantius, *Diuinae institutiones* 5.14.5 (CSEL 19.444): 'eam disputationem, qua iustitia euertitur, aput Ciceronem Lucius Furius recordatur, credo quoniam de re publica disserebat, ut defensionem laudationemque eius induceret, sine qua putabat regi non posse rem publicam'. Lactantius has in mind Cicero, *De re publica* 2.44.70 (above, n. 33).

of justice requires the rejection of false deities. Socrates was imprisoned for having rejected them, and thus pointed to what would later befall Christians who defended true justice and served the one God.[51]

Lactantius' arguments about the relationship between 'true justice' and the knowledge of the true God anticipate Augustine's arguments in the *City of God*. Both sets of arguments also demonstrate the defect in Volkmar Hand's contention that a similarity in Augustine's and Cicero's conceptions of God is responsible for the convergence between their concepts of justice. Hand posits a continuity between Augustine and Cicero at the point at which their reasonings are most dissimilar. As the fount of justice, Augustine's God reveals justice within history through the person and work of Christ.[52] So crucial is Augustine's concern to establish the relationship between Christ and true justice that his ironic dismissal of Rome's claim ever to have been a commonwealth is only of secondary importance within the *City of God*. He is far more interested in demonstrating the interrelationship between the political and theological implications of true justice than with arguing the merits either of Cicero's definition of a commonwealth or of Rome's case for meeting that definition. Hence, his reason for waiting until Book 19 of the *City of God* to disprove Rome's claim becomes even clearer. In Books 2–19 he explores the foundation of true justice as the proper knowledge and love (worship) of the true God. To do this, he distinguishes between pagan cults and philosophical systems (Books 2–10) on the one hand and the Christian religion (Books 11–19) on the other, demonstrating the differing effects they have on the promotion of true justice and piety in the city. In this sense, his critique of pagan religion and philosophy resembles that of Lactantius both in structure and in purpose. When Augustine's delay of his argument against Rome's claim is considered from this point of view, it also becomes clearer why scholarly discussions over

---

[51] See Lactantius, *Diuinae institutiones* 5.14.9–14 (CSEL 19.445–6): 'iustitia quamuis omnes simul uirtutes amplectantur, tamen duae sunt omnium principales quae ab ea diuelli separarique non possunt, pietas et aequitas. [. . .] pietas autem est cognoscere deum . . . si ergo pietas est cognoscere deum, cuius cognitionis haec summa est ut colas, ignorat utique iustitiam qui religionem dei non tenet. [. . .] Plato quidem multa de uno deo locutus est . . . sed nihil de religione: somniauerat enim deum, non cognouerat. quodsi iustitiae defensionem uel ipse uel quilibet alius implere uoluisset, in primis deorum religiones euertere debuit, quia contrariae sunt pietati. quod quidem Socrates quia facere temptauit, in carcerem coniectus est, ut iam tunc appareret quid esset futurum iis hominibus qui iustitiam ueram defendere deoque singulari seruire coepissent'. On *iustitia* in conjunction with *pietas*, see Dihle, 'Gerechtigkeit', 271–2.

[52] The expression *fons iustitiae*, used in reference to Christ, serves Augustine as another logical and textual bridge connecting the reference to Christ as 'rector rei publicae' at *ciu.* 2.21 with his explanation for the establishment of true justice in the city of God at *ciu.* 19.21.

the possibility of his assigning a 'relative' instead of 'absolute' justice to any secular political realm have tended to eclipse his primary concerns at this juncture.[53] Augustine is less interested than his interpreters in discussing the respective merits of a Christian or secular state.[54]

This is not to deny Augustine's concern with justice in political society, but rather to assert an Augustinian conviction about the elusive, provisional character of judgments in the political sphere, given the imperfect nature of human reason and justice, a conception he shares with Plato and Cicero, though he defines justice differently on several occasions.[55] The importance of this definition for Augustine's wider argument concerning the nature and source of true virtue is clear at the opening of Book 19, Chapter 21 of the *City of God*, in his analysis of Cicero's ideas on *consensus iuris*. Augustine observes that, as a concept, 'common agreement about what is right' (*consensus iuris*) resists straightforward definition for Cicero, who is forced to explore its meaning by means of a dialogue. The movement from precise definition

---

[53] *Ciu.* 19.24 is the point of departure for those scholars who have shaped this discussion. G. Hardy, *Le* De civitate dei *source principale du Discours sur l'histoire universelle* (Paris, 1913), and J. Figgis, *The Political Aspects of St. Augustine's City of God* (London, 1921), remain fixed starting points among the most significant studies of the question during the twentieth century. They are followed by W. Kamlah, *Christentum und Geschichtlichkeit. Untersuchungen zur Entstehung des Christentums und zu Augustins Bürgerschaft Gottes*, 2nd rev. edn (Stuttgart, 1951), 327–8, H.-I. Marrou, 'La Théologie de l'histoire', *Augustinus Magister. Congrès international augustinien*, vol. 3 (Paris 1954), 193–204, H.-I. Marrou, 'Civitas dei, civitas terrena, num tertium quid?', *Studia Patristica. Papers presented to the Second International Conference in Patristic Studies held at Christ Church, Oxford*, vol. 2, ed. K. Aland and F. L. Cross (Berlin, 1957), 342–50, F. Cranz, '*De civitate dei* XV, 2 et l'idée augustinienne de la société chrétienne', *Revue des études augustiniennes* 3 (1957), 15–27 = '*De ciuitate dei* XV, 2, and Augustine's Idea of the Christian Society', *Speculum* 25 (1950), 215–25, reprinted in *Augustine: A Collection of Critical Essays*, ed. R. Markus (New York, 1972), 404–21, J. O'Meara, *Charter of Christendom: The Significance of the City of God* (New York, 1961), 101–10, Suerbaum, *Vom antiken*, 170–220, H. Deane, *The Political and Social Ideas of St. Augustine* (New York, 1963), 78–153, 290–1, R. Markus, *Saeculum: History and Society in the Theology of St Augustine*, 2nd edn (Cambridge, 1989), 166–78, G. Lettieri, *Il senso della storia in Agostino d'Ippona. Il* saeculum *e la gloria nel* De civitate dei (Rome, 1988), 197–204, J. Milbank, *Theology and Social Theory: Beyond Secular Reason* (Oxford, 1990), 380–438, van Oort, *Jerusalem*, 115–23, and M. Ruokanen, *Theology of Social Life in Augustine's* De ciuitate dei (Göttingen, 1993), 77–111. Lettieri, *Il senso*, van Oort, *Jerusalem*, and Ruokanen, *Theology* (at the respective pages cited) offer an updated account of the most significant studies which are not cited here.

[54] Deane, *Political*, 99, observes that Augustine never referred to 'relative justice' when speaking about human societies or institutions. See also Marrou, 'La Théologie', 202.

[55] This point is the subject of much of Chapters 4 and 5. In addition to *ciu.* 19.4, 19.21, *ord.* 1.19, 2.22, *diu. qu.* 2, 31.1, *lib. arb.* 1.27, where Augustine repeats the Aristotelian and Ciceronian definitions of justice as 'rendering to each his due', see his discussions of justice at *trin.* 8.9–10 and *en. Ps.* 83.11, where the classical definition is transformed by application of Rom 13:8: 'owe no one anything except to love one another'. For further discussion, see A. MacIntyre, *Whose Justice? Which Rationality?* (Notre Dame, 1988), 146–63. For other studies on Augustine's conception of justice, see below, p. 75 n. 12.

(*definire*) to dialogue (*disputare*) marks an abrupt shift between different modes of reaching right understanding.[56] He approves of Cicero's dialectical strategy, believing that the meaning of *consensus iuris* in the context of *res publica* cannot be pinned down by strict definition, but can only emerge from conversation. Augustine's contemporaries listen to a debate by then classical.[57]

Which passages of *De re publica* does Augustine have in mind? To judge from a number of direct references, he at least has in mind Philus' arguments in Book 3 against the idea that a commonwealth cannot survive without injustice and that justice is to be found in the 'interests of the stronger'.[58] Also, when Augustine explicitly links the concepts of true justice and commonwealth to Christ, 'founder and ruler of the commonwealth' (*conditor rectorque rei publicae*), he consciously alludes to Cicero's description of the ideal statesman, the *rector rei publicae*, whose function is to promote justice, and all civic virtues, within the community.[59] Augustine's close reading of Cicero's text leads him to stress how much justice in political society depends upon the influence exerted by the statesman in evoking a consensus. Consequently, those passages of *De re publica* which link the statesman with the promotion of justice will be of key interest to Augustine in describing the

[56] Augustine alerts his readers to the transition with the conjunction 'however' (*autem*). See *ciu.* 19.21 (CCL 48.687–8): 'breuiter enim rem publicam definit esse rem populi. quae definitio si uera est, numquam fuit Romana res publica, quia numquam fuit res populi, quam definitionem uoluit esse rei publicae. populum enim esse definiuit coetum multitudinis iuris consensu et utilitatis communione sociatum. quid autem dicat iuris consensum, disputando explicat'. I would place more distance between the act of defining (*definire*) a term and that of discussing, or even debating (*disputare*), its meaning than is suggested in most translations of this passage. Augustine adds that Cicero defined *res publica* briefly (*breuiter*). Compare T. Bögel, 'Definio', with I. Lackenbacher, 'Disputo', *Thesaurus linguae latinae*, vol. 5:1, ed. M. Leumann et al. (Leipzig, 1909–34), 342–50 and 1443–50, respectively.

[57] Cicero, *De re publica* 1.7.2: 'de re publica disputatio'.

[58] See *ciu.* 2.21, 19.21. See Cicero, *De re publica* 2.44.70 (Scipio), 3.8.12–20.31 (Philus defending the propositions that the republic requires injustice and that justice consists in the interest of the strongest) followed by Laelius (3.22.33–24.41), and Scipio (3.30.42–31.43) contra. F. Cancelli, 'La giustizia tra i popoli nell'opera e nel pensiero di Cicerone', *La giustizia tra i popoli nell'opera e nel pensiero di Cicerone. Convegno organizzato dall'Accademia Ciceroniana, Arpino, 11–12 ottobre 1991*, ed. F. Cancelli et al. (Rome, 1993), 25–51, at 25, rightly warns that *De re publica* 3 exists today for the most part in a fragmentary condition, and that its passages have been reconstructed from Christian writers who did not always intend to approve, but mainly to refute and criticize, the viewpoints expressed therein.

[59] See Cicero, *De re publica* 5.3.5: 'sic noster hic rector . . . summi iuris peritissimus, sine quo iustus esse nemo potest . . .' in the context of the surrounding passage. R. Heinze, 'Ciceros "Staat" als politische Tendenzschrift', *Hermes* 59 (1924), 73–4 = *Vom Geist des Römertums*, 3rd edn (Stuttgart, 1960), 142–3 (citing Cicero, *De oratore* 1.211), defends the view that *rector rei publicae* refers to an ideal type and that for this reason Cicero has no one particular in mind. Heinze refutes earlier scholarly views which saw in *De re publica* a plea from Cicero that Pompey become dictator. P. Krarup, *Rector rei publicae. Bidrag til fortokningen af Ciceros De re publica* (Copenhagen, 1956), 132–3, 200, supports Heinze. See Zetzel, *Cicero*, 27 n. 56.

relationship between the *rector ciuitatis dei* and the meaning of the justice that he establishes in that city. For Augustine, as for Cicero before him, this task requires that the statesman assimilate the virtues of the ideal orator.

CICERO'S STATESMAN: VIRTUE AND ELOQUENCE

Cicero understands political leadership as a successful blend of statecraft and eloquence, and maintains that the ability to communicate the principles of government requires not only practical experience (*usus*) but also an enthusiasm for learning and teaching such as that found among philosophers.[60] He therefore discourages an absolute separation between philosophers and statesmen; he cannot accept the Epicurean insistence that the sage (*uir sapiens*) ought to avoid involvement in political affairs (1.6.10–11).[61] In his view, statesmen are even more effective than philosophers in convincing members of a society to observe its laws (1.2.3). With this reference to the weaker persuasive power of philosophical discourse, Cicero turns to consider the Greek dispute between philosophy and rhetoric as part of his discussion of the ideal statesman in *De re publica*. He states that justice and its related virtue, piety (*pietas*), are found in society insofar as statesmen, not philosophers, are able to translate them into customs and laws (1.2.2). What emerges from *De re publica* is a portrait of the statesman as skilled at communicating ideas yet also capable of bridging the gap between erudition and its practical application to political life. Cicero's statesman, while versed in the liberal arts,[62] is a sage only in the sense that he is an ardent student of politics.[63] More important is his ability to clarify the law. He combines eloquence (*eloquentia*) and wise counsel (*consilium*) in the manner of Pericles, who pacifies the Athenians during a solar eclipse by

---

[60] See Cicero, *De re publica* 1.8.13: 'sed etiam studio discendi et docendi essemus'. Note the exchange in the following section (1.9.14) between Tubero and Scipio over the value of leisure (*otium*) for the sake of discussion.

[61] References given in parentheses within this chapter refer to Cicero's *De re publica*. K. Büchner, *M. Tullius Cicero. De re publica* (Heidelberg, 1984), 305, points out that the full breadth of meaning in *sapientia* for Cicero, following Roman usage, ranges widely from philosophical wisdom to outright cunning. See also U. Klima, *Untersuchungen zu dem Begriff sapientia. Von der republikanischen Zeit bis Tacitus* (Bonn, 1971), 14, 21, who refers to Cicero's use of the term in relation to 'Situationsklugheit' and 'praktische Lebensklugheit'. Klima (129) also observes that at *De officiis* 3.54–5, Cicero juxtaposes 'uir bonus' and 'uir utilis', thereby suggesting that *sapientia* possesses 'eine rein utilitaristische Auffassung'. See Cicero, *De re publica* 3.8.12, for Philus' description of *sapientia* over against *iustitia*. See also *De re publica* 3.9.16, 3.15.24: the Roman Empire was established by 'sapientia' and not by 'iustitia' understood as 'suum cuique tribuere'.

[62] See Cicero, *De oratore* 1.16.72.

[63] Note the plea at *De re publica* 1.6.11 for the sage to 'descendere ad rationes ciuitatis'.

telling them what he had learned of eclipses from Anaxagoras.[64] Cicero acknowledges Pericles as a teacher whose learning freed his people from irrational fears.[65]

Cicero argues that only the statesman who ponders the heavens and considers the meaning of eternity will attain the wisdom required to resist the lure of fortune or military glory, and says that true statesmen undertake such obligations solely out of a rational sense of duty.[66] Scipio's speech (1.17.26–9) represents Cicero's endorsement of the speculative, philosophical side of the statesman who through ascetic retirement and meditation achieves a contentment equalled only by the enjoyment he experiences in discussing new discoveries with the learned (1.17.28). This statesman prefers wisdom above all else, and avoids any matter that does not touch upon the eternal and the divine. Laelius' rebuttal to Scipio should not be seen as a refutation by Cicero so much as a limitation of the quest for wisdom (*sapientia*) to those disciplines useful for governing (1.20.33).[67] Laelius' observation that Aelius Paetus Catus' pursuit of wisdom does not lead him to seek the leisure (*otium liberale*) of the philosophers but to advance the legal affairs (*negotia*) of his clients in the courtroom (1.18.30) underscores the statesman's obligation to direct his philosophical speculation toward the practical concerns of oratory.[68] Hence, Laelius taunts Scipio, that 'eminent statesman', urging him to bring his discourse (*oratio*) down out of the clouds, and to 'speak about the commonwealth' (1.21.34). He recalls that the admittedly more valuable practical experience he received from the Romans was augmented by the opportunity to learn philosophy from the Greeks, and that both types of learning prepared him to speak competently on the matter (1.22.35). Cicero concludes this discussion by allowing Philus to synthesize Scipio's qualifications for the task: a gifted intellect, experience as a statesman, education, competence in political science, and eloquence (1.23.37).[69] Following Laelius' and Philus' description of his qualities as an ideal

---

[64] *De re publica* 1.16.25: 'Pericles ille, et auctoritate et eloquentia et consilio princeps ciuitatis suae.' See *De re publica* 1.34.51, where Cicero states that in the case of aristocracies, the salvation of the republic lies in the wise counsel of its rulers: 'certe in optimorum consiliis posita est ciuitatium salus'.

[65] *De re publica* 1.16.25: 'quod cum disputando rationibusque docuisset, populum liberauit metu'.

[66] *De re publica* 1.17.27; see also Plato, *Republic* 347B.

[67] This point is reinforced further on when Laelius remarks about the advantage to Scipio of having conversed with Panaetius and Polybius: 'duobus Graecis uel peritissimis rerum ciuilium' (1.21.34). I. Hadot, *Arts libéraux dans la pensée antique* (Paris, 1984), 52–7, concludes that the 'liberal arts' which Cicero recommends for the statesman do not coincide with the seven liberal arts as commonly designated during the Middle Ages, but concern only those disciplines required for 'un homme libre': Greek and Latin, history, philosophy (including dialectic), rhetoric, and Roman law.

[68] See also Ennius, *Annali* 10, Cicero, *De oratore* 1.45.198, *Libri tusculanarum disputationum* 1.18.

[69] See also *De re publica* 2.40.67, where Laelius refers to Scipio as 'prudens' and therefore an ideal statesman. Krarup, *Rector*, 125, 199, argues that *prudentia* is more crucial than *sapientia* to the statesman.

statesman, Scipio defines the commonwealth (1.25.39) in the specific context of *consensus iuris*.

Once Cicero relates the definition of commonwealth to agreement about what is right, the pivotal attributes of the ruler as wise and just become self-evident. In a monarchy, he explains, the sovereign should be 'just and wise' (1.27.43: *aequus et sapiens*): Cyrus was 'the justest and wisest of kings' (1.27.43), as were rulers such as Romulus in Rome's earliest history.[70] The justice of the ideal statesman is free from passions (*cupiditates*) and enjoys total moral transparency. The ruler must also obey the laws he imposes upon others (1.34.52). However, just and wise rulers in the strictest sense of these terms are rarely to be found, as they must have 'almost divine powers' (1.29.45). Cicero equates Ennius' 'best king' (*optimus rex*) with his own 'just king' (*rex iustus*), whom he in turn assimilates to the gods because of the king's effect on the nation, providing it with life, honour, and glory through his own justice.[71] By the time he reaches the conclusion of Book 1, Cicero has provided a careful characterization of the ideal statesman as a just and wise orator, a political leader whose dedication and skill in statecraft, combined with zeal for learning, are matched by force and eloquence in his speech. When these qualities are accompanied by moral integrity (*iustitia*), the statesman is able to elicit agreement where rights are concerned (*consensus iuris*), a political condition which provides a social cohesion rooted in order and results in security (*salus*) for the commonwealth.[72]

Much of the remaining five books of *De re publica* reinforce this argument.[73] Cicero-Scipio's eulogy of Cato at the outset of Book 2 repeats the

---

[70] *De re publica* 1.37.58: 'Iustissimus [Servius Tullius], et deinceps retro usque ad Romulum'. Krarup, *Rector*, 189, notes that Cicero's *rex iustissimus* in the form described here 'strongly resembles Cicero's *rector rei publicae*'.

[71] *De re publica* 1.41.64. But see Krarup, *Rector*, 136–7, where the description of the *rector* as *uir iustus* is found wanting among the synonyms which are listed for the term. While it is a fact that Cicero uses the term *iustus* infrequently in *De re publica*, he does seem to view the *rector* as *iustus* in passages such as 1.41.64. E. Lepore, *Il princeps ciceroniano e gli ideali politici della tarda repubblica* (Naples, 1954), 103 n. 229, notes the importance of *De re publica* 5.3.5 for this linkage. M. Fuhrmann, 'Cum dignitate otium. Politisches Programm und Staatstheorie bei Cicero', *Gymnasium* 67 (1960), 497–500, argues that the replacement of *dignitas* with *iustitia* as the principal quality of the statesman in *De re publica* reflects Cicero's concern over the political turmoil in Rome contemporary with the writing of the work (56–51 BC) and, in particular, his opposition to dictatorship.

[72] It follows that the failure of political leadership to maintain these standards leads to the dissolution of the commonwealth. See *De re publica* 1.26.42: 'nullis interiectis iniquitatibus aut cupiditatibus posse uidetur aliquo esse non incerto statu'. See also 1.28.44, 1.31.47 and, especially, 1.33.50: 'ceteras uero res publicas ne appellandas quidem putant iis nominibus, quibus illae sese appellari uelint. cur enim regem appellem Iouis optimi nomine hominem dominandi cupidum aut imperii singularis, populo oppresso dominantem, non tyrannum potius?'.

[73] *De re publica* was available in its complete form at least until the seventh century. See L. D. Reynolds (ed.), *Texts and Transmission: A Survey of the Latin Classics* (Oxford, 1983), 131–2. Today we possess only about one-quarter of the original text of the six books comprising *De re publica*. Books 1 and 2 are mostly complete, as is Book 6. Books 3–5 are largely fragmentary.

principal motifs of the portrait of the ideal statesman as a just and wise orator. Scipio reports having been enamoured of Cato's eloquence, praising his political and military experience, his passion both for learning and teaching, and the manner in which his life and words harmonized with one another. This final reference alludes to moral integrity, a principal feature of the Ciceronian *uir iustus* (2.1.1). Cicero's ideal statesman possesses sufficient self-knowledge and capacity for moral improvement to serve as a model and a standard by which others may measure their own progress in civic virtues.[74]

This same passage marks the beginning of Cicero's examination of the ideal statesman in an aesthetic-ethical mode. The statesman is drawn into himself (*se contemplare*), while calling on others to imitate him. Cicero depicts the intelligence and achievement of the statesman in visual terms, as the 'splendour of life and character', adding that it is this moral effect which enables the statesman metaphorically to serve as a mirror (*speculum*) to other citizens.[75] Cicero then describes the commonwealth in musical terms. The statesman is like a conductor who achieves a political harmony that resembles musical harmony. From various distinct orchestral or vocal sounds (*ex distinctis sonis*), he imposes, or better still, elicits a productive harmony (*concentus*).[76] Trained ears are able to detect deviation from this careful balance (2.42.69). A similar harmony and concord are produced in the political community when the different classes of people reach a consensus, an agreement which would be impossible without justice (2.42.69).[77] Agreement about what is right (*consensus iuris*) draws symmetry out of asymmetry, harmony out of cacophony, unity out of class rivalry.

Cicero thus introduces a connection between justice and decorum, by which elements of an artistic composition are judged appropriate or fitting (*congruere*) to the whole.[78] He describes statecraft more as an art than as a science. He thus compares the recovery of the decadent commonwealth

---

[74] *De re publica* 2.42.69: 'ut ad imitationem sui uocet alios, ut sese splendore animi et uitae suae sicut speculum praebeat ciuibus'. Krarup, *Rector*, 190, identifies the ideal citizen in this passage with Cicero's *rector rei publicae*.

[75] See *De re publica* 2.42.69 (as above, n. 74).

[76] *De re publica* 2.42.69: 'isque concentus ex dissimillimarum uocum moderatione concors tamen efficitur et congruens'. See Krarup, *Rector*, 123.

[77] Krarup, *Rector*, 191, suggests that Cicero had in mind the harmony that exists within the human soul.

[78] On decorum in classical rhetoric, see H. Lausberg, *Handbuch der literarischen Rhetorik. Eine Grundlegung der Literaturwissenschaft*, 2nd edn (Munich, 1973), 507–11 (§§ 1055–62), 516–19 (§§ 1074–7), H. DeWitt, 'Quo virtus: The Concept of Propriety in Ancient Literary Criticism', unpublished dissertation, Oxford University, 1987, I. Rutherford, 'Decorum I. Rhetorik', *Historisches Wörterbuch der Rhetorik*, vol. 2, ed. G. Veding et al. (Darmstadt, 1994), 423–34.

to the restoration of a beautiful painting, a process that requires an artist's knowledge of 'form' (*forma*).[79] Cicero's use of the Platonic terminology of form at this point underscores the importance of the artist's reliance upon intuition rather than upon strictly fixed rules concerning representation. 'Form' also allows Cicero to distinguish between a thing and its definition. He complains, for example, that although Romans continue to identify themselves in terms of *res publica*, their use of this word (*uerbum*) lacks any correspondence to its reality (*res*).[80]

At the opening of Book 5, Cicero points to certain 'outstanding men' (*uiri optimi/excellentes*) who, because they embody the mores of a past and more perfect commonwealth (5.1.1), are alone able to effect its restoration.[81] It is the task of these outstanding citizens (*optimates*) to restore or conserve the commonwealth by employing the techniques of oratory. Cicero's 'artistic' depiction of the function of the statesman (5.1.1–5.6.8, 2.42.69) highlights the importance of oratory to his concept of statecraft.[82] Pompilius Numa's place in Roman history is secure, he says, because he composed laws and promoted justice and piety (5.2.3).[83] By accepting the civic responsibility for defining equity (*explanatio aequitatis*) through proper interpretation of the law (*iuris interpretatio*),[84] Numa demonstrates a keen grasp of the relationship between the form of the commonwealth and the eloquent discourse which is necessary for its proper functioning.

In his description of the ideal statesman, Cicero suggests how the gap between philosophy and rhetoric might be bridged. He would carefully

---

[79] See Cicero, *De re publica* 5.1.2: 'nostra uero aetas cum rem publicam sicut picturam accepisset egregiam, sed iam euanescentem uetustate, non modo eam coloribus eisdem, quibus fuerat, renouare neglexit, sed ne id quidem curauit, ut formam saltem eius et extrema tamquam liniamenta seruaret'. Augustine copies this text at *ciu.* 2.21 (CCL 47.54).

[80] See Cicero, *De re publica* 5.1.2. Note that Augustine also incorporates this text at *ciu.* 2.21. Büchner, *M. Tullius Cicero*, 393, notes parallels at *De re publica* 1.34.51 and *De legibus* 2.5.13: 'legis nomen'.

[81] Büchner, *M. Tullius Cicero*, 391–2, following Heck, *Bezeugung*, 123, reads 'iuste' for 'fuse' at *De re publica* 5.1.1: 'nam neque uiri, nisi ita morata ciuitas fuisset, neque mores, nisi hi uiri praefuissent, aut fundare aut tam diu tenere potuissent tantam et tam fuse'. Büchner suggests that Cicero has in mind Cincinnatus and Scipio Africanus among others. Moreover, he is persuaded of the centrality of the concept of *iustitia* to Cicero's argument at *De re publica* 5.1.1 because of the semantic link between *morata ciuitas* and *mores*. E. Bréguet, *Cicéron. La République*, vol. 2 (Paris, 1980), 80, sees the relationship between the commonwealth and the mores of its leading citizens as already having been established at *De re publica* 1.34.47: 'talis est quaeque res publica, qualis eius aut natura aut uoluntas, qui illam regit'.

[82] I have been highly influenced in this section and throughout the remainder of this chapter by A. Michel, *Rhétorique et philosophie chez Cicéron. Essai sur les fondements philosophiques de l'art de persuader* (Paris, 1960).

[83] Krarup, *Rector*, 115, notes that the *rector* must be skilled at delivering both a theoretical and a practical explanation of *iustitia*.

[84] *De re publica* 5.2.3. On the synonymity of *aequitas* and *iustitia* in Roman legal usage see above, p. 12 n. 34.

regulate the education of the statesman to prevent it from becoming overly speculative (thus avoiding Epicurean retirement), but he insists that the statesman have sufficient knowledge about rights (*iura*) and laws (*leges*) to be a legal expert (*iuris peritus*).[85] Rhetoric serves the statesman as an instrument for creating and reinforcing those cultural forms (including political, educational, and legal traditions) which both legitimate the established political order and generate sufficient social pressure among citizens to ensure that they adhere to these forms. The Roman passion for personal honour and glory and the corresponding dread of shame and disgrace predispose ordinary citizens to the arguments of their political leaders, which are founded upon honour and reputation.[86] Manipulation of these passions through oratory enables the statesman to give shape to the social and political order required by the commonwealth.[87] Cicero thus assigns to the orator a responsibility to promote the public good. Cato's two-pronged definition of the orator, 'a good man, skilled at speaking' (*uir bonus dicendi peritus*),[88] gives the term a lasting affiliation with two related qualities. Because he is *peritus dicendi*, the true orator speaks effectively and eloquently. This skill requires a knowledge of the traditional techniques of eloquence. However, the first term of the definition, *uir bonus*, implies that the orator's moral worth is vital to his task. The ideal orator is also *optimus*, a man both generous, as implied by *ops*, and magnanimous.[89] Cicero realizes the extent to which the statesman establishes consensus about what is right through his oratory. The reader of *De re publica* is led to conclude that Cicero's orator par excellence is the statesman himself.[90]

---

[85] *De re publica* 5.3.5: 'summi iuris peritissimus, sine quo iustus esse nemo potest'. See Lepore, *Il princeps*, 103, who suggests that the justice with which the statesman is vested in this passage is perhaps equivalent to the justice (*dikaiosune*) of the Platonic and Academic-Peripatetic traditions.

[86] On this point, see J. Lendon, *Empire of Honour: The Art of Government in the Roman World* (Oxford, 1997).

[87] *De re publica* 5.4.6: 'hanc ille rector rerum publicarum auxit opinionibus perfecitque institutis et disciplinis, ut pudor ciuis non minus a delictis arceret quam metus'. Büchner, *M. Tullius Cicero*, 395–6, notes that this description of order constituting the commonwealth is immediately followed by a discussion of more practical matters (5.5.7). He suggests that the content of the statesman's function indicated at 5.4.6 corresponds to the creation of *iuris consensus*, whereas the more mundane matters discussed at 5.5.7 correspond to a responsibility for shared utility (*communio utilitatis*).

[88] See Cicero, *Libri tusculanarum disputationum* 5.28, Quintilian, *Institutio oratoria* 2.15.34–5, 12.1.

[89] Michel, *Rhétorique*, 15. See also, H. Strasburger, 'Optimates', *Paulys Real-Encyclopädie der klassischen Altertumswissenschaft*, vol. 18:1 (Stuttgart, 1939), 773–98, J. Hellegouarc'h, *Vocabulaire latin des relations et des partis politiques*, 2nd edn (Paris, 1972), 500–2. Cicero's discussion at *Pro Sestio* 96–8 is generally regarded as the 'locus classicus' for his elaboration of the optimate ideal. See also Cicero, *De legibus* 2.30: 'continet enim rem publicam consilio et auctoritate optimatium semper populum indigere'. G. Achard, *Pratique, rhétorique et idéologie politique dans les discours* optimates *de Cicéron* (Leiden, 1981), gives texts and studies on optimate discourse in Cicero.

[90] See Heinze, 'Ciceros', 75: 'Wenn Cicero sein Ideal staatsmännischer Tätigkeit dadurch veranschaulicht, daß er das Bild des *rector* zeichnet, so braucht dies nicht anders aufgefaßt zu werden,

CONCLUSION

In Book 19 of the *City of God*, Augustine picks up the thread of the argument concerning justice and the Roman commonwealth which he began in Book 2, and concludes that, according to Cicero's definition, Rome never possessed the characteristics of a true commonwealth because it lacked true justice. His choice of Cicero's treatise as a foil to reach his own definition of the just society stems in part from the text's discussion of civic virtues as practised by the ideal statesman. It provides a philosophical common ground for Augustine's exchanges with public officials before or during his composition of the first books of the *City of God*.

The themes in Augustine's correspondence with public officials which concern *De re publica* – the nature of civic virtue and the role of the statesman in promoting it within the commonwealth – constitute the primary framework for his use of *De re publica* in the *City of God*. Both of the passages from Cicero's text which he cites in Book 2, Chapter 21 of the *City of God* are related to the statesman and his role in promoting justice in the commonwealth. In the first passage (*De re publica* 2.42.69) Cicero likens the role of justice in the commonwealth to harmony in musical composition. This passage illustrates the function of the statesman in evoking the 'common agreement about what is right' which is essential to the commonwealth. In the second passage (*De re publica* 5.1), Cicero laments the absence in Rome of those 'outstanding men' (*uiri optimi*) whose mores embodied those of a past and more perfect commonwealth. His discussion of the *optimates*, both in *De re publica* and elsewhere in his writings, demonstrates the linkage in his portrait of these men between civic virtues and skilful eloquence.

Augustine's criticism of Roman justice, like that of Lactantius, maintains that true justice became possible in Roman society only after the advent of Christ. In the following two chapters, we shall see that the central role in the advancement of a just society which Cicero assigns in *De re publica* to the just and eloquent statesman offers Augustine the backdrop and model for his own account of the role of Christ in the creation and maintenance of a just society. Augustine presents Christ as both the only

als wenn er sein Ideal rednischer Kunst in der Person des *orator* darstellt, oder wenn Antisthenes, Platon, Aristoteles ihr Ideal politischer Tätigkeit in der Person des *politikos* vor Augen gestellt haben.' Lepore, *Il princeps*, 56, further develops the linkage 'orator–princeps', suggesting that the two roles represent 'elementi di reciproca illuminazione'. So, too, Michel, *Rhétorique*, 63: 'Dans l'orateur se trouveront réunis le *rector rei publicae* et le *princeps civitatis*.' See also L. Wickert, 'Neue Forschung zum römischen Prinzipat', *Aufstieg und Niedergang der römischen Welt*, vol. 2:1, ed. H. Temporini (Berlin/New York, 1974), 3–76, Büchner, *M. Tullius Cicero*, 414–15.

completely just human being ever to have lived and the only exponent of virtue whose teaching effectively establishes justice in other human beings. This relationship between justice and oratory in Augustine's conception of Christ as the ideal statesman owes more to Cicero than has been previously acknowledged.

At the same time, we shall see that Augustine distances his explanation of Christ's role in establishing the just society from Cicero's conception of the ideal statesman in relation to the commonwealth. As one would expect, at the heart of this relationship in Augustine's view is Christ's role in healing human beings of the effects of original sin. Augustine thus opposes Cicero's key assumption – one that is also common to the ancient world – that human beings are able to act justly on the strength of their own reason and will. Much of his argument in the *City of God* insists that the injustice of Roman society thoughout its history can be traced to this assumption and its consequences, chief among which is the inability of presumptuous human beings to know and love God, the source of justice. It is this human weakness that Christ overcomes in establishing the just society.

CHAPTER 2

Justice and the limits of the soul

Augustine's views on justice and society stem more from his analysis of the capacities and limits of the human soul than from his thinking about social and political structures. Human beings, he believes, are just insofar as they know and love God.[1] Crucially, at an early point in his episcopal career, Augustine concluded that man's natural capacity to know and love God is impeded by ignorance and weakness, two permanent, debilitating effects of original sin on the soul.[2] In his later writings, he generally associates these spiritual defects with concupiscence.[3] His most significant observations in the *City of God* concerning the failure of Roman justice arise from his treatment of ignorance and weakness in relation to the pursuit of the true virtue through which God is known and loved. In this chapter, we shall explore Augustine's conclusions concerning the effects of ignorance and weakness on human beings who desire to live justly. Moreover, we shall examine how Augustine understands fear of death as the epitome of the effects of original sin on the soul, and how he believes that this fear is

---

[1] This point is made in especially clear terms at *spir. et litt.* 64 (below, pp. 168–70 nn. 98–103).

[2] See *s. dom. m.* 2.7, *c. Faust.* 22.78. Augustine pairs *ignorantia* with *difficultas* at *lib. arb.* 3.50–8, 3.64, 3.70. The similar usages suggest that the terms are somewhat interchangeable. See also *pecc. mer.* 2.2, *nat. et gr.* 33, 81, *perf. ius.* 1. The importance of the couplet as a theme is suggested at *ciu.* 10.24, 20.6 (CCL 48.707): 'uel ignorando uel sciendo nec faciendo quod iustum est'. On the theme in general, see J. Chéné, 'Le Péché d'ignorance selon saint Augustin', and 'L'Ignorance et la difficulté, état naturel et primitif de l'homme', *Œuvres de saint Augustin*, vol. 24: *Aux moines d'Adrumète et de Provence*, ed. J. Chéné and J. Pintard (Paris, 1962), 769–71, 829–31, M. Alflatt, 'The Responsibility for Involuntary Sin in Saint Augustine', *Revue des études augustiniennes* 10 (1975), 171–86, I. Bochet, *Saint Augustin et le désir de Dieu* (Paris, 1982), 85–101, Lettieri, *Il senso*, 70–85, and J. Doignon, 'Souvenirs cicéroniens (Hortensius, consolatio) et virgiliens dans l'exposé d'Augustin sur l'état humain d'"ignorance et de difficulté" (Aug., *lib. arb.* 3, 51–54)', *Vigiliae christianae* 47 (1993), 131–9.

[3] See, for example, *pecc. mer.* 2.2–4, *spir. et litt.* 34, 51. J. Rist, *Augustine: Ancient Thought Baptized*, 2nd edn (Cambridge, 1995), especially 102, 320–7, points out that although Augustine frequently associates *concupiscentia* with lust, in his later, anti-Pelagian writings it may still hold this meaning, but it can also connote something akin to a 'weakness for' or 'proneness to' an evil, without the full force of longing expressed as 'lust'. See also G. Bonner, 'Concupiscentia', *Augustinus-Lexikon*, vol. 1, ed. C. Mayer (Basle, 1986–94), 1113–22. At *pecc. mer.* 2.45, Augustine argues that concupiscence endures in the soul until death.

reflected in the inability of human beings to know and love God through the mystery of the incarnation. Finally, we shall show that Augustine bases his criticisms of Ciceronian and other Roman conceptions of virtue in the false attitudes toward God which he holds that this fear of death produces in them.

When Augustine uses the term 'ignorance' in the context of original sin, he refers to an incapacity to know oneself, others, and God with utter moral clarity.[4] Ignorance therefore prevents the soul from seeing itself in relation to the highest good, or understanding completely the motivations behind its own moral choices.[5] Misled, perhaps, by the false assumption that Augustine is more concerned with the will than the intellect, scholars generally interpret original sin as moral weakness, thereby relegating ignorance to the status of a 'junior partner', or discounting it altogether.[6] Yet for Augustine, it is at least as clear an indicator as moral weakness for assessing the consequences of original sin upon human activity. It causes what he regards as the foundational distortion of moral reason, its erroneous understanding of its own integrity.[7] Ignorance thus represents the inability to understand what justice clearly requires in particular circumstances, further accentuated by its own self-deception.[8] Moral weakness, on the other hand, explains the soul's overall inability or unwillingness to act justly.[9] For Augustine, ignorance and weakness, like the intellect and

---

[4] On *ignorantia* in general, see *diu. qu.* 64.7, *lib. arb.* 3.51–3, *pecc. mer.* 1.65, 2.26, 2.48; as an obstacle to self-knowledge, see *ep.* 140.52, *en. Ps.* 30.2.1.13, 61.21, 106.6, 118.4.5, *s. Guelf.* 32.8; as an obstacle to knowledge of others: *en. Ps.* 30.2.1.13, *s. Guelf.* 12.3, *spec.* 23; as an obstacle to knowledge of God: *ep.* 140.81, 186.16, *spec.* 34, *en. Ps.* 41.2, 118.9.1, *ciu.* 11.1. At *spir. et litt.* 64, Augustine illustrates his understanding of *ignorantia* through the paradox of not knowing what justice requires even though Christ has given the double commandment of love (Mt 22:37–9) as an instruction. See my discussion below, pp. 168–70.

[5] On the loss of recognition of the *summum bonum* as a result of the Fall, see *en. Ps.* 70.2.6–8, *pecc. mer.* 2.27. On the importance of correctly symbolizing it, see *ciu.* 10.19, where Augustine discusses its bearing on the proper worship of God.

[6] Noteworthy for its attempt to correct this view is J. Lössl, *Intellectus gratiae. Die erkenntnis-theoretische und hermeneutische Dimension der Gnadenlehre Augustins von Hippo* (Leiden, 1997).

[7] See *en. Ps.* 30.2.1 (CCL 38.190–202), especially 30.2.1.6 (CCL 38.194–6). Individuals who lack the proper knowledge of God fail to recognize God as the source of justice, which they wrongly locate in themselves. At *spir. et litt.* 4, 17, 19, and 31, respectively, he refers to this moral self-delusion as presumption (*praesumptio*), pride (*superbia*), vanity (*uanitas*), and hypocrisy (*hypocrisis*). See *ciu.* 17.4 along with the comments of Lössl, *Intellectus*, 420 n. 36. The best general introduction to this topic remains that of G. Evans, *Augustine on Evil* (Cambridge, 1982), 29–90, but see also Y. de Montcheuil, 'L'Hypothèse de l'état originel d'ignorance et de difficulté d'après le *De libero arbitrio* de saint Augustin', *Bulletin de littérature ecclésiastique* 23 (1933), 197–221, J. Mausbach, *Die Ethik des heiligen Augustinus*, 2nd edn (Freiburg, 1929), 2:226–39.

[8] See *spir. et litt.* 64, *perf. ius.* 9, *ench.* 24 (CCL 46.63): 'ignorantia rerum agendarum'.

[9] Augustine believes that *infirmitas* pertains to a kind of cartel of personal desires and fears in competition with the divine will. See *pecc. mer.* 2.3.

will to which they correspond, ought not to be considered as separate spiritual disorders. Although he describes them both as defects (*uitia*) which restrict the scope of the will in the practice of justice, he understands the two conditions to interact with each other.[10] He also correlates intellect and will, so that the moral object of knowledge is also in some respect an object of love, and, conversely, that which is not known cannot be loved.[11]

In Augustine's view, these moral debilitations impede the formation of a just society, primarily because they obstruct the knowledge and love of God, the supreme good. Longing for knowledge and love of God is diminished by the moral self-deception and self-reliance which result from these twin effects of original sin. Human beings who pretentiously believe themselves capable of acting justly on the strength of their own insights and efforts are thus impeded from seeking God, who alone is the source of justice. At the same time, it is axiomatic for Augustine that God is knowable exclusively through mystery (*mysterium, sacramentum*), and that divine self-revelation through the incarnation constitutes the only true mystery.[12] God chooses mystery as the form of his self-revelation in order to cure the soul by diminishing the pretentions of moral self-reliance with which it is afflicted.[13] Only the soul that struggles by faith and humility to know and love God through mystery achieves the self-knowledge necessary to recognize and repent of its self-deceptions. As the soul undergoes this moral conversion, it gains a truer understanding of itself in relation to God and neighbour, and is thereby enabled to understand and love justice.[14]

Knowing God through mystery requires approaching divinity through the incarnation.[15] This is the conclusion that Augustine reveals at the end of Book 10 of the *City of God*, by which point he has described the failure

---

[10] Augustine states that the will presents a greater difficulty than the intellect for acting justly. See *spir. et litt.* 5. However, the two faculties are interrelated. See *pecc. mer.* 2.26. See also *lib. arb.* 3.53, *pecc. mer.* 2.48, *nat. et gr.* 81, *trin.* 10.11 (CCL 50.324): 'cum amore cogitat'. I discuss this interaction further below, pp. 73–5.

[11] See *spir. et litt.* 64. See also J. Burnaby, *Amor Dei: A Study of the Religion of St. Augustine* (London, 1938), 155–6, A. Dihle, *The Theory of Will in Classical Antiquity* (Berkeley, 1982), 125–31, Bochet, *Saint Augustin*, 93–5. See *trin.* 8.6–12.

[12] See *ep.* 187.34 (CSEL 57.113): 'Non est enim aliud dei mysterium, nisi Christus.' I discuss the interchangeability of the terms *mysterium* and *sacramentum* below, pp. 151–3.

[13] See, for example, Augustine's discussion of the importance of figurative language as an element in the interpretation of the scriptures at *Gn. adu. Man.* 2.5–6, and my discussion of this point below, pp. 133–9.

[14] I discuss this aspect of Augustine's thought in Chapter 5.

[15] At *ciu.* 10.24 (CCL 47.297), Augustine refers to the incarnation as 'sacramentum magnum'. See below, p. 64 n. 158.

of non-Christian religions and philosophies to lead the soul to true knowledge and love of God, and thus to true happiness. A summary statement
of this position opens Book 11, in which he begins the second part of the
City of God, concerning the origins, course, and ends of the two cities.
Here Augustine asserts that although man, created in the image and likeness of God, can be brought close to God by natural reason and intelligence, he is also impeded from doing so by faults which weaken his ability
to endure God's light, until his soul is 'renewed and healed day by day'
through faith in Christ.[16] By embracing the mystery of the incarnation,
believers come to know God as the divine trinity which first revealed itself
to the Hebrew nation prior to Christ's birth.[17] Inasmuch as this mystery
is the pivotal pathway to God, it also leads the way to love, justice, and
similar divine qualities which have their source in God. In this way, Augustine equates the task of knowing justice with that of knowing God. This
knowledge requires that the soul approach the divine mystery through the
virtues of faith and humility, which counter the vices of ignorance and
weakness.

In Augustine's view, the exercise in virtue which this knowledge involves
is rendered all the more difficult by fear of death (*timor mortis*). Fear of
death epitomizes the effects of ignorance and weakness upon the soul.
Because of it, the soul is repelled by the darkness of a religious mystery
in which God is believed to have died as a particular human being. In
Books 1–10, Augustine argues that true virtue can be apprehended by the
soul only through imitation of this divine vulnerability to death.[18] Yet
he is aware that reflection upon this mystery leads human beings to fear
their own death more acutely, thus making it more difficult for them to
embrace faith in God through Christ. For this reason, he acknowledges
that spiritual beings venerated by non-Christian religions, in which the
threat of death is either absent or obscured, are more attractive to human
beings as mediators of salvation and objects of worship. Yet even in their

---

[16] See *ciu.* 11.2 (CCL 48.322): 'sed quia ipsa mens, cui ratio et intellegentia naturaliter inest, uitiis
quibusdam tenebrosis et ueteribus inualida est, non solum ad inhaerendum fruendo, uerum etiam
ad perferendum incommutabile lumen, donec de die in diem renouata atque sanata fiat tantae
felicitatis capax, fide primum fuerat inbuenda atque purganda. In qua ut fidentius ambularet ad
ueritatem, ipsa ueritas, deus dei filius, homine assumpto, non deo consumpto, eandem constituit
et fundauit fidem ut ad hominis deum iter esset homini per hominem deum. hic est enim mediator
dei et hominum, homo Christus Iesus. per hoc enim mediator, per quod homo, per hoc et uia'.

[17] See *ciu.* 10.24–5 (below, p. 94 n. 90). See also my discussion of Israel below, pp. 107–10.

[18] I discuss this point together with *ciu.* 10.29 below, pp. 94–107. See also R. Dodaro, 'Il *timor mortis*
e la questione degli *exempla virtutum*: Agostino, *De civitate Dei* 1–x', *Il mistero del male e la libertà
possibile (III): Lettura del* De civitate dei *di Agostino. Atti del VII Seminario del Centro Studi Agostiniani
di Perugia*, ed. L. Alici et al. (Rome, 1996), 7–47.

most intellectually compelling forms, these deities do not demand the degree of faith and humility before death that the knowledge and love of God through the Christian mystery requires. As a further consequence, non-Christian philosophies and religions give the soul a false security, in effect encouraging it to flee the vulnerability to death which understanding of the Christian mystery requires, and to immerse itself in the vain pursuit of heroism.

Augustine's well-known argument in Book 19, in which he concludes that true justice does not exist without true piety (19.23–7),[19] explains why his discussions in the first ten books regarding the soul's efforts to overcome obstacles to the true knowledge and worship of God are crucial to his understanding of the creation and preservation of a just society. Equally important to his understanding of these points, however, is his argument that ignorance and weakness afflict the soul to such an extent that the virtues that form a just society cannot be acquired through teachings or examples concerning virtue unless they are accompanied by grace, through which the knowledge and love of God is communicated to the soul. As a consequence, a just society requires more than the statesman envisioned by Cicero, who exemplifies justice and eloquently urges its pursuit. It requires, instead, a statesman whose example of virtue also heals the soul of these fundamental defects. Throughout the first ten books of the *City of God*, Augustine observes that the teachings and practices recommended by ancient philosophies and religions fail to provide both the means for knowing and loving God and an efficacious remedy for fear of death, encouraging instead its avoidance or suppression. Only the true philosophy (*uera philosophia*) of the Christian religion offers a pathway to God which promotes true virtue in the face of the soul's anxiety before death. In doing so, this true philosophy provides the pattern for the just society, demonstrating at the same time the structure of that society in relation to Christ. In Books 1–5, he addresses the inability of Roman gods to provide happiness (*beatitudo, felicitas*) in the present life, while in Books 6–10, he examines their inability to provide happiness after death. At the same time, in Books 1–7 he demonstrates the failure of non-Christian religions to lead human beings to this happiness, whereas in Books 8–10 he argues the same point relative to non-Christian philosophies.[20] Both overlapping sets of divisions form part of the longer

---

[19] Throughout this chapter, references placed in parentheses within the text refer to passages in the *City of God*.

[20] On the structure of *De ciuitate dei* in general and in its parts, see Augustine's own comments at *ciu.* I praef., 1.1, 1.35, 1.36, 2.2, 4.1–2, 4.34, 5.12, 5.26, 6 praef., 6.1, 10.1, 10.18, 10.32, 11.1, 15.1, 17.24, 18.1, 18.54, 19.1, *ep.* 184A.5, *retr.* 2.43, together with G. P. O'Daly, *Augustine's* City of God: *A Reader's*

argument extending from Book 2 to Book 19 against the assumption that Rome had ever been a commonwealth, given that it had never practised true justice.[21] Augustine uses passages in Books 1–10 concerning ignorance and weakness to illustrate the failure of ancient religions and philosophies to help their adherents to live justly.

Augustine understands death as a penalty which all human beings inherit as a consequence of original sin.[22] He distinguishes between what he terms the 'first death' (*prima mors*), in which the soul separates from the body, and the graver 'second death' (*secunda mors*), by which he means eternal damnation following divine judgment.[23] He argues that although eternal damnation, the most severe punishment for original sin, is remitted by God in baptism, no one is spared the first death.[24] Had God cancelled this penalty, conversion to Christianity and acceptance of baptism would be motivated merely by the desire to pass to an afterlife without enduring the pain of death. Under these circumstances, faith, which involves the struggle to believe Christ's promises in the face of death, could not exist.[25]

Guide (Oxford, 1999), 67–73. See also G. Bardy, 'Introduction générale à *La Cité de Dieu*', *Œuvres de saint Augustin*, vol. 33: *La Cité de Dieu, Livres I–V: Impuissance sociale du paganisme*, ed. G. Bardy and G. Combés (Paris, 1959), 7–163, at 35–52, J.-C. Guy, *Unité et structure logique de la Cité de Dieu de saint Augustin* (Paris, 1961), 10–22, van Oort, *Jerusalem*, 74–7, 171–5.

[21] See *ciu.* 2.21 in conjunction with 19.21–7.

[22] See, for example, *c. Fort.* 15, *duab. an.* 13.19, *Gn. adu. Man.* 2.26, *lib. arb.* 3.56, *uera rel.* 48. *s.* 6.7, 165.7, 212.1, 231.2, 361.17, 343.2. Later, in his writings against the Pelagians, Augustine insists that all human beings die because they inherit both the sin and the penalty of the first parents. See *pecc. mer.* 1.8, 1.21, 2.55, 3.19–21, *gest. Pel.* 23–4, *gr. et pecc. or.* 2.2–3, 2.11–20, *nupt. et conc.* 2.46–8, 2.58, *c. ep. Pel.* 4.6–8, *c. Iul. imp.* 1.25, 2.236, 3.94, 6.7, 6.27, 6.36. For Augustine's views on death in general and the evolution of his thought in its regard, see, in particular, J.-M. Girard, *La Mort chez saint Augustin: grandes lignes de l'évolution de sa pensée* (Fribourg, 1992), E. Rebillard, *In hora mortis. Evolution de la pastorale chrétienne de la mort aux IVe et Ve siècles* (Rome, 1994), especially 51–70, 143–67, 225–32. See also G. Bonner, 'Adam', *Augustinus-Lexikon*, vol. 1, ed. C. Mayer (Basle, 1986–94), 63–87.

[23] See *ciu.* 13.2, 13.5, 13.8, 13.12 (CCL 48.395): 'quoniam prima [mors] constat ex duabus, una animae, altera corporis; ut sit prima totius hominis mors, cum anima sine Deo et sine corpore ad tempus poenas luit', 13.15, 13.23, 20.6, 20.9, 21.3, 21.11, *pecc. mer.* 1.4–8, 1.13, 1.55, 3.5, *c. ep. Pel.* 4.8, *c. Iul. imp.* 1.106, *s.* 231.2, 306.5, 344.4, *s. Guelf.* 31.5, *en. Ps.* 48.2.2. On *mors secunda*, see Rev 2:11, 20:6, 20:14, 21:8. Cf. Ambrose, *De bono mortis* 2.3. See also J. Plumpe, 'Mors secunda', *Mélanges De Ghellinck*, vol. 1: *Antiquité* (Gembloux, 1951), 387–403, M.-F. Berrouard, 'La Seconde Mort', *Œuvres de saint Augustin*, vol. 73A: *Homélies sur l'Evangile de saint Jean XXXIV–XLIII*, ed. M.-F. Berrouard (Paris, 1988), 523–5, P. Porro, 'La morte, il tempo, il linguaggio: in margine al XIII libro del *De civitate deï*', *Interiorità e intenzionalità nel De civitate dei di Sant'Agostino*, ed. R. Piccolomini (Rome, 1991), 117–31, Girard, *La Mort*, 158–9, Rebillard, *In hora mortis*, 66–7.

[24] See *pecc. mer.* 2.45.   [25] See *ciu.* 13.4, *pecc. mer.* 2.50–6, *nat. et gr.* 25.

This last observation allows Augustine to offer a positive understanding of fear of death as a divine instrument for the perfection of virtue.[26] Faith and humility, as virtues which counter ignorance and weakness, can be strengthened in their exposure to this anxiety.[27] Augustine employs the symbol of a 'conflict of faith' (*certamen fidei*) in order to indicate the painful transformation in which the soul, confronted with its fear and unable to overcome it, repents of its pretensions to moral strength and avails itself of divine grace.[28]

Augustine reasons that, in fearing death, the soul fears the diminishment of the goods which it most desires. In this regard, he distinguishes in Platonic fashion between temporal goods (*bona temporalia*) which cannot endure beyond death, such as health, wealth, friendship, political liberty, even social status or reputation, and permanent goods (*bona aeterna*), such as happiness and virtue, which transcend death.[29] Although he recognizes that this fear is generally associated with the hour of death, he suggests that it is actually experienced most strongly while one is still living relatively well.[30] Accordingly, he proposes that when the rich young man of Matthew 19 asks Jesus what he must do to inherit eternal life, he does so because the prospect of death leads him to fear the loss of the many temporal goods in his possession.[31] Threats to permanent goods, on the other hand,

---

[26] See *ciu.* 13.4 (CCL 48.388): 'Nunc uero maiore et mirabiliore gratia saluatoris in usus iustitiae peccati poena conuersa est [. . .] sic per ineffabilem dei misericordiam et ipsa poena uitiorum transit in arma uirtutis, et fit iusti meritum etiam supplicium peccatoris.' See also *ciu.* 9.5, *c. Faust.* 22.20, 22.79, *pecc. mer.* 2.45, 2.54–6, *c. ep. Pel.* 4.6, *c. Iul. imp.* 6.27. For a concise treatment of the theme in Augustine, see C. Straw, '*Timor mortis*', *Augustine through the Ages: An Encyclopedia*, ed. A. Fitzgerald et al. (Grand Rapids, 1999), 838–42 (with bibliography).

[27] See *pecc. mer.* 2.50, 2.54, *s. Guelf.* 33.3 (faith); *pecc. mer.* 2.27, 3.23 (humility). On the connection between original sin and humility, see O. Schaffner, *Christliche Demut. Des hl. Augustinus Lehre von der Humilitas* (Würzburg, 1959), 166–72.

[28] See *ciu.* 13.4, *pecc. mer.* 2.51, 2.53–4, *perf. ius.* 16, *c. ep. Pel.* 3.5, *en. Ps.* 30.2.3.

[29] See *exp. prop. Rm.* 58, *s.* 125.7, 177.10. See also *an. quant.* 73 and *ep.* 140.16–19, where Augustine extends the theme of fear of death into a discussion of the conflict between temporal and permanent goods. At *ep.* 155.4, he applies this principle to political life by reminding the vicar of Africa, Macedonius, that mortal life is to be endured in the hope of attaining eternal goods. See *ciu.* 10.16 (CCL 47.289), where Augustine cites Plotinus, *Enneads* 1.6.7 on this point. See also Rebillard, *In hora mortis*, 53–5. On the distinction between eternal and temporal goods, see Plato, *Apology* 29D, 30B, and W. Jaeger, *Paideia: The Ideals of Greek Culture*, vol. 2: *In Search of the Divine Centre*, tr. G. Highet (New York, 1943), 38–40, and 146–7, on Socrates. The most relevant Neoplatonic reference is to the doctrine of Plotinus, *Enneads* 1.2.1–7 (on the virtues), 3.2.13.18–29 (on providence), 6.7.15–42 (on the Good and the multiplicity of goods). For Plotinus, worldly goods constitute a hierarchy of goods ordered and governed by divine providence.

[30] See *s.* 38.7 (CCL 41.481): 'et tunc maxime pungit timor mortis, quando nobis bene est. nam quando male est, non timemus mortem. quando nobis bene est, tunc magis timemus mortem'.

[31] See *s.* 38.7 (CCL 41.482): 'ille qui delectabatur diuitiis suis, et propterea quaerebat a domino quid boni faceret ut uitam aeternam consequeretur, quia a deliciis ad delicias migrare cupiebat, et has quibus delectabatur relinquere formidabat'.

evoke fear of the second death, eternal damnation, to which even baptized Christians are subject should they fail to lead virtuous lives. Augustine argues that fear of death in this case is salutary, because it reminds believers of the need for spiritual vigilance.[32] Fear which is related exclusively to the first death, however, is morally ambiguous. It exerts an undetected but pervasive influence on the soul, and prompts actions aimed at warding off threats to human security. Human beings are right to safeguard those temporal goods which they justly possess. Yet when a conflict arises between possession of temporal and permanent goods, the spiritual anxiety which results signals a grave challenge to Christian faith and morals.[33] Fear of death, in such cases, represents the most potent, insidious, and ubiquitous form in which ignorance and weakness act upon the soul. In Augustine's view, most human beings suffer some form of morally dangerous anxiety over death, which he calls 'the most terrifying of all fears' and likens to a 'daily winter'.[34] In the midst of such a conflict, ignorance and weakness induce the soul to suppress or redirect the anxiety, often through efforts to distract itself or to secure possession of temporal goods through injustices committed at the cost of permanent goods, such as virtue. He cites cases in which echoes of this fear prompt men to tell lies, to seek to amass fortunes, and to aspire to high positions in public office, all the while reasoning that deception, wealth, or power will ward off death. Still other men hope that influential patrons will protect them against this threat.[35] Augustine

---

[32] See, for example, *s.* 62.1–2, 93.6–10, *s. Guelf.* 33.4, *an. quant.* 73.

[33] See, for example, *s.* 177.3 (SPM 1.66) 'iter mortalitatis commune est uniuersis nascentibus, iter pietatis non commune est omnibus: illud enim ambulant omnes nati: istum non nisi renati. ad illud pertinet nasci, crescere, senescere, mori. propter hoc necessarius est uictus et tegumentum. Sufficientes sint huius itineris sumptus. quare te grauas? Quare tantum portas in uia breui, non unde ad hanc uiam finiendam iuueris, sed unde potius hac uia finita grauius onereris?' See also *ciu.* 5.18, where Augustine discusses a hypothetical moral conflict between the desire to leave one's wealth to one's children and the possibility that, in some cases, the virtues of faith and justice require that such worldly riches be given to the poor.

[34] See *ciu.* 22.6 (CCL 48.813): 'sed inmensarum variarumque poenarum et ipsius mortis, quae plus ceteris formidatur', *s.* 38.7 (CCL 41.481): 'hiemps cotidiana'. Cicero, *Libri tusculanarum disputationum* 1.91, says that death 'cotidie imminet'. At *c. Iul. imp.* 6.14 (PL 45.1530), Augustine says that human beings fear death naturally: 'ut etiam hi qui spe fideli futurae uitae gaudia concupiscunt, in hac tamen uita cum mortis timore luctentur'. His point is, perhaps, most vividly argued at *en. Ps.* 30.2.12. See below, n. 35. See also, *s.* 108.4, 177.3 (above, n. 33), *s. Guelf.* 33.4. Girard, *La Mort*, 208, concludes, 'La mort n'est pas seulement un événement ponctuel; elle est en quelque sorte présente au long de la vie même de l'homme, soit par la peur qu'il en ressent, soit par la décrépitude qui se réalise peu à peu.'

[35] See *en. Ps.* 30.2.1.12 (CCL 38.199–200): 'quis obseruat uanitatem? qui timendo mori moritur. timendo enim mori mentitur, et moritur antequam moriatur, qui ideo mentiebatur ut uiueret. mentiri uis, ne moriaris; et mentiris, et moreris; et cum uitas unam mortem quam differre poteris, auferre non poteris, incidis in duas, ut prius in anima, postea in corpore moriaris [. . .] *odisti obseruantes uanitatem superuacue. ego autem*, qui non obseruo uanitatem, *in domino speraui* (Ps 30[31]:7). speras in pecunia,

allows that, in some cases, death can be delayed for a time, but he points out that efforts to overcome death altogether are doomed to fail.[36] Death is truly defeated only when the soul desires God over all other goods, thereby accepting the first death in order to avoid the second. As virtues which counteract ignorance and weakness, faith and humility alone relieve the soul of anxiety before death: faith by directing the soul to disregard temporal goods when their possession conflicts with that of permanent goods, and humility by leading the soul to abandon reliance upon its own strength in seeking permanent goods. God alone provides the soul with this strength.[37]

Ignorance and weakness and their relation to fear of death offer Augustine theoretical categories for analysing three related themes in the first ten books of the *City of God*. He correlates the inability of ancient philosophies and religions to impart true knowledge and love of God with their failure to offer efficacious solutions to fear of death, and he does so in tandem with his rejection of the value of the examples of virtue offered by Rome's most outstanding citizens (*optimi/praeclari uiri*).[38] This view emerges from Augustine's understanding of the relationship between happiness as the primary aim of human life, political objectives such as security (*salus*) as temporal expressions of this happiness, and death as the essential negation of both. Because he believes that happiness is predicated upon the knowledge and love of God as the supreme good, he concludes that fear of

---

obseruas uanitatem; speras in honore et sublimitate aliqua potestatis humanae, obseruas uanitatem; speras in aliquo amico potente, obseruas uanitatem. in his omnibus cum speras, aut tu exspiras'. See also *s. Guelf.* 31.4 (below, n. 37), where Augustine specifies 'worldly ambition' (*ambitio saeculi*) among other means employed in the effort to evade death.

[36] See, for example, *ep.* 127.2, *s.* 109.1, *s. Guelf.* 33.4.

[37] See *s. Guelf.* 31.4 (MA 1.561): 'contemnunt plerumque homines mortem per concupiscentiam carnis; contemnunt mortem per concupiscentiam oculorum, contemnunt mortem per ambitionem saeculi: sed omnia ista de saeculo sunt. qui contemnit mortem propter caritatem dei, nullo modo id potest implere sine adiutorio dei'.

[38] Throughout his political writings, Cicero employed stock Roman and Greek examples of virtue (*exempla uirtutis*) to persuade his audience of the value and attainability of the heroic ideal in the service of the commonwealth. For example, he opened the first book of *De re publica* with a string of patriotic examples of *optimi uiri* during the Punic Wars. Useful studies on the rhetorical structure of the *exemplum* and on its use in Roman literature are provided by H. Litchfield, 'National *exempla virtutis* in Roman Literature', *Harvard Studies in Classical Philology* 25 (1914), 1–71, I. Kapp and G. Meyer, 'Exemplum', *Thesaurus linguae latinae*, vol. 5:2, ed. G. Dittmann et al. (Leipzig, 1931–53), 1326–50, Lausberg, *Handbuch*, 227–34, K. Stierle, 'Geschichte als exemplum – exemplum als Geschichte. Zur Pragmatik und Poetik narrativer Texte', *Geschichte, Ereignis und Erzählung*, ed. R. Koselleck and W.-D. Stempel (Munich, 1973), 347–75, J. Martin, *Antike Rhetorik. Technik und Methode* (Munich, 1974), 119–21, and R. Honstetter, *Exemplum zwischen Rhetorik und Literatur. Zur gattungsgeschichtlichen Sonderstellung von Valerius Maximus und Augustinus* (Konstanz, 1981). Litchfield, 'National', 6, gives Seneca, *Epistula* 98.12 as the first instance of *exempla uirtutum* as a category or class.

death epitomizes the fundamental threat to the formation of a just society. Justice is not found wherever fear of death impedes action aimed at the attainment of lasting happiness. Virtue is therefore necessary to overcome fear of death, all the more so because it leads human beings to choose permanent over temporal goods. Augustine understands that Rome's model citizens (*optimates*) are praised in literature as examples of virtues, and that their role in promoting a just society depends upon the aims and efficacy of the philosophical and religious means by which they ward off fear of death. Against the backdrop of these philosophical and religious traditions, Augustine invents a Christian concept of civic virtue, in part by distinguishing it from the virtue described by ancient philosophies and religions. His argument rests upon his belief that the concept of virtue must itself be redefined and transformed in a Christian key, thus redefining the just society itself.

He begins to lay out his argument in Book 1, where he answers the pagan charge that the Christian God failed to protect Rome and its inhabitants, even the Christians themselves, from Alaric's disastrous sack of AD 410.[39] He acknowledges that it was this accusation that moved him to write the *City of God*.[40] Furthermore, he explains, this charge enables him to explore the relationship between knowledge of God and fear of death. At first he answers his adversaries with a series of philosophical clichés, as if to remind them that according to their own traditions, death is unavoidable, so that it should not matter how one dies.[41] These same traditions affirm that, when considered rationally, death should not be considered an evil for those who live virtuously. On the other hand, those individuals who have not led a morally upright life should fear divine judgment (1.11). To provide an example from Roman history to make these points, he turns to Marcus Atilius Regulus. Regulus represents the 'most noble example' of courage (*uirtus*), and is important as a limit case in Augustine's argument because his combination of piety and valour in the face of death at the hands of his city's enemies arguably exceeds that of all other Roman heroes.[42]

---

[39] The accusation is discussed throughout Book 1. See, especially, *ciu.* 1.1, 1.3, 1.7, 1.9, 1.10, 1.35, 1.36. See also *ciu.* 2.2, 4.1, *retr.* 2.43.1. In sermons preached shortly after the tragedy, Augustine indicates his awareness that a number of Christians, as well as pagans, express this view. See *exc. urb.* 3, *s. Denis* 21.3, as well as the studies indicated by O'Daly, *Augustine's City*, 29 n. 7. On the historical background to Alaric's activities, see J. Matthews, *Western Aristocracies and Imperial Court: A.D. 364–425* (Oxford, 1975), 284–306, and Heather, *Goths and Romans*, 193–218. See also *ep.* 136.2, 138.8–9, and my discussion below, pp. 136–9.

[40] See *retr.* 2.43.1, *ciu.* 1.1.

[41] See *ciu.* 1.11. For similar statements in Cicero, see, for example, *De senectute* 67–71, *Libri tusculanarum disputationum* 1.100–18.

[42] See *ciu.* 1.15 (CCL 47.17): 'quam ob rem nondum interim disputo, qualis in Regulo uirtus fuerit; sufficit nunc, quod isto nobilissimo exemplo coguntur fateri non propter corporis bona uel earum

Augustine recounts the military commander's decision to honour his oath to return voluntarily to the Carthaginians in order to face torture and death,[43] concluding that the Romans do not criticize their own gods when they allow the most atrocious of deaths even to their staunchest devotees (1.15, cf. 2.23). He goes on to note that the prophets Daniel and Jonah, like the holy men Shadrach, Mesach, and Abednego, suffered captivity and even physical torture for the sake of their religion (Dan 3:12–30), but were not abandoned to die by their God, as Regulus apparently was by his (1.14–15). This brief comparison of Christian and Roman heroes and the structure of their piety adumbrates the more extensive contrast which he draws in passages in this and in later books between the two sets of exemplars of virtue.[44] In this connection, he admits not knowing whether Regulus worshipped the gods for the sake of happiness in this life or in the next, but he believes it at least possible that the Roman commander sought happiness in the practice of virtue, and not for its reward. He admits that if this has been the case, Regulus has indeed acquired true virtue (*uera uirtus*).[45] Once again Augustine moves on without further comment, thus indicating his intention to postpone discussion of the quality of Regulus' virtue until later. It is clear, however, that his aim in building a case in favour of the commander's example of virtue lies solely in its usefulness for subverting the Roman conception of piety, which linked devotion to the gods with the acquisition of temporal goods, among them, material prosperity and security for the city.[46]

When, shortly thereafter, he considers the suicide of Lucretia, he employs a dual apologetic strategy similar to his discussion of Regulus. By initially alluding to the extent to which pagan literature extols Lucretia's decision to

rerum, quae extrinsecus homini accidunt, colendos deos, quando quidem ille carere his omnibus maluit quam deos per quos iurauit offendere', 1.24 (CCL 47.26): 'inter omnes suos laudabiles et uirtutis insignibus inlustres uiros non proferunt Romani meliorem'. See also *ciu.* 2.23, 2.29, 3.18, 3.20, 5.18. O'Daly, *Augustine's City*, 79 n. 10, indicates other references to Regulus in Roman and Christian writings. Throughout this chapter I use the term 'hero' synonymously with *uir optimus*, and I apply it to Romans such as Marcus Regulus, even though Augustine, following convention, used the Latin term *heros*, a loan-word from Greek, only to refer to men like Hercules or Romulus, who became divinities after death (cf. *ciu.* 2.14).

[43] See *ciu.* 1.15, 1.24. O'Daly, *Augustine's City*, 248–9, comments that it is 'difficult if not impossible' to determine whether Augustine employs Livy directly (through the *Periochae*) or the Livian tradition as his source for this account. He notes that Cicero, *De officiis* (cf. 3.99–111), may also have played a role.

[44] See, for example, *ciu.* 1.19, 1.22, 1.24, 2.29, 5.12–14, 5.18, 8.27.

[45] See *ciu.* 1.15 (CCL 47.17): 'si autem dicunt M. Regulum etiam in illa captiuitate illisque cruciatibus corporis animi uirtute beatum esse potuisse, uirtus potius uera quaeratur, qua beata esse possit et ciuitas'. Cicero, *Libri tusculanarum disputationum* 5.14, allows the view that Regulus' virtue under torture did not afford him happiness.

[46] See *ciu.* 1.15 (above, n. 45). See also *ciu.* 2.23. O'Daly, *Augustine's City*, 78–9, explains the rhetorical elements supporting Augustine's use of Regulus as counter-example.

commit suicide, he seeks to soften pagan criticism of Christian women who killed themselves in order to avoid rape at the hands of Alaric's forces (1.19, cf. 1.16–17). At the same time, he expresses relief that Lucretia's example did not induce those Christian women who had suffered rape during the siege to take their own lives subsequently, out of shame.[47] Augustine is aware that Christian writers in the past have also lauded Lucretia's example, and that some, such as Ambrose, have even praised Christian virgins who committed suicide to avoid rape.[48] His criticism of Lucretia's action thus reveals his determination to undermine the structure of virtue on which her value as a moral example depends, for pagans and Christians alike.[49] He accepts what he takes to be the prevalent view that she did not consent to her own violation. For this reason, he surmises that her decision to commit suicide arose from her need to dramatize her innocence publicly in order to counter any judgment by her social peers that she had at least consented to, and perhaps even enjoyed, the sexual acts involved in the rape (1.29). Her suicide was therefore motivated by the need to preserve a good reputation and even to obtain praise (1.19). For this reason, Augustine aligns her with Marcus Porcius Cato 'the Younger', whose suicide masks a will to avoid the public disgrace he would have suffered at being pardoned by Julius Caesar (1.23).

Against these two negative examples, Augustine praises Christian women during the sack of 410 who suffered rape but did not allow the loss of a good reputation to destroy them, because their consciences assured them of approval in the sight of God (1.19). Greatness of soul (*magnitudo animi*) is found not in the counterfeit valour exercised in taking one's own life to avoid public shame, but in a fortitude which holds human judgment in contempt when it defames character unjustly (1.22). These women enjoy a consolation (*consolatio*) that is 'great and true' because it is interior, a consolation that transcends exterior approval.[50] Augustine applies this same principle to those of the women who, prior to their assault, relished the

---

[47] See *ciu.* 1.19.

[48] See Ambrose, *De uirginibus* 3.7, 32–7 (AD 337). See also Ambrose, *l. 2, ep. 7* (Maur. 37).38 (CSEL 82 X/1.62), concerning the virgin martyr Pelagia of Antioch. The declaration that Ambrose attributes to Pelagia finds a parallel at Philo, *Quod omnis probus liber sit* 17.116, who in turn depends upon Euripides, *Hecuba* 548.

[49] This point is convincingly demonstrated by D. Trout, 'Re-Textualizing Lucretia: Cultural Subversion in the *City of God*', *Journal of Early Christian Studies* 2:1 (1994), 53–70. Among Christian writers citing Lucretia favourably as an example, Trout identifies Tertullian, *Ad martyras* 4 (he cites other texts at 61 n. 36), Jerome, *Aduersus Jouinianum* 1.46, 1.49, and Paulinus of Nola, *Carmina* 10.192 to Ausonius. See also I. Donaldson, *The Rapes of Lucretia: A Myth and its Transformation* (Oxford, 1982), A. Droge and J. Tabor, *A Noble Death: Suicide and Martyrdom among Christians and Jews in Antiquity* (San Francisco, 1992).

[50] See *ciu.* 1.27, 1.22 (CCL 47.23): 'stultam uulgi opinionem'. On Augustine's concept of consolation, see M. Beyenka, *Consolation in Saint Augustine* (Washington, 1950), Y.-M. Duval, 'Consolatio',

praise they received on account of their reputation for virginity, chastity, and purity. He hears reports that this celebrity had led some of them to resent sharing this status with a growing number of similarly inclined women.[51] These rumours offer him yet another opportunity to insist upon the need to reconstruct virtues like chastity by anchoring them in faith and humility.[52] Crucial to this reconstruction is the conception of virtue as a 'gift of God' (*donum dei*), not a personal achievement.[53] Women who remained virtuous in these circumstances were able to do so only because they had received 'divine assistance'.[54] Jealousy can only be felt by those for whom virtue is a personal achievement, and who are more concerned with exterior approval or condemnation than the interior discourse between God and the soul.[55] This is the first of many points in the *City of God* where Augustine, in his effort to steer Christians away from the urge to heroism as exemplified in pagan models such as Lucretia, insists upon divine grace rather than human effort as the foundation of virtue.[56] His criticism of Lucretia also provides his first opportunity to contrast the exterior rhetoric of public opinion (*gloria, laus, honor*) with the interior, divine rhetoric in relation to the construction of civic virtue and, by extension, of the just society.

It is useful in understanding his critique of Lucretia's example of virtue to observe how, in general terms, he connects it with ignorance and weakness. He argues, for example, that suicide reveals a weakness (*infirmitas*)

Augustinus-Lexikon, vol. 1, ed. C. Mayer (Basle, 1986–94), 1244–7. For its application to fear of death, see especially *en. Ps.* 30.2.1.3.

[51] See *ciu.* 1.28 (CCL 47.29): 'uerum tamen interrogate fideliter animas uestras, ne forte de isto integritatis et continentiae uel pudicitiae bono uos inflatius extulistis et humanis laudibus delectatae in hoc etiam aliquibus inuidistis'.

[52] At *ciu.* 1.28 (CCL 47.29), Augustine acknowledges that he has no confirmation of the accuracy of these reports: 'non accuso quod nescio, nec audio quod uobis interrogata uestra corda respondent'. At *exc. urb.* 1–2, 9 (AD 410/11) and *s.* 113A.11, he interprets the distress that religious celibates encountered during the sack of Rome as a corrective against pride. Writing on virginity c. AD 401, he admits to hearing it said that he is more concerned with humility than virginity. See *uirg.* 52 (CSEL 41.297): 'hic dicet aliquis: non est hoc iam de uirginitate, sed de humilitate scribere'. See also *retr.* 2.23. He couples humility and virginity when speaking about the latter as a state of Christian life in relation to marriage, especially when writing in the context of the Jovianian controversy. See *uirg.* 45, *b. coniug.* 30, *en. Ps.* 99.13, 75.16, *s.* 354.8–9, and my discussion below, pp. 190–1. See also Schaffner, *Christliche Demut*, 74–9, F. Consolino, 'Modelli di santità femminile nelle più antiche Passioni romane', *Augustinianum* 24 (1984), 83–113.

[53] See *ciu.* 1.28 (CCL 47.29): 'quarum uero corda interrogata respondent numquam se de bono uirginitatis uel uiduitatis uel coniugalis pudicitiae superbisse, sed humilibus consentiendo de dono dei cum tremore exultasse'.

[54] See *ciu.* 1.28 (CCL 47.29): 'si peccantibus non consensistis, diuinae gratiae, ne amitteretur, diuinum accessit auxilium'.

[55] On this point in general, see R. Markus, '*De civitate dei*: Pride and the Common Good', *Proceedings of the Patristic, Medieval and Renaissance Conference*, ed. P. Pulsiano (Villanova, 1987–8), 1–16.

[56] See *ciu.* 5.19, 5.20, 5.26, and especially 17.4. I discuss this contrast in more detail below, pp. 107–10, 191–3.

in the face of physical hardship or disgrace.[57] Examples of virtue which are 'proposed by pagans who do not know God (*ignorare deum*)' are not permitted 'to those who worship the one true God'.[58] Augustine here signals his view that the moral value of a heroic example depends upon the extent to which the virtue that motivates it has been informed by the knowledge and love of the true God. In part, this qualification refers to the obedience which is owed to divine precepts. Suicide specifically contradicts divine law; those who worship God therefore reject it.[59] Such devotion to God involves more, however, than obedience to divine commandments. In discussing the virtue of Rome's Christian women during the sack, Augustine notes that the divine consolation which they experienced was neither contradicted nor erased by the darkness which they experienced in searching to understand God's reasons for permitting such violence.[60] Both states, consolation and darkness, co-exist in the soul and spring from God. Their interaction reinforces the humility through which the soul recognizes that the origin of its virtue is God, not itself.[61] This opaque, divine presence, in which the ways and judgments of God are hidden from human scrutiny, is not to be confused with divine absence as it is experienced in the veneration of Roman deities, who are worshipped so that such atrocities as the sack of Rome may be avoided altogether.[62] Instead, it stimulates the religious

---

[57] See *ciu.* 1.19 (CCL 47.21): 'non est pudicitiae caritas, sed pudoris infirmitas', 1.22 (CCL 47.23): 'magis enim mens infirma deprehenditur, quae ferre non potest uel duram sui corporis seruitutem uel stultam uulgi opinionem'. He subsequently recalls that Cato's friends objected in similar terms to his decision to commit suicide. See *ciu.* 1.23 (CCL 47.24): 'qui hoc fieri prudentius dissuadebant, inbecillioris quam fortioris animi facinus esse censuerunt, quo demonstraretur non honestas turpia praecauens, sed infirmitas aduersa non sustinens?'.

[58] See *ciu.* 1.22 (CCL 47.24): 'quaelibet exempla proponant gentes, quae ignorant deum, manifestum est hoc non licere colentibus unum uerum deum'. For an overview of the historical and ethical issues behind Augustine's analysis of Lucretia's suicide, consult O'Daly, *Augustine's* City, 77–9. See also R. Klesczewski, 'Wandlungen des Lucretia-Bildes im lateinischen Mittelalter und in der lateinischen Literatur der Renaissance', *Livius. Werk und Rezeption. Festschrift für Erich Burck zum 80. Geburtstag*, ed. E. Lefevre and E. Olshausen (Munich, 1983), 313–35.

[59] See *ciu.* 1.17, 1.20, 1.21, 1.22, 1.25, 1.26, 1.27, 1.29.

[60] See *ciu.* 1.28 (CCL 47.28): 'habetis magnam ueramque consolationem, si fidam conscientiam retinetis non uos consensisse peccatis eorum, qui in uos peccare permissi sunt. quod si forte, cur permissi sint, quaeritis, alta quidem prouidentia creatoris mundi atque rectoris, *et inscrutabilia sunt iudicia eius et inuestigabiles uiae eius*' (Rom 11:33).

[61] See *ciu.* 1.28 (CCL 47.29): 'in utroque consolamini, pusillanimes, illinc probatae hinc castigatae, illinc iustificatae hinc emendatae [. . .] utrisque igitur, quae de carne sua, quod turpem nullius esset perpessa contactum, uel iam superbiebant uel superbire, si nec hostium uiolentia contrectata esset, forsitan poterant, non ablata est castitas, sed humilitas persuasa'.

[62] See *ciu.* 1.29 (CCL 47.30): 'illi uero, qui probitati eius insultant eique dicunt, cum forte in aliqua temporalia mala deuenerit: *ubi est deus tuus?* (Ps 41[42]:4) ipsi dicant, ubi sint dii eorum, cum talia patiuntur, pro quibus euitandis eos uel colunt uel colendos esse contendunt. nam ista respondet: deus meus ubique praesens, ubique totus, nusquam inclusus, qui possit adesse secretus, abesse non motus; ille cum me aduersis rebus exagitat, aut merita examinat aut peccata castigat mercedemque mihi aeternam pro toleratis pie malis temporalibus seruat'. See also *ciu.* 1.22, 2.3.

faith through which believers acknowledge that God has not abandoned them, even when he permits their enemies to defeat them.[63] Key to their acceptance of this perspective is their faith that, in Christ, God has already suffered the greatest conceivable humiliation.[64] By this same logic, the example of these Christian women outshines even that of Regulus. Regulus is a military hero, obliged by an oath to kill those whom he conquers; had he been able to do so, he would have killed the Carthaginians who killed him. These anonymous Christian heroines, on the other hand, demonstrate a still more courageous acceptance of death: in imitation of Christ's vulnerability to death, they have forsworn any opportunity to kill their enemy who threatened them, or to kill in revenge for evil suffered.[65]

By the end of Book 1, Augustine has elicited the main themes of his subsequent reconstruction of civic virtue. Roman heroes such as Regulus and Lucretia exemplify an artificial virtue in the face of death, which is grounded in a false conception of God. Such 'virtue' is manufactured by the soul itself, sustained either by a love for virtue or, more often, by the thirst for glory. Comparison of pagan virtue with its Christian alternative reveals that, in its idealized form, the latter is the gift of God and is sustained by a mystery which exhibits and – as he will say more explicitly in Book 10 – communicates divine vulnerability to the believer. Once healed of the pride which afflicts pagan heroes, Christians renounce counterfeit forms of virtue, which only serve to mask fear.

Masking fear of death is the concluding theme of Book 1. Augustine suggests that the Roman elite indulge in various forms of luxury (*luxuria*) accompanied by a variety of illicit pleasures (*uoluptates*) to distract them from the inevitability of death. He makes this point indirectly by recalling Scipio Nasica Corculum's decision during the Third Punic War (149–146 BC) to spare Carthage so that Rome would not be bereft of mortal enemies.

---

[63] See *ciu.* 1.28 (CCL 47.29–30): 'nec ideo deum credant ista neglegere, quia permittit quod nemo inpune committit. quaedam enim ueluti pondera malarum cupiditatum et per occultum praesens diuinum iudicium relaxantur et manifesto ultimo reseruantur [. . .] et fide inconcussa non de illo sentiunt, quod ita sibi seruientes eumque inuocantes deserere ullo modo potuerit'.

[64] See *ciu.* 1.24 (below, n. 65).

[65] See *ciu.* 1.24 (CCL 47.25–6): 'porro si fortissimi et praeclarissimi uiri terrenae patriae defensores deorumque licet falsorum, non tamen fallaces cultores, sed ueracissimi etiam iuratores, qui hostes uictos more ac iure belli ferire potuerunt, hi ab hostibus uicti se ipsos ferire noluerunt et, cum mortem minime formidarent, uictores tamen dominos ferre quam eam sibi inferre maluerunt: quanto magis christiani, uerum deum colentes et supernae patriae suspirantes, ab hoc facinore temperabunt, si eos diuina dispositio uel probandos uel emendandos ad tempus hostibus subiugauerit, quos in illa humilitate non deserit, qui propter eos tam humiliter altissimus uenit, praesertim quos nullius militaris potestatis uel talis militiae iura constringunt ipsum hostem ferire superatum'. Augustine extends this criticism of Regulus at *ciu.* 3.18 (CCL 47.86), observing that his 'craving for praise and glory' (*auiditas laudis/gloriae*) led him to impose conditions upon the Carthaginians that were so harsh that they could not accept them. See my discussion below, pp. 184–5.

Scipio's action demonstrated that the best of the Romans understood the utility of fear in keeping their compatriots aware that their vices represented a real threat to their security.[66] Romans, however, continue to seek to protect their access to a more comfortable life through personal ambition and the conquest of other nations.[67] Fear of death expresses itself as the fear of a loss of status and comfort which has been typical of Rome since the decline of the republic.[68] Empire is thus a murky, ambivalent symbol in Augustine's thought. To a limited extent, he interprets it as a sign of at least temporary divine favour. In the long run, however, the cost in resources and human suffering of maintaining and expanding the Empire reveals an underlying, ever-increasing social anxiety about annihilation.[69] In effect, the overdependence upon military force characteristic of empire institutionalizes and internalizes the visible, permanent security threat which Scipio Nasica Corculum saw in Carthage. Thus, a vicious circle links the threat of annihilation with an ever-growing political and military response to foreign threats, disseminating anxiety throughout the Empire to such an extent that even the inhabitants of Roman Africa are alarmed by the Visigothic assault on Rome. Owing to this increased anxiety, Romans create cultural rituals which mask this threat.

Among these practices, Augustine in particularly critical of theatre, especially as apparent in Roman priesthoods and cults, for its power to distract its audiences from this anxiety. He once again recalls Scipio Nasica Corculum, who, as *pontifex maximus*, persuaded the Roman senate in 155 BC

---

[66] See *ciu.* 1.30, cf. 2.18. At *ciu.* 3.28 (CCL 47.95), Augustine makes a parallel point in reference to the usefulness which Sulla saw in introducing a reign of terror during the 'peace' which followed his defeat of Marius: 'haec facta sunt in pace post bellum, non ut acceleraretur obtinenda uictoria, sed ne contemneretur obtenta. pax cum bello de crudelitate certauit et uicit'. See also *ciu.* 4.3.

[67] See *ciu.* 1.30 (CCL 47.30): 'cur enim adflicti rebus aduersis de temporibus querimini christianis, nisi quia uestram luxuriam cupitis habere securam et perditissimis moribus remota omni molestiarum asperitate diffluere? neque enim propterea cupitis habere pacem et omni genere copiarum abundare, ut his bonis honeste utamini, hoc est modeste sobrie, temperanter pie, sed ut infinita uarietas uoluptatum insanis effusionibus exquiratur, secundisque rebus ea mala oriantur in moribus, quae saeuientibus peiora sunt hostibus'. See also *ciu.* 1.31, 2.20, 4.3. At the beginning of *ciu.* 1.30, Augustine misidentifies P. Cornelius Scipio Nasica Corculum with his father, P. Cornelius Scipio Nasica. Augustine depends on Sallust for much of this account. See the discussion by O'Daly, *Augustine's City*, 240–6, and H. Hagendahl, *Augustine and the Latin Classics*, 2 vols. (Göteborg, 1967), 2:634–6.

[68] Thus, accusations against the Christian religion on account of the sack of Rome betray a longing for freedom from adversity which threatens the loss of luxury and comfort. See *ciu.* 1.30 (above, n. 67). Augustine makes the same point using stronger language at *ciu.* 2.20 (CCL 47.52): 'tantum efficiant, ut tali felicitati nihil ab hoste, nihil a peste, nihil ab ulla clade timeatur'. At *ciu.* 2.18, he opposes Sallust's thesis that there was ever a time in the history of the Romans when 'justice and goodness prevailed among them as much by nature as by law' (*Bellum Catilinae* 9.1), arguing that even during the republic what little social order existed depended upon a fear of annihilation by war and not love of justice. See also *ciu.* 2.21, where he appeals to Cicero in making the same point.

[69] On the Roman Empire as an expression of divine favour, see *ciu.* 1.36, 3.11, 4.33. On the increase of anxiety associated with the growth of the Empire, see *ciu.* 1.30, 2.18, 3.9–10, 3.28, 4.3, 4.15.

to abandon the project of building a theatre at Rome to house spectacles intended, in part, to appease the gods during a plague (1.31, 1.33, cf. 2.5, 2.8). Augustine suspects that Scipio, unanimously chosen as 'best citizen' (*optimus*) by his peers, feared to arouse the displeasure of demons by taking an even stronger public stand than he did against the theatrical shows.[70] Such moral weakness in the Roman priest-statesman is explained by the fact that God had not yet revealed to the nations the teaching (*doctrina*) which 'cleanses the heart by faith', so that 'through humble piety' human beings might search beyond the heavens and 'be freed from the oppressive domination of demons'.[71] He will later argue that Christian martyrs and evangelists demonstrate the requisite valour in this regard, and do not fear to speak out against demonic oppression (2.29, 4.30). Augustine wonders whether anyone in the future will believe that, while the whole Empire grieved at Alaric's sack of Rome, refugees from the city who arrived in Africa flocked to the amphitheatres in Carthage, still eager for stage plays, as if oblivious to Rome's misfortune (1.32). To the extent that Roman religion colludes with theatrical performances in distracting even the political elite from the threat of annihilation, it ensures its own inefficacy in promoting civic virtue (1.31–2).

DECEPTORES ET DECEPTOS

Books 2–4, in which Augustine explicitly considers Roman religion, develop these themes further. Book 2 opens with the lament that intellectual blindness (*caecitas*) and moral obstinacy (*peruicacia*) – further echoes of ignorance and weakness – impede the soul from accepting sound doctrine (*doctrina salubris*) and divine assistance (*adiutorium diuinum*), which, when received in faith, enable the mind to perceive errors and arrive at religious and moral truth. Here, for the first of many occasions in the *City of God*, Augustine couples divine teaching with grace as a remedy (*medicina*) for the weakened condition of human reason.[72] Roman religion is characterized by an ignorance that is not able to distinguish the true God from false gods

---

[70] See *ciu.* 1.31. See also G. Bardy, 'Le Théatre à Rome', *Œuvres de saint Augustin*, vol. 33: *La Cité de Dieu, Livres I–V: Impuissance sociale du paganisme*, ed. G. Bardy and G. Combès (Paris, 1959), 780–1, for historical sources.

[71] See *ciu.* 1.31 (CCL 47.32): 'nondum enim fuerat declarata gentibus superna doctrina, quae fide cor mundans ad caelestia uel supercaelestia capessenda humili pietate humanum mutaret affectum et a dominatu superborum daemonum liberaret'. See R. Markus, *The End of Ancient Christianity* (Cambridge, 1990), 107–23, W. Weismann, *Kirche und Schauspiele. Die Schauspiele im Urteil der lateinischen Kirchenväter unter besonderer Berücksichtigung von Augustin* (Würzburg, 1972), 123–95.

[72] See *ciu.* 2.1 (CCL 47.35): 'si rationi perspicuae ueritatis infirmus humanae consuetudinis sensus non auderet obsistere, sed doctrinae salubri languorem suum tamquam medicinae subderet, donec diuino adiutorio fide pietatis inpetrante sanaretur, non multo sermone opus esset ad conuincendum quemlibet uanae opinationis errorem his, qui recte sentiunt et sensa uerbis sufficientibus explicant'.

in spite of the obviously immoral practices which accompany pagan cultic rituals, and the corresponding absence of any moral teaching by these gods (2.4, 2.6, 2.7, 2.13, 2.16, 2.19, 2.22).[73] Augustine mentions mystery religions in passing by dismissing the relevance to his argument of whatever moral teachings may be privately communicated to adherents during their induction into these cults (2.6). His point is that Roman religion lacks structures for any formal, public discourse concerning virtues. He argues further that what weak moral foundation Rome does possess derives from its laws, not from its religion (2.7, 2.14, 2.16). In reply to the objection that it is by philosophers and not the gods that moral instruction ought to be taught, he concedes a limited value to the mind's investigation of moral truths, aided by dialectic, especially in those rare instances when this reflection is also assisted to some degree by grace, as it was in the case of certain philosophers. However, he objects that this method cannot achieve significant results while still at a remove from the 'way of humility' (*uia humilitatis*), by which he refers to the incarnation as divine mystery.[74] Yet another reason for preferring that Christianity, and not philosophical schools or civil law, should provide society with a clear framework for virtue is religion's superior power of persuasion.[75] Roman society squanders the moral capital in the natural rhetorical force of religion. Young boys who are required to read comedies and tragedies as part of a liberal education (2.8) are often moved by the examples of the gods to imitate their misdeeds (2.7, cf. 2.12, 2.20). Augustine recalls his own youthful enthusiasm for this literature and its 'morals'.[76] He constrasts the absence of moral discourse in Roman religion with Christianity's efforts to teach precepts for virtuous living primarily through the scriptures and preaching (2.6, 2.19, 2.25, 2.28).

The modern reader of the *City of God* is apt to be surprised at the importance of demons in Augustine's discussion of true religion. In ancient society their place in the universe as intermediaries who communicated

---

Note, too, that *doctrina* and *adiutorium* parallel the effects of Christ's example as *iustus* and his graced mediation as *iustificare*. See my discussion of these points in Chapters 3 and 5.

[73] O'Daly, *Augustine's City*, 80–1, recalls Augustine's acknowledgement (*ciu.* 2.1) that his depiction of Roman religion is selective and polemical.

[74] See *ciu.* 2.7 (CCL 47.40): 'quantum autem humanitus inpediti sunt, errauerunt, maxime cum eorum superbiae iuste prouidentia diuina resisteret, ut uiam pietatis ab humilitate in superna surgentem etiam istorum conparatione monstraret'. Augustine has in mind philosophers whom he classes generally as 'Platonists' (*platonici*). See my discussion, which concerns especially Books 8–10, below, pp. 63–6. References to studies on Christ as *uia* in the thought of Augustine are given below, p. 72 n. 1.

[75] See, for example, *ciu.* 2.8 (CCL 47.41): 'quis igitur in agenda uita non ea sibi potius sectanda arbitretur, quae actitantur ludis auctoritate diuina institutis, quam ea, quae scriptitantur legibus humano consilio promulgatis?'.

[76] See *ciu.* 2.4. See also *conf.* 1.14–16, 1.20–9.

between the gods and human beings was taken for granted.[77] In theory they could be good or evil, but Augustine tends to align *daemon* with *daemonium* (as at Jas 2:19 and 1 Cor 10:20) and, therefore, to treat them as evil.[78] All deities to whom cultic sacrifices are offered, he believes, are demons.[79] Resentment over imperial edicts banning non-Christian cults, coupled with the fact that many Romans blamed the Christians for Alaric's victory over Rome on the grounds that the church had supported these prohibitions (and thus angered the demons), ensured the prominence of demons in the *City of God*.[80] Augustine charges that demons communicate religious falsehoods to human beings, and are therefore dangerous to the soul, because they reinforce religious and moral ignorance and weakness (2.4–6, 2.9–10, 2.16, 2.19, 2.26). Livy's account of the *haruspex* Postumius, who read animal entrails in order to reassure Lucius Cornelius Sulla about his plans to advance against the army of Gaius Marius during the first of the Civil Wars (88–82 BC), and who later instructed Sulla to eat a portion of the entrails from yet another sacrifice to Mars at Tarentum, provides Augustine with the basis for his charge that the gods proper to Roman sacrifices were in reality evil demons. Their sole power consists in deceiving the Romans into deepening their own ruinous drive for self-glory, as evidenced by the career of Sulla 'Felix'.[81] Demons thus seduce the masses into worshipping them (2.10, cf. 4.29) by means of promises of temporal and eternal rewards which cannot be fulfilled.[82] Finally, even Rome's best citizens (*uiri optimi*) are deceived by Cybele, the 'Mother of the Gods'.[83]

---

[77] See *ciu.* 8.20. Plato, *Symposium* 195, credits 'demons' with this task.

[78] See *ciu.* 9.19. He regarded all demons as fallen angels: *ciu.* 5.9, *c. Max.* 2.12.2, *s. Dolbeau* 23.13. See also J. den Boeft, 'Daemon(es)', *Augustinus-Lexikon*, vol. 2, ed. C. Mayer (Basle, 1996–2002), 213–22, at 213–14, J. Pépin, 'Influences païennes sur l'angelologie et la démonologie de saint Augustin', *'Ex Platonicorum persona'. Etudes sur les lectures philosophiques de saint Augustin* (Amsterdam, 1977), 29–37, Evans, *Augustine*, 98–111, and S. MacCormack, *The Shadow of Poetry: Vergil in the Mind of Augustine* (Berkeley, 1998), 133–74.

[79] See *en. Ps.* 96.11, in conjunction with 1 Cor 8:4, 10:19–20. At *ciu.* 2.11 (CCL 47.43), Augustine asserts that all pagan gods are evil spirits.

[80] See *ciu.* 2.2, 2.3, 2.4, 2.19.

[81] See *ciu.* 2.24–5. Livy's report is lost, but is related by Cicero, *De diuinatione* 1.33.72, and Plutarch, *Sulla* 9.

[82] See, for example, *ciu.* 2.5. See also *ciu.* 4.31 (CCL 47.125): 'hac tamen fallacia miris modis maligni daemones delectantur, qui et deceptores et deceptos pariter possident, a quorum dominatione non liberat nisi gratia dei per Iesum Christum dominum nostrum'. At *ciu.* 9.15, Augustine objects that the immortality 'possessed' by the demons and promised as a reward to their devotees is a deception because it does not offer beatitude. On this point, see G. Remy, *Le Christ médiateur dans l'œuvre de saint Augustin*, 2 vols. (Lille, 1979), 1:256–72, 1:230–4, on beatitude.

[83] See *ciu.* 2.5 (CCL 47.38): 'Romanas occupatura mentes quaesiuit optimum uirum, non quem monendo et adiuuando faceret, sed quem fallendo deciperet [. . .] quo modo igitur nisi insidiose quaereret dea illa optimum uirum, cum talia quaerat in suis sacris, qualia uiri optimi abhorrent suis

In Augustine's view, demons are principally responsible for the collusion between Roman religion and theatre which even their own historians had judged corrosive of public morals and security. He faults demons for ordering stage plays in their honour which contain obscenities that human beings are apt to imitate (2.8–10, 2.13, 2.14, 2.19, 2.25–6, cf. 4.1, 4.26). Rome's most outstanding citizens (*optimi uiri*) and priests, such as Scipio Nasica Corculum and Cicero, who take these demons to be gods and accede through weakness to their demands, also bear responsibility for the detrimental effects of theatre on Roman morals (2.5, 2.27, cf. 4.26, 4.30). Demons posing as gods even allow lies to be told against them, to seduce human beings into imitating their alleged misdeeds, as though they exemplify just conduct (2.10, 2.12, cf. 2.25, 4.1, 4.26–7). Plato decreed that poets who told such untruths about the gods were to be banned from his ideal republic.[84] Rome's moral and political decline, from the time of its foundation through the imperial period, can, according to Augustine, be traced in large part to these effects of the theatre.[85]

Aware of the theatre's capacity to distort public images of Roman citizens (principally its political leaders), Augustine echoes Cicero's approval in *De re publica* of the ancient Roman laws prohibiting poets from praising or slandering any living citizen, as well as his criticism of the Greeks for their refusal to enact similar laws (2.9, 2.12, 2.14, cf. 2.10, 4.26). By prohibiting actors from holding public office as well, the Romans once again opposed Greek practices (2.13–14).[86] Augustine in part accepts this Roman perspective. He does not explain his position explicitly, but the context of his remarks suggests that he views the indecencies which these actors performed on stage as diminishing the dignity proper to public offices or honours (2.11, 2.13, 2.27, 2.29). While accepting the Roman stance on poets and actors, however, he turns it back against them, noting that, in the case of poets, the Romans failed to prohibit them from slandering the gods (2.11). They ought to be ashamed, he says, at the fact that they worship gods who commit acts the performance of which earns actors banishment from public life, while it earns honours for the poets who record them

---

adhibere conuiuiis?' On the cult of Cybele at Carthage, see J. Rives, *Religion and Authority in Roman Carthage from Augustus to Constantine* (Oxford, 1995), 65–72, 163–9. See also O'Daly, *Augustine's City*, 81–2.

[84] See *ciu.* 2.14–15 in conjunction with Plato, *Republic* 398A, 568B, 605A, 607B. Cf. Plato, *Timaeus* 29C–30. See also *ciu.* 8.14.

[85] See, especially, *ciu.* 2.14 (CCL 47.46): 'uel insita extirpanda curarent dii tales, qui etiam seminanda et augenda flagitia curauerunt, talia uel sua uel quasi sua facta per theatricas celebritates populis innotescere cupientes, ut tamquam auctoritate diuina sua sponte nequissima libido accenderetur humana'. See also *ciu.* 2.13, 2.16, 2.18, 2.19.

[86] See W. Beare, *The Roman Stage*, 3rd edn (London, 1964), 166–8, 237–40.

(2.13–14). Sensitive as ancient Romans are to decorum in public life, how can they fail to understand its greater religious significance in relation to the gods?[87] Plato, Marcus Porcius Cato, and other philosophers are worthier of divine honours than the Roman gods, says Augustine, because whereas they provide society with moral instruction, the gods either seduce people away from virtue (2.7, 2.14) or, as in the case of those gods who were once human beings, such as Romulus/Quirinus, fail to achieve the virtue which Plato exhibits through his teachings (2.15, 2.17). Behind Augustine's argument, one senses a further charge concerning the origin of the virtue which public officials are expected to exemplify. He is preparing the ground for a broader criticism: because the gods exemplify vice and not virtue, they cannot be sources of virtue. As a consequence, Rome's best citizens see no alternative but to seek virtue exclusively from within themselves.[88]

Fear of death emerges in this context as part of Augustine's refutation of Sallust's claim that Roman gods did not need to provide their devotees with a moral code because 'justice and goodness (*ius bonumque*) prevailed among them as much by nature as by law'.[89] Augustine refutes this judgment in part by arguing that the evidence which Sallust presents in the *Historiae* undermines rather than supports his conclusion. The social order which Sallust detects during periods of relatively high public morality, such as between the Second and Third Punic Wars, following the banishment of Rome's kings, lasts only as long as an external threat to Rome's political and military security exists. Any semblance of civic virtue in Roman society at such times derived not from a natural inclination to virtue, but from the fear of annihilation either by enemies or by the demons who posed as gods (2.18, 2.22, cf. 3.16, 4.15, 5.13).

Demons cannot even be trusted to communicate truthfully about the security of Rome and the safety of its leaders. Roman historians report that demons deceived Sulla about his personal safety (2.24). Moreover, the

---

[87] See *ciu.* 2.12 (CCL 47.43–4): 'quod erga se quidem satis honeste constituerunt, sed erga deos suos superbe et inreligiose; quos cum scirent non solum patienter, uerum etiam libenter poetarum probris maledictisque lacerari, se potius quam illos huiusce modi iniuriis indignos esse duxerunt seque ab eis etiam lege munierunt, illorum autem ista etiam sacris sollemnitatibus miscuerunt'. See my discussion below, pp. 121–2 on divine dignity and oratory.

[88] He hints at this conclusion at *ciu.* 2.14 (CCL 47.46), by affirming that the Romans' own laws are morally superior to whatever they might have hoped to receive from the gods: 'nequaquam igitur leges ad instituendos bonos aut corrigendos malos mores a diis suis possent accipere seu sperare Romani, quos legibus suis uincunt atque conuincunt'. At *ciu.* 2.16, he approves of the Roman refusal to accept that Apollo was the source of the moral teaching behind the laws which Lycurgus instituted for the Spartans.

[89] See *ciu.* 2.17–19, citing Sallust, *Bellum Catilinae* 9.1. Augustine rebuts Sallust with examples selected from his *Historiae*. O'Daly, *Augustine's City*, 240–6, discusses throroughly Augustine's use of Sallust and provides references to further relevant studies, among which see especially Hagendahl, *Augustine*, 2:631–49.

demons who were thought responsible for protecting Troy were probably guilty of collusion in its destruction by Fimbria in 85 BC (3.7). The Romans find it easy to blame their unwise political decisions on the seductions of demons, yet they remain ignorant of the true God.[90] Searching for security during the anxious years of their territorial expansion, the Romans found hope for divine protection in the multiplication of the gods and sacred images. In doing so, however, they only distanced themselves further from knowledge and love of the true God and from the civic order which monotheism brings (3.12–14, 3.18, 4.8, 4.10–11, 4.13–14). Pantheism, which, Augustine says, results from a variation within the logic of polytheism, likewise misunderstands the nature of true piety (4.12–13). Much of Augustine's criticism of public and private divination also follows from his belief that the Romans ignored the true God and the implications this had for their security. He recalls that auguries and auspices failed to prevent Roman defeats on the battlefield.[91] He mockingly cites as proof of this misplaced trust the order of Mithridates VI Eupator Dionysus, king of Pontus (120–63 BC), that all Roman citizens found in Asia Minor should be put to death. 'Had all the victims failed to heed the auguries? . . . Were there no household or public gods for them to consult?'[92]

In his first four books, in particular, Augustine explores the debilitating effects of ignorance as inculcated by Roman religion, either in terms of the lack of divine revelation or instruction which blinded the Romans or through outright deceptions practised by evil spirits or political and religious leaders. In all cases, ignorance of the true God among the populace is reinforced through athletic contests, local religious festivals, theatre arts, and literature (2.4–8, 2.14, 2.26, 3.17, 4.26; cf. also 7.33–4), which are intended, in large part, to assuage fear of death.[93] The Romans compound the disasters of their polytheism when they create deities from divine

---

[90] See *ciu.* 1.33 (CCL 47.33): 'sed in uobis plus ualuit quod daemones impii seduxerunt, quam quod homines prouidi praecauerunt', 3.15 (CCL 47.80): 'nisi forte quispiam sic defendat istos deos, ut dicat eos ideo mansisse Romae, quo possent magis Romanos punire suppliciis quam beneficiis adiuuare, seducentes eos uanis uictoriis et bellis grauissimis conterentes'.

[91] At *ciu.* 3.21, Augustine mentions the defeat of the consul Gaius Hostilius Mancinus by a much smaller force of Numantines in 137 BC. He asks rhetorically why the auspices withheld offering better military advice to Roman commanders. See Cicero, *De oratore* 1.40.181. See also his remarks at *ciu.* 3.20 in relation to Hannibal's defeat of the Saguntines. At *ciu.* 4.29, he recounts the failures of auspices and auguries to avert defeat during the later period of the Roman Empire.

[92] See *ciu.* 3.22 (CCL 47.91): 'num et isti omnes auguria contempserant? num deos et domesticos et publicos, cum de sedibus suis ad illam inremeabilem peregrinationem profecti sunt, quos consulerent, non habebant?' The massacre took place in summer 88 BC during the First Mithridatic War (88–85 BC). See Livy, *Epitome* 78.

[93] See, for example, *ciu.* 3.18 (CCL 47.85): 'tunc magno metu perturbata Romana ciuitas ad remedia uana et ridenda currebat. instaurati sunt ex auctoritate librorum Sibyllinorum ludi saeculares'.

attributes (4.15–25, 4.28, cf. 5.12.3). Who, Augustine asks, is fool enough to believe that Virtue and Felicity are the names of distinct, divine beings, and not simply gifts of the one, true God (4.24)? On account of their human weakness (*infirmitas*) the Romans reason only to the point of recognizing that the happiness they seek depends upon divine favour. Not knowing (*ignorare*) the name of the God of happiness, they turn Happiness into a god.[94]

Having argued that demons cannot bring temporal happiness as they claim to do, Augustine turns his attention in Books 6–10 to their inability to lead human beings to eternal life. Demons, he says, are the enemies of religious truth (6.6, 6.8, 8.20, 8.22, 9.23). They promote the seductive fantasy of euhemerism, the belief 'that the gods were once human beings' (6.18).[95] On account of such deceptions, demons are regarded as gods and are offered public, obscene rituals as acts of worship (7.26, 7.33). Roman forms of worship are conditioned by demonic threats; Varro's civil theology has encouraged them to inhabit unseemly images such as human phalluses in order to dupe the foolish into fearing them.[96] In this way they deceived Numa Pompilius into establishing diverse forms of divination as religious ceremonies (7.35). With their miraculous feats, such as prognostication, they trick people into thinking them divine, making it more difficult for them to discover the true God (8.22, 10.16, 10.26). Demons even went so far as to attempt to seduce Christ (9.21, cf. Mt 4:1–11).

Theurgy is likewise founded on demonic deceptions.[97] St Paul explains the ecstatic experiences occasioned by theurgic rituals in this way: 'Satan

---

[94] See *ciu.* 4.25. At *ciu.* 8.23–4, Augustine cites Hermes Trismegistus' condemnation in *Asclepius* (about which, see O'Daly, *Augustine's City*, 117–18) of false religion among the Egyptians, who are criticized for 'making gods' and thus for misunderstanding the nature of the true God and of true worship.

[95] At *ciu.* 8.26, Augustine observes that in all of pagan literature one scarcely finds a mention of any god who was not first a human being. He discusses euhemerism elsewhere at *ciu.* 2.5, 2.15, 2.18 (Romulus), 3.4, 3.15 (Romulus), 8.18, 22.6, 22.10 (Hercules, Romulus). See G. Bardy, 'L'Euhémérisme', *Œuvres de saint Augustin*, vol. 33: *La Cité de Dieu, Livres I–V: Impuissance sociale du paganisme*, ed. G. Bardy and G. Combès (Paris, 1959), 785, A. Mandouze, 'Saint Augustin et la religion romaine', *Recherches augustiniennes* I (1958), 187–223, at 202–10, K. Thraede, 'Euhemerismus', *Reallexikon für Antike und Christentum*, vol. 6, ed. T. Klauser (Stuttgart, 1966), 877–90, O'Daly, *Augustine's City*, 105–6.

[96] See *ciu.* 7.27. Numa Pompilius feared demons whom he took to be gods (*ciu.* 7.34). See also the summary statement against Varronian civil theology at *ciu.* 8.5.

[97] See *ciu.* 10.9 (CCL 47.281): 'cum sint utrique ritibus fallacibus daemonum obstricti sub nominibus angelorum', 10.10 (CCL 47.283): 'immo uero malignorum spirituum cauenda et detestanda fallacia, et salutaris audienda doctrina'. At *ciu.* 10.16, Augustine argues that demons involved in theurgic rites desire to be worshipped themselves, rather than that God be worshipped. See also *ciu.* 10.19, 10.24, 10.26. Finally, not being pure themselves, such demons are not able to purify the human soul. See *ciu.* 10.27. On theurgy generally and concisely, see S. Lilla, 'Theurgy', *Encyclopedia of Early Christianity*, vol. 2, ed. A. Di Berardino, tr. A. Walford (Cambridge, 1992), 835–6 (with indication of additional studies).

transforms himself to look like an angel of light' (10.10, cf. 2 Cor 11:14). In his *Letter to Anebo*, Porphyry admits the existence of a class of spiritual beings who deceive human beings by appearing as demons, gods, or even the spirits of the deceased. He adds that some experts hold these spiritual beings responsible for the various phenomena experienced by theurgists during their rituals.[98] Augustine concludes that the deceptions arranged by evil demons falsify the happiness produced by these rites, thereby rendering them useless as worship of the true God (10.12). Since they themselves are impure, these spiritual creatures are capable only of deceiving human beings into believing that they can be purified by theurgical rites (10.27). Indeed, demons have been known to deceive their faithful through performance of miracles that serve only to enchance their power over their devotees.[99]

Augustine's examination of Roman religious literature in the *City of God* describes priests and other public officials as involved either in disseminating or in failing to denounce falsehoods concerning the temporal and permanent goods to be achieved through religious practices.[100] Following his accusations in this regard concerning Scipio Nasica Corculum in Book 1, he charges the *Septemuiri epulones* with reducing sacred rites to farces during the sacrificial banquet in honour of Jupiter.[101] This is but one of a number of arguments throughout Books 1–7 which illustrate Augustine's strategy of identifying Roman priests with poets and actors, and their religious rituals with theatrical shows.[102] Apart from the isolated case

[98] See *ciu.* 10.9 together with 10.11. O'Daly, *Augustine's City*, 126–7, points out that Porphyry's criticisms of demons in the so-called *Letter to Anebo* do not pertain to theurgy per se. Augustine employs a variation of the polemical device known as retortion in order to conflate the discussion of demons in this work with that of theurgy elsewhere in his writings (see Augustine's reference to *De regressu animae* at *ciu.* 10.29). See my discussion below, p. 64 n. 161. On Augustine's knowledge of the *Letter to Anebo*, see P. Courcelle, *Late Latin Writers and their Greek Sources*, tr. H. Wedeck (Cambridge, Mass., 1969), 185–6.

[99] See *ciu.* 10.16. He makes this charge in order to distinguish the misleading phenomena experienced in conjunction with theurgy from miracles attested in the scriptures. I discuss theurgy further below, pp. 95–104.

[100] The literature on Roman priesthoods is vast. A good starting point is provided by M. Beard, J. North, and S. Price, *Religions of Rome*, vol. 1: *A History* (Cambridge, 1998). See also J. Scheid, *Religion et piété à Rome* (Paris, 1985), M. Beard and J. North, *Pagan Priests: Religion and Power in the Ancient World* (London, 1990), 1–71, 179–255, and J. Scheid, 'The Priest', *The Romans*, ed. A. Giardina (Chicago, 1993), 55–84.

[101] See *ciu.* 6.7. The rites were conducted during the 'Roman Games' in September and the 'Plebeian Games' in mid November. For background, see Weismann, *Schauspiele*, 169, 103–4 (similar criticism from earlier Latin patristic sources). On the *epulones* see K. Latte, *Römische Religionsgeschichte* (Munich, 1960), 398–9 and Beard et al., *Religions*, 100–1; on the *epulae Iouis*, see Beard et al., *Religions*, 40, 63, 66–7.

[102] See, for example, his criticisms of Cicero at *ciu.* 2.27 and of Varro at *ciu.* 4.27. For more detailed discussion of this general point, see R. Dodaro, '*Christus sacerdos*: Augustine's Polemic against

of the *Septemuiri epulones*, his complaint in this regard exclusively concerns the pontiffs, whom he associates with religious rituals consisting of
lewd gestures and symbols from poetry and theatrical performances.[103]
He relies largely upon Varro's *Antiquitates rerum diuinarum* for his accusations, but disputes the Roman historian's claim that mythical theology
differs in character from civil or political theology,[104] because priests have
allowed their taste for sexual indecencies to empty their rites of any sacred
content.[105]

Augustine's discussion of civil religion in Books 4–5 makes clear that
he understands the extent to which ancient Roman religious and political
establishments are intermingled, in particular in the involvement of the
priesthoods with the senate and the magistracies.[106] Priests are responsible for maintaining good relations between the gods and the city, not as
mediators, but as advisors to civil officials.[107] Their crucial role in Roman
society affords priests a wide range of influence, from the official cult to

Roman Pagan Priesthoods in *De ciuitate dei*', *Augustinianum* 33:1–2 (1993), 101–35, at 106–11, and
O'Daly, *Augustine's City*, 105–7.

[103] See *ciu.* 4.27. At *ciu.* 3.18, he claims that the pontiffs reinstated the *ludi saeculares* during the most
intense phase of the First Punic War (249 BC). See the remarks of G. Bardy, 'Les Jeux séculaires',
Œuvres de saint Augustin, vol. 33: *La Cité de Dieu. Livres 1–V: Impuissance sociale du paganisme*,
ed. G. Bardy and G. Combés (Paris, 1959), 797–8, Beard, North, and Price, *Religions*, 71–2, 201–6
(on their later revival during the Augustan age). See also *ciu.* 2.8, 2.12, 8.20. On *ludi* in general, see G.
Wissowa, *Religion und Kultus der Römer*, 2nd edn (Munich, 1912), 449–67, G. Piccaluga, *Elementi
spettacolari nei rituali festivi romani* (Rome, 1965), S. Weinstock, *Divus Julius* (Oxford, 1971), 282–6.
On *ludi scaenici*, see Tertullian, *De spectaculis*, J. H. Waszink, 'Varro, Livy and Tertullian on the
History of Roman Dramatic Art', *Vigiliae christianae* 2 (1948), 224–42, Piccaluga, *Elementi*, 55–6.
On the pontifical college in general, see Wissowa, *Religion*, 501–23, Latte, *Römische*, 195–212.

[104] See *ciu.* 6.6–9. At *ciu.* 6.9, he declares civil theology to be nothing more than a fantasy and a hoax.
See also *ciu.* 8.20, where he accuses civil authorities and the pontiffs of colluding with the theatre
and with poets.

[105] See *ciu.* 6.7–8, in regard to the priests of Cybele. See also *ciu.* 2.4–5, 2.26, 7.26, and the discussion by
Mandouze, 'Saint Augustin', 187–223, at 194, on 'prêtres chatres'. O'Daly, *Augustine's City*, 105–6,
rightly refers to Augustine's strategy against Varro in Books 6–7 as 'reductionist', meaning that he
wants to blur the distinction between Varro's mythical and civil theologies, and as 'tendentious'
insofar as Augustine 'concentrates on rites where obscene and perverted elements can be isolated'
(as at 6.8–9), while he also 'adduces obscene, frivolous, and degrading episodes involving gods in
myths and theatrical productions'. In doing so, Augustine adheres to the norms governing polemic
literature of his day.

[106] See G. Szemler, *The Priests of the Roman Republic: A Study of Interactions between Priesthoods and Magistracies* (Brussels, 1972), 34–41. See also L. Schumacher, 'Die vier hohen römischen Priesterkollegien
unter den Flaviern, den Antoninen, und den Severern (69–235 n. Chr.)', *Aufstieg und Niedergang
der römischen Welt*, vol. 2:16.1, ed. W. Haase (Berlin, 1978), 655–819, especially 809, and G. Szemler,
'Priesthoods and Priestly Careers in Ancient Rome', *Aufstieg und Niedergang der römischen Welt*,
vol. 2:16.3, ed. W. Haase (Berlin, 1986), 2314–31, particularly at 2324, where he maintains that, in
reality, priests were 'controllers, directors, possibly manipulators of all facets of daily life'. Szemler,
Priests, 35–6, attempts to schematize the manner in which such influence was directly exerted.

[107] A. Wardman, *Religion and Statecraft among the Romans* (London, 1982), traces this influence from
the late republic to the fourth century.

popular morality.[108] They sustain this political intervention through their involvement in civil-religious ceremonies and discourses connected with public life.

Having dealt with the pontiffs, Augustine considers more directly the theme of divine–human mediation that is the task of the augurs and *haruspices*.[109] In criticizing these Roman priests, he treats a different aspect of the relationship between priesthood and politics in ancient Rome.[110] Unlike the pontiffs, whose activities around the theatrical spectacles at games are intended to entertain and appease the gods, thus enhancing the security of Rome, augurs and *haruspices* ensure the city's security both by revealing the will of the gods regarding specific decisions or actions to be taken and, where possible, by controlling and manipulating these gods.[111]

Augustine singles out Cicero for particularly harsh criticism on the issue of augury. He repeats the Roman statesman's report of Cato's amazement that one augur could pass another on the street without bursting into laughter, and contrasts it with the fact that Cicero himself was an augur.[112] Augustine accuses Cicero of complicity in the politically expedient deception of the Roman people over auguries and other forms of divination, suggesting that he acted in this way for fear of opposing the religious conventions of his city. Augustine dismisses as 'eloquent' but ultimately disingenuous Cicero's attempt in *De natura deorum* to distinguish traditional Roman religion, the *religio maiorum*, from superstition (4.30). Once again, Augustine's analysis of this aspect of Roman religion hinges upon the ignorance and weakness of its devotees and defenders alike, and upon the deceptive but convincing

---

[108] Cicero captures much of the sense of the significance of the priesthoods at *De domo sua* 1: 'Cum multa diuinitus, pontifices, a maioribus nostris inuenta atque instituta sunt, tum nihil praeclarius, quam quod eosdem et religionibus deorum immortalium et summae reipublicae praeesse uoluerunt, ut amplissimi et clarissimi ciues republica bene gerenda religiones, religionibus sapienter interpretandis rem publicam conseruarent.' See R. Düll, 'Rechtsprobleme im Bereich des römischen Sakralrechts', *Aufstieg und Niedergang der römischen Welt*, vol. 1:2, ed. H. Temporini (Berlin, 1972), 283–94, especially 288.

[109] Beard et al., *Religions*, 20, hold that it is not possible to determine clearly the relationship between these two priestly groups. On augury, see Wissowa, *Religion*, 523–34, G. Dumézil, 'Augur', *Revue des études latines* 35 (1957), 126–51 = G. Dumézil, *Idées romaines* (Paris, 1969), 79–102, J. Linderski, 'The Augural Law', *Aufstieg und Niedergang der römischen Welt*, vol. 2.16.3, ed. W. Haase (Berlin, 1986), 2190–225, Beard et al., *Religions*, 21–4. On haruspication, see Wissowa, *Religion*, 543–9, Latte, *Römische*, 157–60, B. MacBain, *Prodigy and Expiation: A Study in Religion and Politics in Republican Rome* (Brussels, 1982), 43–59.

[110] Beard et al., *Religions*, 27, point out that 'from the third century [BC] onwards . . . it is clear that priests were drawn from among the leading senators'.

[111] Linderski, 'Augural Law', 2207, suggests that the activity of augurs 'expresses an active, bold but careful attitude of the Romans towards supernatural powers; one should do whatever one could to appease them, but also whenever it was possible one should try to gain control over them'.

[112] See *ciu.* 4.30 (CCL 47.123): 'Cicero augur inridet auguria.' The reference is to Cicero, *De diuinatione* 2.37.

religious and political discourse which reinforces the general preference for worship of false gods in the hope of ensuring security and peace.

He lodges similar charges against Varro, whom he accuses of weakly conforming to popular custom by including stage shows among religious rites, and of outright deception in classifying tales about the gods which he knew to be false as authentic religion. Augustine attributes Varro's dishonesty to a general Roman moral subservience to demons (4.31). He concludes that the only motive for such error by Cicero and Varro lay in their recognition of the political advantages to be gained in using religion to control the populace. Political leaders (*principes ciuitatis*) perpetuate such large-scale deception in order to strengthen the bonds of civil society and reinforce their power over their subjects. In doing so, they victimize the weak (*infirmus*) and uneducated (*indoctus*).[113]

OPTIMI UIRI

Augustine returns in Book 5 to the theme which he introduced in Book 1, the relation between religious and philosophical conceptions of virtue and the remedies which they offer to fear of death. In his analysis, he distinguishes between the virtues of Roman heroes, such as Marcus Regulus, and those of Christian martyrs. Consistent with his understanding of fear of death, he locates the fundamental distinction between the two sets of virtues in their responses to the spiritual conflict between possession of temporal and possession of permanent goods. Traditional Roman heroes set the love of human praise (*amor laudis humanae*) before all other aims, whereas the martyrs are motivated principally by a love of truth (*amor ueritatis*).[114] The conflict between these two loves is paralleled by the conflict between desire for glory (*cupiditas gloriae*) and love of justice (*dilectio iustitiae*).[115]

While recognizing that both the Christian martyrs and Roman heroes voluntarily embrace gruesome deaths for the sake of their respective

---

[113] See *ciu.* 4.32 (CCL 47.126): 'sic et homines principes, non sane iusti, sed daemonum similes, ea, quae uana esse nouerant, religionis nomine populis tamquam uera suadebant, hoc modo eos ciuili societati uelut aptius alligantes, quo similiter subditos possiderent. quis autem infirmus et indoctus euaderet simul fallaces et principes ciuitatis et daemones'. See also *ciu.* 3.4, 7.34. In Augustine's view, Porphyry could be associated with Cicero and Varro, insofar as the Neoplatonist philosopher deceives the masses into practising theurgic arts, even while recognizing that contemplation is purer when it is unaccompanied by superstitious rites. See *ciu.* 10.27–8.

[114] See *ciu.* 5.14 (below, p. 56 n. 129). Note that the distinction which Augustine draws between *amor laudis humanae* and *amor ueritatis* adumbrates the theme of the two cities/two loves which he introduces at *ciu.* 14.28. Augustine summarizes his view of the Ciceronian ideal at *ciu.* 4.29–30.

[115] See *ciu.* 5.14 (below, p. 56 n. 129).

ideals, Augustine argues that their different attitudes to death distinguish the natures of their respective virtues. To persuade themselves to
die valiantly, Roman heroes believe that they will attain a kind of immortality.[116] Thus they die while clinging to a temporal form of glory consisting
of popular approval and praise.[117] Citing *De re publica*, Augustine represents as emphatic and unconditional Cicero's insistence that Roman statesmen should be 'nourished on glory' before all else, and that they should
avoid disgrace at all costs.[118] He is aware of the reasoning underpinning
Cicero's conclusion that the desire for praise deters statesmen from reckless
self-indulgence.[119] Nevertheless, he charges that the Roman philosopher's
counsel implicitly directs political leaders to act only in such a way as to win
popular support, without regard for what is good or true.[120] In Augustine's
view, the Romans have subverted virtue by anchoring it to glory. Desire for
glory is a byproduct of ignorance and weakness; the longing for it always
counteracts justice.[121] In the end, the soul easily mistakes human glory for
transcendence. Roman heroes sacrifice their lives in pursuit of the security (*incolumitas*) of the earthly city. They nevertheless recognize that they

---

[116] See *ciu.* 5.14 (below, p. 56 n. 129). At *ciu.* 3.4, he recalls Varro's opinion that courageous men
are emboldened when they see themselves as sons of the gods, to the advantage of their political
communities. See my remarks and references to studies concerning euhemerism above, p. 49 n. 95.

[117] See *ciu.* 5.12 (CCL 47.142): '"laudis auidi, pecuniae liberales erant, gloriam ingentem, diuitias
honestas uolebant" [Sallust, *Bellum Catilinae* 7.3]; hanc ardentissime dilexerunt, propter hanc
uiuere uoluerunt, pro hac emori non dubitauerunt'. Augustine refers here to the earliest epoch of
Roman heroes.

[118] See *ciu.* 5.13 (CCL 47.147): 'etiam Tullius hinc dissimulare non potuit in eisdem libris quod de
re publica scripsit, ubi loquitur de instituendo principe ciuitatis, quem dicit alendum esse gloria
et consequenter commemorat maiores suos multa mira atque praeclara gloriae cupiditate fecisse.
huic igitur uitio non solum non resistebant, uerum etiam id excitandum et accendendum esse
censebant, putantes hoc utile esse rei publicae'. See Cicero, *De re publica* 5.7.9. Augustine insists
that Cicero maintains this position unequivocally, even in his philosophical writings: 'quamquam
nec in ipsis philosophiae libris Tullius ad hanc peste dissimulet, ubi eam luce clarius confitetur.
cum enim de studiis talibus loqueretur, quae utique sectanda sunt fine ueri boni, non uentositate
laudis humanae, hanc intulit uniuersalem generalemque sententiam: "honos alit artes, omnesque
accenduntur ad studia gloria iacentque ea semper, quae apud quosque improbantur"', citing Cicero,
Libri tusculanarum disputationum 1.4. See also Cicero, *Libri tusculanarum disputationum* 2.58–9.

[119] See *ciu.* 5.13, 5.19. Augustine omits any mention of Cicero's criticism of excessive love for glory, as at
De re publica 6.25.2 (about which, see Zetzel, *Cicero*, 248–9). Cicero's position on the relationship
between glory and political office is complex. Pursued with moderation, glory can be an 'instructor
in virtue' for political leaders, but sought for its own sake it leads to domination (*dominatio*). See,
for example, Cicero, *Libri tusculanarum disputationum* 1.91: 'non gloriae cupiditate . . . sed uirtutis'.
See also A. Haury, 'Cicéron et la gloire, une pédagogie de la vertu', *Mélanges de philosophie, de
littérature et d'histoire ancienne offerts à Pierre Boyancé* (Rome, 1974), 401–17.

[120] See *ciu.* 5.14 (below, n. 121), 5.20.

[121] See *ciu.* 5.14 (CCL 47.147): 'huic igitur cupiditati melius resistitur sine dubitatione quam ceditur.
tanto enim quisque est deo similior, quanto et ab hac inmunditia mundior. quae in hac uita etsi
non funditus eradicatur ex corde, quia etiam bene proficientes animos temptare non cessat: saltem
cupiditas gloriae superetur dilectione iustitiae, ut, si alicubi iacent quae apud quosque improbantur,
si bona, si recta sunt, etiam ipse amor humanae laudis erubescat et cedat amori ueritatis'.

forfeit this security in death, so that they die for the sake of glory, confusing it with immortality.[122]

In distinguishing the Christian martyr from the Roman hero, Augustine examines the opposing goal (*finis*) which each group pursues. Key to this opposition is the contrast between true and false virtue (*uirtus*), which he understands mainly as courage.[123] He sees the root of this contrast in the opposition between true and false piety, which is symbolized in the difference between divine and human glory.[124] True virtue has as its goal the acquisition of permanent goods, such as eternal life; therefore it culminates in the knowledge and love of God. The aims of false virtue, on the other hand, do not transcend the horizon of the earthly city. Because the goal of Roman virtue is the attainment of temporal benefits, such as victory for Rome and glory for themselves, Roman heroes necessarily forfeit permanent goods, such as true piety and the happiness which it imparts.[125] Thus, in confronting death, they avoid any exercise of faith, hope, or love – those virtues which conduct the soul to the true God and therefore to true happiness.[126] Augustine reasons further that hopes for immortality in the form of glory betray a masked fear of death which amounts to a

---

[122] See *ciu.* 5.14 (CCL 47.148): 'sed cum illi essent in ciuitate terrena, quibus propositus erat omnium pro illa officiorum finis incolumitas eius et regnum non in caelo, sed in terra; non in uita aeterna, sed in decessione morientium et successione moriturum: quid aliud amarent quam gloriam, qua uolebant etiam post mortem tamquam uiuere in ore laudantium'.

[123] See, for example, Cicero, *Libri tusculanarum disputationum* 2.43: 'Appellata est enim ex uiro uirtus; uiri autem propria maxime est fortitudo, cuius munera duo sunt maxima, mortis dolorisque contemptio.'

[124] On the dependence of *uera uirtus* upon *uera pietas*, see *ciu.* 5.14 (CCL 47.148): 'hos secuit sunt martyres, qui Scaeuolas et Curtios et Decios non sibi inferendo poenas, sed inlatas ferendo et uirtute uera, quoniam uera pietate, et innumerabili multitudine superarunt'. See also *ciu.* 5.19 (below, p. 57 n. 131). I discuss this relationship more extensively below, pp. 184–92. Divergences between Augustine's concept of glory and non-Christian, Roman concepts are treated by A. Vermeulen, *The Semantic Development of Gloria in Early-Christian Latin* (Nijmegen, 1956), especially 47–51, 80–90, 111–14, 187–212, Hand, *Augustin*, 16–22, L. Swift, 'Defining "Gloria" in Augustine's *City of God'*, *Diakonia: Studies in Honor of R. T. Meyer*, ed. T. Halton (Washington, 1986), 133–44 = *The City of God: A Collection of Critical Essays*, ed. D. Donnelly (New York, 1995), 277–88, L. Swift, 'Pagan and Christian Heroes in Augustine's *City of God'*, *Augustinianum* 27:3 (1987), 509–22, J. Velasquez, '*Gloriosissimam ciuitatem dei*. Algunas consideraciones en torno a *gloria'*, *Augustinus* 31 (1986), 285–9, Lettieri, *Il senso*, 215–17, C. Alonso Del Real, '*De ciuitate dei V: exempla maiorum, uirtus, gloria'*, *L'etica cristiana nei secoli III e IV: eredità e confronti* (Rome, 1996), 423–30, P. M. Hombert, *Gloria gratiae. Se glorifier en Dieu, principe et fin de la théologie augustinienne de la grâce* (Paris, 1996), 25–31, 226–51, K. Pollmann, 'Augustins Transformation der traditionellen römischen Staats- und Geschichtsauffassung (Buch i–v)', *Augustinus. De ciuitate dei*, ed. C. Horn (Berlin, 1997), 25–40.

[125] See, especially, *ciu.* 5.19 (CCL 47.155–6): 'dum illud constet inter omnes ueraciter pios, neminem sine uera pietate, id est ueri dei uero cultu, ueram posse habere uirtutem, nec eam ueram esse, quando gloriae seruit humanae; eos tamen, qui ciues non sint ciuitates aeternae, quae in sacris litteris nostris dicitur ciuitas dei, utiliores esse terrenae ciuitati, quando habent uirtutem uel ipsam, quam si nec ipsam'.

[126] See, especially, *ciu.* 22.6.

subtle denial of death. While appearing courageous, Roman heroes fear
death in the guise of defeat or dishonour. Under these conditions, fear
of death does not act as a means to the perfection of virtue, because the
soul cannot overcome the pride which prevents it from abiding the loss of
honour through an acknowledged dependence upon God alone. Augustine
contrasts the apostles to Roman heroes, suggesting that the former, by
preaching Christ in places where they expected personal dishonour as well
as the rejection of their message, did not die for the sake of an earthly
glory, but in ignominy.[127] They accepted that Christ's death was widely
viewed as a humiliation, and that their own deaths would fail to reverse
the widespread rejection of the Christian religion; they remained unaware
of God's hidden plan to use their deaths to promote its expansion. As
a consequence, they died without the false consolation of human praise,
the precise aim that spurs Roman statesmen to heroic deaths. In those
cases where their preaching was welcomed by unbelievers, they did not
ascribe this success to their own efforts, but to the grace of God, whom
they glorified.[128] Augustine points out that Christ taught the apostles to
sacrifice the desire for glory as an end in itself, and to direct their good
works instead to the acquisition of eternal life: 'Take care not to perform
your just deeds before others, so as to be seen by them, or you will have no
reward with my Father, who is in heaven' (Mt 6:1). The contrast between
the motivations of the apostles and Roman heroes is further heightened by
the fact that, prior to death, the apostles perceived the reward (*merces*) of
eternal life only through faith, so that it did not negate the darkness of death
that they encountered in martyrdom. Consequently, the Christian martyrs,
in confronting this darkness, did not console themselves with a surrogate
immortality in the form of glory.[129] Aware, however, of the danger that his
earlier quotation of Mt 6:1 might be understood as urging that good works
be hidden from view in order to preserve humility, Augustine pairs it with

---

[127] See *ciu.* 5.14 (CCL 47.148): 'qui cum in his locis praedicarent Christi nomen, ubi non solum
improbabatur (sicut ille ait: iacentque ea semper, quae apud quosque improbantur), uerum etiam
summae detestationis habebatur [. . .] inter maledicta et opprobria, inter grauissimas persecutiones
crudelesque poenas non sunt deterriti a praedicatione'.

[128] See *ciu.* 5.14 (CCL 47.148): 'non in ea tamquam in suae uirtutis fine quieuerunt, sed eam quoque
ipsam ad dei gloriam referentes, cuius gratia tales erant, isto quoque fomite eos, quibus consulebant,
ad amorem illius, a quo et ipsi tales fierent, accendebant'.

[129] See *ciu.* 5.14 (CCL 47.147): 'tam enim est hoc uitium inimicum piae fidei, si maior in corde sit
cupiditas gloriae quam dei timor uel amor, ut dominus diceret; *quo modo potestis credere gloriam ab
inuicem expectantes et gloriam quae a solo deo est non quaerentes*' (Jn 5:44). See also *ciu.* 5.16 (CCL
47.149): 'merces autem sanctorum longe alia est etiam hic opprobria sustinentium pro ueritate
dei, quae mundi huius dilectoribus odiosa est'. See *pecc. mer.* 2.50, 2.54, where Augustine, citing a
number of passages from the Epistle to the Hebrews (11:1, 11:13, 11:39–40), argues that the martyrs'
deaths are noteworthy for the struggle they involve over faith in what is unseen.

another biblical precept: 'Let your works shine in the sight of others, so that they may see your good works, and glorify your Father, who is in heaven' (Mt 5:16). He stresses that the public character of the apostles' just deeds allows God to be glorified. As a consequence, unbelievers come to know and love the true God, because they understand that the good works of the apostles that they observe have their source in God.

Throughout the *City of God*, Augustine grounds the acquisition of virtue by human beings in the divine gift of grace and pardon. To underscore the contingent nature of virtue, he looks to piety (*pietas*), the virtue which in the classical Roman view unites civic virtues with religious devotion to the gods.[130] As he argued earlier in Book 1, in Book 5 he urges the view that unlike Roman piety, Christian piety is a gift of God. Central to Augustine's conception of true piety as practised by statesmen is their public acknowledgement of the limits of their virtue through prayer to God for forgiveness of their sins.[131] By means of this prayer, piety purifies the intention behind other virtues, such as justice, with the result that these, too, are rendered true.[132]

EXEMPLUM UIRTUTIS

By the close of Book 7, Augustine has criticized various ways in which traditional Roman religion sees the relationship between the soul's longing to overcome fear of death, its growth in virtue, and the foundation of a just society. The centre of his criticism throughout is the source of virtue. He finds that Roman religious theory (as in the mythical and civil theologies identified by Varro or the accounts of divination offered by Cicero) as well as practice (as in the piety demonstrated by Rome's *optimi uiri*) invariably embraces understandings of virtue arising from human initiative and accomplishment, which he dismisses as forms of pride. In Books 8–10, he turns to the Platonic concept of mediation in order to show that virtue originates outside the soul, and to place greater distance between virtue and human autonomy.

[130] On the classical Roman concept of *pietas*, see T. Ulrich, *Pietas (pius) als politischer Begriff im römischen Staate bis zum Tode des Kaisers Commodus* (Breslau, 1930), D. Kaufmann-Bühler, 'Eusebia', *Reallexikon für Antike und Christentum*, vol. 6, ed. T. Klauser et al. (Stuttgart, 1966), 985–1052.

[131] See *ciu.* 5.19 (CCL 47.156): 'tales autem homines uirtutes suas, quantascumque in hac uita possunt habere, non tribuunt nisi gratiae dei, quod eas uolentibus credentibus petentibus dederit, simulque intellegunt, quantum sibi desit ad perfectionem iustitiae, qualis est in illorum sanctorum angelorum societate, cui se nituntur aptare'. He adds that the hope of the saints has been placed in the grace (*gratia*) and mercy (*misericordia*) of God. See also *ciu.* 5.20. On the relationship between *uera uirtus* and *uera pietas*, see also above, p. 55 nn. 124, 125.

[132] I develop this point below, pp. 208–12.

Prior to rejecting Roman accounts of virtue, Augustine explicitly criticizes the Peripatetic and Stoic approaches to fear of death in relation to just conduct. Significantly, these comments appear in Book 9, in which he argues that happiness and virtue exist in the soul only as a consequence of divine mediation.[133] In the first half of this book he returns to the subject of demons, insisting that they are unfit to act as mediators (9.3). He supports this conclusion by citing Apuleius that demons lack rational control over their own passions. As a result, they are inferior to certain exemplary philosophers or sages who, although mortal beings, are able to suppress those emotional disturbances which distort rational, moral judgments.[134] This assertion provides Augustine with the opportunity to discuss the inadequacy of Stoic and Peripatetic positions on reason in relation to virtue.

He accepts the premise that both schools place the practice of justice prior to personal security and wellbeing as the proper moral aim of their adherents.[135] To choose a more just behaviour over self-preservation in those situations in which they are in conflict, the sage must confront his fear of death. In this regard, Augustine allows for slight differences between the approaches urged by the two schools. He notes that although the Stoics insist that the sage suppress strong emotions which affect the mind, the Peripatetics allow a limited vulnerability to such passions. He concludes that these differences are ultimately unimportant because both schools oblige the sage to ward off fear of death completely so that it does not adversely influence judgment and conduct.[136] Moreover, both claim that

---

[133] See Guy, *Unité*, 68–9, in conjunction with *ciu.* 9.2–7.

[134] At *ciu.* 9.3, he charges that demons lack the sage's deeper commitment to wisdom and justice. See also *ciu.* 9.6. Augustine's source is Apuleius, *De deo Socratis* 12, but J. Brachtendorf, 'Cicero and Augustine on the Passions', *Revue des études augustiniennes* 43 (1997), 289–308, rightly points out that he distorts Apuleius' point.

[135] See *ciu.* 9.4 (CCL 47.253): 'ambo sane, si bonorum istorum seu commodorum periculis ad flagitium uel facinus urgeantur, ut aliter ea retinere non possint, malle se dicunt haec amittere, quibus natura corporis salua et incolumis habetur, quam illa committere, quibus iustitia uiolatur'.

[136] See *ciu.* 9.4 (CCL 47.252): 'de uerbis eos potius quam de rebus facere controuersiam'. J. Wetzel, *Augustine and the Limits of Virtue* (Cambridge, 1992), 117–22, in the wider context of his remarks (112–26), discusses the problems for modern interpretation posed by Augustine's tendency in representing ancient philosophical schools to force 'many characters to speak under one roof', without paying attention to differences within and between the schools (117). He rightly insists that Augustine is 'an astute interpreter of the philosophy that came his way' (121). At the same time, Wetzel cautions readers about the futility of expecting too much historical precision in Augustine's account (120). Finally, he appreciates the importance of accepting that the full scope of Augustine's theology of grace can only be understood as a counterpoint to the 'common enterprise' into which he unites pagan philosophical schools (120). For other discussions of the historical (in)accuracy of Augustine's portrayal of Platonic-Peripatetic and Stoic views on the passions, see G. Bardy, 'Les Passions chez Aristote et chez les stoïciens', *Œuvres de saint Augustin*, vol. 34: *La Cité de Dieu, Livres VI–X: Impuissance spirituelle du paganisme* (Paris, 1959), 608–9, Hagendahl, *Augustine*, 2:512–14, G. P. O'Daly, *Augustine's Philosophy of Mind* (London, 1987), 46–50, O'Daly, *Augustine's City*, 118–20. See also Brachtendorf, 'Cicero and Augustine', especially 296–300.

reason provides sufficient strength and insight to repress this fear and act virtuously.[137] In a tale from Aulus Gellius which Augustine recounts, a Stoic sage fears for his life while aboard a ship during a storm at sea; he overcomes his panic by reasoning that his good consists in clinging not to life or to bodily integrity, but to virtues such as justice.[138] This is a correct judgment in Augustine's view. However, he denies the Stoic belief that reason alone can lead to virtuous action, and offers an alternative model for just behaviour in the situation which Gellius describes.[139] Significantly, he prefaces these remarks with the affirmation that the divine scriptures, which he says encompass Christian knowledge, subject the mind of the believer to God who governs (*regere*) and assists (*iuuare*) it, while they also subject the passions to the mind so that they may be restrained and redirected in the service of justice (*usus iustitiae*).[140] Augustine does not

[137] See *ciu.* 9.4 (CCL 47.253): 'quae si ita sunt, aut nihil aut paene nihil distat inter Stoicorum aliorumque philosophorum opinionem de passionibus et perturbationibus animorum; utrique enim mentem rationemque sapientis ab earum dominatione defendunt'. In regard to the Peripatetic position specifically, see Augustine's observations at ibid. (CCL 47.251): 'has ergo perturbationes siue affectiones siue passiones quidam philosophi dicunt etiam in sapientem cadere, sed moderatas rationique subiectas, ut eis leges quodam modo, quibus ad necessarium redigantur modum, dominatio mentis inponat'. Concerning the position of the Stoics, see ibid. (CCL 47.253): 'sapientis autem, quamuis eas necessitate patiatur, retinet tamen de his, quae adpetere uel fugere rationabiliter debet, ueram et stabilem inconcussa mente sententiam'.

[138] See *ciu.* 9.4 (CCL 47.253): 'nam profecto si nihili penderet eas res ille philosophus, quas amissurum se naufragio sentiebat, sicuti est uita ista salusque corporis: non ita illud periculum perhorresceret, ut palloris etiam testimonio proderetur. uerum tamen et illam poterat permotionem pati, et fixam tenere mente sententiam, uitam illam salutemque corporis, quorum amissionem minabatur tempestatis inmanitas, non esse bona, quae illos quibus inessent facerent bonos, sicut facit iustitia'. Cf. Aulus Gellius, *Noctes Atticae* 19.1. Brachtendorf, 'Cicero and Augustine', 297–300, demonstrates that Augustine's version of the anecdote differs from Gellius' insofar as the former maintains, while the latter does not, that the Stoic sage in question is subject to passions.

[139] The closing lines of *ciu.* 9.4 (CCL 47.253) indicate the conclusion concerning the mind's functions which Augustine rejects: 'ita mens, ubi fixa est ista sententia, nullas perturbationes, etiamsi accidunt inferioribus animi partibus, in se contra rationem praeualere permittit; quin immo eis ipsa dominatur eisque non consentiendo et potius resistendo regnum uirtutis exercet'.

[140] See *ciu.* 9.5 (CCL 47.254): 'non est nunc necesse copiose ac diligenter ostendere, quid de istis passionibus doceat scriptura diuina, qua christiana eruditio continetur. deo quippe illa ipsam mentem subicit regendam et iuuandam mentique passiones ita moderandas atque frenandas, ut in usum iustitiae conuertantur'. Note the similarity between Augustine's position on the moral utility of passions as stated both here and at *ciu.* 14.9 and the representation of the Peripatetic position which Cicero explicitly rejects at *Libri tusculanarum disputationum* 4.43–6. O'Daly, *Augustine's Philosophy*, 48–9, explains Augustine's view that along with the reasoning faculty of the soul, the irrational faculty was also created by God, so that its affections are natural and good, provided they are governed by reason. O'Daly also points out that Lactantius, *Diuinae institutiones* 6.17, and Ambrose, *De officiis ministrorum* 2.19, hold similar views to Augustine. See also A. Solignac, 'Passions et vie spirituelle', *Dictionnaire de spiritualité*, vol. 12, ed. A. Rayez and C. Baumgartner (Paris, 1983), 345–7. On the other hand, Brachtendorf, 'Cicero and Augustine', 300, concludes in conjunction with *ciu.* 9.4–5 that 'Augustine is not interested in a positive evaluation of the passions', but only in adopting the Peripatetic assumption 'that the passions are unavoidable because they are a part of human nature'. He maintains, moreover, that Augustine's interest in using Gellius' anecdote lies in imputing to the Stoics the view that passions are unavoidable, so that the sage can be said

venture further explanation at this point regarding the precise way in which scripture directs the mind and passions in the pursuit of virtue. But what he claims in Books 9 and 14 about the mind's subordination to God and its role in the moral transformation of passions cannot be assessed properly without this explanation of the role of scripture being taken into account.[141] Returning to Gellius' anecdote, Augustine suggests that the sage might have allowed his own fear of death to steer him toward compassion for fellow passengers in danger of dying. He insists that from a Christian point of view, one who acts on this compassion has performed a just deed even though his judgment, which philosophers believe should always be dominated by reason, had been swayed by emotion.[142] Augustine admits that Cicero and even the Stoic philosophers Zeno and Chrysippus occasionally affirm the desirability of emotions such as compassion as motives for acting virtuously, but he charges that Stoic and Peripatetic authorities present an inconsistent picture of the role of emotions in guiding reason to moral judgment.[143] In letters to public officials, he similarly acknowledges awareness of Roman philosophical traditions concerning the role of compassion in just conduct, but largely dismisses them as inconsequential.[144]

> to stand in need of salvation and an afterlife. Although I do not agree with Brachtendorf regarding Augustine's assessment of the passions, I endorse his view regarding Augustine's anti-Stoic use of Gellius' anecdote. More specifically, however, Augustine wants to refute the Stoic insistence on the autonomy of reason in acting virtuously as part of his wider argument in Books 8–10 concerning the need for divine mediation in acting virtuously. In this regard, see my summary of Wetzel's remarks (above, p. 58 n. 136).

[141] See, for example, *ciu.* 14.9 where Augustine cites several scriptural passages demonstrating the positive role which passions play in the life of the apostle Paul. However, even this discussion presupposes a deeper account of the relation of scripture to the moral transformation of emotions. I treat this matter more extensively in Chapters 4 and 5.

[142] See *ciu.* 9.5 (CCL 47.254): 'denique in disciplina nostra non tam quaeritur utrum pius animus irascatur, sed quare irascatur; nec utrum sit tristis, sed unde sit tristis; nec utrum timeat, sed quid timeat. irasci enim peccanti ut corrigatur, contristari pro adflicto ut liberetur, timere periclitanti ne pereat nescio utrum quisquam sana consideratione reprehendat. nam et misericordiam Stoicorum est solere culpare; sed quanto honestius ille Stoicus misericordia perturbaretur hominis liberandi quam timore naufragii'. Brachtendorf, 'Cicero and Augustine', 299–300, insists that Augustine misrepresents Cicero at this point. Cicero believes that passions can enter the soul involuntarily, but that before any passion can be said to move the soul, the mind must give consent to it.

[143] See *ciu.* 9.5, 14.9 (CCL 48.425–6): 'uerum his philosophis, quod ad istam quaestionem de animi perturbationibus adtinet, iam respondimus in nono huius operis libro, ostendentes eos non tam de rebus, quam de uerbis cupidiores esse contentionis quam ueritatis. apud nos autem iuxta scripturas sanctas sanamque doctrinam ciues sanctae ciuitatis dei in huius uitae peregrinatione secundum deum uiuentes "metuunt cupiuntque, dolent gaudentque", et quia rectus est amor eorum, istas omnes adfectiones rectas habent'. Augustine quotes Vergil, *Aeneid* 6.733. His assertions regarding the positive, Christian outlook on anger (*ira*) and compassion (*misericordia*) can be contrasted with Cicero's presentation of the negative, Stoic position at *Libri tusculanarum disputationum* 3.19–20. See also the remarks of Lettieri, *Il senso*, 73–8.

[144] See, for example, his discussion at *ep.* 104.16 to Nectarius, and 138.9–10 to Flavius Marcellinus. His reason for commenting favourably upon Cicero's endorsement of compassion in the judge or ruler

Scholars dispute the extent of Augustine's dependence upon Cicero's *Tusculan Disputations* for his portrait of the sage in Books 9 and 14 of the *City of God*.[145] Yet even if direct dependence upon the *Tusculanae* cannot be proven, its explanation of the reasoning processes by which the sage overcomes fear of death epitomizes what Augustine finds most objectionable in such philosophical accounts. In assessing the importance of Cicero's text for the *City of God*, it is useful first to recall the attention that the Roman philosopher pays to the themes of death and fear of death.[146] Early on in the work he introduces the thesis that pain can be suppressed either through outright endurance, as when fear is simply banished from the mind, or through the application of philosophical reasoning.[147] Cicero likens the study of philosophy to a medicine for the soul (*medicina animi*) which enables reason to overcome the suasive power of emotions.[148] One of the more significant intentions behind the *Tusculanae* is to reconcile the functions of rhetoric and philosophy in overcoming fear of death.[149] Central to this aim is the role which Cicero assigns to examples of courage (*exempla*

may largely be apologetic, insofar as it supports the view that the Christian perspective represents less discontinuity with traditional Roman ethics than public officials might at first conclude. I take up the question of Augustine's views concerning pagan accounts of virtue below, pp. 183–6, 194–200.

[145] Hagendahl, *Augustine*, 2:511, 2:514, offers the strongest case for direct dependence. He concludes that the exposition of Stoic thought at *ciu.* 9.4–5 and 14.3–9 is largely drawn from Books 3, 4, and 5 of Cicero's *Libri tusculanarum disputationum*, and that Augustine must have had a copy of the text in front of him as he wrote these chapters. M. Testard, 'Saint Augustin et Cicéron. A propos d'un ouvrage récent', *Revue des études augustiniennes* 14 (1968), 47–67, at 59, dismisses Hagendahl's view, concluding instead that Augustine's portrait of the sage includes well-known philosophical teachings and historical events, and that it is not possible to exclude doxographies and manuals as his sources. O'Daly, *Augustine's Philosophy*, 50–2, especially n. 140, acknowledges that Books 3 and 4 are Augustine's 'principal source for his philosophical views on the emotions', and Brachtendorf, 'Cicero and Augustine', 295–303, seems also to assume this dependence. On Augustine's earlier use of the *Tusculanae*, see M. Miotti, '*De beata vita* di Agostino. Rapporto con il V libro delle *Tusculanae Disputationes* di Cicerone', *Scritti offerti a R. Iacoangeli*, ed. S. Felici (Rome, 1992), 203–25.

[146] The entire first book of the *Tusculanae* is dedicated to the theme of *contemptio mortis*. See, in particular, 1.89, 1.91, 1.111–18. The themes of death and fear of death return frequently throughout the remainder of the work, either directly or as background for a related argument. See, for example, 2.2, 2.43, 2.47, 2.59, 3.66, 3.72, 4.37–44, 4.64, 5.5, 5.14, 5.15–20. See also Hagendahl, *Augustine*, 1:148–9, 1:179–84, 1:341–4, 2:511–16, M. Testard, *Saint Augustin et Cicéron*, vol. 1: *Cicéron dans la formation et dans l'œuvre de saint Augustin*. vol. 2: *Répertoire des textes* (Paris, 1958), 1:243.

[147] See Cicero, *Libri tusculanarum disputationum* 2.31, 2.42–65, respectively, for the statement of the thesis (*propositio*) and its demonstration (*confirmatio*). See also MacKendrick, *Philosophical*, 152–3, on the structure of Book 2.

[148] See Cicero, *Libri tusculanarum disputationum* 3.6: 'Est profecto animi medicina, philosophia; cuius auxilium non ut in corporis morbis petendum est foris, omnibusque opibus viribus ut nosmet ipsi nobis mederi possimus elaborandum est. quamquam de uniuersa philosophia, quanto opere et expetenda esset et colenda, satis, ut arbitror, dictum est in Hortensio'.

[149] Cicero, ibid., 1.117, acknowledges the role of *eloquentia* in urging human beings not to fear death. However, at 1.7, he states his intention to demonstrate that rhetorical skill must be combined with philosophical conviction in treating fear of death. See also 2.5.

uirtutis) in the face of severe pain or death. Orators generally draw upon stock examples from among *optimi uiri* as rhetorical ornamentation for their discourses. Cicero, however, deploys them in the *Tusculanae* not only in order to heighten the eloquence of his text, but to provide models of the philosophical reasoning process through which fear of death is suppressed.

His assurance that this reflection offers a therapy for fear of pain and death is founded upon his view of the sage's capacity to suppress fear through acts of reason prior to and during the contest with death.[150] At the centre of his confidence lies his Stoic conviction that by acting on its own strength alone, reason becomes perfected virtue (*uirtus perfecta*) and is, consequently, able to command the irrational part of the soul.[151] Crucially, Cicero argues that heroic individuals achieve the virtue through which they are able to accept suffering and death with equanimity by reflecting both upon philosophical principles which teach how fear is to be overcome and upon well-known examples that demonstrate how such principles have been successfully applied in the past. In illustrating this reasoning process, he begins with the precept that the virtuous man avoids any base, slack, or unmanly behaviour which could weaken his resolution. The sage who wishes to steel himself in the face of death reflects upon this and similar principles in conjunction with examples of heroism such as Zeno of Elea, a philosopher who suffered torture rather than betray his accomplices in a plot to overthrow a tyrant. Cicero points out that while thinking about moral principles and examples of this nature, the sage typically engages in a kind of conversation (*sermo*) with himself which includes debate (*contentio*) and demonstration (*confirmatio*).[152] These three technical terms indicate distinct modes of discourse. Cicero specifies them in this context because he wants to underscore his view that reason is not spontaneously swayed by the moral principles which it presents to itself, but that it must be convinced by argument in order to suppress fear. Moreover, it is unlikely to be persuaded solely as a consequence of reflection upon unadorned philosophical principles. In order to counteract fear, reason must be moved to do so by examining moral principles within the context of a wider 'indirect discourse'. 'Indirection' in this context refers to philosophical

---

[150] See ibid., 2.51.   [151] See ibid., 2.47.
[152] See ibid., 2.51: 'In quo vero erit perfecta sapientia – quem adhuc nos quidem vidimus neminem, sed philosophorum sententiis qualis hic futurus sit, si modo aliquando fuerit, exponitur – is igitur sive ea ratio, quae erit in eo perfecta atque absoluta, sic illi parti imperabit inferiori, ut iustus parens probis filiis; nutu quod volet conficiet, nullo labore, nulla molestia; eriget ipse se, suscitabit, instruet, armabit, ut tamquam hosti sic obsistat dolori. Quae sunt ista arma? Contentio, confirmatio sermoque intimus, cum ipse secum: "Cave turpe quiddam, languidum, non virile." Obversentur species honestae viro: Zeno proponatur Eleates . . . de Anaxarcho Democritio cogitetur . . .'

argument which relies on figurative expressions, such as metaphors and other tropes, or historical examples to persuade its intended audience to adopt a position. As a blend of philosophical and rhetorical arguments with ancient roots, the 'techniques of indirection in philosophy have to do with what is indicated by the text but not spelled out or made explicit in it'.[153] For example, Cicero pairs philosophical principles with historical examples, even though the latter are more traditionally associated with the orator's craft than with the philosopher's. To this end, he assigns Zeno's example a double role. It provides the sage with a demonstration of the soundness of moral principles that prescribe means for offsetting fear of pain and death in the pursuit of a higher good, while also encouraging him to imitate the hero and embrace this good even at the cost of death. Cicero notes that military heroes engage in a similar kind of interior discourse when they 'reflect (*cogitare*) with all their heart' on the honour they stand to achieve by dying bravely. He cites the example of the three Decii, whose fear of injury was quelled by their anticipation of the 'fame and glory of death'.[154] Cicero acknowledges that no one with such perfected reason has yet been known to exist, but he maintains that the ideal is achievable, and that it may be observed to a large degree in figures such as Zeno of Elea, Anaxarchus of Thrace, Callanus, and Marius. Such is the authority of these courageous men that others can be inspired to follow their example.[155]

PHILOSOPHY

Augustine's admiration for and debt to certain Platonic schools of philosophy is well known even if the nature and extent of his involvement with them are still widely debated among scholars.[156] He admits that the Platonists possess a correct concept of the one, true God.[157] They equate the attainment of happiness with 'participation in the light of God, the creator

---

[153] J. Mason, *Philosophical Rhetoric: The Function of Indirection in Philosophical Writing* (London, 1989), xi.

[154] See Cicero, *Libri tusculanarum disputationum* 2:58–9: 'Ad ferendum igitur dolorem placide atque sedate plurimum proficit toto pectore, ut dicitur, cogitare quam id honestum sit . . . Fulgentes gladios hostium videbant Decii, cum in aciem eorum irruebant: his levabat omnem vulnerum metum nobilitas mortis et gloria.'

[155] See ibid., 2.53: 'Cur ergo postea alii? Valuit auctoritas.'

[156] For a recent account of scholarly debates concerning Augustine's debt to Platonism and an indication of the pertinent studies, see R. Crouse, '*Paucis mutatis verbis*: St Augustine's Platonism', *Augustine and his Critics*, ed. R. Dodaro and G. Lawless (London, 1999), 37–50. For treatment of the question in relation to the *City of God*, see van Oort, *Jerusalem*, 237–44.

[157] See *ciu.* 8.3, 8.5, 8.6, 8.8, 8.9–12, 10.1 At *ciu.* 8.5, Augustine asserts that the doctrine of the Platonists surpasses that of Varro's mythical and civil theologies. He applies the tag 'Platonici' to Plato, Apuleius, Plotinus, Porphyry, and Iamblichus. See *ciu.* 8.12 and O'Daly, *Augustine's City*, 115, 257–9.

of the soul and of the entire world', and affirm that only those who adhere with undivided love to God as the supreme good can attain blessedness (10.1, cf. 8.3–11). He approves of these and other Platonic insights in which he sees the beginnings of philosophical solutions to some of the problems which ignorance and weakness engender in the soul, including fear of death.

Yet he also observes that Platonic accounts of mediation and participation err through their attachment to the worship of multiple gods (8.12, 10.1), and in their refusal to accept the incarnation of Christ as the great mystery (*magnum sacramentum*).[158] As a consequence, Platonists succumb to ignorance (*error*) and are given to weakness (*euanescere, resistere non audere*) where moral and spiritual activity is concerned.[159] They reject the incarnation as unsuitable for God, as a violation of decorum.[160] Augustine recognizes that in their concern to liberate the soul from the body and from passions such as fear of death, they promote an ascesis which culminates in contemplation of the intelligible world and the return of the human intellect to God. Some among these philosophers, such as Porphyry, advocate theurgy as a means of purifying the soul.[161] As a therapy for fear of death, such attempts to know and worship God, either through contemplation alone or through theurgy, are regarded by Augustine as doomed to failure for two reasons. First, in both cases, practitioners disparage the humility by which God, in Christ, becomes a human being, vulnerable to death.

---

[158] See *ciu.* 10.24 (CCL 47.297): 'noluit intellegere dominum Christum esse principium, cuius incarnatione purgamur. eum quippe in ipsa carne contempsit, quam propter sacrificium nostrae purgationis adsumpsit, magnum scilicet sacramentum ea superbia non intellegens, quam sua ille humilitate deiecit uerus benignusque mediator'.

[159] See *ciu.* 10.3 (CCL 47.274). See also *ciu.* 10.19 against the worship of deities other than God.

[160] At *ciu.* 8.18, 8.20, Augustine alludes to Plato, *Symposium* 203A, in affirming that for the Platonists, 'no god has dealings with human beings'. On the incarnation and decorum, see also *ciu.* 10.28, 10.29 (CCL 47.305): 'sed huic ueritati ut possetis adquiescere, humilitate opus erat, quae ceruici uestrae difficillime persuaderi potest [. . .] an forte uos offendit inusitatus corporis partus ex uirgine? neque hoc debet offendere, immo potius ad pietatem suscipiendam debet adducere, quod mirabiliter mirabiliter natus est'.

[161] See *ciu.* 10.9 and my discussions of theurgy below, pp. 95–104. Augustine probably has in mind the work of Porphyry, which he refers to as *De regressu animae* (see *ciu.* 10.29). J. O'Meara, *Porphyry's Philosophy from Oracles in Augustine* (Paris, 1959), believes that Augustine's source was a different, lost work of Porphyry, the *Philosophy from Oracles*. This conclusion is disputed by P. Hadot, 'Citations de Porphyre chez Augustin (A propos d'un ouvrage récent)', *Revue des études augustinennes* 6 (1960), 205–44. O'Daly, *Augustine's* City, 257 n. 54, observes that although Hadot is generally regarded as having refuted O'Meara's thesis, it nonetheless 'remains plausible'. On Porphyry's relation to theurgy, see H. Lewy, *Chaldean Oracles and Theurgy: Mysticism, Magic and Platonism in the Later Roman Empire*, rev. edn, ed. M. Tardieu (Paris, 1978), 449–66, and A. Smith, 'Porphyrian Studies since 1913', *Aufstieg und Niedergang der römischen Welt*, vol. 2.36.2, ed. W. Haase (Berlin, 1987), 717–73, at 763, who concludes that in the final analysis, Porphyry's attitude toward theurgy remains 'unclear to us', and that 'he himself may not have been entirely clear where he stood'.

In scorning this divine humility, they reject the grace which overcomes ignorance and weakness.[162] For Augustine, only this grace enables the soul to attain some measure of true knowledge and love of the true God, and to understand how true virtue confronts death.

In regard to theurgists, Augustine objects that they rely upon intermediary, spiritual beings who, because they are not God, cannot mediate the knowledge of God and the attendant blessedness which together heal the twin effects of original sin.[163] He charges that whereas Porphyry professes to be a lover of strength and wisdom (*uirtutis et sapientiae amator*), in reality he leads human beings astray from Christ, the true strength and wisdom of God (*dei uirtus et sapientia*).[164] Augustine recognizes the presence of a certain conception of grace in Porphyry's thought, insofar as the philosopher acknowledges that 'it is granted' (*esse concessum*) only to a few to reach God on the strength of their intelligence alone. He accepts, moreover, that Porphyry's affirmation reflects the truth concerning the grace of God and human insufficiency. Porphyry even uses the word 'grace' in this connection, he observes, and holds that God's providence and grace supply all that is needed for the perfection of wisdom in life after death for those accustomed to contemplation.[165] Finally, Augustine is aware of Porphyry's claim that intermediary, spiritual beings which are summoned through theurgical rites are able to purify only the lower part of the soul, known as the 'spiritual soul', and not the higher part, the 'intellectual soul', which can be purified only by what Plotinus referred to as the 'principles' (10.9, 10.27). Nevertheless, he argues that Porphyry fails to consider what precisely is granted within his concept of grace, and by what means it

---

[162] See *ciu.* 10.27 (CCL 47.302), where Augustine equates Porphyry's rejection of salvation through Christ with an insistence that human beings should rely upon their own, weak virtue in attempting to live justly: 'ea quippe dixit, quae etiam multum proficientium in uirtute iustitiae possunt propter huius uitae infirmitatem, etsi non scelera, scelerum tamen manere uestigia, quae non nisi ab illo saluatore sanantur, de quo iste uersus expressus est'.

[163] B. Studer, 'La *cognitio historialis* di Porfirio nel *De ciuitate dei* di Agostino (*ciu.* 10, 32)', *La narrativa cristiana antica. Atti del XXIII Incontro di studiosi dell'antichità cristiana, Roma 5–7 maggio 1994* (Rome, 1995), 520–53, at 550, notes a relationship between Augustine's reflection on the Ciceronian link between justice and *res publica* and his polemic against Porphyry and Neoplatonic theurgists, who fail to worship God correctly.

[164] See *ciu.* 10.28 (CCL 47.303).

[165] See *ciu.* 10.29 (CCL 47.304): 'confiteris tamen gratiam, quando quidem ad deum per uirtutem intellegentiae peruenire paucis dicis esse concessum. non enim dicis: paucis placuit, uel: pauci uoluerunt; sed cum dicis esse concessum, procul dubio dei gratiam, non hominis sufficientiam confiteris. uteris etiam hoc uerbo apertius, ubi Platonis sententiam sequens nec ipse dubitas in hac uita hominem nullo modo ad perfectionem sapientiae peruenire, secundum intellectum tamen uiuentibus omne quod deest prouidentia dei et gratia post hanc uitam posse compleri'. P. Courcelle, *Les Lettres grecques en Occident. De Macrobe à Cassiodore* (Paris, 1948), 227–8, suggests that Augustine learned of these usages while reading Porphyry's *De regressu animae*.

is communicated. Porphyry's understanding of grace is inadequate when compared with the supreme model of grace (*summum exemplum gratiae*) which is found in the incarnation (10.29). Porphyrian mediation of immortality and happiness through spiritual beings which are only created beings, no matter how exalted they are above human beings, is infinitely inferior to the direct mediation of virtue between God and the soul through Christ (10.25).

'YOU SHALL BE LIKE GODS' (GN 3:5)

As we have seen, in Augustine's view, Roman religion and non-Christian philosophies alike fail to inform their adherents about either the true God or the nature of true worship. This ignorance, coupled with the weakness of the soul, prevents human beings from practising true virtue. Augustine's proof for his conclusion that the Roman commonwealth has never succeeded in attaining true justice depends upon these arguments in Books 1–10. However, he is also concerned there to show that, as permanent defects of the soul caused by original sin, ignorance and weakness make human beings vulnerable to deception about true religion by demons or other human beings. This deception, which is communicated through different forms of discourse, such as oratory, religious ritual, games and theatrical spectacles, philosophy and literature, is, moreover, the primary means of ensuring continued ignorance and weakness. For Augustine, the soul's affliction by ignorance and weakness is the reason that language is able to invent and sustain a counterfeit concept of justice.

Augustine never abandons the conviction, dear to classical rhetoricians, that human behaviour is largely conditioned by the effects of language on the soul.[166] With Cicero, he accepts that rational judgment is all too easily swayed by well-argued and seemingly plausible falsehoods.[167] He recognizes that moral ignorance and weakness correlate negatively to the three functions of rhetoric: teaching (*docere*), moving or persuading (*mouere*,

---

[166] Surprisingly, a thorough, up-to-date treatment of rhetoric in Augustine is still lacking, but see L. Pizzolato, *Capitoli di retorica agostiniana* (Rome, 1994). Though dated, J. Finaert, *Saint Augustin rhéteur* (Paris, 1939), and H.-I. Marrou, *Saint Augustin et la fin de la culture antique*, 4th edn (Paris, 1958), 3–157, retain their usefulness in this regard. Among specific studies of Augustine's familiarity with rhetoric, see also L. McNew, 'The Relation of Cicero's Rhetoric to Augustine', *Research Studies of the State College of Washington* 25:1 (1957), 5–13, J. Oroz Reta, *San Agustín y la cultura clásica* (Salamanca, 1963), E. Fortin, 'Saint Augustine and the Problem of Christian Rhetoric', *Augustinian Studies* 5 (1974), 85–100, G. Kennedy, *Classical Rhetoric and its Christian and Secular Tradition from Ancient to Modern Times* (Chapel Hill, 1980), 149–60, and G. Mainberger, *Rhetorica I. Reden mit Vernunft: Aristoteles, Cicero, Augustinus* (Stuttgart, 1987), 316–72.

[167] See *doctr. chr.* 4.4–11.

persuadere), and pleasing (*delectare*).[168] He understands that, in hidden ways, ignorance and weakness impede efforts to teach justice, to persuade others to practise it, and to elicit delight in it.[169] Cicero may be excused for concluding erroneously that nature itself is to blame for the human incapacity to overcome moral evil, because he could not have understood the stealthy interference in moral reasoning and the will which arises from the consequences of original sin: 'Perceiving the problem, he misdiagnosed it.'[170]

Augustine's insistence that a just society requires that its members be healed from the effects of original sin stems in part from his conclusions about the relationship of original sin to language and to the practice of virtue. Political discourse in the earthly city (*ciuitas terrena*) has its roots in the 'city' governed by the devil (*ciuitas diaboli*). As such, it is patterned ultimately on Satan's rhetoric. Book 14 of the *City of God*, in particular, employs the Genesis narrative of the Fall as a metaphor for the disruption of political community which is caused by the presence of a deceptive rhetoric.[171] Accordingly, Satan arouses in Eve and Adam a preference for

---

[168] Compare Cicero, *Orator* 21.69, on the *officia oratoris* in general (*probare, delectare, flectere*) with Augustine, *rhet.* 2–3, where he discusses the function of the orator to persuade (*persuadere*) the audience in relation to his function to teach (*docere*), and with *doctr. chr.* 4.96 (*docere, delectare, flectere*). At *doct. chr.* 4.67–71, the interrelationship of the functions is apparent in Augustine's insistence that effective teaching (*docere*) involves pleasing an audience (*delectare*). See A. Primmer, 'The Function of the Genera Dicendi in De doctrina christiana: 4', *De doctrina christiana. A Classic of Western Culture*, ed. D. W. H. Arnold and P. Bright (Notre Dame, 1995), 68–86. See also B. Kursawe, *Docere – delectare – movere: Die officia oratoris bei Augustinus in Rhetorik und Gnadenlehre* (Paderborn, 2000), especially 99–152. At *doctr. chr.* 4.14–15, Augustine treats 'docere–mouere' as a rhetorical scheme concerned with overcoming defects in understanding (*nescire*) and will (*torpere*), echoes of ignorance and weakness. See Hagendahl, *Augustine*, 351 n. 4, and Testard, *Saint Augustin*, 1:268–9, on Augustine's substitution of the obligation *docere* for Cicero's *probare*.

[169] See *ench.* 24 (CCL 46.63): 'porro animus cum adipiscitur concupita, quamuis perniciosa et inania, quoniam id errore non sentit, uel delectatione morbida uincitur, uel uana etiam laetitia uentilatur'.

[170] See *c. Iul.* 4.60 (PL 44.767): 'rem uidit, causam nesciuit', citing Cicero, *De re publica* 3. See also *c. Iul.* 4.61, 4.77–8. Cicero makes a similar point with regard to the natural weakness of the mind at *Libri tusculanarum disputationum* 2.47. On Cicero's Stoic ethics, see M. Schofield, 'Two Stoic Approaches to Justice', *Justice and Generosity: Studies in Hellenistic Social and Political Philosophy. Proceedings of the Sixth Symposium Hellenisticum*, ed. A. Laks and M. Schofield (Cambridge, 1995), 191–212. Augustine's argument that it is not nature itself but the Fall which is responsible for the corruption of morals can be found at a number of locations in his work, for example, *ciu.* 11.17 and 13.3. His distinction between human nature and evil in Book 14 of the *City of God* is intended as a refutation of Manichean and Platonic dualisms. At *ciu.* 11.15 he argues similarly that the devil cannot have been evil by nature. See H.-I. Marrou and A.-M. La Bonnardière, 'Le Dogme de la résurrection des corps et la théologie des valeurs humaines selon l'enseignement de saint Augustin', *Revue des études augustiniennes* 12 (1966), 111–36.

[171] On the Fall in Augustine as a polyvalent symbol, see P. Ricoeur, *The Conflict of Interpretations: Essays in Hermeneutics*, ed. D. Ihde (Evanston, 1974), 283–6. Compare the description of Augustine's reading of Genesis which follows with Cicero's mythic account of the origins of political community through rhetoric at *De inuentione* 1.2.2.

self-delusion through deceitful but persuasive speech, culminating in the false promise, 'You shall be like gods' (Gn 3:5).[172] Satan's is, therefore, the archetypal seduction because it embodies the form of all future misdirection of the soul.[173] Similarly, it constitutes the prototype for all secular political discourse, in that it displaces within the soul the original blessing of life lived for the sake of authentic spiritual communion, and introduces in its stead the illusion of self-sufficiency and of satisfaction with a lack of moral rectitude.

In Augustine's view, this retreat into a rival 'creation' by Adam and Eve inaugurates the realm of the essentially private.[174] Such, indeed, was the political form of Satan's own pride: a self-deception which rejected the exclusive divine claim to hegemony, and substituted the domain of self-rule. Satan's rival city remains eternally devoid of truth because its genesis represents an act of usurpation.[175] Augustine's insistence upon the fundamental mendacity of Satan's actions is intended to establish the eloquent lie as the cause of social and political disruption characteristic of the earthly city, where he holds sway.[176] Genesis 3 marks the primordial transition of natural desire away from beatitude in human existence, as it was ordered, toward the 'mimetic desire' of longing to have what God alone possesses.[177] Augustine maintains that human beings seek to create good works out of their own capacities, but that these attempts, which stem from the original

---

[172] See *ciu.* 14.2 (CCL 48.432): 'fallacia sermocinatus', 15.22 (CCL 48.487): 'fallacia seductae illae feminae persuaserunt peccatum uiris'. See also *trin.* 4.15, 11.8, *ciu.* 14.13, 22.30. Augustine's insistence that Satan could not have seduced Adam and Eve unless they were predisposed by virtue of an already erring will is intended to underscore the full autonomy of their decision, not to minimize the force of the rhetoric which occasioned their choice. See W. Babcock, 'The Human and the Angelic Fall: Will and Moral Agency in Augustine's *City of God*', *Augustine: From Rhetor to Theologian*, ed. J. McWilliam (Waterloo, 1992), 133–49.

[173] See, for example, *ciu.* 14.3 (CCL 48.417): 'peccatorum suasor et instigator occultus'. See also *en. Ps.* 103.4.6.

[174] See *en. Ps.* 103.2.11 (CCL 40.1498): 'et miseri audiendo dimiserunt quod commune erat, unde beati erant, et ad suum proprium redacti, cum uolunt peruerse esse similes deo – hoc enim eis dixerat: *Gustate, et eritis sicut dii* [Gn 3:5] –, appetentes quod non erant, quod acceperant amiserunt'. See O. O'Donovan, *The Problem of Self-Love in St. Augustine* (New Haven, 1980), 93–111.

[175] See *ciu.* 14.4. At *ciu.* 11.33 (CCL 48.353), Augustine describes the rival 'angelic society' (*societas angelica*) gathered around Satan. See *Io. eu. tr.* 17.16 (CCL 36.178–9), where Satan's deed is described as 'usurpatio'.

[176] See *ciu.* 14.3 (CCL 48.418): 'pater mendacii'. At *trin.* 12.13, Augustine links Satan with the invention of seductive language.

[177] See *ciu.* 14.11, where Augustine describes Satan's sin as consisting in envy of God and, later, of human beings. At *ciu.* 22.30 (CCL 48.865) he notes that human beings similarly desire what God possesses: 'quoniam ipse est deus, quod nobis nos ipsi esse uolumus'. See also *trin.* 10.7; *s.* 264.3 (PL 38.1214): 'cui ergo erat rapina aequalitatis Dei? primo homini, cui dictum est, *Gustate, et eritis sicut dii* [Gn 3:5]. uoluit per rapinam tendere se ad aequalitatem, et per poenam perdit immortalitatem'. The term 'mimetic desire' is borrowed from R. Girard, *Violence and the Sacred*, tr. P. Gregory (Baltimore, 1977), especially 145–9.

act of defiance, are doomed to failure.[178] When good does result from human efforts, it is because they are never without divine assistance.[179] Knowledge and love of God, the proper worship of God, are impeded by the dissonance of this free-floating selfhood.[180] Augustine describes the sin of Adam and Eve as self-worship as opposed to the correct worship of God.[181] He believes that as a consequence of this erroneous self-love, human beings are never quite free of the lie at the foundation of all disordered desire, 'You shall be like gods.' Whether he employs the term 'pride' (*superbia*), 'avarice' (*auaritia*), or 'desire' (*cupiditas*) to describe seminal injustice of the sort implicit in 'original sin',[182] the phenomenon at the root of all sin remains for Augustine linguistic or rhetorical in character: in every sin one detects the contours of a lie.[183]

Consequently, the egoistic conception expressed in the term 'my own' enters human consciousness and language as a reference to a self detached from its proper mooring in God's providential order.[184] God's command not to eat the fruit of a given tree was intended to remind Adam and Eve of the necessity of enjoying a selfhood within the limits of its relation to God, an obedience (*oboedientia*) understood in its deepest sense of hearing the divine Word.[185] Violation of this order constitutes the primal injustice (*iniustitia*).[186] The conceit by which human beings subvert the divine social order, thereby rejecting worship of the true God, results in the establishment of new terms for a just social order. Determination of shared utility

---

[178] See *ciu.* 14.11 (CCL 48.431),: 'defectus potius fuit quidam ab opere dei ad sua opera quam opus ullum, et ideo mala opera, quia secundum se, non secundum deum'.

[179] See, for example, *ciu.* 22.30.

[180] See *ciu.* 11.1 (CCL 48.321): 'huic conditori sanctae ciuitatis ciues terrenae ciuitatis deos suos praeferunt ignorantes eum esse deum deorum'. This specific application of *ignorantia*, of not being able to know the true God and of preferring false religion, occurs as a specific result of the Fall. See also *ciu.* 14.9.

[181] See *ciu.* 14.13.   [182] See especially *trin.* 12.14–15.

[183] See *ciu.* 14.4 (CCL 48.418): 'unde non frustra dici potest omne peccatum esse mendacium'. See also *s. Denis* 20.2 (CCL 41.219): 'facit enim consuetudinem loqui mendacium; etiam si non uis, illa loquitur mendacium', *Io. eu. tr.* 5.1 (CCL 36.40): 'nemo habet de suo, nisi mendacium et peccatum'.

[184] See *ciu.* 14.1 (CCL 48.41): God had intended that human society should consist 'in unitatem concordem pacis uinculo conligandum'. But man broke away from attachment to divine order. See also *ciu.* 14.13. At *en. Ps.* 103.2.11 (CCL 40.1497), Augustine opposes the philosophical consequences of this pseudo-autonomy as the 'privatization' of truth, whereby 'my truth' stands in opposition to 'your truth': 'quod sentio, sentis . . . non habeo quasi priuatum meum, nec tu priuatum tuum. ueritas nec mea sit propria, nec tua, ut et tua sit et mea . . .'. See also *lib. arb.* 132, *trin.* 10.7, 12.14, *Gn. adu. Man.* 2.24, and R. Holte, *Béatitude et sagesse. S. Augustin et le problème de la fin de l'homme dans la philosophie ancienne* (Paris, 1962), 248–50.

[185] See, especially, *ciu.* 14.15, but also *ciu.* 14.12 (CCL 48.434): 'sed oboedientia commendata est in praecepto', and *ciu.* 13.20.

[186] See *ciu.* 14.12 (CCL 48.434): 'tanto maiore iniustitia uiolatum est [praeceptum], quanto faciliore posset obseruantia custodiri'.

(*utilitas communis*) will henceforth require measured calculation[187] which must ceaselessly concern itself with the principle of 'just desert' or 'merit', as expressed in the conventional conception of justice as 'giving to each his or her due' (*suum cuique reddere*).[188] Recognition that this understanding of justice runs counter to the New Testament realignment of justice with love of God and neighbour demonstrates to Augustine that the classical definition of justice arose from the deformation of another, purer justice. The language of justice in the city of God will have to be purified of its association with this 'privatized' sense of justice.[189]

CONCLUSION

Commentators on the *City of God* are right to interpret the arguments of the first ten books as corresponding with Augustine's stated intentions: (1) to demonstrate the inefficacy of pagan gods in providing for temporal or permanent happiness, and (2) to confute charges against the Christian religion for its responsibility in the sack of Rome in 410. However, Augustine's numerous references to ignorance and weakness in his discussion of pagan religion and philosophy reveal his concern to show that as a result of original sin, the human being is incapable of knowing and loving God without God's direct mediation. Augustine argues that fear of death, which is natural to human beings as a result of original sin, epitomizes this ignorance and weakness and is largely responsible for the inability of pagans to accept that God has united himself with man and suffered death in Christ. Instead, Augustine asserts, pagan Romans have looked to other forms of religion and philosophy, which promise alternative ways to

---

[187] See Aristotle, *Nicomachean Ethics* 5.3.8.29–31: justice involves 'proportion', which is an 'equality of ratios'.

[188] At *diu. qu.* 31.1, Augustine gives Cicero's version (*De inventione* 2.160) of the classical definition of justice: 'iustitia est habitus animi, communi utilitate conseruata, suam cuique tribuens dignitatem'. See Aristotle's discussion of δικαιοσύνε at *Nicomachean Ethics* 5.1.10.10 and 5.2.2.18, where his use of the verb πλεονεκτέω 'to claim more than one's due', implies a right to 'one's due'. He develops the principle of desert in terms of distributive justice at 5.3.7–17. See the discussion of *pleonexia* by A. MacIntyre, *After Virtue*, 2nd edn (Notre Dame, 1984), 106 and 111–13. For Augustine, private property and possession are results of the Fall, a point well illustrated by Deane, *Political*, 42–8.

[189] Augustine indicates realignment of *iustitia* with *caritas* at *nat. et gr.* 84 (CSEL 60.298): 'caritas ergo inchoata, inchoata iustitia est . . . caritas magna magna iustitia'. Further detail of this transformation is given at *en. Ps.* 83.11, where he spells out the 'duty' implied by the classical definition of justice, 'give to each his or her due', as 'works of justice', which are also 'works of charity'. See also *trin.* 14.12, where he contrasts his understanding of justice with that of Cicero in *Hortensius*. *Res publica* is thus refocused away from concern for private advantage toward care for the *res communis*. See also *ep.* 140.63 (CSEL 44.210): 'ista est communio cuiusdam diuinae caelestisque rei publicae; hinc saturantur pauperes non sua quaerentes, sed quae Iesu Christi, id est non commoda priuata sectantes sed in commune, ubi salus omnium est, consulentes'.

purification of the soul than through such a direct divine vulnerability to death. Against these alternatives, Augustine holds that God is knowable exclusively through the mystery (*mysterium, sacramentum*) of the incarnation. In his view, God chooses mystery as the form of his self-revelation to man in order to cure the soul of ignorance and weakness by diminishing the pretensions of moral self-reliance with which they afflict it. Only the soul that struggles by faith and humility to know and love God through mystery achieves the purification necessary to recognize and repent of its self-deceptions. Augustine argues that in the case of pagan Romans, the ease with which they are deceived about worship is heightened by the ability of their priests and statesmen, acting in collusion with demonic spirits, to persuade them to embrace false piety in their search for temporal security. In this way, they not only fail to come to know and love themselves, their neighbours, and, above all, the true God; they also fail to look beyond the immediate, temporal benefits promised by polytheism (such as security and material prosperity) in order to learn to seek eternal goods (such as happiness in God). In accord with Augustine's argument that no commonwealth can exist without true justice, and that true justice demands rendering to God the true worship that is his due, the analysis contained in Books 1–10 of the *City of God* concerning the inherent inability of human beings to know or worship God demonstrates Augustine's wider argument concerning the nature of the just society and Rome's inability to achieve it.

In the chapter which follows, we shall examine the solution that Augustine offers to the problem in establishing a just society that results from ignorance and weakness in the human soul. Augustine proposes Christ as the statesman (*rector rei publicae*) whose unique condition as God and man means that he alone in history is capable of sustaining a just society, because he alone is both completely just and capable of healing other human beings from original sin, thus making them just. Augustine argues that human beings are united to Christ when they accept in faith and humility that virtue derives only from the mediation of Christ's grace. Thus united with Christ as members of his body, these believers form the just society.

CHAPTER 3

Christ and the formation of the just society

Augustine's decision to establish the just society in Christ is fundamental to his way of thinking. Being, unity, truth, goodness, and beauty inevitably conduct the soul to God and, therefore, to Christ as the way to God.[1] The same logic obtains for justice.[2] Augustine maintains that justice cannot be known except in Christ, and that, as founder (*conditor*) and ruler (*rector*), Christ forms the just society in himself. United with Christ, members of his body constitute the whole, just Christ (*Christus totus iustus*), which is the city of God, the true commonwealth, and the locus for the revelation of justice.[3] It will be argued in this chapter that, in Augustine's view, Christ creates this just society through his mediation of divine humility to human beings through his incarnation. Christ's virtue takes hold in human beings when they believe in the mystery of the incarnate God. In this chapter we shall also see that, for Augustine, this faith in the incarnation requires believers (1) to reject the concept of an autonomous moral reason in the soul, (2) to affirm that the source of their virtue is Christ, and (3) to accept that perfect human virtue can be found only in Christ.

---

[1] As, for example, at *ciu.* 9.15, 10.21, 10.29, 10.32, 11.2, 22.24. On Christ as *uia* in relation to justice, see *en. Ps.* 31.2.18, 103.4.6. See also *an. quant.* 76, *lib. arb.* 2.26, *spir. et litt.* 5, *nat. et gr.* 36. On Christ as the *uia* which leads pilgrims to the city of God, see *en. Ps.* 90.2.1. On the motif 'homeland-way' (*patria-uia*), see M.-F. Berrouard, 'Le Christ, patrie et voie', *Œuvres de Saint Augustin*, vol. 71: *Homélies I–XIV sur l'Evangile de Saint Jean*, ed. M.-F. Berrouard (Paris, 1969), 848–50. See also L. Galati, *Cristo la via nel pensiero di S. Agostino* (Rome, 1956), O. Du Roy, *L'Intelligence de la foi en la Trinité selon saint Augustin* (Paris, 1966), 96–105, 451–4, O. Brabant, *Le Christ: centre et source de la vie morale chez s. Augustin* (Gembloux, 1971), 79–83, Remy, *Le Christ*, 1:28–34, G. Madec, *La Patrie et la voie. Le Christ dans la vie et la pensée de saint Augustin* (Paris, 1989), 37, 44–8, 161–2, 171–2, 239–41, M.-F. Berrouard, 'Saint Augustin et le mystère du Christ chemin, vérité et vie. La médiation théologique du Tractatus 69 in Iohannis Euangelium sur Io. 14, 6a', *Augustiniana* 41 (1991), 431–49, B. Studer, *The Grace of Christ and the Grace of God in Augustine of Hippo: Christocentrism or Theocentrism?*, tr. M. J. O'Connell (Collegeville, 1997), 44–7.

[2] On the transcendental nature of justice, see, for example, *en. Ps.* 61.21 (CCL 39.789): 'respice ergo, transcende, uade illuc ubi semel locutus est deus; et ibi inuenies fontem iustitiae, ubi est fons uitae'.

[3] On Christ as founder and ruler of the city of God, see *ciu.* 2.21 (CCL 47.55). On the theme *Christus totus iustus*, see *en. Ps.* 30.2.3.5 (CCL 38.215–16) and my discussion below, pp. 97–9, 105–7.

Before moving deeper into this discussion, we should keep in mind two general points in Augustine's thought regarding Christ's role in revealing justice, the first concerning Christ's person and work, the second concerning the nature of justice. Regarding Christ, Augustine makes a series of interrelated claims. Christ is the only completely just man ever to have lived. Moreover, he alone justifies other human beings by purifying and healing the soul of ignorance and weakness.[4] Only as a result of such purification and healing is man able to live justly in imitation of Christ. Grasping these points is essential to understanding how Augustine believes that ignorance and weakness may be overcome in the soul, in order that it may come to know and love justice. As noted in the previous chapter, Augustine pairs ignorance and weakness with the intellect and the will. However, he also envisages a dynamic element in their relationship.[5] In a real sense, ignorance and weakness interact with each other to such a degree that it is impossible to determine clearly to which of them any particular moral failing should be assigned. Thus, as suggested in the last chapter, Augustine bases his criticism of Roman religion on the assumption that the faith and humility required for the apprehension of the mystery of God incarnate have proven too strenuous for non-Christians, who approach divinity in less rigorously intellectual and moral terms. In Augustine's scheme, does this choice on their part represent a failure of the intellect or of the will? In cases where ignorance is willed (that is, consented to) because its object imposes an excessive intellectual and moral burden on the inquirer, Augustine hesitates to fault ignorance or weakness alone, as if both defects were not in some sense interrelated in the act itself. For example, he speaks of ignorance and weakness together when discussing the failure of pagans to understand the nature of God as mystery.[6] His explanation of Porphyry's rejection of the incarnation as a religious truth acknowledges the necessity

---

[4] Thus, Augustine applies the label 'just and justifying' (Rom 3:26) to Christ. See, for example, *ciu.* 17.4 (below, p. 109 n. 152). See also *ciu.* 9.17 and 10.24, where other terms denote these same attributes. B. Studer, 'Le Christ, notre justice, selon saint Augustin', *Recherches augustiniennes* 15 (1980), 123 n. 223, observes that Augustine applies this Pauline expression more often to Christ than to God. On justification (*iustificatio*) as 'making just' (*iustum facere*), see, for example, *gr. et lib. arb.* 1.13, *en. Ps.* 105.5 (below, p. 95 n. 91), *s. Dolbeau* 19.3 (D 158): 'de te dici potest ut sis iustus, numquam auditur ut sis et iustificans. quid est enim iustificans, nisi iustum faciens? sicut uiuificans uiuum faciens, sicut saluificans saluum faciens, sic et iustificans iustum faciens'.

[5] E. Katayanagi, 'The Last Congruous Vocation', *Collectanea augustiniana. Mélanges T. J. van Bavel*, vol. 2, ed. B. Bruning et al. (Leuven, 1991) = *Augustiniana* 41 (1991), 645–57, at 650, citing *trin.* 10.18, argues in a similar vein that 'Augustine indeed distinguishes the will from the intellect, but not as though each were located externally', by which he means that '[w]hen man feels persuaded, then the intellect works not only externally, but also inwardly, within the will'.

[6] See, for example, my discussion above, pp. 37–41, concerning the contrast between the reactions of Lucretia and of Christian virgins during the sack of Rome to their respective rapes. See also above,

of faith and humility in order to accept the seemingly irrational and indecorous proposition that, in Christ, God united himself with man and died. Faith and humility each require a close interrelationship between the intellectual and voluntary elements proper to each virtue. Thus, pondering a truth that is accepted on faith so as to understand it more deeply requires that one already believe it, an axiom for which Augustine finds support at Isa 7:9, 'Unless you believe you will not understand.'[7] Faith, in this sense, can be described as an initial stage in knowledge, one that involves a focused assent of the will, as opposed to a general trust in what is visible and more easily accessible to understanding.[8] Likewise, to perceive even partially the reasonableness and beauty of the idea that, in becoming man, God acted humbly, one must practise an intellectual form of humility. In *De trinitate*, Augustine will argue in an analogous manner that in order to understand justice, one has to be just.[9]

The interaction of justice and grace in Christ's example mirrors this dynamic interrelationship between intellect and will, and therefore between ignorance and weakness. Augustine identifies two erroneous ways of conceiving the effect of Christ's sacraments, examples, and grace upon the intellect and will which must be avoided in order that this process of justification may be understood. Enlightenment of the intellect and healing of the will are not separate operations performed within the soul; nor, therefore, do they occur as distinct steps in a process. Grace heals the will of its weakness concerning justice in the same act in which the intellect is enlightened about the nature and content of justice, as both are understood in Christ's example.[10] Augustine informs us in Book 8 of *De trinitate* that the mind perceives justice to the degree that the form of justice which Christ's example presents to the mind becomes an object of desire, and is both known and loved.[11] However, Augustine's understanding of this process also clearly implies that for the full effects of Christ's example and grace to be perceived by both intellect and will, the obstacles to understanding and loving virtue represented by ignorance and weakness must simultaneously be overcome. For this to occur, Augustine insists that the justice

---

p. 44 n. 74, concerning Augustine's accusation at *ciu.* 2.7 against the Platonists for rejecting the *uia humilitatis* as the only means to arrive at true piety.

[7] See, for example, *Acad.* 3.43, *ord.* 2.26–7, *sol.* 1.12–14.23, *an. quant.* 12, *c. Faust.* 12.46, and the discussions by E. TeSelle, 'Credere' and 'Fides', *Augustinus-Lexikon*, vol. 2, ed. C. Mayer (Basle, 1996–2002), 119–31 and 1333–40, respectively.

[8] See *spir. et litt.* 54, *ench.* 20, *praed. sanct.* 5.   [9] See *trin.* 8.6–13 and my discussion below, pp. 157–9.

[10] This is the burden of Augustine's argument against the Pelagians at *gr. et pecc. or.* 1.12, which I discuss below, pp. 168–71.

[11] See my discussion of *trin.* 8 below, pp. 156–9.

presented to the mind by Christ's example should somehow also deflate the pretensions to justice which the soul, under the effects of original sin, manufactures and to which it obsessively clings. In this sense, the justice which is understood by the enlightened intellect and loved by the purified will is known not simply in the manner in which it is loved, but also to the extent that it has converted the soul from its intellectual and volitional attachment to a counterfeit justice. Moreover, approached in this way, ignorance and weakness do not constitute two distinct defects of the soul, but two alternative conceptions of the same defect. Christ's grace thus enables his example to demonstrate to the soul the extent to which its prior concepts of justice are nothing more than reflections of the soul's own particular form of self-righteousness.

Christ continues by means of his grace and teaching to instruct, admonish, and assist the members of his 'city' in the practice of justice. These rhetorical emphases (instruction, exhortation, correction) constitute his examples of justice and related virtues, and represent aspects of his mediation. As a result of this understanding of Christ's example and grace, Augustine disagrees with Cicero on the proper role of the statesman. For Cicero, the statesman who wishes to construct and promote a just society must act justly while also speaking persuasively about justice. For Augustine, discourse about justice cannot sustain a just society unless the statesman who offers it is also capable of purifying his listeners' souls. Such healing inevitably involves disabusing them of the false conceptions of justice which contribute to their own moral presumption.

The second aspect of Augustine's theology which is crucial to understanding Christ's role in founding and governing the just society is the meaning of the term justice (*iustitia*) and its various cognates. These concepts possess a religious significance for Augustine which is derived from the scriptures and earlier Christian authors.[12] Justice in its fundamental,

---

[12] For New Testament background to the concept of justice, see below, n. 14. For the patristic background, see especially J.-M. Aubert, 'Justice', *Dictionnaire de spiritualité*, vol. 8, ed. A. Rayez et al. (Paris, 1974), 1622–38. See also A. Descamps, *Les Justes et la justice dans les évangiles et le christianisme primitif: hormis la doctrine proprement paulinienne* (Louvain, 1950), A. Davids, 'Het begrip gerechtigheid in de oude kerk', *Tidjschrift voor theologie* 17 (1977), 145–70, Dihle, 'Gerechtigkeit', 233–360, Buchheit, 'Die Definition, 356–74, H. Merkel, 'Gerechtigkeit. IV', *Theologische Realenzyklopädie*, vol. 12, ed. G. Krause and G. Müller (Berlin, 1984), 420–4, A. McGrath, *Iustitia dei. A History of the Christian Doctrine of Justification: The Beginnings to the Reformation* (Cambridge, 1986), 17–36. For treatments specific to Augustine, see, in particular, Studer, 'Le Christ', but also J. Plagnieux, 'Le Binome *iustitia-potentia* dans la sotériologie augustinienne et anselmienne', *Spicilegium beccense* 1 (1959), 141–54, F.-J. Thonnard, 'Justice de Dieu et justice humaine selon s. Augustin', *Augustinus* 12 (1967), 387–402, R. Evans, *Four Letters of Pelagius* (New York, 1968), 76–7, J. Christes, 'Christliche und heidnische-römische Gerechtigkeit in Augustins Werk *De ciuitate*

Christian sense means to stand in right relationship to God and, therefore, to obey God and his commandments.[13] Yet because the greatest commandment is to 'love God and neighbour as oneself' (Mt 22:37–9), Augustine argues that justice is interchangeable with love (*caritas*).[14]

By equating justice with love, Augustine follows a number of early Christian authorities including Cyprian, Lactantius, and Ambrose. Unlike these authors, however, he identifies justice as a central issue in a number of theological controversies which have engaged him since the first years of his priesthood. As early as his treatise against the Manichean Faustus (AD 397/9), for example, he insists that justice is only acquired gradually in this life, never completely, and that the lack of its perfection in an individual must not be taken to indicate its absence altogether.[15] Shortly after the beginning of his controversy with the Pelagians over original sin and its consequences for human nature and Christ's grace, Augustine argues in a similar vein that biblical figures renowned for their justice, such as Job and Paul, need not have been completely faultless during their lives in order to serve as fitting examples of justice.[16] Augustine's response to their

---

dei', *Rheinisches Museum* 126 (1980), 163–77; A. McGrath, 'Divine Justice and Divine Equity in the Controversy between Augustine and Julian of Eclanum', *Downside Review* 101 (1983), 312–19. On Cicero's influence upon Augustine's concept of justice, see Hagendahl, *Augustine*, 1:543–5. For a much-abbreviated, summary treatment, including references to further studies, see R. Dodaro, 'Justice', *Augustine through the Ages: An Encyclopedia*, ed. A. Fitzgerald et al. (Grand Rapids, 1999), 481–3.

[13] See Studer, 'Le Christ', 105 n. 49, citing: *agon.* 7, *en. Ps.* 61.62, 32.2.1.2, 124.9, *s.* 18.9, 34.3, 278, *ciu.* 19.21, *ep.* 120.20.

[14] See, for example, *nat. et gr.* 84 (above, p. 70 n. 189). On the concept of justice in its New Testament contexts, see E. Käsemann, 'Gottesgerechtigkeit bei Paulus', *Zeitschrift für Theologie und Kirche* 58 (1961), 367–78, G. Jeremias, *Der Lehrer der Gerechtigkeit* (Göttingen, 1963), L. Ruppert, *Jesus als der leidende Gerechte? Der Weg Jesu im Lichte eines alt- und zwischentestamentlichen Motivs* (Stuttgart, 1972), J. Ziesler, *The Meaning of Righteousness in Paul* (Cambridge, 1972), B. Przybylski, *Righteousness in Matthew and his World of Thought* (Cambridge, 1980).

[15] See *c. Faust.* 22.27.

[16] See *pecc. mer.* 2.22, *perf. ius.* 23–30. I recognize that the expression 'Pelagian' and its cognates are somewhat ambiguous. I shall try where possible to distinguish the positions of Pelagius, Celestius, Julian of Eclanum, and others connected with this ascetical movement. The fundamental guide to the movement and the writings which it produced remains O. Wermelinger, *Rom und Pelagius. Die theologische Position der römischen Bischöfe im pelagianischen Streit in den Jahren 411–432* (Stuttgart, 1975). For a more general, concise outline, see F. Nuvolone and A. Solignac, 'Pélage et pélagianisme', *Dictionnaire de spiritualité*, vol. 12:2, ed. A. Rayez et al. (Paris, 1986), 2889–942. See also O. Wermelinger, 'Neuere Forschungskontroversen um Augustinus und Pelagius', *Internationales Symposium über den Stand der Augustinus-Forschung*, ed. C. Mayer and K.-H. Chelius (Würzburg, 1989), 189–217, and now A. Kessler, *Reichtumskritik und Pelagianismus. Die pelagianische Diatribe de duitiis: Situierung, Lesetext, Übersetzung, Kommentar* (Freiburg, 1999), 4–24. However, see also the superb introductions and notes by R. Teske in Augustine, *Answer to the Pelagians. The Works of Saint Augustine: A Translation for the 21st Century*, vols. 1:23–6, tr. R. Teske, ed. J. Rotelle (New York, 1997–99).

arguments about justice and sinlessness (*impeccantia*) closely parallels his earlier reply to Faustus. Do the positions regarding justice and its relationship to grace that Augustine articulates during the Pelagian controversy represent any meaningful shift from those which he had already expressed in his dispute with the Manicheans or Donatists, or with the Platonic or Stoic thinkers known to him? Furthermore, the years of his dispute with the Pelagians are the very years in which he wrote the *City of God* (AD 412–26/7). The coincidence of these two major theological preoccupations raises the further question of how his differences with the Pelagians may have influenced his account in the *City of God* of Christ's responsibility for the origin of a just commonwealth.

As a consequence of the polemical context in which Augustine's understanding of justice is based, his religious and moral use of terms such as 'justice' (*iustitia*) and its allied civic virtues, such as piety (*pietas*) and mercy (*misericordia*), consistently overlaps with his political usage of them. Thus, even when he speaks of Christ in an overtly political context, his treatment of Christ's justice unites political and religious concerns.[17] From AD 411 onward, his conception of justice, and therefore of the just man or woman (*uir iustus, femina iusta*), is especially coloured by his opposition to the Pelagians.[18] Following the onset of this controversy he becomes more emphatic about the specific effects of the grace of Christ upon the believer's gradual growth in justice. While it is true that Augustine employs terms such as 'true justice' (*uera iustitia*) prior to AD 411, it is in the clarification of his position vis-à-vis the Pelagians that he arrives at the mature conception of justice present in the *City of God*.[19] Consequently, when Augustine reflects upon themes such as justice or the just statesman in Ciceronian terms, and then shifts his thinking to justice as it should be practised by those who would inhabit the city of God, he does not abandon his positions on justice which emerge from the dispute with the Pelagians. Instead, he

---

[17] See, for example, *c. Iul.* 4.25–6, where he denies that the Roman heroes Gaius Fabricius Luscinus, an unidentified Scipio (perhaps P. Cornelius Scipio Africanus Major) and Romulus could be called 'just'. In this regard, see also *ciu.* 2.29 in conjunction with *ep.* 104.2 and *ciu.* 5.18.

[18] See Studer, 'Le Christ', 102–15.

[19] For earlier uses of *uera iustitia*, see, for example, *conf.* 3.7, *c. Faust.* 5.8, 26.5, *op. mon.* 22. Most occurrences of the expression postdate the onset of the Pelagian controversy, and the majority of these are found in anti-Pelagian works, as at *pecc. mer.* 2.45, *nat. et gr.* 14, 70, *c. ep. Pel.* 3.21, 3.23, *gr. et pecc. or.* 1.27, 1.52, 2.45, *corrept.* 20, *c. Iul.* 4.17, 4.19, 4.21, 4.26, 6.11, *c. Iul. imp.* 1.39, 2.105, 3.37, 6.18. Among these texts, *c. Iul.* 4.17 and 4.26 clearly delineate the overlap between anti-Pelagian and political concerns. See above, n. 17. See also my discussion of *ciu.* 19.27 (below, pp. 111–12).

employs them to correct the concept of justice which he found in Roman authors such as Cicero.[20]

When considering Christ's person and work in an anti-Pelagian context, Augustine at times draws a parallel between the two pairs 'just and justifying' and 'ignorance and weakness'. In so doing he asserts that, as a truly just man, Christ offers the only perfect example of justice that can cure ignorance, while as the God-man he offers the grace by which the soul is enabled to understand and imitate his example.[21] Analysis of the *City of God* with these principles in mind reveals that the interrelationship between these two conceptual pairings forms the structure of Augustine's claim that Christ alone brings into being the justice which is found in his city. Without Christ's grace no society can be just.

Perhaps the most concise statement of Augustine's argument in this regard occurs in Book 20 of the *City of God*. All human beings are born into original sin, Augustine says, and continue thereafter to sin either because they do not know how to act justly or because they fail to do so through moral weakness. To this assertion he adds that Christ is the only human being ever to have lived without sin ('unus uiuus . . . nullum habens omnino peccatum') – a reference to Christ's unique status as a 'just man' (*iustus*) – and that he died for the sake of our justification (*propter iustificationem nostram*), without which human beings could never achieve justice. Christ, who was perfectly just because he had no sin, died and rose from the dead in order to make it possible for other human beings to be just. His death brought about forgiveness of sins and enabled human beings to live no longer for themselves, but for him.[22] Augustine's statement echoes the

---

[20] O'Meara, *Charter*, 91–110, especially 96–101, argues that Augustine fully intends to link the theological (Pauline) and historical (Ciceronian) conceptions of justice. O'Meara perhaps goes too far in suggesting (98) that the seam between the two conceptions becomes apparent at *ciu.* 4.3, where Augustine identifies the justice of the classic aphorism 'remota itaque iustitia' with the justice referred to at 2 Pet 2:19–21. O'Meara also refrains from suggesting any role for the Pelagian controversy in shaping Augustine's views of justice in *De ciuitate*. But see the highly suggestive remarks on the conjunction of theological and historical conceptions of justice, along with their anti-Pelagian emphases, in O. O'Donovan, 'Augustine's *City of God* XIX and Western Political Thought', *Dionysius* 11 (1987), 89–110, especially at 99–100.

[21] This thesis is demonstrated by Studer, 'Le Christ', especially 109–10, 131. On the uniqueness of Christ's status as 'just' meaning 'without sin', see *pecc. mer.* 2.1, 2.34, *perf. ius.* 24, *en. Ps.* 32.2.26, 50.9, *Io. eu. tr.* 41.7, 41.9, 84.2.

[22] See *ciu.* 20.6 (CCL 48.707): 'omnes itaque mortui sunt in peccatis, nemine prorsus excepto, siue originalibus siue etiam uoluntate additis, uel ignorando uel sciendo nec faciendo quod iustum est; et pro omnibus mortuis uiuus mortuus est unus, id est nullum habens omnino peccatum; ut, qui per remissionem peccatorum uiuunt, iam non sibi uiuant, sed ei, qui pro omnibus mortuus est propter peccata nostra et resurrexit propter iustificationem nostram, ut credentes in eum, qui iustificat inpium, ex inpietate iustificati, tamquam ex morte uiuificati, ad primam resurrectionem, quae nunc est, pertinere possimus'.

argument in his writings against the Pelagians that ignorance and weakness impede the capacity of human beings to act justly. His position that all human beings are dead as a result of original sin is pointedly anti-Pelagian in its intent.

Pelagius rejects the reality of original sin and therefore sees no conflict between it and man's capacity either to know what justice requires or to fulfil its obligations. God, in his view, creates human nature capable of living justly.[23] Moreover, against the example provided by Adam, God provides Christians with the example of Christ and the scriptures, which offer a full account of the obligations of justice and a number of examples of its achievement in the just men and women of the Old Testament. These examples confirm both that the complete avoidance of sin and a life of perfect justice are possible, and that God acts justly in expecting Christians to adhere to his law without moral failure.[24]

Clearly, Augustine and Pelagius disagree over the precise role of Christ in exemplifying perfect justice and in enabling Christians to follow his example. Pelagius accepts without reservation the doctrine that through his death and resurrection, Christ extends to human beings the possibility of eternal life; he likewise confesses that baptism in Christ is essential for salvation in that it cleanses the soul from sins acquired during one's lifetime. *Pace* Augustine, he does not deny the importance of grace in order to be sinless; instead, he disagrees with Augustine over the specific ways that grace aids the soul in knowing and willing the moral good.[25] Moreover, he holds that other human beings beside Christ have offered examples of

---

[23] See, for example, Pelagius, *Epistula ad Demetriadem* 2.2, 3.2.

[24] See ibid., 5.1–8.4 on Old Testament examples of justice. At *gest. Pel.* 24 and 26, Augustine argues that during the synod at Diospolis (AD 415), Pelagius had defended the thesis that before the coming of Christ, certain individuals named in the scriptures had lived holy and just lives. Augustine also asserts that, whereas during the synod Pelagius did not maintain that any of these individuals had been sinless, such a claim can be found in his writings.

[25] At *gest. Pel.* 20–2, Augustine accuses Pelagius of employing an ambiguous notion of grace, and he rejects what he terms Pelagius' identification of grace with created human nature or knowledge of the Law. See also *ep.* 177.2 (CSEL 44.670–1), in which five African bishops including Augustine complain to the bishop of Rome, Innocent I, that Pelagius' understanding of grace does not 'follow the usage of the church' (*ecclesiastica consuetudo*). However, Pelagius acknowledges the necessity of grace in order to be sinless before two ecclesiastical tribunals as well as in his *libellus fidei* for the bishop of Rome. See, especially, Pelagius, *Libellus fidei ad Innocentiam papam* 13 (PL 45.1718). On the polemical techniques which Augustine uses in formulating this kind of argument, see E. Rebillard, 'Sociologie de la déviance et orthodoxie. Le cas de la controverse pélagienne sur la grâce', *Orthodoxie, christianisme, histoire / Orthodoxy, Christianity, History: travaux du groupe de recherches 'Définir, maintenir et remettre en cause l'"orthodoxie" dans l'histoire du christianisme'*, ed. S. Elm et al. (Rome, 2000), 221–40, and R. Dodaro, 'The Theologian as Grammarian: Literary Propriety in Augustine's Defense of Orthodox Doctrine', *Studia patristica: Papers Presented at the Thirteenth International Conference on Patristic Studies, Oxford University, 16–21 August 1999*, vol. 38 (Leiden, 2001), 70–83.

sinlessness and justice. Although his group of exemplary people includes a number of pagans, it is the patriarchs and prophets of the Old Testament who, along with Christ, have offered the clearest examples of justice. What Pelagius and his associates do not grasp, from Augustine's point of view, is the disproportionate character of the relationship between Christ's example and that of other just human beings, a disparity which follows logically from Christ's unique unity of divine and human natures. Thus Pelagians also reject the need for justification by Christ as Augustine understands this.

Augustine's disagreement with the Pelagians over Christ's person and work in relation to justice emerges most clearly in the *City of God* in the passage from Book 20 referred to above. The Pelagians are not Augustine's primary audience in this work; nonetheless, after the controversy begins in AD 411, Augustine's positions on education in virtue and the promotion of civic virtues in society are, in large part, aimed at confuting Pelagian arguments.[26] Consequently, his analysis in Books 2–19 of the effects of moral ignorance and weakness on the practice of justice, and of the contrary effects of Christ's redemptive activity for the promotion of justice, is shaped by the Pelagian controversy.

ADUERSARII GRATIAE

Yet at times in his writings after the onset of the controversy, Augustine denies that he significantly revised his thinking about the relationship between human nature and Christ's grace even from the time of his earliest writings. For example, when Pelagius in *De natura* quotes a passage from Augustine's *De libero arbitrio* (AD 387–95) in support of the position that the human will can avoid sin completely, Augustine replies that his earlier claim regarding the capacity of the human will to choose good and avoid evil did not make grace unnecessary. He charges Pelagius with quoting the passage from *De libero arbitrio* out of context, and counters that if Pelagius had also quoted other passages from the same work 'there would remain no dispute between us'.[27] He thus implies that, taken as a whole, *De libero arbitrio* already contains the essential rebuttal of Pelagian positions, in particular, concerning man's natural capacity to avoid sin (*impeccantia*).[28]

---

[26] One detects, for example, echoes of his arguments against the Pelagians in his correspondence with public officials such as Macedonius (*ep.* 155.5: AD 413/414) and Boniface (*ep.* 185.37–8: AD 417).

[27] See *nat. et gr.* 80–1, where Augustine also cites the passage in question from Pelagius' work *De natura*. Augustine composed this work in AD 415.

[28] See *nat. et gr.* 81. Pelagius was confident that human beings possessed a natural capacity to avoid all sin (*impeccantia*) and that they were capable of attaining a condition of perfected justice (*iustitia*

In his *Retractationes* (AD 428), written near the end of his life, Augustine insists even more forcefully that he could have employed arguments from *De libero arbitrio* against the Pelagians if the movement had existed at the time of the work's composition.[29] He protests that the reason for the absence of a full discussion of grace in his earlier work is that it was intended solely to provide an explanation for the nature of evil, and to defend free will against the Manicheans.[30] He also claims that, while not itself the primary subject of this treatise, the concept of grace pervades his argument.[31] He identifies several passages, including his assertion that virtues (he names justice explicitly), which he calls 'great goods', have their origin in God, and that God should be praised not only for bestowing goods of this magnitude upon human beings, but also for his gift of intermediate goods, among which are free will and even lesser goods.[32] He cites a passage from *De libero arbitrio* in which he had noted that although human beings fall into sin of their own free will, they cannot free themselves from it of their own free will: to do so requires faith in Christ.[33] Finally, he claims to have included among the three levels of goods created by God 'the good *use* of free will, which is virtue'.[34] This conclusion cannot be found in *De libero arbitrio* in so many words. However, in Book 2 he reasons that, when free will acts in accord with the changeless good, it becomes virtuous.[35] His argument in the *Retractationes* thus extends this reasoning from *De libero arbitrio* by placing the use of free will, when it acts virtuously, in the category

---

perfecta). See *gest. Pel.* 16–20, and the conclusion of Nuvolone and Solignac, 'Pélage', 2927–8, Augustine faults his adversaries for failing to accept that Christ alone among all human beings is capable of giving an example of true, complete justice because he alone has lived without sin.

[29] See *retr.* 1.9.6 (CCL 57.28): 'ecce tam longe antequam Pelagiana heresis exstitisset, sic disputauimus, uelut iam contra illos disputaremus'. In a related incident during the same year, a certain Hilary (or Euladius) informs Augustine that some monks of Marseilles were citing earlier works of his, among them *De libero arbitrio*, in support of their views on the relation of grace to free will, views which opposed those which they had read in Augustine's *De correptione et gratia* (AD 426/27). See *ep.* 226.3–8. At *persev.* 52, Augustine insists that, although they are written before the Pelagian controversy, the earlier works indicated by the Gallic monks express views consistent with those found in his current writings on these subjects.

[30] See *retr.* 1.9.2 and 1.9.4 (on the nature of evil), 1.9.3 (against the Manicheans). G. Madec, *Introduction aux 'Révisions' et à la lecture des œuvres de saint Augustin* (Paris, 1996), 43–4, citing *lib. arb.* 2.4, 3.16, and *retr.* 1.9.2, 1.13.1, argues that the work 'is not expressly directed against the Manicheans'. Instead, he detects there a crossroad of intersecting perspectives, philosophical and religious, that demonstrate Augustine's early views on original sin, virtue, and grace in relation to significant philosophical and religious movements with which he was familiar, among them Platonism and Stoicism, in addition to Manicheism.

[31] See *retr.* 1.9.4.

[32] See *retr.* 1.9.4, quoting from *lib arb.* 2.50 and 2.54. At *lib. arb.* 2.50–2, free will is classed as an 'intermediate good'. See also *retr.* 1.9.6.

[33] See *retr.* 1.9.4, quoting from *lib arb.* 2.54.

[34] See *retr.* 1.9.6. Augustine does not quote a specific passage from *lib. arb.* at this point.

[35] See *lib. arb.* 2.53.

of goods which are created and bestowed upon human beings by God. On this reading, *De libero arbitrio* subordinates the virtuous use of free will to the agency of divine grace.

Scholars recognize that there are serious problems with Augustine's claim that his anti-Pelagian writings continue the position on free will and grace which he previously sketched in *De libero arbitrio*. His somewhat awkward attempt to argue that in the earlier work he had subordinated the virtuous use of free will to the agency of divine grace simply does not hold up to close textual scrutiny. On the contrary, Pelagius is right to identify in *De libero arbitrio* forthright, unqualified affirmations of the will's ability to avoid sin altogether. He would find nothing in this work with which to disagree, including Augustine's statement that conversion from sin requires faith in Christ.[36]

Although Augustine may overstate the value of *De libero arbitrio* in refuting Pelagius, the work does hint at many of the essential elements of his later, anti-Pelagian arguments concerning the central role of Christ's grace in promoting virtue within the human soul. To dramatize his point that human virtue depends upon a divine initiative, Augustine employs the metaphor of a rhetorical contest between God and Satan. He describes God in this early treatise as 'speaking outwardly by means of the divine law and inwardly to the depths of the heart' of the believer who begs God for assistance. Thus, God calls out to (*uocare*) the wayward, teaches (*docere*) believers, consoles (*consolare*) those who hope, and encourages (*adhortare*) those who love, while he also hears and responds to (*exaudire*) those who pray for guidance and strength. In this way, Augustine argues, God prepares a glorious future in a 'most blessed city' (*ciuitas beatissima*) for those who by means of faith overcome the 'malicious persuasion' through which Satan, described in political terms as a king (*rex*), had seduced Adam away from happiness into misery.[37] Here for the first time in his writings, Augustine refers to a 'city' which comes into being as a consequence of a victory in a contest between two persuasive discourses. This metaphor returns later in the *City of God*, where Augustine argues that God's discourse overcomes

---

[36] See *lib. arb.* 2.54.

[37] See *lib. arb.* 3.57 (CSEL 74.137) 'et opem a creatore inplorandam, ut conantem adiuuet, qui uel extrinsecus lege, uel in intimis cordis allocutione conandum esse praecepit et praeparat ciuitatis beatissimae gloriam triumphantibus de illo qui primum hominem ad istam miseriam perduxit uictum pessima suasione; quam miseriam isti suscipiunt ad eum uincendum optima fide'. The reference to Satan as *rex* occurs in the following sentence. Reference to this passage is missing from the accounts of the earliest treatments of *ciuitas* in Augustine offered by U. Duchrow, *Christenheit und Weltverantwortung. Traditionsgeschichte und systematische Struktur der Zweireichelehre* (Stuttgart, 1970), especially 186–243: 'Herkunft und Anfänge der civitas-Lehre Augustins', and by van Oort, *Jerusalem*, 108–15, especially at 110–11.

the force of ignorance and weakness in the soul by stimulating faith and humility.[38] Moreover, within his argument in *De libero arbitrio* that God reveals the means for acquiring salvation to all peoples in all ages, Augustine indicates the importance of humbly confessing (*humiliter confiteri*) one's weakness in order to receive divine assistance in the struggle against sin.[39] The connection in this passage between humility, the confession of sins, and divine assistance in the soul's efforts to overcome moral ignorance and weakness anticipates Augustine's later, anti-Pelagian views. Nevertheless, throughout the third book of *De libero arbitrio*, he omits those specific explanations of grace which ultimately locate justification in the person and redemptive work of Christ. For example, he acknowledges that the inferior part of the soul requires divine assistance in order to act in conjunction with the higher part of the soul in perceiving 'the good of a just deed' and acting upon it, and that such divine assistance is available to the one who asks for it.[40] In taking this position, Augustine concludes that divine mercy, and not the soul's own resources, is necessary for overcoming ignorance and difficulty. However, his explanation of this process lacks any reference to the importance of the grace of Christ, a characteristic feature even of his earlier writings against the Pelagians.[41] Augustine also gives the impression in this passage from *De libero arbitrio* that, although the soul is enabled to 'mature with the fruits of wisdom and justice' through divine assistance, in the end happiness is attained only when the individual wills to reach out for it.[42] He is therefore still far from any conception of Christ as 'just and justifying', much less as the founder and ruler of the city that exemplifies true justice.

Toward the end of his life Augustine is again intent on emphasizing the continuity of his position on grace. He describes the first treatise he wrote as a bishop, *De diuersis quaestionibus ad Simplicianum* (AD 395/6), as if he had written it against the Pelagians.[43] In this work, in fact, he reversed the position he had elaborated earlier in a Pauline commentary,[44] by explaining the conversion of the will from evil to the good as the exclusive result of divine grace, which God offers to some human beings and not to others,

---

[38] See my discussion above, pp. 28–30.

[39] See *lib. arb.* 3.53 and 3.58, where emphasis is also placed upon the importance of humble confession of sins and prayer as means for overcoming ignorance and weakness. In Chapter 5 (below, pp. 172–6). I offer an analysis of confession of sins as the form of speech which for Augustine most clearly expresses the condition of just men and wormen. See also my discussion of *De sancta uirginitate* below, pp. 190–1.

[40] See *lib. arb.* 3.65.   [41] See, for example, *nat. et gr.* 4.

[42] See *lib. arb.* 3.65.   [43] See *perseu.* 52. See also *praed. sanct.* 8 (AD 428/9).

[44] See *ex. prop. Rm.* 60. Augustine wrote the commentary in AD 394/5.

regardless of their individual merits. He thus abandons the position he
held even as late as *De libero arbitrio*, that the soul's movement from sin
to virtue depends upon free choice. *Ad Simplicianum* is widely recognized
as a watershed in Augustine's thought on grace and free will, which not
only colours the presentation of his conversion in the *Confessions*, but sets
the tone for all of his subsequent writing on these topics.[45] As his writing
during the Pelagian controversy shows, he would like his readers to accept
that from this point onward his position on the relation of grace to free
will remains consistent.

Most scholars, however, posit a certain development and even substantial changes within Augustine's views on grace during the years that follow
Ad Simplicianum.[46] One of the clearest examples of this change in Augustine's thinking is the new interpretation of Rom 7:15–24 which emerges
in his writings during his controversy with Pelagius. Prior to this dispute,
Augustine refrained from applying the sentiments expressed in this passage
to Paul, because he did not wish to accuse the apostle of concupiscence.
In his earliest writings, he maintains that Paul was describing the interior,
spiritual struggles of the unbaptized only. Later, during the years leading up
to the Pelagian controversy, he gradually assents to the view that Paul was
describing the spiritual distress even of Christians as they struggle against
concupiscence.[47] In making this clear, however, he still considers Paul to

---

[45] For important discussions of this change, see W. Babcock, 'Augustine's Interpretation of Romans
(AD 394–396)', *Augustinian Studies* 10 (1979), 55–74, J. P. Burns, *The Development of Augustine's
Doctrine of Operative Grace* (Paris, 1980), in particular 37–44, 111–20, P. Fredriksen, 'Beyond the
Body/Soul Dichotomy: Augustine on Paul against the Manichees and the Pelagians', *Recherches
augustiniennes* 23 (1988), 87–114, Wetzel, *Augustine*, 155–60.

[46] See, for example, Burns, *Development*, 7–15, and J. Wetzel, 'Pelagius Anticipated: Grace and Election
in Augustine's *Ad Simplicianum*', *Augustine from Rhetor to Theologian*, ed. J. McWilliam (Waterloo,
1992), 121–32, Wetzel, *Augustine*, especially 187–90. Not all scholars agree about the nature and
significance of these changes. Thus, Katayanagi, 'Congruous', challenges Burns's thesis concerning
a profound change after AD 418 affecting Augustine's understanding of the role of 'interior grace'.
Hombert, *Gloria*, opposes in more general terms any conceptual distinction between the 'early'
and 'late' Augustine in regard to his teachings on grace, and he holds that this doctrine does not
change after *Ad Simplicianum*. Lössl, *Intellectus*, agrees that the division between 'early' and 'late'
Augustinian views is misplaced, and accepts that *Ad Simplicianum* lays out the constant, essential
lines of Augustine's views on grace, but concludes that they undergo development as a result of
theological controversies after AD 397, in particular the Pelagian controversy. Evidently, the relative
meanings and emphases placed on the terms employed by scholars in outlining their positions,
'development', 'change', 'continuity', etc., greatly determine the divergence between their positions
as stated.

[47] See *diu. qu.* 66.7. See also *exp. prop. Rm.* 46, *exp. Gal.* 46, *Simpl.* 1.1.1–17. M.-F. Berrouard, 'L'Exégèse
augustinienne de Rom., 7, 7–25 entre 396 et 418 avec des remarques sur les deux premières périodes
de la crise pélagienne', *Recherches augustiniennes* 16 (1981), 101–96, at 108–20, 132–40, 171–6, cites
a large number of texts spanning Augustine's career in which he applies these verses to Christians
generally in order to demonstrate that they experience moral and spiritual distress in spite of living
'under grace'.

be speaking only vicariously, on behalf of those Christians whose justice is far from perfect, and not about himself.

Marie-François Berrouard maintains that Augustine changed his position concerning the application of this passage to Paul sometime in AD 417 after reading Pelagius' *Pro libero arbitrio*. This treatise is Pelagius' answer to Jerome, who contended that Paul's affirmations at Rom 7:15–25 counter Pelagius' thesis asserting the natural capacity of human beings to avoid all sin.[48] In support of his argument, Jerome suggested that at Rom 7:15 ('I do not know what I do, for I do not do what I want; rather, I do what I hate') and at Rom 7:23 ('I observe another law in my lower self which wars against the law in my conscience'), Paul spoke for himself as well as for all the baptized.[49] Jerome concluded that at Romans 7 Paul described a continuing, personal struggle with concupiscence. In *Pro libero arbitrio*, Pelagius objected that by attributing this interior struggle to the apostle, Jerome has broken with the practice of earlier Christian authorities, who interpreted Paul as speaking on behalf of Jews alone, because they were sinning under the old law.[50] In Berrouard's view, this dispute between Pelagius and Jerome reaches Augustine in AD 417, when Augustine reads Pelagius' treatise. At this time Augustine adopts Jerome's position on Romans 7 because he sees that his own interpretation of the passage runs perilously close to supporting Pelagius' defence of the power of human freedom over sin, while he is also encouraged to do so by Jerome's stance.[51] Thus for Berrouard and other scholars, it is not until Augustine writes *De nuptiis et concupiscentia* against Julian of Eclanum in AD 418/19 that he first identifies Paul explicitly as the subject of these verses.[52] Meanwhile, Julian writes to Rome

---

[48] See Jerome, *ep.* 133.2.

[49] At *gr. et pecc. or.* 1.43 (AD 418), Augustine acknowledges that he read this argument in the third book of Pelagius' *Pro libero arbitrio*.

[50] See *gr. et pecc. or.* 1.43. Cf. Pelagius, *Pro libero arbitrio* 3 (PLS 1.1542–3).

[51] Berrouard, 'L'Exégèse', 194, insists that during the years of his controversy with the Pelagians leading up to this point, Augustine's identification of Paul as the subject of these verses remains 'more or less latent'. In my view, however, B. Delaroche, *Saint Augustin lecteur et interprète de saint Paul dans le* De peccatorum meritis et remissione (*hiver 411–412*) (Paris, 1996), 264–8, rightly reads Augustine's interpretation of Rom 7:19–20 and 7:24–5 at *pecc. mer.* 2.16–20 (AD 411) as already directly implicating Paul in the spiritual distress which these verses describe. Delaroche offers no reasoning in defence of his position, but see R. Dodaro, '"*Ego miser homo*": Augustine, the Pelagian Controversy, and the Paul of Romans 7:7–25', *Augustinianum* 44(2004), 135–44, where I provide arguments in support of this view. It should be noted, however, that dating Augustine's change in viewpoint back to the composition of *De peccatorum meritis* does not diminish, but reinforces, the importance of Berrouard's demonstration that the Pelagian controversy provides Augustine with the reason for this change.

[52] See *nupt. et conc.* 1.30 (CSEL 42.242): 'idem apostolus loquens uelut ex suae personae introductione nos instruit dicens *non enim quod uolo*' (Rom 1:15), in the context of *nupt. et conc.* 1.30–6. O. Bardenhewer, 'Augustinus über Röm. 7.14ff.', *Miscellanea agostiniana*, vol. 2 (Rome, 1931), 879–83,

during the following year and accuses Augustine of calumnizing Paul.[53] Augustine rebuts the charge in a long section in Book 1 of *Contra duas epistulas Pelagianorum*, acknowledging and defending his new position.[54] In spite of this declared change of view, however, in the final analysis Augustine merely admits that he regards his more recent interpretation as 'more probable'.[55]

Clearly, Augustine reaches this position with great difficulty. He risks seeming to diminish the heroic stature of Paul by weakening the exemplary appeal of his virtue, even at a time when preachers are stressing the value of Paul and other Christian martyrs as examples of virtue, in the face of moral laxity among Christians. Julian's charge that Augustine calumnizes Paul probably reflects the thinking of many Christians, who regard the saint as an unparalleled example of virtue. Augustine's difficulty in admitting his change of view in regard to Romans 7 is therefore significant not only as an index of his reluctance to accuse Paul of concupiscence, but more importantly as an indication of a change in his understanding of grace. With the advent of the Pelagian controversy, Christian martyrs become limit cases for Augustine. He employs them to underscore Christ's unique freedom from concupiscence, which no other human beings can share, and mankind's resultant need for Christ's grace in order to know and choose the moral good against the pull of concupiscence. Had Augustine not been pressed by the Pelagian party to accept a more univocal understanding of the relationship between Christ's justice and that of martyrs and saints like Paul, he would not have needed to modify his interpretation of Romans 7, or to emphasize the extent to which even the saints require grace to overcome concupiscence and its effects. Augustine is conscious that, in responding to the Pelagian challenge to his postion on grace, he is redefining basic Christian conceptions of moral perfection, heroism, and the imitation of Christ.

Augustine's new emphasis on the necessity of grace even to Paul appears in another significant change in his representation of Paul's experience of

---

at 880, and Berrouard, 'L'Exégèse', 102–3, 189–90, cite *nupt. et conc.* 1.30–7 as the first text in which Augustine states explicitly that Paul is speaking at Romans 7 about his own condition. Hombert, *Gloria*, 209, dates the change to AD 417, with the preaching of *s.* 151–6.

[53] See Berrouard, 'L'Exégèse', 192, citing *c. ep. Pel.* 1.13.

[54] See *c. ep. Pel.* 1.13–24. Augustine acknowledges the changed perspective at 1.22. See also *c. Iul.* 6.70.

[55] See *retr.* 2.1.1 (CCL 57.84): 'Harum prior est *de eo quod scriptum est: Quid ergo dicemus? Lex peccatum est? Absit, usque ad illud ubi ait: Quis me liberabit de corpore mortis huius? Gratia dei per Iesum Christum dominum nostrum* [Rom 7:24–5]. In qua illa apostoli uerba: *Lex spiritalis est, ego autem carnalis sum* [Rom 7:14] et cetera, quibus caro contra spiritum confligere ostenditur, eo modo exposui, *tamquam homo describatur adhuc sub lege nondum sub gratia constitutus* [cf. Rom 6:14]. Longe enim postea etiam spiritalis hominis – et hoc probabilius – esse posse illa uerba cognoui.'

concupiscence. This too may be traced to the Pelagian controversy, and concerns Paul's fear of death. In a series of sermons, treatises, and biblical commentaries which he composed after his first contact with Pelagian ideas, he admits that even martyrs such as Peter and Paul experienced fear of death as a natural consequence of their conflict with concupiscence. At the same time he insists that, although their fear of death clearly represents a failure of virtue, it does not vitiate their saintly status. Instead, their interior struggle to accept martyrdom in spite of their fear purifies their virtue, thereby contributing to its perfection in death.[56] Primary among Augustine's scriptural proofs for this argument are Jn 21:18–19 ('when you were young you girded yourself and went wherever you willed, but when you will be older, they will gird you and take you where you do not want to go'), alluding to Peter's martyrdom, and, in reference to Paul's fear of death, 2 Cor 5:4 ('We groan, being weighed down, inasmuch as we do not wish to be stripped, but to be clothed over on top, so that what is mortal may be swallowed up by life'). Only after AD 411 does Augustine begin to employ these passages to support this contention.[57] Previously, in fact, he never so much as suggested that Peter and Paul feared death.[58] With his revised view of Paul's concupiscence, Augustine's acknowledgement that both apostles never overcame fear of death in their earthly life represents a direct rebuttal

---

[56] See, for example, *s. Guelf.* 31.3 (MA 1.560): 'attendite martyrum gloriam: nisi mors amara esset, martyrum gloria nulla esset. si nihil est mors, quid magnum martyres contemserunt'?, *c. Iul. imp.* 6.14 (PL 45.1531): 'concupiscentias carnis ne perfeceritis; ubi certamen nobis potius, quod contra carnem aduersantem debeamus exercere, proposuit, ut concupiscentias eius non perficiamus consentiendo, sed resistendo uincamus'. See also *ciu.* 13.4 and 20.17, along with other references to Augustinian texts given above, p. 33 n. 29.

[57] Augustine cites Jn 21:18–19 in conjunction with Peter's fear of death at *ep.* 140.27, *en. Ps.* 68.1.3, 30.2.1.3, 89.7, *s.* 173.2, 297.1–2, 299.8, 344.3, *s. Guelf.* 31.3, *s. Casin.* 1.133.8, *Io. eu. tr.* 123.5, *c. Iul imp.* 2.186. He cites 2 Cor 5:4 in conjunction with Paul's fear of death at *ep.* 140.16, *en. Ps.* 68.1.3, 78.15, *s.* 173.2, 277.8, 299.9, 344.4, *Io. eu. tr.* 123.5, *ciu.* 20.17, *c. Iul. imp.* 2.186, 6.14, 6.21. Each of these Augustinian texts postdates AD 411, and in many of them both scriptural passages are found. More or less explicit references to Pelagian positions are found in a number of these texts, specifically, *ep.* 140 (about which, see below, pp. 159–64), *s.* 299, and *c. Iul. imp.* 2.186, 6.14, 6.21. For a fuller exposition of this argument, see R. Dodaro, '*Christus iustus* and Fear of Death in Augustine's Dispute with Pelagius', *Signum pietatis. Festgabe für Cornelius P. Mayer OSA zum 60. Geburtstag*, ed. A. Zumkeller (Würzburg, 1989), 341–61, and Rebillard, *In hora mortis*, 55–66.

[58] Prior to the onset of the Pelagian controversy, Augustine was more optimistic about the capacity of Christians to overcome fear of death. See, for example, *diu. qu.* 25 (CCL 44A.32): 'sapientia dei hominem ad exemplum quo recte uiueremus suscepit. pertinet autem ad uitam rectam, ea quae non sunt metuenda non metuere. mors autem metuenda non est'. See also *an. quant.* 73, *c. Adim.* 21, *f. et symb.* 11. During this period, Augustine's position on fear of death was in harmony with that of other Latin Christian authors, who regarded fear of death as a passion of the soul which saintly Christians could overcome. See, for example, Tertullian, *De testimonio animae* 4, *Ad martyras* 2.1, Cyprian, *De mortalitate* 2–7, Ambrose, *De bono mortis* 5, 31, 48, *De fuga saeculi* 34, 53, *De excessu fratris* 2.47. See also Dodaro, *Christus iustus*, 345–6, and Rebillard, *In hora mortis*, 11–28 (principally on Ambrose).

of Pelagian arguments that human beings, by imitating Christ, can be fully just and avoid sin altogether.[59]

Augustine knew of the viewpoint, circulating at Carthage in connection with the baptismal controversy, that human beings are naturally subject to death, not as a penalty for Adam's sin.[60] In his commentary on the Pauline epistles, Pelagius implies that Christ himself was not immortal.[61] Moreover, Pelagius clearly does not consider fear of death as a punishment imposed by God. Instead, he thinks that through the exercise of reason, Christians can control this fear, which is but a debilitation of faith and fortitude. Thus, for Pelagius, Christ's example urges Christians not to run away in the face of death, whereas Paul exemplifies the triumph of joy over fear of death.[62] In his *Epistula ad Demetriadem*, Pelagius tells a young, consecrated virgin that the purity of her conscience, along with her ascetic practices, should make her all but certain that she will possess the eternal reward promised

---

[59] Fundamental to Augustine's views on fear of death in the years following AD 411 is the argument of the Pelagians that death is not a collective punishment for the sin of Adam. See, for example, *pecc. mer.* 2.49–51, 3.19–23, *nat. et gr.* 23–6, *gr. et pecc. or.* 1.55, *c. ep. Pel.* 4.6–7, *c. Iul.* 1.21–8.

[60] See *pecc. mer.* 2.48, 2.51, *ep.* 140.64. The question whether Pelagius denies any causality between Adam's sin and his death is, however, disputed by scholars. G. Bonner, 'Rufinus of Syria and African Pelagianism', *Augustinian Studies* I (1970), 31–47, at 41, holds that the doctrine that Adam would have died whether he sinned or not was taught by Celestius, not Pelagius. R. Evans, *Pelagius: Inquiries and Reappraisals* (London, 1968), 72 n. 17, argues that, strictly speaking, Pelagius accepts that death is caused by Adam's sin. As evidence, he cites Pelagius, *Expositio in Rom 5, 12*, in A. Souter (ed.), *Pelagius's Expositions of Thirteen Epistles of St. Paul* (Cambridge, 1922), 45: 'quo modo, cum non esset peccatum, per Adam aduenit'. However, J. Valero, *Las bases antropológicas de Pelagio en su tratado de las* Expositiones (Madrid, 1980), 319–20, suggests that Pelagius' commentary on Romans 5 (the text that Evans has in mind) pertains exclusively to moral or spiritual death (*muerte moral*), and not to physical death, which, he holds, Pelagius treats only superficially in commenting upon 1 Cor 1:25 and 1 Cor 15:21–2. There, Pelagius indicates no causality between Adam's death and universal mortality; rather, the two are only chronologically related. See also Pelagius, *Expositio in 1 Cor 15, 21–22*, in Souter, *Pelagius's*, 217, 'sicut per Adam mors intrauit, quia primus ipse est mortuus, ita et per Christum resurrectio, quia primus resurrexit, et sicut ille morientum forma est, it [et] iste [est] resurgentium'. Valero, *Las bases*, 319, argues that the assertion 'per Adam mors intrauit' suggests to Pelagius only that Adam was the first human being to die. Finally, Augustine reports that in his treatise *De natura*, Pelagius denies explicitly that Adam's sin plays any role in his death. See *nat. et gr.* 23 (CSEL 60.248): 'nec ipse primus homo ideo morte damnatus est; nam postea non peccauit'. See also Valero, *Las bases*, 319 n. 38.

[61] See Pelagius, *Expositio in 1 Cor 1, 25*, in Souter, *Pelagius's*, 135: 'mortem, quam nec gigantes euadere potuerunt, cruci fixi infirmitas superauit'. Valero, *Las bases* 319, points out that Pelagius calls it scandalous that Jews expect the Messiah to be immortal. See Pelagius, *Expositio in 1 Cor 1, 23*, in Souter, *Pelagius's*, 134: 'scandalum illis est auire Christum mori potuisse, quem illi quasi immortalem expectant'.

[62] On Christ's example, see Pelagius, *Expositio in Phil. 2, 21*, in Souter, *Pelagius's*, 402: 'non curantes de corpore uel exemplo Christi, qui pro omnium salute mori minime recusauit'. At *pecc. mer. 3.1*, Augustine acknowledges having read Pelagius' entire Pauline commentary. On Paul's example, see Pelagius, *Expositio in Phil. 2, 17*, in Souter, *Pelagius's*, 401: 'sed etiam si occidar, quia sacrificium [et obsequium] fidei uestrae obtuli deo, uincit profectus uestri gaudium tristitiam poenae uel mortis. siue: iam non timeo mori, sacrificio uestrae fidei consummato. siue: quia uestrae fidei ministraui'.

her for a life of virtue, so that she should confidently experience joy and not fear in the face of death.[63] Finally, in his treatise *De uita Christiana*, Pelagius explicitly affirms that, for those who are just, death is a final repose from toil and not a punishment.[64]

Against these views, Augustine insists that Christ is the only human being completely free from concupiscence and, consequently, from moral ignorance and weakness. He is therefore the only human being who is by nature free from fear of death. Christian martyrs, like all human beings except Christ, suffer from original sin and its consequences; as a result they are never completely free from moral ignorance and weakness, or from the fear of death which these defects cause. They are unable to imitate Christ's example completely.[65] In a sermon which has strong anti-Pelagian echoes, Augustine sets out the major lines of this argument. He begins by attributing death and fear of death to original sin.[66] He points out that, although Christ's words and example strengthen the martyrs' resolve not to fear death, nevertheless, they continue to love life. For this reason, they continue to fear death – even Peter, Prince of the Apostles, feared death at the moment of his martyrdom.[67] Christ, by contrast, enjoyed a natural freedom from fear of death. He feared death only because he willed to experience what other human beings unavoidably feel when confronted with mortality.[68] It is through Christ's divine assistance (*adiutorium dei*) alone that the martyrs, ineluctably afflicted by concupiscence, are able to

---

[63] See Pelagius, *Epistula ad Demetriadem* 30 (PL 30.45–6). On Augustine's reading of this letter, see *gr. et pecc. or.* 1.40–4. I discuss this letter and Augustine's reaction to it in more detail below, pp. 189–91.

[64] See Pelagius, *De uita christiana* 5 (PL 50.389): 'Vides ergo hac solutionem corporis justis et Dei cultoribus requiem esse, non poenam; et cum dissoluuntur, liberari eos potius quam perire. Et idcirco ipsam solutionem qui fideles sunt nec timent nec uerentur, sed uenire magis desiderant et exoptant, per quam sibi requiem intelligunt exhiberi, non poenam'.

[65] See *Io. eu. tr.* 84.2 (CCL 36.537): 'postremo etsi fratres pro fratribus moriantur, tamen in fraternorum peccatorum remissionem nullius sanguis martyris funditur, quod fecit ille pro nobis; neque in hoc quid imitaremur, sed quid gratularemur contulit nobis'.

[66] See *s. Guelf.* 31.1. A. Kunzelmann, *Die Chronologie der Sermones des hl. Augustinus* (Rome, 1931), 460, and H.-J. Frede, *Kirchenschriftsteller. Verzeichnis und Sigel*, 4th edn (Freiburg, 1995), 241, date the sermon to AD 410/12. H. Drobner, 'The Chronology of St. Augustine's *Sermones ad populum*', *Augustinian Studies* 31:2 (2000), 211–18, and 'The Chronology of St. Augustine's *Sermones ad populum* II: Sermons 5 to 8', *Augustinian Studies* 34:1 (2003), 49–66, rigly warns against accepting uncritically the standard dating schemes for Augustine's *sermones ad populum*. Nevertheless, on the strength of internal evidence, there seems to be no doubt that Augustine is already reacting in this sermon against various propositions which he will later associate with the Pelagians. For other Augustinian texts linking fear of death with original sin, see above, p. 33 n. 26.

[67] See *s. Guelf.* 31.2–3, citing Jn 21:18.

[68] See *s. Guelf.* 31.3 (MA 1.560): 'et ille qui potestatem habebat ponendi animam suam, et potestatem habebat iterum sumendi eam [Jn 10:18], tamen ut in se nos transfiguraret, *tristis est*, inquit, *anima mea usque ad mortem* [Mt 26:38]. Petro etiam beato, *cum senueris*, inquit, *alter te cinget, et feret quo tu non uis* [Jn 21:18], etiam cum senueris'.

muster whatever virtue they display in their deaths.[69] Fear of death thus acts as an 'instrument of virtue' (*instrumentum uirtutis*), insofar as it directs martyrs to distrust their own virtue as a means of achieving moral freedom, and to hope in Christ alone.[70]

Sermons which Augustine preached on the feast of Saints Peter and Paul following AD 411 highlight how Christ's example of virtue in the face of death is infinitely more authentic than that of the apostles. In one such sermon, Augustine reminds his congregation of Paul's confession that the purpose of God's becoming man is the salvation of sinners, among whom he, Paul, is the first (1 Tim 1:15), a distinction which Paul deserves, in Augustine's view, if for no other reason, because of his earlier persecution of Christians (Acts 9:4).[71] Turning to Peter, whose temerity in promising to die for Christ leads Christ to predict his denial, Augustine interprets Christ's intervention with Peter (Jn 13:37–8) as a reminder to all believers of the necessity of Christ's assistance in order to die as a martyr.[72] Thus, by predicting that Peter would fear death at the time of his martyrdom (Jn 21:18), Christ is also indicating in a more general sense that human nature is inherently weak and subject to this same fear. Death remains a struggle for the Christian faithful and saints alike[73] – Christ alone is without sin.[74] After all, he argues, if Peter 'despite such great perfection' fears his own death, 'what wonder if there be some panic involved in the suffering even of the just, even of saints?'[75]

Augustine's attribution to Paul both of the concupiscence described at Rom 7:15–24 and of the fear of death which is its consequence occurs with greater clarity and force in his writings as the Pelagian controversy progresses. As early as *De peccatorum meritis et remissione* in AD 411/12, he

---

[69] See *s. Guelf.* 31.4 (MA 1.561): 'ut non eam possent martyres pro ueritate et pro aeterna uita contemnere, nisi illo adiuuante qui iubebat ut contemnerent. [. . .] contemnunt plerumque homines mortem per concupiscentiam carnis; contemnunt mortem per concupiscentiam oculorum, contemnunt mortem per ambitionem saeculi: sed omnia ista de saeculo sunt. qui contemnit mortem propter caritatem dei, nullo modo id potest implere sine adiutorio dei'.

[70] See *s. Guelf.* 31.2. Parallel discussions of the 'conflict of faith' (*certamen fidei*) which fear of death occasions in the soul are given above, p. 33 n. 28. In addition to these texts, see also *ciu.* 9.4, where fear of death, with other passions, is acknowledged for its potential utility in promoting justice within the soul (*usus iustitiae*).

[71] See *s.* 299.6.   [72] See *s.* 299.7.

[73] See *s.* 299.10 (PL 38.1375): 'mortem autem etiam et fidelibus et sanctis relinquit ad luctam'.

[74] See *s.* 299.8 (PL 38.1373–4): 'Ergo in nostra natura et culpa et poena. Deus naturam sine culpa fecit, et si sine culpa persisteret, nec poena utique sequebatur. Inde uenimus, inde utrumque traximus, et hinc multa contraximus. In nostra igitur natura et culpa et poena: in Iesu carne et poena sine culpa, ut et culpa sanaretur et poena. *Alter te*, inquit, *cinget*, et feret *quo tu non uis* [Jn 21:18]. Poena est haec: sed per poenam tenditur ad coronam'.

[75] See *en. Ps.* 30.2.1.3 (CCL 38.192): 'ergo si Petrus apostolus tanta perfectione quo nollet iit uolens . . . quid mirum si est aliquis pauor in passione etiam iustorum, etiam sanctorum?'

begins to discuss the virtues of the saints in terms inferior to, and dependent upon, Christ; prior to his initial engagement with Pelagian views on death, freedom, and grace, he refrains from characterizing the saints' virtues in such extreme terms. His decision to set Christ's virtue and that of the saints in radical discontinuity to each other reflects a deepening difference with Pelagius and his associates over the nature and function of Christ's person and work in the promotion of virtue. Augustine does not initially charge Pelagius with a heterodox understanding of Christ as far as the tenets of the Christian creeds are concerned.[76] Pelagius confesses that Christ is both fully God and fully man, that he is the saviour, and that human beings are redeemed from sin by his death and resurrection.[77] However, Augustine recognizes major differences between his and Pelagius' understanding of Christ's person and work in the promotion of virtue within the souls of human beings. Augustine's later expositions on the virtues of the saints, in particular of Paul, underscore these differences.

For Augustine, such differences are ultimately rooted in the unity of Christ's two natures, another point of disagreement with Pelagius. When examined against the backdrop of his positions on original sin, Augustine's understanding of this unity of Christ's two natures requires that his human nature be seen as completely and uniquely free from original sin. In Augustine's view, this freedom distinguishes Christ's human nature from that of all other human beings. Pelagius and his associates reject Augustine's understanding of original sin, and for this reason do not posit a radical difference between Christ's humanity and that of all other human beings. Pelagius assumes that human beings are able to imitate Christ's moral example with greater or lesser success, depending upon their will to do so and upon other factors, such as the quality of the moral guidance provided to them.

Sometime before his dispute with Pelagius, Augustine decided that Christ's divine and human natures are substantially united to each other,

---

[76] See *ep.* 140.83. At a point later in their dispute, however, he accuses the Pelagians of denying the incarnation. See *s.* 183.12 (PL 38.992): 'quid dicis, Pelagianista? audite quid dicit. uidetur confiteri Christum in carne uenisse: sed discussus inuenitur negare. Christus enim in carne uenit, quae similitudo esset carnis peccati, non esset caro peccati. apostoli uerba sunt: *misit deus filium suum in similitudinem carnis peccati* [Rom 8:3]. non in similitudinem carnis, quasi caro non esset caro; sed *in similitudinem carnis peccati* [Rom 8:3], quia caro erat, sed peccati caro non erat. iste autem Pelagius et ceteram carnem omnis infantis carni Christi conatur aequare. non est, carissimi. non pro magno commendaretur in Christo similitudo carnis peccati, nisi omnis cetera caro esset caro peccati. quid ergo prodest, quia dicis Christum in carne uenisse, et omnium infantium carni eum conaris aequare?'

[77] I agree on this point with J. Dewart, 'The Christology of the Pelagian Controversy', *Studia patristica*, vol. 17, ed. E. Livingstone (Oxford, 1982), 1221–44, at 1224, who cites in support of this assertion, among other scholars, J. Rivière, 'Hétérodoxie des Pélagiens en fait de rédemption?', *Revue d'histoire ecclésiastique* 41 (1946), 5–43.

and that the category of a single 'person' (*una persona/unitas personae*) best expresses the form of this union.[78] To his account of the unity of natures in Christ's unique person, Augustine adjoins the concept of a dynamic interrelationship between Christ's two natures. This interrelationship implies an exchange of characteristics, whereby the attributes proper to one nature can be predicated of the other. Accordingly he asserts that, in Christ, God assumed human flesh and mortality. Similarly, Augustine claims that Christ's human nature was endowed with divine characteristics such as immortality and beatitude.[79] In his discussion of the unity of Christ's natures 'in one person' and of the exchange that takes place between these natures thus united, Augustine is careful to stress that the integrity of each nature is maintained, so that neither is perceived as having been absorbed into the other. This is essential to his description of the manner by which virtues, which have their origin in God, are mediated to human beings through Christ's divine and human natures.[80] Crucially, as Augustine further clarifies during his controversy with the Pelagians, it is only as a consequence of its unity with his divine nature that Christ's human nature is completely free of sin.[81] For Augustine, Christians are thus obliged to affirm that Christ differs from all other human beings, insofar as he is entirely free of sin, original or personal.[82] For this reason, Christ is the only

---

[78] T. van Bavel, *Recherches sur la christologie de saint Augustin. L'humain et le divin dans le Christ d'après saint Augustin* (Fribourg, 1954), 20–6, argues that between AD 400 and 411, Augustine develops an account of the unity of Christ's divine and human natures, first in terms of a union of grace, but later as a substantial union in terms of a single personhood (*una persona*). H. Drobner, *Person-Exegese und Christologie bei Augustinus. Zur Herkunft der Formel* Una Persona (Leiden, 1986), shows that Augustine originally employs the term *persona* in conjunction with prosopographical exegesis in order to identify the speaker of a particular biblical passage. See my discussion of this point below, pp. 105–7. Drobner (153–69) further demonstrates that by AD 411, Augustine transfers the meaning of *persona* from its grammatical context to an ontological one, which can be used in order to represent this unity of natures in Christ.

[79] See E. Franz, 'Totus Christus. Studien über Christus und die Kirche bei Augustin', unpublished dissertation, Evangelisch-Theologische Fakultät der Rheinischen Friedrich-Wilhelms-Universität Bonn, 1956, 140–62, van Bavel, *Recherches*, 47–63, Studer, *Grace*, 42–3, citing *Io. eu. tr.* 27.4, *s.* 80.5, *s. Casin.* 2, 76.3, *c. s. Arrian.* 8.6. This teaching is sometimes referred to as *communicatio idiomatum* or *circumincessio*.

[80] I discuss this point in great detail below, pp. 154–68.

[81] See *ench.* 40, *praed. sanc.* 30, and the discussion by van Bavel, *Recherches*, 85–101, especially 96–7.

[82] Christ's unique freedom from sin and its consequences occurs especially as a theme in Augustine's writings against the Pelagians. See *pecc. mer.* 1.57, 1.60, 2.57 (CSEL 60.125): 'Solus unus est qui sine peccato uisit inter aliena peccata', *spir. et litt.* 1.1, *nat. et gr.* 15, *perf. ius.* 12.29, *nupt. et conc.* 1.13, 1.27, *c. Iul. imp.* 2.56. See also *ep.* 179.44, 187.10, *ench.* 28, 34–40, *c. s. Arrian.* 9.7, *ciu.* 20.26, in conjunction with F.-J. Thonnard, 'Le Don d'intégrité et l'état de justice originelle', *Œuvres de saint Augustin*, vol. 23: *Premières polémiques contre Julien*, ed. F.-J. Thonnard et al. (Paris, 1974), 717–21, and Studer, 'Le Christ', 122–4.

human being in history who is completely just (*solus iustus*).[83] Augustine will now insist that 'the martyr stands far removed from Christ'.[84]

In order to strengthen his argument against the Pelagians that Christ's total freedom from sin and fear of death is not a function simply of his human nature, but that it is grounded in the substantial unity between his human and divine natures, Augustine begins in AD 411 to speak of Christ explicitly as 'one person' (*una persona*) when discussing the uniqueness of his virtue as compared to that of all other human beings.[85] Although, as mentioned earlier, he clearly arrives at such an understanding prior to the beginning of this dispute, he only begins to employ this precise terminology after his first contact with Pelagian thought.[86] More importantly, he does so principally in contexts which are predominantly anti-Pelagian.[87] By insisting in these terms that Christ, the God-man, is a unique being, Augustine intends to demonstrate the flaws in Pelagius' understanding of Christ. He suggests that if Pelagius believes Christ's human nature to be

---

[83] See *ciu.* 17.4 (below, p. 109 n. 152), *Io. eu. tr.* 41.9, *en. Ps.* 36.2.14, 50.9 (below, p. 177 n. 130), 98.7, *s.* 161.9.

[84] See *Io. eu. tr.* 84.2 (CCL 36.537–8): 'in ceteris enim quae dixi, quamuis nec omnia dicere potui, martyr Christi longe impar est Christo. quod si quisquam se, non dico potentiae Christi, sed innocentiae comparabit, non dicam et alienum se putando sanare, sed suum saltem nullum habere peccatum; etiam sic auidior est quam ratio salutis exposcit, multum est ad illum, non capit tantum'.

[85] However, van Bavel, *Recherches*, 93, comments that, 'dès sa conversion, saint Augustin met en relief la différence entre le Christ-Homme et les autres saints'. His argument, however, is more concerned with establishing this 'différence' in Augustine's thought than with dating it back to his conversion. Moreover, it seems that in the fuller context of van Bavel's discussion (93–101), 'saints' should be understood as referring to all the baptized, and not to human beings especially regarded by Christians for their superior holiness, such as Paul. Finally, in the texts which he cites in support of this observation, one finds a marked difference in the argument between those that might be dated prior to the onset of the dispute with Pelagius (for example *exp. Gal.* 24, *uirg.* 37, and perhaps *en. Ps.* 44.7) and those that were assuredly composed after AD 411, and, in particular, in the context of this dispute (e.g., *gest. Pel.* 32, *c. Iul. imp.* 4.47, 4.84, 5.57). In the earlier cases cited, Augustine affirms the difference between Christ and other human beings only in general terms; whereas, in most of the latter cases, involving specifically anti-Pelagian writings, he clearly excludes any symmetry even between Christ and saints of the stature of Paul (*gest. Pel.* 32), while he also affirms that only Christ is completely sinless (*c. Iul. imp.* 5.57), and that this status arises in Christ as a result of the unity 'in one person' between his two natures (*c. Iul. imp.* 4.84).

[86] See, for example, *pecc. mer.* 1.60 and *s.* 294.9 (below, p. 94 n. 88), along with *ep.* 140.12. Each of these texts was composed at some time between AD 411/12. See also *c. s. Arrian.* 7.6–9.7, *ench.* 35–6, *perseu.* 67. For indications of other texts, see Drobner, *Person-Exegese*, 241–53. Van Bavel, *Recherches*, 20, observes that, 'l'on ne puisse attester avec certitude l'apparition de la formule *una persona* qu'en 411, tandis que *unitas personae* semble déjà familière à saint Augustin dès 400. A partir de cette dernière date, la doctrine de l'union personnelle se confirme de plus en plus et elle peut être considerée comme définitive'.

[87] See, for example, *pecc. mer.* 1.60, *s.* 294.9, *perseu.* 67, *corrept.* 30, *c. Iul. imp.* 4.84. I would also argue from the context of the arguments that the reference to Christ's 'one person' at *ep.* 140.12, 187.10, and *ench.* 36 reflects opposition to positions which Augustine associates with the Pelagians.

morally comparable in all respects to that of all human beings, then he must have no proper conception of the unity and dynamic interrelationship between Christ's human and divine natures. Otherwise, he would agree with Augustine that Christ's complete freedom from sin as a human being must be explained in terms of this interrelationship, and that his two natures can be thought to interact in this way only if they are united with each other in a manner that is unique in human history and that defies rational explanation. To affirm that God unites himself with all human beings in precisely the same way that one finds in Christ is to deny the uniqueness of the incarnation, either because its special grace is not exclusive to Christ or because it must not involve a radical unity between Christ's natures. Only a failure to acknowledge Christ's essential unity can lead one to understand his human nature as sufficiently detached from his divine nature as to be morally similar to that of all human beings. For this reason, Augustine accuses Pelagius and his associates of positing 'two Christs', one divine, the other human.[88]

CHRISTUS MEDIATOR

Augustine's first clear assertion in the *City of God* of Christ's role as the divine mediator of justice occurs in Book 10.[89] There he opposes claims related to Porphyry's explanations of spiritual purification by returning once again to the consequences of original sin on the soul. He asserts that Christ purifies and heals the soul in order to dispel the 'darkness of ignorance' (*tenebris ignorantiae*) by which the intellect is 'shrouded' (*obuolutus*) and 'unable to know' (*nequaquam percipere*) God in the form of mystery. Christ is able to accomplish this mediation because in his human nature he is just (*iusta*) and sinless (*non peccatrix*).[90] Although Augustine does not mention the term 'justify' (*iustificare*) in Book 10, the concept is expressed by the

---

[88] See, for example, *pecc. mer.* 1.60 (CSEL 60.61): 'ne quasi duo Christi accipiantur, unus deus et alter homo, sed unus atque idem deus et homo', *s.* 294.9 (PL 38.1340): 'quia in hoc utroque non duo Christi sunt, nec duo filii dei sed una persona, unus Christus dei filius, idemque unus Christus, non alius, hominis filius; sed dei'.

[89] On Christ as the divine mediator of justice in general in Augustine, see Remy, *Le Christ*, 1:436–56, 1:503–38, Studer, 'Le Christ', 122–39, Madec, *La Patrie*, 98–104 (along with the other studies cited at 103 n. 39).

[90] See *ciu.* 10.24 (CCL 47.298): 'quod utique carnales, infirmi, peccatis obnoxii et ignorantiae tenebris obuoluti nequaquam percipere possemus, nisi ab eo mundaremur atque sanaremur per hoc quod eramus et non eramus. eramus enim homines, sed iusti non eramus; in illius autem incarnatione natura humana erat, sed iusta, non peccatrix erat. haec est mediatio qua manus lapsis iacentibusque porrecta est; hoc est semen dispositum per angelos, in quorum edictis et lex dabatur, qua et unus deus coli iubebatur et hic mediator uenturus promittebatur'. At *ciu.* 10.25 (CCL 47.298), Augustine expands upon the latter point, indicating that it was 'through faith in this mystery' that the just men

terms 'purify' (*mundare*) and 'heal' (*sanare*), as Augustine employs them in relation to Christ.[91]

Throughout Book 10, Augustine rejects theurgy as a threat to the Christian faith, insofar as it offers a parallel explanation to that of Christianity for the unity of prayer and sacrament in the course of spiritual purification. He claims, for example, that although theurgic rites had been banned for some time by imperial law, they are still being practised privately in his own day,[92] and states that his critique of Porphyrian theurgy is intended for the benefit of those who are currently practising it.[93] Augustine also opposes a tendency among certain opponents of Christianity, such as Porphyry, to deny that Christ is the unique, incarnate Word and Son of God, as he is represented in Catholic doctrine, but to represent him instead in positive terms as one sage, 'divine man', or thaumaturge among many others in history. In an important study, Goulven Madec argues that at around the time Augustine wrote *De consensu euangelistarum* (c. AD 399) this pagan view of Christ recirculated in Africa, in an effort to present Christ as a defender of traditional Roman polytheism.[94] Contemporary efforts to depict Christ's miracles as a form of magic also contribute to the threat to the Christian religion that Augustine perceives in the practice of pagan Neoplatonic theurgy in his own day.[95]

and women recalled in the Old Testament were purified through pious living: 'huius sacramenti fide etiam iusti antiqui mundari pie uiuendo potuerunt'.

[91] See the passages cited above, n. 90. On *mundare* and *sanare* as synonyms for *iustificare*, see, for example, *s.* 292.6 (PL 38.1324): 'Christus sanat, Christus mundat, Christus iustificat: homo non iustificat . . .', *en. Ps.* 105.5 (CCL 40.1556): 'deinde, quia deus iustificat, id est, iustos facit, sanando eos ab iniquitatibus suis', *nat. et gr.* 29 (CSEL 60.254–5): 'ipse autem deus, cum per mediatorem dei et hominum hominem Christum Iesum spiritaliter sanat aegrum uel uiuificat mortuum, id est iustificat inpium'. See also *c. litt. Pet.* 3.66, *pecc. mer.* 1.55, *spir. et litt.* 15, *nat. et gr.* 12, *c. litt. Pet.* 3.52, 3.67, *gr. et pecc. or.* 2.28, *c. Iul. imp.* 2.30, 2.212. Augustine's reason for avoiding the term *iustificare* here may have to do with the fact that Book 10 is composed with Porphyry's hostility to Christianity in mind, in the context of which this exclusively Christian term might not have been as useful for his apologetic purposes.

[92] See *ciu.* 10.9, 10.16, and 10.28, along with J.-B. Clerc, '*Theurgica legibus prohibita*: à propos de l'interdiction de la théurgie (Augustin, *La Cité de Dieu* 10, 9, 1.16, 2; *Code théodosien* 9, 16, 4)', *Revue des études augustiniennes* 42 (1996), 57–64. See also *s. Dolbeau* 26.28. In his correspondence with Augustine (*ep.* 233–5), Longinianus appears to have been a devotee of some form of theurgy. See P. Mastandrea, 'Il "dossier Longiniano" nell'epistolario di sant'Agostino (epist. 233–235)', *Studia patavina* 25 (1978), 523–40.

[93] See *ciu.* 10.29.

[94] See G. Madec, 'Le Christ des païens d'après le *De consensu euangelistarum* de saint Augustin', *Recherches augustiniennes* 26 (1992), 3–67, at 48–67. See also P. Courcelle, 'Propos anti-chrétiens rapportés par saint Augustin', *Recherches augustiniennes* 1 (1958), 149–86.

[95] Madec, 'Le Christ', 47, notes, for example, Augustine's opposition at *ciu.* 10.9 to the assertion of any connection between the miracles that God performed for the Israelites, as recorded in the scriptures, and the 'magic' produced by theurgists who conjure demons. See also my discussion below, pp. 203–4.

Augustine distinguishes his idea of mediation in Christ and Porphyry's account of theurgy in two essential ways. First, he says, purification of the soul is not a gift that God bestows upon man 'downward' through a hierarchy of intermediary, spiritual beings, as theurgists assume. Instead, by becoming man in Christ, God allows all human beings who are reborn in Christ to participate directly in his own divine nature, thus liberating them from mortality and misery by uniting them, not with angelic beings, but with himself.[96] This explanation of the unity between God and man as it is found in Christ constitutes the core element of Augustine's understanding of 'mystery' (*mysterium, sacramentum*), and he rejects alternative explanations.[97] Second, human beings cannot apprehend religious truth in the form of mystery unless they cease to rely on their own intellect, and humbly acknowledge their complete dependence upon God's direct intervention in their souls.[98] Clinging to other forms of spiritual purification and to other accounts of the genesis of virtue when one is directly confronted with the reality of this divine mystery constitutes an act of pride, and impedes the birth of true virtue in the soul.[99] Both points raised by Augustine in his effort to distinguish Christian faith in Christ as the sole mediator of virtue from philosophical explanations of theurgic mediation set forth faith and, especially, humility, as the principal content and effect of salvation. Faith and humility correspond to, and offset, the twin defects of original sin, namely ignorance and weakness; on account of them, human efforts to live life justly are prone to failure.

Thus, Augustine's most complete statement in the *City of God* about the form in which true virtue is born in the soul and fear of death is overcome does not occur until his discussion of Platonic mediation in Book 10. As he argues in earlier books in opposition to Roman religion, he insists here against non-Christian, philosophical accounts of salvation that faith and

---

[96] See *ciu.* 10.23, 9.15. On Porphyry's arguments, see Remy, *Le Christ*, 1:234–43.

[97] On this point, see *ep.* 187.34 (above, p. 29. n. 12).

[98] See *ciu.* 10.29 (CCL 47.305): 'o si cognouisses dei gratiam per Iesum Christum dominum nostrum ipsamque eius incarnationem, qua hominis animam corpusque suscepit, summum esse exemplum gratiae uidere potuisses [. . .] gratia dei non potuit gratius commendari, quam ut ipse unicus dei filius in se incommutabiliter manens indueretur hominem et spiritum dilectionis suae daret hominibus homine medio, qua ad illum ab hominibus ueniretur, qui tam longe erat inmortalis a mortalibus, incommutabilis a commutabilibus, iustus ab inpiis, beatus a miseris. et quia naturaliter indidit nobis, ut beati inmortalesque esse cupiamus, manens beatus suscipiensque mortalem, ut nobis tribueret quod amamus, perpetiendo docuit contemnere quod timemus. sed huic ueritati ut possetis adquiescere, humilitate opus erat'.

[99] See *ciu.* 10.28 (CCL 47.303): 'mittis ergo homines in errorem certissimum, neque hoc tantum malum te pudet, cum uirtutis et sapientiae profitearis amatorem; quam si uere ac fideliter amasses, *Christum dei uirtutem et dei sapientiam* [1 Cor 1:24] cognouisses nec ab eius saluberrima humilitate tumore inflatus uanae scientiae resiluisses'. See Remy, *Le Christ*, 1:141–51.

humility are the key virtues which enable believers to know and love God in the mystery of the incarnation. It is through their faith in this mystery that believers receive Christ's gift of humility.[100] This divine humility is essential to the soul's purification and healing because it alone enables human beings to overcome the moral presumption which results from ignorance and weakness. Chastened in this manner, believers learn how to confront death. Augustine insists that humility is required for submission to the truth of the incarnation through which believers obtain the healing and purification that allow them to experience blessedness and confront their fear of death.[101]

With these principles in mind, Augustine introduces into this discussion of Christ's mediation the concept of the 'whole Christ, head and body' (*totus Christus caput et corpus*), which, adapting Paul, he identifies as the church (Col 1:18, 24).[102] He develops this image, at least in part, in order to stress Christ's unity with the church against the Donatists, for whom the church exists only where it can be found 'without stain or wrinkle' (Eph 5:27):

---

[100] At *ciu.* 10.9 (CCL 47.281), Augustine distinguishes faith in this mystery from participation in theurgic rites: 'fiebant autem simplici fide atque fiducia pietatis, non incantationibus et carminibus nefariae curiositatis arte conpositis, quam uel magian uel detestabiliore nomine goetian uel honorabiliore theurgian uocant'. See also *ciu.* 10.22 (CCL 47.296): 'hac dei gratia, qua in nos ostendit magnam misericordiam suam, et in hac uita per fidem regimur, et post hanc uitam per ipsam speciem incommutabilis ueritatis ad perfectionem plenissimam perducemur'.

[101] See *ciu.* 10.29 (CCL 47.305): 'gratia dei non potuit gratius commendari, quam ut ipse unicus dei filius in se incommutabiliter manens indueretur hominem [. . .] et quia naturaliter indidit nobis, ut beati inmortalesque esse cupiamus, manens beatus suscipiensque mortalem, ut nobis tribueret quod amamus, perpetiendo docuit contemnere quod timemus. sed huic ueritati ut possetis adquiescere, humilitate opus erat'. See the remarks of Schaffner, *Christliche Demut*, 93–120.

[102] See *ciu.* 10.6, 10.20. See also *en. Ps.* 90.2.1 (CCL 39.1266): 'corpus huius capitis ecclesia est, non quae hoc loco est, sed et quae hoc loco et per totum orbem terrarum; nec illa quae hoc tempore, sed ab ipso Abel usque ad eos qui nascituri sunt usque in finem et credituri in Christum, totus populus sanctorum ad unam ciuitatem pertinentium; quae ciuitas corpus est Christi, cui caput est Christus'. See also *en. Ps.* 30.2.3.5 (CCL 38.216), where Augustine associates with 'the whole, just Christ' (*totus Christus iustus*) those of his members who, in imitation of Christ, disdain temporal honours and accept humiliations from those who seek such honours. Moreover, at *en. Ps.* 61.4 (below, p. 107 n. 144), he refers to Christ's unity with the members of his body as 'hanc quasi rempublicam'. Franz, 'Totus', 122 and 129, describes how Augustine establishes a 'Relationseinheit' between Christ and the church. He cites *s.* 341.11, where Augustine refers to 'the whole Christ' as the 'third mode' of Christ's existence, following that of the eternal Word and the incarnate Christ. Parallel references are found at *s. Dolbeau* 22.2 and 22.19. In regard to this theme, see also M. Reveillaud, 'Le Christ-Homme, tête de l'Eglise. Etudes d'ecclésiologie selon les *Enarrationes in Psalmos* d'Augustin', *Recherches augustiniennes* 5 (1968), 67–94, P. Borgomeo, *L'Eglise de ce temps dans la prédication de saint Augustin* (Paris, 1972), 211–18, T. van Bavel and B. Bruning, 'Die Einheit des "Totus Christus" bei Augustinus', *Scientia augustiniana. Studien über Augustinus, den Augustinismus und den Augustinerorden. Festschrift A. Zumkeller OSA zum 60. Geburtstag*, ed. C. Mayer (Würzburg, 1975), 43–75. See also Remy, *Le Christ*, 1:738–80, C. Müller, *Geschichtsbewußtsein bei Augustinus. Ontologische, anthropologische und universalgeschichtlich/heilsgeschichtliche Elemente einer augustinischen 'Geschichtstheorie'* (Würzburg, 1993), 221–5.

that is, where its members, particularly its bishops, are free of serious sin. Augustine's frequent reference to *Christus totus* during this campaign leads him to a deeper appreciation of the image's capacity to depict a series of complex interrelationships between Christ and the members of his church. Accordingly, he insists that the holiness of the church and its ministers and sacraments is sustained by Christ alone. As 'head of the body', Christ purifies its members from sin.[103] By developing this principle, Augustine argues that clerics and lay Christians alike are purified through the sacrifice that Christ offers as the one, true priest, and not as a result of any ritual act that church members perform on their own behalf. In connection with this last, fundamental point, Augustine insists that, as the one, true priest, Christ is the sole mediator between God and man. Although bishops are called 'priests' (*sacerdotes*), they do not perform the unique, priestly function of mediation which only Christ can accomplish.[104] Through the image of the 'whole Christ', Augustine explains that cultic acts which remit sins, such as baptism, are in reality performed by Christ, who acts through Christian priests. Augustine's frequent insistence on this point is due, in part, to his conclusion that the Donatists, by erroneously attributing to their bishops the power of obtaining forgiveness of sins through intercessory prayer, establish the latter as mediators on a par with Christ. Augustine knows, for example, that the Donatist bishop, Parmenian, regards the ideal bishop as a 'mediator' between God and man, and he complains that 'Donatists put Donatus in the place of Christ.'[105] Behind the Donatist conception of the cultic role of bishops stands their conviction that the holiness of the church is, in effect, guaranteed by the bishop, inasmuch as he obtains divine forgiveness for the sins of the church's lay members through intercessory

---

[103] See *c. litt. Pet.* 2.239, *s.* 157.3, *s. Dolbeau* 22.19, *en. Ps.* 118.22.4, *trin.* 1.24, and, in particular, *pecc. mer.* 1.60 (CSEL 60.61): 'fideles eius fiunt cum homine Christo unus Christus, ut omnibus per eius hanc gratiam societatemque ascendentibus ipse unus Christus ascendat in caelum, qui de caelo descendit. sic et apostolus ait: *sicut in uno corpore multa membra habemus, omnia autem membra corporis, cum sint multa, unum est corpus, ita et Christus* [1 Cor 12:12]. non dixit: ita et Christi, id est corpus Christi uel membra Christi, sed: *ita et Christus,* unum Christum appellans caput et corpus'.

[104] G. Bonner, '*Christus sacerdos*: The Roots of Augustine's Anti-Donatist Polemic', *Signum pietatis. Festgabe für Cornelius P. Mayer OSA zum 60. Geburtstag,* ed. A. Zumkeller (Würzburg, 1989), 325–39, notes the connection in Augustine's anti-Donatist writings conveyed by the theme '*Christus sacerdos*' between the uniqueness of Christ's sacrificial offering as the one, true priest (*uerus sacerdos*) and his freedom from all sin, original or personal.

[105] See *s. Dolbeau* 26.52 (D 409): 'Unde mihi uenit in mentem cum magno dolore commemorare ausum fuisse Parmenianum, quondam donistarum episcopum, in quadam epistula sua ponere episcopum esse mediatorem inter populum et deum', ibid., 26.55 (D 410): 'Et hoc isti dicere nec timent nec erubescant, quod mediator sit episcopus inter deum et homines', ibid., 26.45 (D 401): 'Donatum donatistae pro Christo habent.'

prayer. The reasoning by which Donatists view their bishops as mediators leads them to conclude that the prayers of bishops remit sins only if the bishops themselves are sinless. As biblical support for this argument, the Donatists cite 1 Sam 2:25: 'If the people sin, the priest prays for them; if, however, the priest sins, who shall pray for him?'[106] Against this reasoning, Augustine protests that only Christ obtains the forgiveness of sins, and that, in offering intercessory prayer, bishops do not act as mediators. His insistence that Christ is the only true high priest because he alone is able to offer freely to God the death of a perfectly just man as a propitiatory sacrifice for the justification of others is, therefore, also intended to counter this Donatist view.[107] Moreover, he opposes the sharp, Donatist distinction between the intercessory roles of bishops and laity in the church by insisting that Christ, as high priest, incorporates into his body the whole church, and not just priests.[108] Augustine adds that the apostles, who never refer to themselves as mediators, ask lay members of the church to pray for the forgiveness of their sins.[109]

Augustine's efforts to deny any mediatorial status even to saintly bishops are matched by his determination to deny a similar dignity to theurgists.[110] Whether in their attempts through prayer, ritual acts, and incantations to influence spiritual beings, or in their will to overcome their own passions and temptations and unite themselves with various divinities in order to achieve purification and interior peace, theurgists delude themselves by believing that their supernatural practices and the mental states which

---

[106] See *c. litt. Pet.* 2.240, 2.241, and, in particular, *s. Dolbeau* 26.54, and *en. Ps.* 36.2.20 (CCL 38.362). In this latter text, Augustine offers an example of the Donatists' error in this regard, from his point of view. The passage reproduces a letter from the Maximinianist synod of Cebarsussa (24 June 393) which denounces Primian, the Donatist bishop of Carthage, for failing to live up to the ideal standards of the bishop 'qui in omnia sanctus et in nullo reprehensibilis haberetur'. For further discussion of this Donatist view on bishops and the holiness of the church, see, especially, M. Tilley, 'Sustaining Donatist Self-Identity: From the Church of the Martyrs to the *Collecta* of the Desert', *Journal of Early Christian Studies* 5:1 (1997), 21–35.

[107] See, for example, *c. litt. Pet.* 2.241, *c. ep. Parm.* 2.15, *s. Dolbeau* 26.43 (D 398): 'Praelibauit tamquam de capite quod offerret deo, *sacerdos in aeternum* [Heb 5:6] et *propitiatio pro peccatis nostris* [1 Jn 2:2].' See also *s. Dolbeau* 26.49, 26.54, 26.55.

[108] See *s. Dolbeau* 26.49 (D 404–5): 'Nos autem omnes episcopi sacerdotes ideo dicimur, quia praepositi sumus. Universa tamen ecclesia corpus est illius sacerdotis. Ad sacerdotem pertinet corpus suum. Nam et apostolus Petrus ideo dicit ad ipsam ecclesiam: *Plebs sancta, regale sacerdotium* [1 Pt 2:9].' See also *s. Dolbeau* 26.53, 26.57.

[109] See *en. Ps.* 36.2.20, *s. Dolbeau* 26.57 (D 412): 'Isti se non dicunt mediatores et pro eis orant a quibus pro se orari uolunt. On this point, see also J. Carola, '*Solvitis et uos*: The Laity and their Exercise of the Power of the Keys according to Saint Augustine of Hippo', unpublished dissertation, Institutum Patristicum Augustinianum, Rome, 2001.

[110] On this point, see R. Dodaro, '*Christus sacerdos*: Augustine's Preaching against Pagan Priests in the Light of *S. Dolbeau* 26 and 23', *Augustin prédicateur (395–411), Actes du Colloque International de Chantilly (5–7 septembre 1996)*, ed. G. Madec (Paris, 1998), 377–93.

these rites induce derive from real power and aim at true virtue.[111] As with the Donatist bishops, Augustine contrasts the theurgists' claim to a form of mediation with the attitude of the apostles and martyrs. When the saints exorcize evil spirits or perform healing miracles, they profess to do so in the name of Christ, the one true priest and mediator, acting through his power and virtue alone.[112] Furthermore, they vehemently oppose attempts by unbelievers to honour them or to erect cults in their names.[113] Augustine admits that a certain amount of veneration may be appropriate to some human beings, as long as one always remembers that it is only human beings who are being honoured.[114] With theurgists in mind, Augustine warns contemporary Christians that they might be tempted to hold a high opinion of themselves as a result of great spiritual achievements, such as the performance of miracles, were it not the case that they,

---

[111] See *ciu.* 10.22 (CCL 47.296): 'non enim nisi peccatis homines separantur a deo, quorum in hac uita non fit nostra uirtute, sed diuina miseratione purgatio, per indulgentiam illius, non per nostram potentiam; quia et ipsa quantulacumque uirtus, quae dicitur nostra, illius est nobis bonitate concessa'. At *ciu.* 10.21, Augustine charges, on the basis of an unidentified statement of Porphyry, that in order to be aided by good spirits, theurgists must oftentimes first mollify evil spirits. He cites Vergil, *Aeneid* 7.310, on Aeneas' attempt through song and suppliant gifts to soothe the feelings of Juno. See MacCormack, *The Shadows of Poetry*, 165. At *s. Dolbeau* 26.27–8, Augustine describes the ritual process by which theurgists first become aware of their need for spiritual purification, and then pursue it through additional rituals aimed at communion with spiritual beings who provide mediation. For reference to the two aims of theurgy, supplication of spiritual beings and liberation from the passions, see, in particular, E. Dodds, 'Theurgy and its Relationship to Neoplatonism', *Journal of Roman Studies* 37 (1947), 55–69, at 56 = *The Greeks and the Irrational* (Berkeley, 1956), 283–311, at 284, and E. Des Places, *La Religion grecque* (Paris, 1969), 324.

[112] See *ciu.* 10.22 (CCL 47.296): 'uera pietate homines dei aeriam potestatem inimicam contrariamque pietati exorcizando eiciunt, non placando, omnesque temptationes aduersitatis eius uincunt orando non ipsam, sed deum suum aduersus ipsam. non enim aliquem uincit aut subiugat nisi societate peccati. in eius ergo nomine uincitur, qui hominem adsumpsit egitque sine peccato, ut in ipso sacerdote ac sacrificio fieret remissio peccatorum, id est per mediatorem dei et hominem, hominem Christum Iesum, per quem facta peccatorum purgatione reconciliamur deo'.

[113] See *ciu.* 10.19 (CCL 47.294), where Augustine recalls the incident reported at Acts 14:8–18 in which Paul and Barnabas eschew attempts to worship them as gods following their performance of a healing miracle: 'nam Paulus et Barnabas in Lycaonia facto quodam miraculo sanitatis putati sunt dii, eisque Lycaonii uictimas immolare uoluerunt; quod a se humili pietate remouentes eis in quem crederent adnuntiauerunt deum'. See also *s. Dolbeau* 26.13 and *s.* 273.8, where Augustine also refers to a similar example in the case of Peter, who directs pagans to honour God for the miracle that the apostle performed (cf. Acts 3:12–13). At *s. Dolbeau* 26.48, Augustine comments in similar terms on the fact that neophyte Christians deposited their belongings at the apostles' feet (cf. Acts 4:35), arguing that this act is not to be interpreted as glorification of the apostles, but of God. See also *s. Dolbeau* 26.46. For comparison of martyrs in relation to 'heroes', see *ciu.* 10.21, along with H. Inglebert, 'Les Héros romains, les martyrs et les ascètes: les *uirtutes* et les préférences politiques chez les auteurs chrétiens latins du IIIe au Ve siècle', *Revue des études augustiniennes* 40 (1994), 305–25.

[114] See *ciu.* 10.4 (CCL 47.276): 'multa denique de cultu diuino usurpata sunt, quae honoribus deferrentur humanis, siue humilitate nimia siue adulatione pestifera; ita tamen, ut, quibus ea deferrentur, homines haberentur'.

like the apostles, live 'under pardon' right up to the time of their deaths.[115] By insisting in the midst of his discussion of theurgy that the apostles and martyrs were pardoned sinners, Augustine reacts against a present tendency to associate them with traditional 'heroes', such as Hercules, who are widely regarded as endowed by the gods with supernatural, spiritual gifts, and who are, consequently, worshipped as deities following their deaths.[116]

Clearly, Augustine is concerned that whenever one gives spiritual or human beings the status of 'mediator', he risks making them objects of religious devotion and imitation, even of envy. He inquires whether spiritual beings desire that sacrifices be offered to themselves or to God.[117] Furthermore, he claims that even Porphyry acknowledges rivalries between spiritual beings who are invoked by theurgists.[118] Finally, he criticizes Porphyry for failing to denounce this envy.[119] In line with this argument, he insists that angels faithful to God do not desire to be worshipped.[120] He portrays Satan as the paradigmatic, false mediator who seduces practitioners of theurgy by boasting that he is superior to Christ because, unlike Christ, he did not become a human being and die in ignominy.[121] Augustine dismisses with equal contempt, and for the same reason, the Donatists' contention that the bishop is a mediator. He compares this claim to an act of adultery in

---

[115] See *ciu.* 10.22 (CCL 47.296): 'non enim nisi peccatis homines separantur a deo, quorum in hac uita non fit nostra uirtute, sed diuina miseratione purgatio, per indulgentiam illius, non per nostram potentiam; quia et ipsa quantulacumque uirtus, quae dicitur nostra, illius est nobis bonitate concessa. multum autem nobis in hac carne tribueremus, nisi usque ad eius depositionem sub uenia uiueremus'. Cf. *pecc. mer.* 1.56. On the admission by the apostles that they are sinners, see, for example, *s. Dolbeau* 26.55 (D 410): 'Sed illud Iohannis adtendite dicentis: *Haec scribo uobis ut non peccetis. Et si quis peccauerit, aduocatum habemus ad patrem* [1 Jn 2:1]. Non diceret *habemus*, nisi quia bene se nouerat et humiliter commendabat. *Et ipse est*, inquit, *exoratio pro peccatis nostris* [1 Jn 2:2]. Non dixit "uestris", quasi se faciens alienum a peccatis.'

[116] See *s. Dolbeau* 26.28 (D 388): 'Nam multa simulacrorum, sicut scriptura dicit, ex honoribus hominum qui magni habebantur uel absentium uel mortuorum instituta sunt.'

[117] See *ciu.* 10.1 (CCL 47.272): 'quo modo credendi sint uelle a nobis religionem pietatemque seruari; hoc est, ut apertius dicam, utrum etiam sibi an tantum deo suo, qui etiam noster est, placeat eis ut sacra faciamus et sacrificemus, uel aliqua nostra seu nos ipsos religionis ritibus consecremus'.

[118] See *ciu.* 10.9 (CCL 47.282): 'ipsamque theurgian, quam uelut conciliatricem angelorum deorumque commendat, apud tales agere potestates negare non potuit, quae uel ipsae inuideant purgationi animae, uel artibus seruiant inuidorum, querelam de hac re Chaldaei nescio cuius expromens'. He continues this argument at *ciu.* 10.10.

[119] See *ciu.* 10.26 (CCL 47.301): 'quid adhuc trepidas, o philosophe, aduersus potestates et ueris uirtutibus et ueri dei muneribus inuidas habere liberam uocem'.

[120] See *ciu.* 10.7.

[121] See *s. Dolbeau* 26.41. See also ibid., 26.15, 26.44, 26.46-7. At *ciu.* 10.24 (CCL 47.297), Augustine argues that other demons make the same claim: 'eum quippe in ipsa carne contempsit . . . quam sua ille humilitate deiecit uerus benignusque mediator, in ea se ostendens mortalitate mortalibus, quam maligni fallacesque mediatores non habendo se superbius extulerunt miserisque hominibus adiutorium deceptorium uelut inmortales mortalibus promiserunt'.

which the bishop usurps the church from Christ, the bridegroom.[122] His concern to defend Christ's unique status as mediator reflects his deep anxiety that individuals who regard other spiritual or human beings as conduits of virtue may themselves yearn for the same exalted role. Augustine sees a link between the desire to imitate outstanding exemplars of virtue and the will to outshine them.[123] Only when it is understood by believers that God mediates goodness to human beings directly, without intermediary spiritual beings such as angels – and certainly not through priests – is it possible to put an end to spiritual rivalries.[124] Augustine contends that the apostles were careful to ensure that they did not receive honours from other human beings. In so behaving, they were conscious of the fact that harm is done to those who worship spiritual or human beings in place of God.[125] He argues that believers should humbly recognize that God has no peers, whether spiritual or human, and they should refrain from aspiring to claim as their own that goodness which can only be God's.[126] They should also stop looking to heroic men and women, renowned during their lives for holiness, as proof that anyone can achieve peace, freedom, or virtue in this life. Christians are comforted by God, Augustine affirms, though they remain subject to afflictions, and they live in the joy of a good hope (Wis 12:19). But he insists that they remain far from freedom from temporal adversity while they live their present life.[127]

In a further effort to distinguish true salvation from Donatist and pagan alternatives, Augustine discusses the nature and aims of the sacrifices which priests offer. Sacrifices, he says, should be offered to God alone, and not to lesser spiritual beings (a clear reference to theurgic rites aimed at appeasing

---

[122] This adulterer, whom Augustine (following Mt 22:11) describes as appearing at the wedding feast without a proper garment, is removed for seeking to draw attention to himself, not to the bridegroom. See *s. Dolbeau* 26.52 (D 407–8): 'Uideamus amicum sponsi zelantem sponso, non se opponentem pro sponso [. . .] non enim habet uestem in qua honoraret sponsum, sed per eum habitum honorem suum quaesiuit in sponsi conuiuio.'

[123] This failing is equally present in spiritual and human beings. See *s. Dolbeau* 26.44 (D 400): 'Qualis est autem malus ille falsusque mediator qui intercludit iter ad deum, tales esse effectant omnes superbi homines: ubicumque sint, similes uolunt esse mediatori suo. Et quomodo uidetis in hominibus, sic et in angelis [. . .] Cum ergo superbi homines se coli uolunt ei, si deus illis praeponatur, irascuntur, imitatores sunt fallacis illius mediatoris.'

[124] See *s. Dolbeau* 26.26 and 26.46. Augustine discusses angels in relation to mediation at *s. Dolbeau* 26.14–16 and 26.46–8. Moreover, at *s. Dolbeau* 26.48, he explicitly states that angels are not models for imitation. See also *ciu.* 10.16, 10.19, 10.25, 10.26.

[125] See *s. Dolbeau* 26.15 (D 378): 'respuerunt honorem qui eis ad superbiam conferebatur, ut ille unus honoretur in omnibus, qui solus sine periculo honorantis honoratus est'.

[126] See *s. Dolbeau* 26.32, 26.44.

[127] See *s. Dolbeau* 26.63. Augustine also observes that practitioners of theurgy do not obtain the peace, freedom, or virtue that they hope to receive through appeal to spiritual beings.

demons).[128] Against such practices, he insists that God intends visible sacrifice only as a symbolic language, which gives visible form to the invisible sacrifice that God desires, not for his own satisfaction, but for the benefit of human beings. Believers should love God as the good which alone brings them happiness, and they should love their neighbour in such a way as to lead their neighbour into the love of God.[129] He cites Ps 50(51):18–19 to illustrate the invisible sacrifice that God desires ('If you had desired sacrifice I would have offered it; but you do not delight in holocausts. The sacrifice offered to God is a broken spirit; God will not despise a heart that is broken and humbled'). Contrition for sins and the desire for divine pardon are the exclusive aims of the only sacrifice which God seeks from human beings. This sacrifice can only be 'offered' in the heart of the believer; no exterior ritual accomplishes it. In making these points, Augustine also intends to clarify the manner in which God ought to be conceived. Unlike spiritual beings such as angels, demons, and minor deities, God is not a contingent being who experiences needs and desires, and who seeks gratification.[130] Human beings can only understand God's 'desires' in a correct manner by believing that he wills their happiness. Inasmuch as God creates human beings to be happy by participating in himself as the supreme good, they can only achieve happiness by clinging to him as their good.[131] In order to love God in this way, however, human beings must know themselves as they really are, sinners in need of God's pardon. Otherwise, pride substitutes

---

[128] See *ciu.* 10.4.

[129] See *ciu.* 10.5 (CCL 47.276): 'nec quod ab antiquis patribus alia sacrificia facta sunt in uictimis pecorum, quae nunc dei populus legit, non facit, aliud intellegendum est, nisi rebus illis eas res fuisse significatas, quae aguntur in nobis, ad hoc ut inhaereamus deo et ad eundem finem proximo consulamus'. A similar argument is found at *ciu.* 10.19. See also *ciu.* 10.3, where Augustine discusses love of neighbour in the context of love of God. On the relationship of neighbour love to love of God, see especially O'Donovan, *Problem*, and R. Canning, *The Unity of Love for God and Neighbour in St. Augustine* (Heverlee-Leuven, 1993), who discusses other relevant studies. My understanding of sacraments (*sacramenta*) as symbolic language is derived, in part, from R. Markus, 'Augustine on Magic: A Neglected Semiotic Theory', *Revue des études augustiniennes* 40 (1994), 375–88, at 382. Markus cites *c. Faust.* 19.11 (CSEL 25/1.510), where Augustine asserts that 'human beings cannot be brought together in the name of any religion, whether true or false, without being associated by means of some shared, visible symbols or sacrament': 'in nullum autem nomen religionis, seu uerum, seu falsum, coagulari homines possunt, nisi aliquo signaculorum uel sacramentorum uisibilium consortio conligentur'.

[130] At *ciu.* 10.16 (CCL 47.290–1), Augustine argues that the fact that God does not need sacrifices is attested by scripture, as well as by their abolition by Christians: 'illis enim multi tanto minus sacrificiis colendi sunt, quanto magis haec expetunt; his uero unus commendatur deus, qui se nullis talibus indigere et scripturarum suarum testificatione et eorundem postea sacrificiorum remotione demonstrat'.

[131] See *ciu.* 10.6 (CCL 47.279): 'opera uero misericordiae non ob aliud fiant, nisi ut a miseria liberemur ac per hoc ut beati simus (quod non fit nisi bono illo, de quo dictum est: *mihi autem adhaerere deo bonum est*)' (Ps 72[73]:28).

self-love for love of God. Augustine affirms that a humble confession of one's true condition (misery) is necessary in order for the grace of Christ's mediation to heal the soul's weakness.[132] Believers are urged to extend the pardon (*misericordia*) that they receive from God to their neighbour. In this way, they glorify God by promoting in their neighbours true love of God.[133]

Against the background of these principles, Augustine characterizes the eucharist as a visible sacrifice in which the invisible sacrifice (compassion, mercy) which God desires of human beings is made manifest. In doing so, he returns to the concept of the 'whole Christ' and to the unity it establishes between Christ as priest and members of his body, the church (Rom 12:3). Augustine couples this image with a second Pauline concept in which Jesus, 'though in the form of God, did not deem equality with God something to be grasped at, but emptied himself and took on the form of a servant' (Phil 2:7).[134] As symbolic language, the eucharist instructs believers that Christ, the true priest, offers in his death the one sacrifice that is acceptable to God.[135] Christ's sacrifice, therefore, also contains the invisible sacrifice that Christians, as members of his body, offer to God when they show compassion to their neighbour. As a consequence, in celebrating the eucharist Christians are reminded that they should not esteem themselves for their virtuous deeds. Instead, they should recognize that the source of their virtue is found not in themselves, but in Christ. By adopting this perspective, they too assume the 'form of a servant', and in imitation of Christ, do not grasp at equality with God.[136]

---

[132] See *ciu.* 10.28 (CCL 47.304): 'sed haec est gratia, quae sanat infirmos, non superbe iactantes falsam beatitudinem suam, sed humiliter potius ueram miseriam confitentes'.

[133] See *ciu.* 10.5. Concerning the obligation to forgive one's neighbour, see also *ep. Io. tr.* 5.8, and *s.* 211, along with H. Pétré, *Caritas. Étude sur le vocabulaire latin de la charité chrétienne* (Louvain, 1948), 136–7, D. Dideberg, *Saint Augustin et la première épître de saint Jean. Une théologie de l'agapè* (Paris, 1975), 67–73, Canning, *The Unity*, 189–91, 198–201, 205–15.

[134] See *ciu.* 10.6. See also *en. Ps.* 30.2.1.3, a key text in this discussion, one in which Augustine also indicates that Christ unites believers with his body, which has assumed the 'form of a servant'. This reference recalls a similar one at *ciu.* 9.15, where Augustine speaks of Christ in the *forma serui* in terms of the ignominious character of Christ's death. Reference to Phil 2:7 is also found at *ciu.* 20.10. See B. Studer, 'Das Opfer Christi nach Augustins *De civitate dei* x, 5–6', *Lex orandi – lex credendi, Miscellanea P. Vagaggini*, ed. G. Békés and G. Farnedi (Rome, 1980), 93–107, and the discussion by A. Verwilghen, *Christologie et spiritualité selon saint Augustin. L'Hymne aux Philippiens* (Paris, 1985), 269–84. Verwilghen, however, seems curiously unaware of the allusion to Phil 2:7 at *ciu.* 10.6.

[135] See *ciu.* 10.20.

[136] See *ciu.* 10.6. On Christ's death as an example of humility, see Schaffner, *Christliche Demut*, 107–20.

CHRIST'S MEDIATION OF VIRTUE

In order to explain how Christ mediates virtue to human beings, Augustine turns again to the image of the 'whole Christ' and harmonizes it with his conception of the unity of Christ's two natures. He first proposes that Christ is able to transfer to himself the 'persons' proper to the members of his body, considered either individually or collectively.[137] He thus claims that Christ experiences the emotions of the members of his body as his own, and that he is consequently able to express them. One must remember, however, that when Augustine uses the term 'person' (*persona*) in this context, he is drawing from the more fundamental, grammatical and theatrical usage of the category, by which it refers to the subject or speaker of a word.[138] As an example of this kind of transfer of 'persons', he cites Acts 9:4, where Christ reproves Saul for persecuting Christians. Christ's question, 'Saul, Saul, why do you persecute me?', indicates to Augustine Christ's own identification with those members of his body whom Saul persecutes. Though Saul never persecutes Christ directly, in assuming the 'persons' of his persecuted members, Christ experiences their suffering, and speaks out 'in their persons' (meaning that he speaks 'as' these members).[139]

Augustine holds that in cases where Christ's statements in the scriptures seem unworthy of him because they reflect a sinful disposition, he can be understood as speaking not for himself (*ex persona sua*), but vicariously, on behalf of all others, as, for example, when he prays on the night before his death that his Father should let this cup pass from him (Mt 26:39), or when, while dying on the cross, he cries out the words of the psalmist, 'My God, my God, why have you forsaken me?' (Mt 27:46, Ps 21[22]:1).[140] Christ

---

[137] See, for example, *ciu.* 17.18 (CCL 48.584–5): 'sed solet in se membrorum suorum transferre personam et sibi tribuere quod esset illorum quia caput et corpus unus est Christus'. See also the observations of Franz, *Totus,* 140–62.

[138] See Drobner, *Person-Exegese,* 24–114.

[139] Additional scriptural passages confirm for Augustine the reality of this transfer between Christ and members of his body. See M. Cameron, *Augustine's Construction of Figurative Exegesis against the Donatists in the 'Enarrationes in Psalmos'* (Ann Arbor, 1996), 272–301, M. Fiedrowicz, *Psalmus vox totius Christi. Studien zu Augustins 'Enarrationes in Psalmos'* (Freiburg, 1997), 312–45.

[140] See *en. Ps.* 21.2.3–4 (CCL 38.123–4); cf. *en. Ps.* 40.6, 142.7, 37.6. For background on Augustine's use of prosopographical exegesis to this effect, see Drobner, *Person-Exegese,* 11–81. A résumé of this argument can be found in H. Drobner, 'Grammatical Exegesis and Christology in St. Augustine', *Studia patristica: Papers of the 1983 Oxford Patristic Conference,* vol. 18:4, ed. E. Livingstone (Kalamazoo, 1990), 49–63. See also Fiedrowicz, *Psalmus,* 234–378, an English summary of which can be found in M. Fiedrowicz, 'General Introduction', *The Works of Saint Augustine: A Translation for the 21st Century,* Part III, vol. 15: *Expositions of the Psalms, 1–32,* tr. M. Boulding, ed. J. Rotelle (New York, 2000), 13–66, at 50–60.

here voices a fear of death which he experiences fully, not on account of his own sin, but on account of the sins of all other human beings. Christ's decision to suffer the consequences of sin leads Augustine to conclude that he also wills to speak about that experience as his own. Thus, he transfers to himself the 'voice' of the suffering members of his body.

Christ's ability to take upon himself the despair of the members of his body is matched by his capacity to transfer back to his members the virtues that are proper to himself. Augustine explains the reciprocal nature of this transfer by reflecting on the meaning of Christ's discourse on the cross. His decision to pray aloud the first verse of Psalm 21(22) as he dies suggests to Augustine that the remainder of this psalm can rightly be attributed to him, including the words 'far from my salvation are the words of my sins'. Augustine notes that the repentant tone of this second verse of the psalm differs from the despair expressed in the first verse: the speaker confesses to having sinned through what he had just said when complaining that God had abandoned him. Augustine reasons that Christ, by speaking these words, repents of the despair that he had voiced in the preceding verse, and transfers to sinful human beings the hope that he properly experiences in his own, unique person (which is to say, in the 'person' formed by the unity of his divine and human natures).[141] Christ's words as he faces death on the cross thus express the transformation through which he makes the sins of all human beings his own, while he also makes his justice their justice.[142] Augustine describes as a 'wondrous exchange' (*mira commutatio*) this transfer by which Christ assumes the fear of death that all members of his body experience, while he communicates back to them his own hope as consolation.[143]

---

[141] See *ep.* 140.15 in conjunction with 140.17 (CSEL 44.167): 'sed haec uerba, quibus humanus dies et uitae huius prolixitas concupiscitur, uerba sunt delictorum et longe sunt ab ea salute, cuius nondum rem sed iam spem gerimus'. In this same section, Augustine specifies that 'the words of my sins' (*uerba delictorum meorum*), which refer to the subject's fear of death, are to be understood as 'the words of fleshly desires' (*uerba desideriorum carnalium*). See *en. Ps.* 21.1.2 (CCL 38.117): 'nam haec uerba sunt non iustitiae, sed delictorum meorum'. See also *en. Ps.* 21.2.4, where Augustine applies the same logic to Christ's prayer at Mt 26:39 ('Father . . . let this cup pass from me'). In commenting upon this latter verse, Augustine alludes to Eph 1:23 in identifying the church as the body of Christ. See also *en. Ps.* 58.1.2, and Drobner, *Person-Exegese*, 129–31.

[142] See *en. Ps.* 21.2.3 (CCL 38.123): '*Deus meus, deus meus, respice me; quare me derelequisti* [Ps 21[22]:2] Quare dicitur, nisi quia nos ibi eramus, nisi quia corpus Christi ecclesia? Utquid dixit: Deus meus, Deus meus, respice me; quare me dereliquisti, nisi quodammodo intentos nos faciens et dicens psalmus iste de me scriptus est? *Longe a salute mea, uerba delictorum meorum* [Ps 21[22]:3]. Quorum delictorum, de quo dictum est: *Qui peccatum non fecit, nec inuentus est dolus in ore eius* [1 Pet 2:22] Quomodo ergo dicit *delictorum meorum*, nisi quia pro delictis nostris ipse precatur, et delicta nostra sua delicta fecit, ut iustitiam suam nostram iustitiam faceret?'

[143] See *en. Ps.* 30.2.1.3 (CCL 38.192): 'Verumtamen quia dignatus est assumere formam serui, et in ea nos uestire se, qui non est dedignatus assumere nos in se, non est dedignatus transfigurare nos in se,

This new description of the divine mediation of virtue in the metaphorical terms of a dialogue between Christ and the members of his body in effect creates an Augustinian model of the just society, the commonwealth that is founded and governed by Christ.[144] Augustine's treatise *De gratia noui testamenti* is a key text in charting this movement, for it traces the consequences of the incarnation as a divine discourse by which human beings are justified.[145] In Christ, the 'voice' of the divine Word (*uox uerbi*) is united with the 'voice' of the man Jesus (*uox carnis*) to become the 'voice of healing' (*uox medicinae*) within the human soul suffering ignorance and weakness as the result of original sin. Christ's justifying prayer becomes the oration of the just society, of the church (*uox ecclesiae*), whereby Christ speaks through the suffering members of his body.[146]

JUST AND JUSTIFYING

Christ's unique capacity to justify human beings as the true mediator returns as a dominant theme in Book 17, Chapter 4 of the *City of God*, in which Augustine describes the Hebrew nation from Abraham until the birth of Christ as a 'quasi-commonwealth' (*quaedam res publica*), one

et loqui uerbis nostris, ut et nos loqueremur uerbis ipsius. Haec enim mira commutatio facta est, et diuina sunt peracta commercia, mutatio rerum celebrata in hoc mundo a negotiatore caelesti.' See also W. Babcock, *The Christ of the Exchange: A Study of Augustine's* Enarrationes in Psalmos (Ann Arbor, 1972).

[144] See *pecc. mer.* 1.60 (CSEL 60.61): 'per unitatem uero personae [. . .] unus Christus, ut omnibus per eius hanc gratiam societatemque'. See also *en. Ps.* 61.4 (CCL 39.773): 'sed debemus intellegere personam nostram, personam ecclesiae nostrae, personam corporis Christi. unus enim homo cum capite et corpore suo Iesus Christus, saluator corporis et membra corporis, duo in carne una [cf. Gen 2:24, Eph 5:31], et in uoce una, et in passione una; et cum transierit iniquitas, in requie una [. . .] ad communem hanc quasi rempublicam nostram'.

[145] *De gratia noui testamenti* = *ep.* 140 (CSEL 45.155–234). For background, see below, pp. 159–60 n. 58. See, especially, *ep.* 140.18 (CSEL 44.168), where the juxtaposition of Eph 5:32 and Mt 19:6: 'erunt duo in carne una; sacramentum magnum . . . in Christo et in ecclesia; igitur non iam duo. sed una caro', with Jn 1:14: 'uerbum caro factum est, et habitauit in nobis', suggests a movement from the notion of the unity of natures 'in una persona Christi' to the formation of the just society in the divine Word become flesh. See also a parallel text at *en. Ps.* 30.2.1.4.

[146] See *ep.* 140.18 (CSEL 44.168–9): 'quid hic quaeris, humana infirmitas, uocem uerbi, per quod facta sunt omnia? audi potius uocem carnis, quae facta est inter omnia, quoniam *uerbum caro factum est et habitauit in nobis* [Jn 1:14]; audi potius medicinae uocem, qua sanaris, ut uideas deum, quem tibi uidendum distulit, hominem autem uidendum adtulit, occidendum obtulit, imitandum contulit, credendum transtulit, ut ista fide ad uidendum deum mentis oculus sanaretur. quid ergo dedignamur audire uocem corporis ex ore capitis? ecclesia in illo patiebatur, quando pro ecclesia patiebatur, sicut etiam ipse in ecclesia patiebatur, quando pro illo ecclesia patiebatur. nam sicut audiuimus ecclesiae uocem in Christo patientis: *deus, deus meus, respice me; quare me dereliquisti?* [Ps 21[22]:2 cf. Mt 27:46] sic audiuimus etiam Christi uocem in ecclesia patientis: *Saule, Saule, quid me persequeris?*' (Acts 9:4).

that foreshadows the 'city of God whose founder and king is Christ'.[147] In the context of this narrative, Augustine turns to Hannah's canticle (1 Sam 2:1–10) as a thanksgiving oration in which the prophetess acknowledges the birth of her son Samuel as a divine gift.[148] In terms stronger even than in Book 10, Augustine insists there that Christ alone mediates justice because he alone is truly just, while he also justifies human beings, thereby uniting them with himself to form the only just society in history. Augustine's commentary on this canticle reflects his principal anti-Pelagian arguments concerning the disparity between divine and human justice.[149] However, there is no reason to exclude the possibility that he also intends his criticisms to apply to other heretical groups, such as the Donatists or Manicheans, or even to pagan philosophies, such as Porphyry's. It is also possible that Augustine frames in anti-Pelagian terms his criticism of several different religious and philosophical movements on issues concerning the divine mediation of virtue. Chapter 4 of Book 17 therefore reveals his logic in framing his criticisms of Roman religion and pagan philosophy throughout Books 1–10 within his critique of Pelagian conceptions of virtue.

According to Augustine's interpretation, Hannah's canticle aims to reject moral self-sufficiency and affirm that the source of strength (*uirtus*) within Christ's 'city' lies in God, not in the self.[150] True security (*salus*) for the city is thus to be attained only through Christ, because 'there is no one who is just as our God' (1 Sam 2:2), a passage which can be read in counterpoint to both Pelagian and pagan conceptions of virtue. Augustine's reference in this chapter to Christ as 'founder and king' (*conditor et rex*) of the city of God echoes the parallel expression 'founder and ruler' (*conditor rectorque*) found in Book 2. In the context of the passages from *De re publica* which Augustine cites in Book 2 regarding Cicero's statesman, his claim in Book 17 that Christ is the foundation of true security in the city of God once again brings the

---

[147] See *ciu.* 16.12–17.24. On the Hebrew nation as 'quaedam res publica', see *ciu.* 7.32, 10.32. See also *ciu.* 17.4 (CCL 48.556): 'ipsam religionem christianam, ipsam ciuitatem dei, cuius rex et conditor Christus', and cf. *ciu.* 2.21 (above, p. 11 n. 28). *Rex* is substituted for *rector* here because in these chapters of Book 17, Augustine is specifically treating the Old Testament period of Hebrew kings.

[148] See *ciu.* 17.4 (CCL 48.555): 'cum gratulationem suam domino fundit exultans, quando eundem puerum natum et ablactatum deo reddit eadem pietate, qua uouerat'. On *pietas* for *iustitia*, see *ciu.* 20.6 (CCL 48.707), where Augustine paraphrases Rom 4:5: 'credentes in eum, qui iustificat impium, ex impietate iustificati'.

[149] Hombert, *Gloria*, 248–9, thinks it 'incontestable' that *ciu.* 17.4 reflects anti-Pelagian concerns.

[150] See *ciu.* 17.4 (CCL 48.557): 'haec dicuntur aduersariis ciuitatis dei ad Babyloniam pertinentibus, de sua uirtute praesumentibus, in se, non in domino gloriantibus [. . .] *arcus potentium infirmatus est, et infirmi praecincti sunt uirtute* [1 Sam 2:4]. infirmatus est arcus, id est intentio eorum, qui tam potentes sibi uidentur, ut sine dei dono atque adiutorio humana sufficientia diuina possint inplere mandata, et praecinguntur uirtute, quorum interna uox est: *miserere mei, domine, quoniam infirmus sum*' (Ps 6:3). See also *en. Ps.* 83.11.

issue of the statesman's relationship to the commonwealth to the fore, and prompts reconsideration of Cicero's well-known assertion that only the wise and just statesman promotes the security of the commonwealth.[151] By applying to Christ the expression from Rom 10:13, 'just and justifying', Augustine distinguishes his concept of the statesman's role in promoting justice within the commonwealth from that of Cicero. For Augustine, the wise and just statesman is found only in Christ, because he alone is 'just *as well as* justifying'.[152]

At the same time, his commentary on Hannah's canticle allows him to emphasize Christ's singular role in providing for the the security of the city of God, where other religious and philosophical systems, in their pride and arrogance, fail to do so. By the time he completes Book 17 in AD 425, Augustine already frequently employs the expression 'just and justifying' in reference to Christ in sharp opposition to Pelagian views.[153] His interpretation of Hannah's canticle as a corrective to explanations of virtue which exaggerate the moral capabilities of the human intellect and will reflects his differences with both pagan and Pelagian accounts. Hannah decries 'boasting' (*gloriari*) and 'haughty, arrogant' speech (*loqui excelsa/magniloquia*). Augustine ascribes this self-glorifying speech to the 'opponents of the city of God', that is, to all groups which 'presume upon themselves, not on God'.[154] He detects ignorance and weakness in the souls of those who view virtues such as prudence as 'products' of human design and effort, and not

---

[151] See, for example, Cicero, *De re publica* 1.34.51: 'quodsi liber populus deliget, quibus se committat, deligetque, si modo salvus esse vult, optimum quemque, certe in optimorum consiliis posita est civitatium salus, praesertim cum hoc natura tulerit, non solum et summi virtute et animo praeessent inbecillioribus, sed ut hi etiam parere summis vellent'.

[152] See *ciu.* 17.4 (CCL 48.557): '*laetata sum in salutari tuo; quoniam non est sanctus, sicut dominus, et non est iustus, sicut deus noster* [1 Sam 2:1]; tamquam sanctus et sanctificans, iustus et iustificans [. . .] qui ut dicit apostolus, *ignorantes dei iustitiam* (id est, quam dat homini deus, qui solus est iustus atque iustificans) *et suam uolentes constituere* (id est uelut a se sibi partam, non ab illo inpertitam) *iustitiae dei non sunt subiecti* [Rom 10:3]'.

[153] Augustine's use of the expression 'just and justifying' in relation to Christ is infrequent prior to AD 411. See *adn. Iob.* 38, *trin.* 1.24, and *c. litt. Pet.* 2.35. Much more frequent is his use of the expression following the beginning of the Pelagian controversy, and, in most cases, with reference to its issues. See, for example, *pecc. mer.* 1.18, 1.43, *spir. et litt.* 15, 16, 21, *c. ep. Pel.* 3.13, *ep.* 140.71, 185.40, *en. Ps.* 36.2.14, 49.2. In this connection, see also Studer, 'Le Christ', 118. See also *ep.* 185.37 and 185.40, where one detects in his use of this expression a confluence of his arguments against both the Donatists and Pelagians, and my discussion of these passages below, pp. 200–2.

[154] Note the linkage of 'praesumere' and 'gloriari' at *ciu.* 17.4 (CCL 48.557). See, for example, his criticism of those 'qui tam potentes sibi uidentur, ut sine dei dono atque adiutorio humana sufficientia diuina possint inplere mandata' (quoted above, p. 108 n. 150). Augustine's polemic against those who believe themselves capable of fulfilling divine commands without God's assistance clearly echoes criticism elsewhere of the Pelagians: *pecc. mer.* 2.7, 2.13, *gr. et pecc. or.* 1.50, *gr. et lib. arb.* 12.24, *corrept.* 9.24. *c. Iul. imp.* 1.106, but also *ep.* 140.36, *en. Ps.* 31.2.1, 31.2.10, 31.2.18, 58.18–19, 143.2, *s.* 100.3; 145.3, 145.5, *c. Max.* 2.12.2.

as gifts of God mediated to man through Christ.[155] It is at this point in Augustine's exposition that the similarity between Pelagian and Ciceronian conceptions of virtue becomes clear. After AD 412, he frequently accuses the Pelagians of presuming on themselves (*praesumere in se*) as the source of virtue. His use of Rom 10:3 at this juncture is a further indication that he is applying an anti-Pelagian analysis to those who he says 'belong to Babylon'.[156]

Augustine's decision to include the Israelites among those 'adversaries' who 'belong to Babylon' reflects the symbolic function he assigns to their history. At some times, Israel symbolizes the city of God,[157] while at others it foreshadows the history and destiny of those political or ecclesial groups that choose to disregard divine sovereignty.[158] In the context of Augustine's interpretation of Hannah's canticle, the employment of Rom 10:3 invites substitution of 'Pelagians' or 'pagans' for the 'Jews' referred to.[159]

---

[155] See *ciu.* 17.4 (CCL 48.560): 'ac per hoc *non glorietur prudens in sua prudentia, et non glorietur potens in sua potentia, et non glorietur diues in diuitiis suis; sed in hoc glorietur, qui gloriatur, intellegere et scire dominum et facere iudicium et iustitiam in medio terrae* [Jer 9:23–4]. non parua ex parte intellegit et scit dominum, qui intellegit et scit etiam hoc a domino sibi dari, ut intellegat et sciat dominum. *quid enim habes*, ait apostolus, *quod non accepisti? si autem et accepisti, quid gloriaris, quasi non acceperis* [1 Cor 4:7]? id est, quasi a te ipso tibi sit, unde gloriaris. facit autem iudicium et iustitiam, qui recte uiuit. recte autem uiuit, qui obtemperat praecipienti deo; et *finis praecepti*, id est, ad quod refertur praeceptum, *caritas est de corde puro et conscientia bona a fide non ficta* [1 Tim 1:5]. porro ista *caritas*, sicut Iohannes apostolus testatur, *ex deo est* [1 Jn 4:7]. facere igitur iudicium et iustitiam ex deo est'.

[156] See *ciu.* 17.4 (CCL 48.557): 'haec dicuntur aduersariis ciuitatis dei ad Babyloniam pertinentibus, de sua uirtute praesumentibus, in se, non in domino gloriantibus, ex quibus sunt etiam carnales Israelitae, terrenae Hierusalem ciues terrigenae, qui, ut dicit apostolus, *ignorantes dei iustitiam* (id est, quam dat homini deus, qui solus est iustus atque iustificans [cf. Rom 3:26]) *et suam uolentes constituere* (id est uelut a se sibi partam, non ab illo inpertitam) *iustitiae dei non sunt subiecti* [Rom 10:3], utique quia superbi, de suo putantes, non de dei, posse placere se deo, qui est deus scientiarum atque ideo et arbiter conscientiarum, ibi uidens cogitationes hominum, quoniam uanae sunt, si hominum sunt et ab illo non sunt'. For anti-Pelagian applications of Rom 10:3, see, for example, *ep.* 140.50, 140.54, 140.71–3, 140.83, 177.14, 196.7, *spir. et litt.* 15, 20, 22, 50, 59, *nat. et gr.* 1, 36, 47, *perf. ius.* 22, *gr. et pecc. or.* 1.46, *gr. et lib. arb.* 24, *c. Iul. imp.* 1.37, 1.141, *ep.* 177.14, *en. Ps.* 30.2.1.6, 30.2.1.13, 58.7, and *s.* 131.10.

[157] See *ciu.* 15.2 and *ep.* 196.16.

[158] See *ciu.* 18.32. M. Pontet, *L'Exégèse de saint Augustin prédicateur* (Paris, 1945), 194, remarks, 'La prophétie devient histoire, l'histoire devient prophétie.' See G. Strauss, *Schriftgebrauch, Schriftauslegung und Schriftbeweis bei Augustin* (Tübingen, 1959), 109–13, on the transposition of events in history. On Augustine's use of Jews as a symbol of religious and political attitudes to justice contrary to his own, see T. Raveau, 'Adversus Iudaeos. Antisemitismus bei Augustinus?', *Signum pietatis. Festgabe für Cornelius P. Mayer OSA, zum 60 Geburtstag*, ed. A. Zumkeller (Würzburg, 1989), 37–51, at 46, Müller, *Geschichtsbewußtsein*, 196–206. See also P. Fredriksen, '*Exaecati occulta iustitia dei*: Augustine on Jews and Judaism', *Journal of Early Christian Studies* 3 (1995), 299–324, and P. Fredriksen, 'Augustine and Israel: *Interpretatio ad litteram*, Jews, and Judaism in Augustine's Theology of History', *Studia patristica: Papers Presented to the Thirteenth International Conference on Patristic Studies held at Oxford, 1999*, vol. 38, ed. M. Wiles and E. Yarnold (Leuven, 2001), 119–35.

[159] In AD 418, Augustine explicitly states at *ep.* 196.7 that Rom 10:3 can be applied to the Pelagians, who are Jews 'not in name, but . . . by virtue of committing the same error'. See also *gr. et lib. arb.* 24–5 (AD 426/27), where Augustine first applies Rom 10:3 to Jews, then to the Pelagians.

Against the backdrop of his discussions in Books 10 and 17 of Christ's role as the high priest and mediator, the just man who justifies the members of his body, Augustine returns in Book 19 to the argument of Book 2 against the assumption that Rome had ever been a commonwealth.[160] He begins a discussion of the nature of virtue, insisting that virtue attributed to the mind and not to God is actually sin.[161] By implication, Augustine suggests that Rome's justice remained consistently deficient because its worship of demons prevented it from seeking virtue in the love of the true God. However, Augustine's well-known dismissal in this chapter of Roman 'virtues' as vices is not the point of his argument; it serves only as a foil for his discussion of the limits of true virtue, and of justice in particular (19.25). Far more significant is his argument that since true virtue resides in God and is not proper to the soul, even Christians who seek virtue in the love of the true God can, because of original sin, know this virtue only imperfectly (19.27). They experience peace, for example, as consolation in the midst of misery, rather than as the true beatitude that is known only after death. 'True justice' for pilgrim members of the city of God consists in sharing with others the forgiveness of sins, rather than in the achievement of a perfected virtue.[162] Given this true, but partial, experience of justice on the part of believers, Augustine concludes that, in the prayer (*oratio*) which characterizes 'the entire city of God on pilgrimage in the world', its citizens cry out in unison, 'forgive us our sins as we forgive those who sin against us' (Mt 6:12).[163] Augustine once again unites Roman pagan and Pelagian conceptions of virtue into a unity in contrast to his own understanding of civic virtue.[164] At the same time, the anti-Pelagian context of his remarks

---

[160] See my discussion of that argument and reference to the relevant passages above, pp. 10–19.

[161] See *ciu.* 19.25 (CCL 48.696): 'proinde uirtutes, quas habere sibi uidetur, per quas imperat corpori et uitiis, ad quodlibet adipiscendum uel tenendum rettulerit nisi ad deum, etiam ipsae uitia sunt potius quam uirtutes. nam licet a quibusdam tunc uerae atque honestae putentur esse uirtutes, cum referuntur ad se ipsas nec propter aliud expetuntur, etiam tunc inflatae ac superbae sunt, et ideo non uirtutes, sed uitia iudicanda sunt'.

[162] See *ciu.* 19.27 (CCL 48.697): 'pax autem nostra propria et hic est cum deo per fidem et in aeternum erit cum illo per speciem. sed hic siue illa communis siue nostra propria talis est pax, ut solacium miseriae sit potius quam beatitudinis gaudium. ipsa quoque nostra iustitia, quamuis uera sit propter uerum boni finem, ad quem refertur, tamen tanta est in hac uita, ut potius remissione peccatorum constet quam perfectione uirtutum'.

[163] See *ciu.* 19.27 (CCL 48.697): 'testis est oratio totius ciuitatis dei, quae peregrinatur in terris. per omnia quippe membra sua clamat ad deum: *dimitte nobis debita nostra, sicut et nos dimittimus debitoribus nostris*' (Mt 6:12).

[164] See *ciu.* 19.27 (CCL 48.698): 'quis ita uiuere se praesumat, ut dicere deo: *dimitte nobis debita nostra* [Mt 6:12] necesse non habeat nisi homo elatus? nec uero magnus, sed inflatus ac tumidus, cui per iustitiam resistit, qui gratiam largitur humilibus. propter quod scriptum est: *deus superbis resistit, humilibus autem dat gratiam*' (Jas 4:6, 1 Pt 5:5). It should be borne in mind, however, that although Augustine quotes Mt 6:12 frequently throughout his anti-Pelagian writings contemporary with the *City of God*, he also cites the passage prior to the Pelagian controversy, notably at *c. ep. Parm.* 2.20,

is demonstrated by his criticism of those who presume that their justice is complete and that they have no need to pray for forgiveness of sins. He reiterates that even in just human beings, reason is not free of concupiscence. Consequently, it does not opt for virtue without a struggle against the effects of original sin.[165] As evidence for this principle, he observes that even when the soul performs a good deed, moral weakness emerges in the act, at least in some minor form, perhaps a casual remark or fleeting thought.[166] Augustine thus closes the argument that he began in Book 2 concerning Rome's status as a commonwealth. In effect, he argues that the just society is penitential. True justice requires believers to seek from God the forgiveness of their sins and the grace to perform good works.[167]

CONCLUSION

Augustine's well-known rejoinder to Cicero that only that city established and governed by Christ can be just requires him, for coherence, to create a new religious myth. Drawing primarily on the Pauline epistles, Augustine envisions a unity between Christ and his followers in which God mediates justice through the incarnate Word, in the form of divine mystery. At the origin of this revelation is the supreme act of divine humility. In order to understand and worship the true God in this mystery, human beings must abandon reliance upon their own capacity to produce and sustain virtue. Faith in a mystery that is impenetrable to reason, accompanied by a humility that renounces the self as the source and repository of virtue, allows members of Christ's body to perceive the hidden, deleterious influence of moral ignorance and weakness on the soul. For Augustine, several consequences

---

Cresc. 2.35, and *c. litt. Pet.* 2.237, against Donatists who refuse to acknowledge the presence of sinners in their sect. See also *uirg.* 48, where the same passage is quoted in an admonition which occurs outside both Donatist and Pelagian contexts. Once again, it ought to be acknowledged that many of Augustine's arguments against the Pelagians apply as well to other Christian conceptions of virtue. See my remarks above, pp. 107–11.

[165] See *ciu.* 19.27 (CCL 48.697): 'quia enim deo quidem subdita, in hac tamen condicione mortali et corpore corruptibili, quod adgrauat animam, non perfecte uitiis imperat ratio, ideo necessaria est iustis talis oratio. nam profecto quamquam imperetur, nequaquam sine conflictu uitiis imperatur'.

[166] It should be noted that this argument is also found in his earlier, anti-Pelagian treatise *De perfectione iustitiae hominis*. See *ciu.* 19.27 (CCL 48.697): 'et utique subrepit aliquid in hoc loco infirmitatis etiam bene confligenti siue hostibus talibus uictis subditisque dominanti, unde si non facili operatione, certe labili locutione aut uolatili cogitatione peccetur'. Cf. *perf. ius.* 44 (CSEL 42.47): '*dimitte nobis debita nostra* [Mt 6:12]. quod, nisi fallor, non opus esset dicere, si numquam uel in lapsu linguae uel in oblectanda cogitatione eiusdem peccati desideriis aliquantum consentiremus'.

[167] See *ciu.* 19.27 (CCL 48.689): 'hic itaque in unoquoque iustitia est, ut oboedienti deus homini, animus corpori, ratio autem uitiis etiam repugnantibus imperet, uel subigendo uel resistendo, atque ut ab ipso deo petatur et meritorum gratia et uenia delictorum ac de acceptis bonis gratiarum actio persoluatur'.

follow from this faith and humility. They enable Christians to struggle continually against moral ignorance and weakness. Aided by Christ's grace, they are enlightened and strengthened by his examples and sacraments. In this way, they are able to advance toward true virtue. Through this moral progress, believers acknowledge their continuing sinfulness. They confess their sins and pray for forgiveness, assured that Christ's death has already won for them the divine pardon which they cannot secure for themselves, either by religious ritual or philosophical reason. They believe that in Christ's death, God has made himself vulnerable to death. As a result, they renounce religious or philosophical attempts to dispel or disguise the spiritual darkness surrounding death as illusory; instead, they are confident that, along with fear, they will also experience the divine consolation that Christ, as head of the body, speaks in them. This 'exchange' of discourse between the head and members symbolizes for Augustine the process of justification itself.

Thus Augustine rejects Cicero's confidence in reason's domination of the mind as it chooses to act virtuously.[168] He illustrates his own view by imagining Christ on the cross, determined to exchange his speech with that of sinful human beings. Against Cicero's view that the source of virtue is reason as it converses primarily within itself, as when it draws inspiration from moral examples, Augustine sees this dialogue as a conversation with Christ. As a result, human virtue is a product of a direct, divine mediation, not of human reason alone. By explaining the genesis of human virtue in this manner, Augustine ensures that it will be conditioned by humility. He seeks to refute philosophical claims to moral and spiritual autonomy, and thus to underscore the soul's moral dependence upon God. He also seeks to overcome the threat to the just society implied in the Pelagian assumption that the practical requirements of justice and attendant virtues can be thoroughly understood. Instead, Augustine argues, virtue can indeed be known and willed, but never perfectly. By acknowledging that perfect virtue is the sole prerogative of Christ, and by stressing confession of sins and thanksgiving for pardon received, the body of Christ, which is the church, can confidently acquire a limited justice during its pilgrimage through the earthly city.

Just how confidently does Augustine suppose Christians can reasonably know the practical requirements of the just life? If Christ must be viewed by believers as a man whose perfect virtue can never be equalled by anyone else in this life, can his followers ever be confident that their understanding

---

[168] See my discussion of Cicero's argument above, pp. 61–3.

of the moral life is correct? If each of their moral judgments is conditioned by ignorance and weakness, should they ever feel justified in acting? Finally, what role do the scriptures, as God's word, play in revealing the requirements of the just life and in offering examples of just conduct capable of inspiring believers? In the next chapter, we shall look at Augustine's approach to the scriptures in relation to the just society. In particular, we shall examine the criteria for interpreting the scriptures which he employs to determine the practical requirements of justice. In his discussion of these criteria, however, Augustine regularly warns that the proper interpretation of the scriptural word is undermined by the same moral presumption that leads human beings to assume the integrity of their own moral judgments. In his view, a true understanding of the moral norms contained in the scriptures, and of their implications for particular moral judgments, depends upon their reception by the soul through grace as it progresses in humility toward an ever more perfect virtue.

CHAPTER 4

Divine eloquence and virtue in the scriptures

In Chapter 1 we observed that Augustine took note of Cicero's emphasis in *De re publica* on the statesman's use of oratory to establish justice in the Roman commonwealth.[1] It is therefore not surprising that in the *City of God* Augustine treats the scriptures in parallel fashion as God's oratory. For example, he acknowledges the role of divine pronouncements (*eloquia*) from the Old Testament in the formation of the Hebrew *res publica*. Augustine claims that these scriptural passages are fulfilled in the New Testament in relation to the city of God.[2] Finally, he argues that the law which God gave to the Hebrew people commanding that he alone be worshipped (Ex 22:20) is fulfilled in God's 'city'. It is a law that he says is 'not obscure', but is 'written in Hebrew' and 'widely known', referring to the diffusion of the Old Testament throughout the Roman Empire. As a result of its obedience to this law, he concludes, the city of God, and not Rome, is where justice is found.[3] Augustine's analogy between the scriptures as a divine discourse and the role of political oratory in Roman society offers a starting point for exploring the many complex processes by which he believes that Christ persuades members of his body to act justly.[4] Augustine is aware of the argument common to Cicero and to Roman culture generally that

---

[1] See *ciu.* 2.21, where Augustine cites Cicero, *De re publica* 2.42.69 and 5.1. See my discussion above, pp. 19–24.

[2] See *ciu.* 18.41 (CCL 48.637–8): 'at uero gens illa, ille populus, illa ciuitas, illa res publica, illi Israelitae, quibus credita sunt eloquia dei [. . .] propheticis, hoc est diuinis, uocibus, quamuis per homines, in illa ciuitate populo commendata sunt, non argumentationum concertationibus inculcata, ut non hominis ingenium, sed dei eloquium contemnere formidaret, qui illa cognosceret'. Augustine offers the same argument at *ciu.* 10.32. He reasons in similar terms at *ciu.* 2.19, 17.4.

[3] See *ciu.* 19.23.

[4] It should be remembered that the 'city of God' (*ciuitas dei*), properly constituted, consists in the angels and saints who live in beatitude with God in eternity. See *ciu.* 11.9, 11.28, 12.9, 15.1, 18.49–50, 20.10, *cat. rud.* 31.37. Members of this 'city' have no need for divine instruction. The scriptures as *eloquium dei* (or *eloquia diuina*) provide guidance in living justly to those persons whose love of God and practice of virtue signify their participation in the earthly pilgrimage toward the city of God. See *ciu.* 1.35, 9.5, 11.1, 20.9, *s.* 105.9. See also W. Blümer, 'Eloquentia', *Augustinus-Lexikon*, vol. 2, ed. C. Mayer (Basle, 1996–2002), 775–97, at 780–1.

examples of Rome's best citizens (*optimi uiri*), as narrated in political oratory and other traditional literature, both define civic virtues and urge their
imitation.[5] His alternative approach to divine oratory provides more, however, than a comparison of biblical examples of virtue with their Roman
counterparts. Augustine's account of the role of the scriptures in the formation of the just society subordinates the force of the speaker's eloquence to
the function of grace within the soul. Against the weight of ignorance and
weakness, he says, reason cannot arrive at particular moral judgments with
the aid of examples alone. God uses sacraments (*sacramenta*) and mysteries
(*mysteria*) as divine figures of speech in order to draw believers through
the language of the scriptures into the hidden aspects of his wisdom and
justice.

These next two chapters will examine Augustine's explanation of the
process through which the human soul comprehends scriptural teaching
concerning the nature of true virtue. His account assumes that Christ mediates to the soul understandings of the deepest aspects of virtue under the
form of mystery. As demonstrated in Chapter 3, the heart of Christ's mediation is formed by the unity of his divine and human natures, and this
unity enables him to communicate virtue to the human soul as if in a
dialogue. Without this mediation, the soul is not able to overcome ignorance and weakness, and it sinfully presumes to understand the scriptural
word. At best, virtue apprehended from the scriptures in this manner only
appears to be virtue. However, as we shall see in the course of these next two
chapters, Augustine warns that Christ's wisdom, through which believers
are gradually able to comprehend the lessons of the scriptures, is imparted
to the soul only partially, through mystery. As will be shown, Augustine
insists as a consequence that the deeper meanings of virtues signified in the
scriptures are only partially knowable to the soul while it still struggles in
this life against the effects of original sin. He argues that the same faith
and humility with which Christians approach the incarnation as mystery is
required in interpreting scriptural sacraments and mysteries, as they reveal
true understandings of virtue.

FOUNDATIONS

Augustine finds a model for this mediated understanding of justice in
the theophanies of the Old Testament. For example, he sees God's

---

[5] Nectarius passionately pleads this point in correspondence with Augustine. See *ep.* 103 and my
discussion above, pp. 6–7 n. 1–3.

self-revelation to Moses on Mount Sinai (for example, at Exodus 33) as communicating the divine presence through a tension between God's self-revelation and hiddenness. Augustine holds that a similar tension characterizes the communication of the divine presence as it is apprehended through sacraments (*sacramenta*) in the scriptures and liturgy.[6] He maintains that a divine communication within the soul is essential for a true understanding of virtues, such as justice, which even the finest examples of virtue as proposed by Cicero and other Roman authors cannot provide. Augustine, therefore, couples the force of biblical examples with the effect of grace on the mind, a pairing which he frequently refers to as a sacrament.[7] For Augustine, the relationship between examples and sacraments parallels the relationship between knowledge (*scientia*) and wisdom (*sapientia*). His explanation of these relationships shows how grace illuminates the religious text or symbol in the mind of the believer, not in order to make its meaning clearer, but to accustom the mind to appreciate it as a mystery which can never be fully grasped.

But how are the dynamics of knowing justice in the form of mystery reflected in Augustine's approach to particular moral questions, especially those concerned with a just society? How, for Augustine, can Christians who long to live as citizens in Christ's commonwealth ever know with confidence what justice requires of them? To answer these questions it is useful to examine Augustine's writings concerning the just use of violence, a vexed question that represents a limit case for determining just action.[8] Much of his writing to or about public officials addresses their frequent obligation to judge people accused of serious crimes.[9] Elsewhere he explores the moral dilemmas inherent in the defence of one's homeland, on one occasion arguing that the New Testament does not altogether prohibit recourse to violence, though the Roman concept of a 'just war' does fall far short

---

[6] The term *sacramentum* may well be the most semantically dense term in Augustine's theological vocabulary. Its basic definition is 'sacred sign' (*signum sacrum*). See *doctr. chr.* 3.30–2 (CSEL 80.87–8), *ciu.* 10.5 (CCL 42.277). See also *ep.* 138.7, *ep.* 98.9, *c. Faust.* 19.16. Yet the term's range of meanings, theological and exegetical, extends far beyond its vastly more limited usage within modern Christian theology. See my discussion below, pp. 147–59, as well as the helpful treatment by E. Cutrone, 'Sacraments', *Augustine through the Ages: An Encyclopedia*, ed. A. Fitzgerald et al. (Grand Rapids, 1999), 741–7 (with bibliography).

[7] I develop these points below, in Chapter 5.

[8] Note that at *ciu.* 19.6, as he approaches his argument concerning the lack of true justice in the Roman commonwealth (*ciu.* 19.21–7), he discusses the dilemma facing the magistrate who must decide whether to apply torture in order to seek confession of crimes, or whether to condemn a convicted criminal to death.

[9] Augustine discusses the issue at *ciu.* 19.6. But see also *ep.* 153. For other correspondence, see *ep.* 86, 91.1, 95.3, 100, 104.1, 104.7–10, 133.1–3, 134.2–4, 138.14, 139.2, 151, 155.11, 173.3, 185.21–3, 204.3, 8*, 9*.2, 10*.3–4. See also *en. Ps.* 50, *s.* 13.7–9, and Possidius, *Vita Augustini* 20.

of the standard of non-violence advocated in the Bible.[10] He also recognizes that even ordinary Christians are at times confronted with dilemmas over the just use of violence. In a sermon he preached after the assassination by townspeople (most likely in Hippo) of a public official accused of extorting oppressive duties on imported goods, Augustine reproves heads of households for neglecting to speak out in order to prevent those in their charge from colluding in homicide.[11]

In these and similar cases he discusses, Augustine clearly doubts that reason, impaired as it is by ignorance and weakness, can ever arrive at just judgments. True, in other cases he believes that the mind can achieve complete moral clarity. He is convinced, for example, that lying is always wrong – he states that he cannot imagine a situation in which lying would be justifiable, even in defence of one's homeland.[12] It follows for him that someone who refrains from lying in a given instance has certainly acted justly, as far as the commandment not to lie is concerned. Yet, he recognizes that, owing to the effects of original sin, many moral obligations cannot easily be determined.[13] Augustine believes that few actions are as morally unambiguous as lying: in the vast majority of situations, moral action is far more difficult to define.[14]

A prime example is the decision whether or not to kill. Both natural law and the Decalogue (Ex 20:13, Dt 5:17) make clear that murder is immoral.[15] However, not all homicide is murder for Augustine: just war, the just use of capital punishment, and even God's command to Abraham to sacrifice

---

[10] See *ep.* 138 and my discussion of it below, pp. 135–9.
[11] See *s.* 302. The sermon was preached on the feastday of St Laurence (11 August), but the year is uncertain.
[12] For the general principles, see *mend.* 21.42, *c. mend.* 18.37, *ench.* 18, and the discussions by S. Bok, *Lying: Moral Choice in Public and Private Life* (New York, 1978), 35–6, and C. Kirwan, *Augustine* (London/New York, 1989), 196–204. For the particular case of lies told in the interest of defence of one's homeland, see *c. mend.* 15.32–17.34, where Augustine refuses any justification of Rahab's decision to lie to Jericho officials in her effort to save two Israelite spies (Jos 2). Rist, *Augustine*, 191–9, discusses lying as the primary among a small number of moral absolutes in Augustine's thought. For comparison of Augustine's position on lying with that of other early Christian writers, in particular, Jerome, see B. Ramsey, 'Two Traditions on Lying and Deception in the Ancient Church', *The Thomist* 49 (1985), 504–33.
[13] See, for example, *perf. ius.* 18, where he discusses the negative consequences which often inadvertently arise from deficient moral judgments. Echoes of ignorance and weakness are present in his argument.
[14] At *ep.* 55.23, Augustine discusses the difficulty in arriving at a proper understanding of the obligation to keep the Sabbath holy (Ex 16:29, 20:8, Dt 5:12). See also *ep.* 138, where he discusses difficulties involved in interpreting the various scriptural passages obliging Christians to respond to violence with non-violence (Mt 5:39–41, 1 Thes 5:15, Rom 12:17).
[15] See, for example, *ciu.* 18.41 (CCL 48.637): '*non homicidium facies* [Ex 20:13], *non furaberis* [Ex 20:15], et cetera huius modi, non haec ora humana, sed oracula diuina fuderunt'. See also Rist, *Augustine*, 191, 194–5.

Isaac (Gn 22:2) are all cases in point.[16] Moreover, the moral rectitude of some actions can be undermined solely by the unjust intention of the agent. King David was guilty of murder because he posted Uriah on the front line of battle during a just war (2 Sam 12:2–6). In this case, intention alone differentiates a just deed from a heinous crime.[17] The difficulty of interpreting divine commands in the scriptures and discerning the intentions of the human heart both complicate moral decision-making immeasurably. For these interrelated reasons, Augustine believes, reason cannot arrive at truly just decisions, so long as its grasp is limited to contingent reality alone (*ratio scientiae*). To make just decisions, reason must reflect upon contingent reality against the horizon of transcendence, the abode of divine wisdom. This form of reason as it relates to wisdom (*ratio sapientiae*) requires faith enlightened by grace.[18]

By expressing moral reasoning as a function of both contingent and transcendent reality, Augustine successfully avoids sceptical or rationalist moral positions. Nevertheless, he obviously finds something attractive in both options. How he reconciles his rejection of the possibility of certainty in moral reasoning with his relative confidence about it can only be explained by turning to concepts in his ethics such as grace and mystery or sacrament (*mysterium, sacramentum*). In describing the role of these concepts in moral judgments, however, Augustine relies on analogies with classical rhetoric, principally as proposed by Cicero. This Augustinian turn to rhetoric is paradoxical because moral reflection, in its classical form, was suspicious of rhetorical influences.[19] Yet the titles of many of Augustine's writings which are significant for his ethics, such as *De praesentia dei*, *De spiritu et littera*, and *De doctrina christiana*, in addition to his *Confessions*, hint at his general approach to moral reasoning. From the word of God (*uerbum dei*) to the word of the heart (*uerbum cordis*), a full spectrum of communication metaphors marks out for him the intellectual processes associated with moral reflection.[20] Thus, in *De trinitate* he employs metaphors such as divine presence and communication, along with participation and divine illumination, in order to explain moral decision-making.[21]

---

[16] See, for example, *ciu.* 1.21, *mend.* 13.23, *ep.* 153.17. At *c. Faust* 22.5, Augustine quotes Faustus' complaint against the manner in which Moses violates the commandment not to kill, as evidenced at Ex 2:12, 12:35–6, 17:9. Augustine explicitly replies to this charge at *c. Faust.* 22.78.

[17] See *en. Ps.* 50.8, and my discussion of it below, pp. 174–9.

[18] See further discussion below, pp. 165–71.

[19] On rhetorical influences in philosophy, see Mason, *Philosophical*. Further theoretical background is provided by I. A. Richards, *The Philosophy of Rhetoric* (Oxford, 1964).

[20] See *trin.* 15.17, 15.19, together with W. Beierwaltes, 'Zu Augustins Metaphysik der Sprache', *Augustinian Studies* 2 (1971), 179–95, at 183.

[21] See, for example, *trin.* 8.5–6, where he discusses knowledge of justice in terms related to participation in the good, enjoyment of God's presence, and knowledge and love of God. Later, he describes justice

It is not at the theoretical level alone that Augustine's ethics depend upon an understanding of the role of tropes. He insists that figures of speech in the scriptures constitute necessary features of God's revelation of justice to the human mind. His view of the role of figurative language in the sacred scriptures depends upon a set of arguments which he initially uses against the Manicheans, the most fundamental of which affirms that the Old and New Testaments constitute a unified divine discourse (*eloquium dei*), one that reflects God's intention to impart sound instruction.[22] In affirming the scriptural canon as the basis for the unity of the Old and New Testaments, Augustine argues that scriptural passages are harmonious 'as if from the mouth of one speaker'.[23] He thus confutes the arguments of the Manicheans, who deny the divine inspiration of the Old Testament and significant parts of the New Testament.[24] Much of this Manichean argument springs from contradictions they perceive between various scriptural passages. Against this view, Augustine insists on the logical coherence behind the two testaments as well as between individual scriptural passages or sets of passages which seem to contradict each other.[25] He is certain that qualified, orthodox exegetes are able to resolve difficulties arising either from

as an 'inner truth present to the mind which is capable of beholding it'. See *trin.* 8.9 (CCL 50.283): 'ueritas est interior praesens animo qui eam ualet intueri'.

[22] On the use of tropes in the scriptures as divine discourse, see *doctr. chr.* 3.40. Marrou, *Saint Augustin*, 469–503, and Strauss, *Schriftgebrauch*, especially 109–48, are fundamental on the theme of the scriptures as divine discourse. For the term *eloquia dei* as used in this context, see *ciu.* 18.41, *ep.* 82.5, *trin.* 3.27 (CCL 50.158): 'de scripturis sanctis diuina eloquia', *doctr. chr.* 4.24 (CSEL 80.123): 'sunt ergo ecclesiastici uiri, qui diuina eloquia non solum sapienter, sed eloquenter etiam tractauerunt'. See also *en. Ps.* 103.4.1.

[23] See *c. Faust.* 11.6 (CSEL 25/1.321): 'quia ita sibi omnia in canonica auctoritate concordant, ut tamquam uno ore dicta iustissima et prudentissima pietate credantur et serenissimo intellectu inueniantur et sollertissima diligentia demonstrentur: non liceret de alterutro dubitare'. The same ideas are expressed at *ciu.* 18.41 (CCL 48.636): 'denique auctores nostri, in quibus non frustra sacrarum litterarum figitur et terminatur canon, absit ut inter se aliqua ratione dissentiant. unde non inmerito, cum illa scriberent, eis Deum uel per eos locutum'. See also Strauss, *Schriftgebrauch*, 68–73, O. Wermelinger, 'Le Canon des Latins au temps de Jérôme et d'Augustin', *Le Canon de l'Ancient Testament. Sa formation et son histoire*, ed. J.-D. Kästli and O. Wermelinger (Geneva, 1984), 153–210, and C. Mayer, 'Congruentia testamentorum', *Augustinus-Lexikon*, vol. 1, ed. C. Mayer (Basle, 1986–94), 1195–1201.

[24] See *c. Faust.* 1.2, 4.1, 6.1, 8.1, 9.1, 10.1, 15.1. See also R. Dodaro, '*Quid deceat uidere* (Cicero, *Orator* 70): Literary Propriety and Doctrinal Orthodoxy in Augustine of Hippo', *Orthodoxie, christianisme, histoire = Orthodoxy, Christianity, History: travaux du groupe de recherches 'Définir, maintenir et remettre en cause l'"orthodoxie" dans l'histoire du christianisme'*, ed. S. Elm et al. (Rome, 2000), 57–81, Mayer, 'Congruentia', 1197–8.

[25] See Strauss, *Schriftgebrauch*, 68–73, and R. Dodaro, 'Literary Decorum in Scriptural Exegesis: Augustine of Hippo, *Epistula* 138', *L'esegesi dei padri latini. Dalle origini à Gregorio Magno. Atti del XXVIII Incontro di studiosi dell'antichità cristiana, Roma, 6–8 maggio 1999*, vol. 1: *Parte generale – Oriente, Africa* (Rome, 2000), 159–74. The argument that the unity and divine inspiration of the Old and New Testaments can be explained, at least in part, by virtue of the capacity of the latter to clarify uses of figurative and prophetic language by the former can be traced at least to Origen, as can the rationalization of apparent incongruities between scriptural passages from arguments based on a divine plan. See Origen, *De principiis* 4.1.6–7, 4.2.9.

the use of metaphorical language or from apparent textual inconsistencies in arriving at cogent interpretations of the passages in question.[26]

The Manichean challenges and Augustine's response both depend upon a concept of God as orator speaking within the entire body of the scriptures.[27] Faced with the Manichean charge that much of the Old Testament diminishes God's dignity, Augustine is forced to argue that God composed the scriptures in accord with conventional rhetorical strategies, and that even seeming stylistic defects in the Bible can be explained in terms of the divine author's adherence to rhetorical theory.[28] Consequently, Augustine acknowledges that a divine inspiration stands behind the decisions of the human authors to make use even of elaborate rhetorical schemes, including a variety of literary genres, narrative structures, and figures of speech in communicating moral principles through what is known today as 'philosophical indirection'.[29] By this logic, God is the author of the scriptures in terms not only of their content, but of the rhetorical strategies which they employ.

Many of the Manicheans' difficulties with scripture stem from its frequent, and at times ill-suited, use of figurative language. Augustine considers this objection in the light of the occasional, strategic use of tropes endorsed by classical rhetoric. By suggesting that God, like all good orators, knows how to employ figures of speech in order to retain the readers' attention or to convey a difficult concept, Augustine underscores the cogency (*ratio*) of the figurative language in the scriptures, thereby defending the dignity of the divine orator. This rationale for God's use of metaphors, parables, and enigmas depends upon a more fundamental concept of the orator's duties as conceived by traditional rhetorical theorists: teaching (*docere*), moving or persuading (*mouere*, *persuadere*), and delighting (*delectare*) the

---

[26] See *c. Faust.* 11.6–8, *ep.* 102.38 (CSEL 34/2.578): 'sunt enim innumerabiles, quae non sunt finiendae ante fidem, ne finiatur uita sine fide, sed plane retenta iam fide ad exercendam piam delectationem mentium fidelium studiosissime requirendae et, quod in eis eluxerit, sine typho arrogantiae communicandum, quod autem latuerit, sine salutis dispendio tolerandum'.

[27] See Origen, *Commentarium in Iohannem* 1.1–8 (SC 120.148–53). Origen, *De principiis* 4.2.9, arguing on the basis of divine inspiration of the the the scriptures, affirms the obligation to account for apparent contradictions by searching out 'a meaning worthy of God'. See the discussion by M. Sheridan, '*Digne deo*: A Traditional Greek Principle of Interpretation in Latin Dress', *L'esegesi dei padri latini. Dalle origini a Gregorio Magno. Atti del XXVIII Incontro di studiosi dell'antichità cristiana, Roma, 6–8 maggio 1999*, vol. 1: *Parte generale – Oriente, Africa* (Rome, 2000), 23–40, at 36–9. See also O. Dreyer, *Untersuchungen zum Begriff des Gottgeziemenden in der Antike: mit besonderer Berücksichtigung Philons von Alexandrien* (Hildesheim, 1970).

[28] Such as regarding *abusio* or catachresis. See *doctr. chr.* 3.89, together with Strauss, *Schriftgebrauch*, 115. The gravity of this point is underscored by the fact that many of these literary features caused the young Augustine initially to reject the authority of the scriptures in favour of Manichean myths. See *conf.* 3.9.

[29] On philosophical indirection, see above, pp. 62–3 and n. 153.

audience with his words.[30] Augustine holds that the entire content of the scriptures can be interpreted through rhetorical theory.

SPEAKING FIGURATIVELY

For Augustine, it is precisely the capacity of figurative language to express multiple meanings simultaneously that makes it ideal as a medium for communicating the nature of true justice. He recognizes that, when interpreted literally, biblical precepts for right conduct confound the deeper senses of what justice demands. By way of example, he mentions Christ's encounter with the woman caught in adultery (Jn 8:3–11). The Pharisees and scribes who demand the stoning of the woman can cite divine precepts in support of their judgment (Dt 22:22–4, Lv 20:10).[31] But is the truest form of justice to be found in the harsh, literal application of these precepts, Augustine asks, or does the broader sense of justice embodied in the scriptures as a whole exceed the precepts contained in a few passages read in isolation? Augustine considered questions of interpretation such as these against the backdrop of those Platonic traditions concerned with the transcendental character of knowledge in opting for exegetical practices, such as allegory, in which to anchor his concept of mystery or sacrament.[32]

---

[30] See my discussion of these duties above, pp. 66–7. On the *officia oratoris* in general, see Cicero, *Orator* 21.69, *De oratore* 2.25.115, 2.28.121, 2.29.128, *Brutus* 49.185, *De optimo genere oratorum* 1.3: 'optimus est enim orator, qui dicendo animos audientium, et docet et delectat et permovet: docere debitum est, delectare honorarium, permovere necessarium', Quintilian, *Institutio oratoria* 3.5.2: 'Tria sunt item quae praestare debeat orator, ut doceat moueat, delectet.' See *doctr. chr.* 4.74, citing Cicero, *Orator* 21.69.

[31] See my discussion of this point below, pp. 173–9.

[32] On Augustine's use of allegory, see Marrou, *Saint Augustin*, 9–26, 484–94, J. Pépin, 'Saint Augustin et la fonction protreptique de l'allégorie', *Recherches augustiniennes* 1 (1958), 243–86, at 258–85, Strauss, *Schriftgebrauch*, 130–48, B. Prete, 'I principi esegetici di s. Agostino', *Sapienza* 8 (1966), 552–94; C. Mayer, *Die Zeichen in der geistigen Entwicklung und in der Theologie des jungen Augustinus* (Würzburg, 1969), 118–22, G. Ripianti, 'L'Allegoria o l'intellectus figuratus nel doctrina christiana di Agostino', *Revue des études augustiniennes* 18 (1972), 72–90, C. Mayer, *Die Zeichen in der geistigen Entwicklung und in der Theologie Augustins II: Die antimanichäische Epoche* (Würzburg, 1974), 294–302, C. Mayer, 'Allegoria', *Augustinus-Lexikon*, vol. 1, ed. C. Mayer (Basle, 1986–94), 233–9. To understand sacrament (*sacramentum*) in an exegetical sense as metaphor requires that it be linked in Augustinian terminology with the term 'figure' (*figura*) or 'signification' (*significatio*), and with 'similitude' (*similitudo*). B. Studer, '*Sacramentum et exemplum* chez saint Augustin', *Recherches augustiniennes* 10 (1975), 103–4, provides evidence for this association in Augustine's thought. References to the death and resurrection of Christ considered as sacrament are treated in Augustinian exegetical terminology as *signa translata*. On the meaning and importance of this term for Augustine's exegetical theory see *doctr. chr.* 2.15, along with Mayer, *Die Zeichen . . . II: Die antimanichäische Epoche*, 102–3, K. Pollmann, Doctrina christiana. *Untersuchungen zu den Anfängen der christlichen Hermeneutik unter besonderer Berücksichtigung von Augustinus*, De doctrina christiana (Fribourg, 1996), 180–3, and R. Bernard, '*In figura*: Terminology pertaining to Figurative Exegesis in the Works of Augustine of Hippo', unpublished dissertation, Princeton University, 1984, 39–57. Also helpful

In his treatise *Ad inquisitiones Ianuarii*, the relationship between scriptural and liturgical sacraments as symbols of the just life is more clearly outlined than anywhere else in his writings.[33] In this work, Augustine examines various senses of sacrament as parts of a discourse which began in the scriptures and continues in present-day preaching and ritual of the church. Considering the three-day liturgical commemoration of Christ's death and resurrection concluding with Easter, Augustine defines the exegetical-liturgical category of sacrament as a kind of passage (*transitus*), in order to illustrate the traditional theological connection between Christ's transformation from death to life, and the spiritual transformation from death to life within the believer.[34] By using this idea in several ways and making it the central theme of the treatise, he also explains the just life as a series of interconnected spiritual 'passages' which draw the believer who acts justly into the hidden, yet remotely perceptible, enjoyment of blessedness beyond death. Sacred scripture designates this blessedness, which Augustine calls a 'delight in justice' (*delectatio iustitiae*), as the sole reliable guide for the Christian, who is uncertain how to interpret and fulfil the range of biblical precepts concerning justice. Once again, Augustine endeavours to avoid an overly restrictive interpretation of these precepts. He uses the one commandment which cannot be interpreted literally – the commandment to keep holy the Sabbath – as the key to establishing a fuller sense of justice which lies beyond the limits of language.

First he considers the multiple 'passages' required in order to understand how symbols function in biblical language and liturgical ritual, and then suggests God's reason for employing them. He begins with the moveable character of the date of Easter, which he interprets as a symbol of the

---

in this regard are the observations of Pio de Luis Vizcaíno, *Los hechos de Jesús en la predicación de san Augustín. La retórica clásica al servicio de la exégesis patrística* (Rome, 1983), 187–223, especially 187–206.

[33] The treatise is dated to AD 400. It is more conventionally identified in Augustine's literary corpus as *ep.* 54 and 55 (CSEL 34/2.158–213). The text which concerns us is *ep.* 55. On the importance of this work for Augustine's liturgical theory, see A. Mandouze, 'A propos de *sacramentum* chez saint Augustin. Polyvalence lexicologique et foisonnement théologique', *Mélanges offerts à Mademoiselle Christine Mohrmann*, ed. L. Engles et al. (Utrecht, 1963), 222–32, Mayer, *Die Zeichen . . . II: Die antimanichäische Epoche*, 398–415, Studer, '*Sacramentum*', 95–6.

[34] See *ep.* 55.17 (CSEL 34/2.187): 'in eam nobis ex hac uita fit transitus, quem dominus noster Iesus Christus sua passione praemonstrare ac consecrare dignatus est'. Augustine makes a similar point in a later, parallel text which I discuss in Chapter 5. See *ep.* 140.30 (CSEL 44.181): 'nam ille hanc rem sacramento suae passionis resurrectionisque significans carnem mutauit de mortalitate ad inmortalitatem, uitam uero non mutauit de uetustate in nouitatem, qui numquam fuit in impietate, unde transiret ad pietatem'. See also *c. Max.* 1.2 (PL 42.745), where Augustine applies this interpretation of 'sacrament' or 'mystery' to baptism. In this connection, see Pépin, 'Saint Augustin', and Mayer, *Die Zeichen . . . in der Theologie des jungen Augustinus*, 341–8. On the interchangeable relationship between *sacramentum* and *mysterium*, see my discussion below, pp. 151–3.

'movement' from death to life in Christ. He finds the same symbolism present in the passage of the three days of the Easter celebration, noting that the Hebrew word at the root of the Latin *pascha* means 'passage'.[35] In this way he sees that the outward features of the liturgical celebration, the symbols or sacraments, figuratively highlight the feast's deeper meaning, a transformation within the soul of the believer.[36] Behind his enthusiasm for this liturgical symbolism lies a Platonic sensitivity to the movement from visible to invisible orders of reality.[37] He brings justice into the discussion by speaking metaphorically of Christ as the 'sun of justice' (*sol iustitiae*).[38] Reflecting on this symbolism, he observes that the soul is distracted from its contemplation of this interior light (divine justice) by the external attractiveness of the world (which can include even the performance of good works). Human beings become ever more obsessed with these 'lower' objects, as interest in them is transformed into the desire to possess them. Desire undergoes this corruption both as a result of the attraction of material objects and activities and as a consequence of the approval from others who encourage their possession.[39]

Augustine also defends the ritual use of sacramental ornaments in the eucharist, such as water, bread, oil, and wine, because God similarly employs sacraments in the scriptures.[40] He suggests that both liturgical and biblical sacraments are intended to wean the soul away from its obsession with

---

[35] See *ep.* 55.2 (CSEL 34/2.171): 'sed ab eo, quod transitur, ut dixi, a morte ad uitam, Hebraeo uerbo res [passio] appelata est. in quo eloquio pascha transitus dicitur [. . .] transitus ergo de hac uita mortali in aliam uitam inmortalem, hoc est enim de morte ad uitam in passione et in resurrectione domini commendatur'. On this concept in Augustine and its Latin Christian background, see C. Mohrmann, *Etudes sur le latin des chrétiens*, 2nd edn (Rome, 1962), 1:205–22.

[36] Elsewhere, Augustine underscores the power of liturgy to recall the events of Christ's death and resurrection which are recorded in the the scriptures. See *en. Ps.* 21.2.1 (CCL 38.121): 'passio domini, sicut scimus semel facta est; semel enim Christus mortuus est, iustus pro iniustis [. . .] sed tamen anniuersaria recordatio quasi repraesentat quod olim factum est'.

[37] *ep.* 55.8 (below, n. 38) in conjunction with Plato, *Phaedrus* 250B.

[38] See *ep.* 55.8 (CSEL 34/2.177–8): 'adtende nunc, quod in Prouerbiis legimus: *sapiens sicut sol permanet, stultus autem sicut luna mutatur* [Eccl 27:12]. et quis est *sapiens qui permanet*, nisi sol ille iustitiae, de quo dicitur: *ortus est mihi iustitiae sol* [Mal 4:2], et quem sibi non fuisse ortum in die nouissima plangentes impii dicturi sunt: *et iustitiae lumen non inluxit nobis et sol non ortus est nobis?* [Wis 5:6] nam istum carnis oculis uisibilem *solem oriri facit super bonos et malos* deus, qui *etiam pluit super iustos et iniustos* [Mt 5:45]. ducuntur autem semper ex rebus uisibilibus ad inuisibilia congruae similitudines'. On this theme in general, see M. Wallraff, *Christus verus sol. Sonnenverehrung und Christentum in der Spätantike* (Münster, 2001).

[39] See *ep.* 55.9 (CSEL 34/2.179): 'mutatur ergo in deterius ad exteriora progrediens et *in uita sua proiciens intima sua* [Eccl 10:10]; et hoc terrae, id est eis, *qui terrena sapiunt* [Phil 3:19], melius uidetur, *cum laudatur peccator in desideriis animae suae et, qui iniqua gerit, benedicitur* [Ps 9[10]:24]'. The juxtaposition of Phil 3:19 and Ps 10(11):3 expresses the enhanced rhetorical influence of popular approval upon the spiritually deteriorating 'desires of one's own heart'.

[40] See *ep.* 55.13 (below, n. 41). At *doctr. chr.* 3.87–8, Augustine affirms the general principle that the divine author makes use of rhetorical ornamentation in the scriptures.

the outer, visible world, and draw it into the light of the inner world, symbolized by the sun of justice.[41] Contemplation of this inner light, which Augustine likens to repose in God, symbolizes the soul's desire for divine justice (understood as the unrivalled love of God). When Augustine adds that it is difficult to explain why unadorned truths lack the religious appeal that embellishments of sacred mysteries are able to convey, he once again reveals his conviction in the powerful force of rhetoric upon human beings, who may be led to a deeper love for God by the artful play of signs (*signa*) upon the soul. This ascension to higher orders of reality is represented by two 'passages'. The believer's attention must first be drawn away from baser entertainments into the richness of Christian symbolism. Once this has been achieved, the believer must pass beyond the surface of the symbol, in order to arrive at its inner meaning (*spiritus*). Both 'passages' stimulate the imagination, startling it into fresh awarenesses which excite the desire for a holy rest in God alone.[42]

To clarify his point concerning the parallel relationship between liturgical and scriptural ornamentation and the 'passage' from an outer to an inner reality which they are intended to stimulate, Augustine begins a long discussion of yet another 'passage' symbolized by the Easter triduum: the figurative sense in which the commandment to observe the Sabbath (Ex 20:8, Dt 5:12) should be interpreted.[43] He is aware that the Easter celebration marks the transformation of the Hebrew Sabbath, observed on the last day of the week, to the Lord's day (*dies dominica*). In this sense, the Sabbath itself undergoes a 'passage' from the old to the new dispensation.[44]

---

[41] See *ep.* 55.9 (CSEL 34/2.179): 'ac per hoc spiritus sanctus de uisibilibus ad inuisibilia et de corporalibus ad spiritalia sacramenta similitudinem ducens transitum illum de alia uita in aliam uitam, quod pascha nominatur, a quarta decima luna uoluit obseruari'. See also *ep.* 55.13 (CSEL 34/2.184–5): 'si quae autem figurae similitudinum non tantum de caelo et sideribus sed etiam de creatura inferiore ducuntur ad dispensationem sacramentorum, eloquentia quaedam est doctrinae salutaris mouendo affectui discentium accommodata a uisibilibus ad inuisibilia, a corporalibus ad spiritalia, a temporalibus ad aeterna'. See Augustine's references to the 'similitudines' that he describes as 'congruae' at *ep.* 55.8 (above, n. 38). A similar reference occurs at *ep.* 55.13 (CSEL 34/2.183): 'sed ad rem sacrate significandum similitudines habitas religiosissima deuotione suscipimus sicut de cetera creatura de uentis, de mari, de terra . . . ad sermonem quidem multipliciter, ad celebrationem uero sacramentorum iam christiana libertate parcissime sicut de aqua, de frumento, de uino, de oleo'. See also *ep.* 55.21 (CSEL 34/2.191–2): 'omnia ista pertinent, quae figurate nobis insinuantur; plus enim mouent et accendunt amorem, quam si nuda sine ullis sacramentorum similitudinibus ponerentur'.

[42] See *ep.* 55.21 (CSEL 34/2.192): 'credo, quod ipse animae motus, quam diu rebus adhuc terrenis implicatur, pigrius inflammatur; si feratur ad similitudines corporales et inde referatur ad spiritalia, quae illis similitudinibus figurantur, ipso quasi transitu uegetatur et tamquam in facula ignis agitatus accenditur et ardentiore dilectione rapitur ad quietem'.

[43] See *ep.* 55.22–3.

[44] See W. Rordorf, *Der Sonntag. Geschichte des Ruhe- und Gottesdiensttages im ältesten Christentum* (Zurich, 1962), H. Rahner, *Griechische Mythen in christlicher Deutung*, 3rd edn (Zurich, 1966),

With these transformations, liturgical and theological, as the backdrop to his discussion, he examines the commandment to keep holy the Sabbath, mindful as well that it constitutes an essential feature of the divine instruction concerning the just life. How should Christians understand their obligations regarding this commandment? Is it abrogated in the light of the New Testament? Augustine realizes that the solutions he poses to these questions will bear directly on the larger question concerning the function of the scriptures as a discourse on the nature and obligations of justice.

In framing his discussion, he first claims that, except for the divine commandment to keep holy the Sabbath, no commandment of the Decalogue makes use of any figurative expression (*locutio figurata*), such as metaphor. As a consequence, he notes, all the remaining commandments invite 'literal' interpretations.[45] But Augustine recognizes in the term 'Sabbath' a figure of speech which requires interpretation. As with all symbols, its specific meaning must be determined in a context that goes beyond the historical or literal sense alone. On the surface, the commandment to keep holy the Sabbath requires believers to rest from their labours. Augustine reasons that to arrive at the commandment's deeper meaning, the biblical interpreter must consider other scriptural passages in which God is also seen to be commanding rest. Only in this way can the metaphor be understood and its underlying rhetorical objective be revealed. He defends this approach on the grounds that to adhere to a strict, literal exegesis would expose God's commandment to ridicule, and at the same time preclude enjoyment of the desire for the rest in God alone which the commandment is ultimately intended to induce.

Exegetical principles which Augustine uses to reach this position can be most clearly identified in the first three books of *De doctrina christiana*, which he wrote concurrently with *Ad inquisitiones* and with which it demonstrates strong parallels. Sabbath, as he describes it in *Ad inquisitiones*, is an 'ambiguous metaphorical sign' (*signum ambiguum translatum*). By this he means that it is a symbol or emblem (*res significans*) with

---

101–2, W. Rordorf, 'Die theologische Bedeutung des Sonntags bei Augustin. Tradition und Erneuerung', *Der Sonntag. Ansprung – Wirklichkeit – Gestalt. Festschrift Jacob Baumgartner*, ed. A. Altermatt and T. Schnitker (Würzburg, 1986), 30–43, Wallraff, *Christus*, 93–6.

[45] See *ep.* 55.22 (CSEL 34/2.193): 'non figurate aliud praetendunt et mystice aliud significant, sed sic obseruantur, ut sonant'. 'Literal' is the term traditionally applied to interpretations which are not allegorical or figurative. In *De doctrina christiana*, Augustine employs the term *signa propria*, which is also translated 'literal', but which really refers to signs which are not tropes. See Bernard, 'In Figura', 39–57, 166–7, for a superb discussion of the principal features of Augustine's figurative exegesis.

numerous possible meanings (*res significatae*), each of which contributes to the broader meaning of the biblical commandment.[46] Augustine expresses this judgment only after discounting the suitability of a literal interpretation. He devises a test to determine when the literal interpretation ought to be abandoned in favour of the figurative. Expressions are figurative, he holds, when their literal sense fails to reflect just conduct and the truth acquired through faith. By 'truth of the faith' (*ueritas fidei*) Augustine refers to knowledge of God and neighbour, while 'just conduct' (*honestas morum*) pertains to love of God and neighbour.[47] In other words, when trying to determine whether God intends that a given biblical expression be interpreted literally or figuratively, the reader must ask whether the literal interpretation harmonizes with the greatest divine commandment to love God and one's neighbour as oneself (Mt 22:37–40). If it fails to do so, a figurative interpretation ought to be employed. Literal interpretations of biblical moral precepts should thus give way to figurative interpretations when they fail to conform to an intuition about justice. Augustine first suggests this complex exegetical principle at the close of Book 2 of *De doctrina*, where, however, he also cautions, 'knowledge puffs up, but love builds up' (1 Cor 8:1).[48] His point is that in interpreting the scriptures, one has to avoid relying exclusively on techniques drawn from the study of rhetoric or other disciplines. Augustine holds that, as exegetical criteria, true knowledge and love of God and neighbour counter the ignorance and weakness which obstruct knowledge and love on a moral plane. By citing 1 Cor 8:1, Augustine introduces the importance of humility in arriving at a correct interpretation of any given biblical text. In his view, even the decision whether to press the literal meaning of a biblical passage or to interpret it figuratively constitutes a struggle against the effects of original sin.[49] In

---

[46] See also *ep.* 149.34 (CSEL 44.379), where Augustine defends the usefulness (*utilitas*) of deriving numerous interpretations from 'obscure' passages of the scriptures, provided only that they accord with the truth of the Christian faith.

[47] See *doctr. chr.* 3.33–4 (CSEL 80.88): 'et iste omnino modus est, ut quicquid in sermone diuino neque ad morum honestatem neque ad fidei ueritatem proprie referri potest, figuratum esse cognoscas. morum honestas ad diligendum deum et proximum, fidei ueritas ad cognoscendum deum et proximum pertinet'.

[48] See *doctr. chr.* 2.148. Bernard, 'In Figura', 28, regards this verse as a 'hinge', providing a connection between Books 2–3 of *De doctrina christiana*. Thus, Book 2 concerns knowledge (*scientia*), the rhetorical principles for unlocking *signa ignota*, while Book 3 treats love (*caritas*), the 'theological' dispositions required for distinguishing *signa propria* from *signa translata*. Although Bernard's arrangement of Augustine's plan is overly tidy in my view, I think that he is right to stress the importance of Augustine's citation of 1 Cor 8:1 as providing the rationale for the distinction between proper signs and tropes.

[49] See *doctr. chr.* 3.55–7.

Book 10 of the *City of God*, he employs this line of reasoning by claiming
that even the just men of ancient times (*iusti antiqui*) knew how to interpret
the law figuratively through faith and humility against the influence upon
the soul of ignorance and weakness. As a consequence, they were able to
discern the mystery (*sacramentum*) of the incarnation behind the figurative
language (*mystice loqui*) of the scriptures.[50]

In the case of the commandment to observe the Sabbath, Augustine
rejects a literal interpretation because it leads to the conclusion that God
commands sloth. Insofar as slothful behaviour makes a mockery of right
conduct, the interpretation of the commandement upon which it rests
must be erroneous.[51] In essence, Augustine opts for a figurative instead of a
literal interpretation of the precept because the latter interpretation chafes
against his intuitive sense of justice.[52] He subsequently adheres to the procedures outlined in Book 3 of *De doctrina*, and applies to the figurative
language in question the principles for interpreting ambiguous tropes.[53]
These principles require that the exegete (1) rely upon the content of the
passage itself to give some interpretative direction, (2) compare it with similar (*congruere*) passages whose meanings are more clearly understood, and
(3) adhere to the correct faith (*recta fides*) so that no heterodox interpretation is introduced.[54] These procedures make it clear that Augustine takes for
granted the existence of a recognizable congruence between at least some
ambiguous passages and others whose meanings are clearer. This congruity
provides him with the interpretative key for clarifying the ambiguous passage in question with the help of clearer passages.[55] These latter passages
should contain no expressions which fail to reflect right conduct and the
truth of the Christian faith. Augustine judges that 'Sabbath', a metaphor
(*signum translatum*) which is employed at Ex 20:8 and Dt 5:12, refers to rest
(*requies*). He searches for an interpretation of these two passages in other
passages in which a figurative and not a literal meaning for rest is suggested,

---

[50] See *ciu.* 10.24–5 (CCL 47.297–8).   [51] See *ep.* 55.22. See also *doctr. chr.* 3.22–4.

[52] He repeats the general principle at *spir. et litt.* 6 (CSEL 60.158): 'neque enim solo illo modo intellegendum est quod legimus: *littera occidit, spiritus autem uiuificat* [2 Cor 3:6], ut aliquid figurate
scriptum, cuius est absurda proprietas, non accipiamus sicut littera sonat, sed aliud quod significat
intuentes interiorem hominem spiritali intelligentia nutriamus'.

[53] See *doctr. chr.* 3.84–5.

[54] See the complete discussion at *doctr. chr.* 3.82–6, especially 3.84–5, along with Bernard, 'In Figura',
43–56.

[55] Augustine's concept of 'congruence' seems to derive from moral-aesthetic criteria derived from the
rhetorical doctrine of propriety or decorum (*aptum*). Cicero, *De oratore* 3.39.157, notes that two words
can be termed *similitudines* when the comparison between them is pleasing (*delectare*); alternatively,
no *similitudo* can be said to exist when the listener is repelled (*repudiare*) by the suggestion. For
further discussion of this exegetical method in Augustine, see the discussion below, pp. 136–9, and
Dodaro, 'Literary Decorum'.

and finds them at Ps 45(46):11 ('be still and know that I am God'), and Mt 11:28–9 ('come to me all you who labour and I shall give you rest').[56]

Augustine then examines the concept of Sabbath as a sacrament or symbol of Christ's death and resurrection. He ponders the relationship between the liturgy of the Easter triduum and the three days of Christ's crucifixion, repose in the tomb (= Sabbath), and resurrection. Once again, he sees the 'passage' from sin to justice in certain key scriptural texts as intended to lead the reader to an interior, sacramental participation in the spiritual renewal represented by Christ's death.[57] He points out that the Easter triduum liturgy symbolizes a 'passage' from present to future life, from time to eternity, from activity to rest, and from hardship to joy.[58] These themes correlate with two periods within the Easter triduum, the one consisting of sensory signs – the just deeds signified by the crucifixion (Good Friday) – the other consisting of repose and delight in inaudible, invisible, but permanent, unchanging realities (Easter Sunday). The Sabbath (Saturday) symbolizes the point of union between these two periods or realities in the lives of those who desire to live justly.[59]

The first period, the 'time of the cross' (*tempus crucis*), corresponds in Augustine's view to the first day of the triduum, Friday. The commemoration of Christ's passion on this day symbolizes the believer's observance of the commandments, because they oblige the avoidance of sin and the performance of good works in imitation of Christ.[60] Augustine assigns to this period the spiritual 'passage' from sin to grace, and from the exterior world of sense knowledge and action (such as in the performance of good works) to the interior realm of contemplation and repose. The second period combines the events of the second and third days (marked by the repose in the tomb and the resurrection), and represents them as spiritual

---

[56] See *ep.* 55.22. Note that Augustine examines this same relationship between Sabbath = resurrection (as a typology for eschatological rest) and justice at *ciu.*11.9 and 22.30.

[57] See *ep.* 55.24 (CSEL 34/2.195): 'adtende igitur sacratissimum triduum crucifixi, sepulti, suscitati', *ep.* 55.27 (CSEL 34/2.200): 'haec et ex auctoritate diuinarum scripturarum et uniuersae ecclesiae, quae toto orbe diffunditur, consensione, per anniuersarium pascha celebrantur in magno utique, sicut iam intellegis, sacramento'.

[58] See *ep.* 55.24–5. The suggestion that the sacred triduum constitutes a discourse appears at the beginning of this section.

[59] Compare this argument concerning the unity between the performance of good works and contemplation of God as the fullest expression of the just life with a parallel argument at *ciu.* 19.19, where Augustine also maintains that the just life requires a mixture of good works and contemplation. Note, too, the placement of this argument in relation to his return at *ciu.* 19.21 to discussion of Cicero's concept of the commonwealth and its relationship to true justice.

[60] See *ep.* 55.24. Scriptural texts cited by Augustine concerning mortification and avoidance of sin include Col 3:5, Rom 8:13, Gal 6:14, Rom 6:6. Good works (*opera bona*), essential to justice, are mentioned at the opening of *ep.* 55.25.

realities which 'we do not yet see or possess, but act upon by means of faith and hope'. The reference to faith and hope is important becaue it signals a particular way of participating in the spiritual passages (transformation, renewal) which are figuratively represented in the sacrament. Faith and hope lead to a correct interpretation of this symbolism. As a consequence, they nurture desire for the future rest which follows from just conduct in the present life. In this way, faith and hope constitute a 'grammar' in Augustine's mind for interpreting Ps 45(46):11 ('be still and know that I am God') and Mt 11:28–9 ('come to me all you who labour and I shall give you rest'), the two biblical texts which he identifies as key to understanding the commandment to keep holy the Sabbath.[61] By interpreting this commandment with faith, believers no longer associate Sabbath rest with a literal understanding of Old Testament Sabbath prohibitions concerning their exterior activity. Instead, faith and hope lead them to interpret the commandment as requiring the interior, spiritual renewal symbolized in the liturgies of the second and third days of the Easter triduum.

Augustine thus first contrasts Sabbath rest with the Good Friday agony of crucifixion, which he equates symbolically with the obligation binding Christians to perform good works. He likens rest to a reward or payment (*merces*) for labour. He then softens the boundaries between the believers' earthly toil and their heavenly reward of eternal repose by appealing to Paul's instructions at Rom 12:12 that they 'rejoice now in hope', and at Rom 8:25 that they 'wait with patience'. Augustine thereby harmonizes active performance of good works with the contemplative anticipation of a holy rest in God alone. Faith and hope enable believers, even while toiling in the earthly realm against the consequences of sin, to experience a foretaste of the fuller joy reserved for life after death. In Augustine's view, Paul's instructions direct believers to carry out the tasks which justice demands of them with a cheerful disposition, by looking forward in hope to a future rest.[62]

The complex relationships involved in this joyful, hopeful disposition are taken up in the symbolism of the crucifixion (*figura crucis*) which Augustine interprets through Eph 3:18 ('May you and all the saints be able to

---

[61] On the function of hope in the discernment of justice, see *doctr. chr.* 3.34, where it is presented as binding together the truth of the faith (*ueritas fidei*) and the love of God and neighbour. See also *doctr. chr.* 3.60.

[62] See *ep.* 55.25 (CSEL 34/2.196): 'haec sunt etiam bona opera quidem tamen adhuc laboriosa, quorum merces requies est. sed ideo dicitur: *spe gaudentes* [Rom 12:12], ut cogitantes requiem futuram cum hilaritate in laboribus operemur'. For a more specifically political application of this maxim, see *ep.* 155.4 to the vicar of Africa, Macedonius.

measure, in all its breadth and length and height and depth, the love of Christ, in order to know what surpasses knowledge'). In this section of *Ad inquisitiones*, Augustine draws an extended comparison between the crucified Christ and the just life. Here, as in other works, Augustine focuses on the scriptural presentation of Christ as the principal example (*exemplum*) of the just life.[63] Scholars have noted Augustine's interpretation of Christ's deeds, such as the crucifixion and resurrection, as signs, and therefore as words (*uerba*) within scriptural discourse.[64] Scholars interpret his intention as applying rhetorical analyses to Christ's deeds in order to discover in them the doctrinal or moral teaching which the divine author of the scriptures intends to convey.[65] Christ's hands fixed with nails to the transverse beam of the cross thus symbolize the performance of good works, while the nails which fix the hands to the wood of the cross represent the commandments, the 'things which keep us occupied in this life'.[66] In discussing this aspect of Christ's example, Augustine is concerned that works of justice not be misconstrued by believers as ends in themselves; they do not represent the perfection of the Christian life, but are its obligations, the mere fulfilment of which cannot satisfy the deepest spiritual longings of the believer rightly conceived or nurtured.[67] Good works undertaken to improve the welfare of others advance one's spiritual and moral growth ultimately only if they

---

[63] The quality of the image of Christ crucified as example of the just life is indicated by the Pauline citations which Augustine intersperses throughout his discussion of the image in this part of the treatise. See, for example, *ep.* 55.25. The fundamental study of the role of Christ as *exemplum* in Augustine's exegesis is W. Geerlings, *Christus exemplum. Studien zur Christologie und Christusverkündigung Augustins* (Mainz, 1978). But see also Brabant, *Le Christ*, especially 77–114, 187–99, P. Siniscalco, 'Christum narrare et dilectionem monere', *Augustinianum* 14 (1974), 605–23, Studer, '*Sacramentum*', 102–24, Studer, 'Le Christ', 125–39, Studer, *Grace*, 47–55, and A. Kessler, 'Exemplum', *Augustinus-Lexikon*, vol. 2, ed. C. Mayer (Basle, 1996–2002), 1174–82 (with bibliography). See also de Luis Vizcaíno, *Los hechos*, especially 235–71. The idea of Christ as moral exemplar for Christians is present in Origen, for example, at *Contra Celsum* 8.17.16, 8.23.3, 8.63.33, *De principiis* 3.1.10.4, 3.1.19.31, 4.1.6.8, 4.2.6.4, 4.2.6.13, 4.2.6.40. On the use of moral *exempla* by Jerome, see P. Hamblenne, 'L'*exemplum* formel chez Jérome', *Augustinianum* 36 (1996), 94–145. On *exemplum* as moral paradigm in Roman literature, see the studies indicated above, p. 35 n. 38.

[64] See *Io. eu. tr.* 44.1 (CCL 36.381): 'ea quippe quae fecit dominus noster Iesus Christus stupenda atque miranda, et opera et uerba sunt: opera quia facta sunt; uerba, quia signa sunt', and Strauss, *Schriftgebrauch*, 109–10, who cites other texts. See also de Luis Vizcaíno, *Los hechos*, 40–8 and 33–6, where he discusses the Roman classical background to the association of deeds (*facta*) with speech (*dicta*). On this point, see also Geerlings, *Christus*, 148–55. On the relationship between Augustine's theory of signs and his biblical hermeneutics, see especially R. Lorenz, 'Die Wissenschaftslehre Augustins', *Zeitschrift für Kirchengeschichte* 67 (1956), 213–51, at 232, 236–7, U. Duchrow, *Sprachverständnis und biblisches Hören bei Augustin* (Tübingen, 1965), especially 151–9, 163–6, Mayer, 'Congruentia', 1199–1200, Pollmann, 187–95.

[65] Geerlings, *Christus*, 8, rightly observes that studies of Augustine's ethics have altogether neglected consideration of the value of Christ's example for Augustine's teaching on the moral life.

[66] See *ep.* 55.25.

[67] See my discussion above, p. 104, of Augustine's treatment of good works at *ciu.* 10.6.

are motivated by a longing to transcend the realm of moral contingency.[68] Such desire is symbolized in the upward position of Christ's head as it lay against the uppermost beam of the cross. Augustine sees exemplified in this image the Christian's expectation of recompense from divine justice for good works performed during one's lifetime.[69] Between the hands fixed to the horizontal beam by the nails of the obligations of justice and the head raised in anticipation of future rest are Christ's arms opened across the breadth of the cross. They symbolize the cheerful mien of the just soul, whose desires have been transformed into hope for a future rest in God.[70] In like manner, the extension of Christ's body along the vertical beam of the cross symbolizes long-suffering endurance of trials.[71] Augustine likens Christ's example of perseverance in hanging upright on the cross while waiting to die to Paul's example of resigning himself to enduring the ardours of his apostolate despite his desire for rest after death (Phil 1:23–4).[72] Paul feels obliged to continue preaching the Gospel, although his perspective is altered by the passage of his desire beyond the limits of human achievement to a longing for a holy rest, as a result of which he is bolstered in his undertakings. By taking this position, Augustine resists a sharp distinction between just conduct and its reward in the afterlife. The desire for rest is itself the genesis (and therefore a foretaste) of that rest which is the proper object of any just deed.[73] The rest which the just already enjoy in this life is without doubt a lesser form of ultimate beatitude, attenuated as it is by the threat of time; it cannot be divorced from rest in God, because in Augustine's view death does not interrupt the 'rest' which the just already enjoy

---

[68] See *ep.* 55.25 (CSEL 34/2.197): 'in necessariis deputantur, non in eis, quae per se ipsa appetenda et concupiscenda sunt'. Note that Augustine, in a letter to the vicar of Africa, Macedonius, applies this same principle in conjunction with the civic duties of public officials. See *ep.* 155. 10–12, and my discussion below, pp. 208–12.

[69] See *ep.* 55.25 (CSEL 34/2.196–7): 'per altitudinem autem, cui caput adiungitur, expectationem retributionis de sublimi iustitia dei, *qui reddet unicuique secundum opera sua, his quidem qui secundum tolerantiam boni operis gloriam et honorem et incorruptionem quaerentibus uitam aeternam*' (Rom 2:6–7).

[70] See *ep.* 55.26 (CSEL 34/2.198–9): 'non ergo murmuremus in difficultatibus, ne perdamus latitudinem hilaritatis, de qua dicitur: *spe gaudentes*, quia sequitur: *in tribulatione patientes*' (Rom 12:12).

[71] See *ep.* 55.25 (CSEL 34/2.197): 'itaque etiam longitudo, qua totum corpus extenditur, ipsam tolerantiam significat, unde longanimes dicuntur, qui tolerant',

[72] See *ep.* 55.25 (CSEL 34/2.197): 'unde illud optimum se dicit concupiscere, *dissolui, et esse cum Christo; manere autem in carne necessarium,* inquit, *propter uos* [Phil 1:23–4]. quod ergo ait *dissolui, et esse cum Christo,* inde incipit requies'.

[73] See *ep.* 55.25 (CSEL 34/2.197): 'quod ergo ait *dissolui, et esse cum Christo,* inde incipit requies, quia non interrumpitur resurrectione, sed clarificatur, quae tamen nunc fide retinetur, quia *iustus ex fide uiuit*' (Rom 1:17 = Hab 2:4). At *ciu.* 11.12 (CCL 48.333), Augustine acknowledges that those who live justly can already rightly be called blessed: 'cum hodie non inpudenter beatos uocemus, quos uidemus iuste ac pie cum spe futurae inmortalitatis hanc uitam ducere sine crimine uastante conscientiam, facile inpetrantes peccatis huius infirmitatis diuinam misericordiam'.

in this life. There is undeniably some element of assurance in a promised, future consolation implied by Augustine's reference to a 'reward' (*merces*) after death.[74] However, the experience of rest which he outlines for the just prior to death is not simply satisfaction in advance, but what he elsewhere refers to as 'delight in justice' (*delectatio iustitiae*), a delight in the desire for God.[75] Here Augustine has in mind his earlier discussion of the many human desires which compete with the desire for rest in God alone.[76] Elsewhere he refers to Paul's longing to be with Christ as a 'superior' (*optimum*) desire, adding that as a result of such longing, rest is already enjoyed in faith. Paul's affirmation that 'the just live by faith' (Rom 1:17, Gal 3.11, cf. Heb 10:38, Hab 2:4) should therefore be understood in a double sense: faith guides believers to live justly by enabling them to penetrate the deeper meanings (*res signficatae*) of the sacraments present in the scriptures and in liturgical ritual, while also supporting them in the performance of their just deeds by allowing them sustained contemplation of the ultimate end (symbolized by the reference to the 'sun of justice') to which their just activities are directed.[77]

PRAEPARATIO CORDIS

As he makes clear in *Ad inquisitiones*, Augustine is certain that the scriptures possess the capacity to teach justice through the rhetorical use of sacraments and examples. In holding this view, however, he does not believe that even the most accurate interpretations of the scriptures can ever uncover justice as it is known by God. The same figurative language which renders the biblical text pleasing to read can also frustrate attempts to arrive at clear signification of the truths it contains. Christians are wrong to expect that the

---

[74] Perhaps best expressed in his statement in the section following: *ep.* 55.26 (CSEL 34/2.198): 'sed alia sunt solatia miserorum, alia gaudia beatorum'.

[75] See *ciu.* 13.5 (CCL 48.388): 'auget enim prohibitio desiderium operis inliciti, quando iustitia non sic diligitur, ut peccandi cupiditas eius delectatione uincatur. ut autem diligatur et delectet uera iustitia, non nisi diuina subuenit gratia'. Note the rhetorical contest implicit in this passage between 'delight in justice' (*delectatio iustitiae*) and the biblical law that Augustine, in accord with 1 Cor 15:56, denotes as 'the strength of sin' (*uirtus peccati*).

[76] See *ep.* 55.9.

[77] See *ep.* 55.25 (CSEL 34/2.197–8): 'ea quae nondum uidemus et nondum tenemus, sed fide et spe gerimus, in alio biduo figurata sunt. haec enim, quae nunc agimus tamquam clauis praeceptorum in dei timore confixi, sicut scriptum est: *confige clauis a timore tuo carnes meas* [Ps 118[119]:120], in necessariis deputantur, non in eis, quae per se ipsa appetenda et concupiscenda sunt. unde illud optimum se dicit concupiscere, *dissolui et esse cum Christo; manere autem in carne necessarium*, inquit, *propter uos* [Phil 1:23–4]. quod ergo ait *dissolui et esse cum Christo*, inde incipit requies, quia non interrumpitur resurrectione, sed clarificatur, quae tamen nunc fide retinetur, quia *iustus ex fide uiuit* [Rom 1:17, Hab 2:4]'.

parables, examples, sacraments, and other figures contained in the scriptures make justice transparent to reason. In the *City of God*, he acknowledges that, whereas the angelic knowledge of God is not mediated by language, human reason depends upon linguistic concepts. Consequently, he explains, justice as it is known to the just is ultimately inferior to justice as it is known in the wisdom of God.[78] Knowledge of justice which is mediated by words is always partial and indirect.

Figurative language and other textual difficulties inherent in the scriptures, therefore, allow Augustine to hold his confidence in the authoritative foundation of the scriptures in tension with his belief in the transcendental nature of eternal, divine truths. Obscure or otherwise difficult biblical figures of speech become conceptual stepping stones connecting visible, temporal reality with invisible, eternal reality. Thus he concludes that God, as the divine author, makes skilful use of linguistic and rhetorical forms which, however, render difficult the interpretation of certain passages within the scriptures.[79] At the same time, their inherent interpretative problems both increase the interest and delight with which the reader pursues more intellectually demanding truths,[80] and simultaneously provide the reader with

---

[78] See *ciu.* 11.29 (CCL 48.349): 'illi quippe angeli sancti non per uerba sonantia Deum discunt, sed per ipsam praesentiam inmutabilis ueritatis . . . et tamen omnes . . . ita nouerunt, ut eis magis ista, quam nos ipsi nobis cogniti simus. ipsam quoque creaturam melius ibi, hoc est in sapientia dei tamquam in arte, qua facta est [. . .] multum enim differt, utrum in ea ratione cognoscatur aliquid, secundum quam factum est, an in se ipso; sicut aliter scitur rectitudo linearum seu ueritas figurarum, cum intellecta conspicitur, aliter cum in puluere scribitur; et aliter iustitia in ueritate incommutabili, aliter in anima iusti'.

[79] *Gn. adu. Man.* 2.5–6, in conjunction with 1 Cor 13:12 ('Now I see in a mirror dimly, but then face to face. Now I know in part; then I shall understand fully'), is fundamental for appreciating the relation in Augustine between the use of biblical language, including obscure tropes, and the divine communication of truth. In this passage, he makes clear his view that human beings require the scriptures and their figurative language only as a consequence of the abiding effects of original sin upon the human intellect. See the discussions by Holte, *Béatitude*, 335–8, and F. Van Fleteren, 'Per speculum et in aenigmate: The Use of 1 Corinthians 13:12 in the Writings of Augustine', *Augustinian Studies* 23 (1992), 69–102.

[80] On the rhetorical usefulness (*utilitas*) of obscure symbols, mysteries, and locutions in the scriptures for arousing the reader's interest, see *ciu.* 11.19 (CCL 48.337–8): 'quamuis itaque diuini sermonis obscuritas etiam ad hoc sit utilis, quod plures sententias ueritatis parit et in lucem notitiae producit, dum alius eum sic, alius sic intellegit', *s.* 51.5 (PL 38.336): 'Haec est utilitas secreti. Honora in eo quod nondum intellegis; et tanto magis honora, quanto plura uela cernis', *ep.* 137.18. See Marrou, *Saint Augustin*, 488–92, who points out the ancient rhetorical and philosophical background to Augustine's view that the use of obscure metaphors and locutions in the scriptures gives pleasure (*delectare*) to the reader. See *en. Ps.* 103.1.18 (CCL 40.1490): 'ut semper quaesita etsi cum difficultate, cum maiori iucunditate inueniantur', *mor.* 1.30 (PL 32.1324): 'et quaesitis exerceatur utilius, et uberius laetetur inuentis'. See also B. Studer, '*Delectare et prodesse*, ein exegetisch-homiletisches Prinzip bei Augustinus', *Signum pietatis. Festgabe für Cornelius Petrus Mayer zum 60. Geburtstag*, ed. A. Zumkeller (Würzburg, 1989), 497–513.

the requisite preparation (*praeparatio*) and training (*exercitatio*) to under-take such an investigation.[81]

Augustine presumes an additional motive for God's use of rhetorical indi-rection. Ignorance and weakness so impair moral reasoning that unsound judgments made under their influence can seem just to the person who makes them. As a remedy for this moral blindness, God carefully avoids straightforward explanations of eternal truths. Instead he forces the mind to unravel the meaning of obscure biblical symbols or ambiguous passages referring to justice with difficulty; in doing so it is freed from fixed, erro-neous patterns of thought and drawn into a deeper understanding of justice as mystery. Augustine wonders, for example, what effect the narrative about the woman caught in adultery (Jn 8:3–11) might have if read and pondered by a magistrate about to condemn a convicted criminal to death. How do the dialectical elements of Jesus' response to the Pharisees and scribes invite the judge to revise his own concept of justice in the light of the deeper wisdom behind divine justice?[82]

In Letter 138 to the imperial tribune and notary Flavius Marcellinus (AD 411/12), Augustine exhibits more reservations than he displays in *Ad inqui-sitiones* about the capacity of the scriptures to reveal true justice clearly. His letter responds to two related exegetical issues which had been raised by Rufius Volusianus, the pagan proconsul of Africa, both of which con-cern the reliability of the concept of justice as revealed in the scriptures.[83] First, Volusianus and a circle of his associates at Carthage find inconsistent the New Testament rejection of forms of sacrifice which had earlier been approved in the Old Testament.[84] Second, they are concerned by the obli-gation of non-violence imposed on Christians by four verses of the New Testament: Mt 5:39 ('if anyone strikes you on the right cheek, turn to him the other also'), Mt 5:41 ('if anyone forces you to go with him one mile, go with him two miles'), 1 Thes 5:15 ('see that none of you repays evil for

---

[81] On the function of *exercitatio* relative to scriptural interpretation, see *Gn. adu. Man.* 2.1 (CSEL 91.115): 'quae omnis narratio non aperte, sed figurate explicatur, ut exerceat mentes quaerentium ueritatem, et spirituali negotio a negotiis carnalibus auocet', *diu. qu.* 53 (CSEL 44A.88): 'deus enim noster sic ad salutem animarum diuinos libros sancto spiritu moderatus est, ut non solum manifestis pascere, sed etiam obscuris exercere nos uellet'. See also *ciu.* 20.17, *Io. eu. tr.* 21.12, *trin.* 15.27, Marrou, *Saint Augustin*, 486–9, Pollmann, *Doctrina*, 219–23 (with other relevant studies on *obscuritas* in relation to *delectatio* and *exercitatio* indicated in the notes). On *praeparatio cordis* in relation to scriptural interpretation, see below, p. 139 n. 98.

[82] See *en. Ps.* 50.8–9, *ep.* 153.8–10, *s.* 13.5–8, and my discussion below, pp. 173–9.

[83] See my remarks about Marcellinus and Volusianus above, pp. 7–9, and below, pp. 202–5.

[84] See *ep.* 138.2, together with *ep.* 136.2 (Marcellinus to Augustine). For background on this correspon-dence, see above, pp. 7–8 n. 5, and my discussion below, pp. 202–5.

evil'), and Rom 12:17 ('repay no one evil for evil').[85] Volusianus concludes from these passages that the Christian religion is pacifist, and that it cannot be relied upon to provide the Empire with a strong defence against its enemies.

Augustine's response to Volusianus turns upon the use of rhetorical principles concerned with literary decorum as a means of interpreting individual scriptural passages in harmony with the entirety of the scriptures. Literary decorum has its source in ancient Greek and Latin rhetorical precepts governing the determination of what is suitable and fitting in discourse, and is thus concerned with rhetorical or literary propriety, with harmony between ideas and the language used to express them, or between two separate texts or sets of texts.[86] Augustine gives his most important defintion of decorum in Letter 138, where he compares the *aptum*, that which can be called fitting or appropriate, with the *pulchrum*, the beautiful. There he says that, whereas something can be judged as beautiful (*pulchrum*) without reference to any other object, judgments about whether something can be described as *aptum* depend entirely upon its suitability when viewed in relation to something else.[87] Typically, judgments about decorum concern the relationship of one part to another part and/or to the whole. In traditional Roman rhetoric, decorum is divided into two aspects: the external and internal. Judgments concerning the relationship between (1) the content of a discourse, (2) the style or occasion (*tempus, locus*) of its delivery, and (3) the social status (*dignitas*) of the audience refer to decorum in an external sense. For example, the preacher's decision to avoid telling an off-colour joke during a funeral service reflects a judgment about decorum in an external sense. Decorum in an internal sense is concerned with the

---

[85] See *ep.* 138.9. Augustine responds to Marcellinus' letter (*ep.* 136 within the Augustinian corpus) concerning objections to Christianity which Volusianus has expressed both directly to Augustine (see *ep.* 135) and to Marcellinus. Augustine intends that this letter supplement his earlier reply to Volusianus (*ep.* 137).

[86] Among the key Latin terms used to convey these concepts are *accommodatio, aptum, conuenientia, conuenire, congruere, congruentia, decere, decus, decorum, dignitas, dignum, honestas, honestum*.

[87] See *ep.* 138.5 (CSEL 44.129): 'aptum uero, cui ex aduerso est ineptum, quasi religatum pendet aliunde nec ex semet ipso sed ex eo, cui conectitur, iudicatur; nimirum etiam decens atque indecens uel hoc idem est uel perinde habetur'. See the brief discussion of this letter by Strauss, *Schriftgebrauch*, 90, 102. Augustine's first work, *De pulchro et apto* (AD 380), which dealt with the relationship between the beautiful and the fitting, has been lost. It is perhaps surprising that among his writings in our possession, Letter 138, and not Book 3 of *De doctrina christiana*, is the principal locus for his application of literary decorum to scriptural interpretation. But see *doctr. chr.* 3.29–73 (CSEL 80.87–99) and discussion by Strauss, *Schriftgebrauch*, 92–5. Primmer, 'The Function', 68, is right to point out that 'Augustine devoted more than half of *De doctrina* 4 . . . to a discussion of Cicero's pairing of the *officia* and the *genera.*' However, Book 4 is concerned not with the principles of scriptural exegesis per se, but with instructions regarding the preaching of the scriptures, and thus with preaching styles. Much more important for exegesis is the briefer discussion of decorum in Book 3.

adaptation of the elements which make up a discourse to each other, as in the case between two or more words or between individual words and their intended meanings. In this way, decorum as a rhetorical principle governs the fittingness or suitability of the words to the ideas they are intended to express. Literary decorum is thus an aesthetic-ethical category which pertains to two sets of relationships: (1) the relationship between the discourse and its audience, inasmuch as the speech is intended to persuade, and (2) the relationship between the ideas (*res*) and the words (*uerba*) chosen by the speaker. As a 'virtue' governing rhetorical judgments which are both aesthetic and ethical, literary decorum has as its principal goal the preservation of the dignity of the speaker, the subject matter of the discourse, and the audience. Finally, literary decorum requires subtle and subjective judgments by the author. Classical rhetorical manuals, such as those of Cicero and Quintilian, do not specify the application of decorum in great detail because it cannot be clearly expressed. Classical rhetoricians can only insist upon the virtue's fundamental importance for the orator.[88]

Turning to Volusianus' concerns about scriptural passages prohibiting the use of force in resisting evil, Augustine shows the deeper moral wisdom which can be derived from harmonizing such scriptural passages with those passages that approve of a measured, forceful response in certain situations.[89] As the author of the scriptures, God teaches just behaviour through the skilful deployment of apparent inconsistencies, the unravelling of which delights his hearers while it draws them into deeper appreciations of the beauty of justice. Augustine urges that the scriptures be read from this aesthetic point of view, much like a musical composition in which different time spans are harmonized so that its beauty is appreciated all the more.[90]

Behind this approach lies Augustine's knowledge of philosophical theories concerning music, which claim that music resolves motion and time in music into an eternal and unchanging cosmic whole. In *De musica*, for example, he describes the effect on the soul of hearing successive syllables

---

[88] I have summarized the basic principles of literary decorum and the classical rhetorical works which treat of the subject more fully elsewhere. See Dodaro, '*Quid deceat*'. For further background, see Lausberg, *Handbuch*, 507–11 (§§ 1055–62), 516–19 (§§ 1074–7), DeWitt, '*Quo Virtus*', Rutherford, 'Decorum 1. Rhetorik'.

[89] F. Young, *The Art of Performance: Towards a Theology of Holy Scriptures* (London, 1990), especially 45–65 and 88–133, offers a highly suggestive account of scriptural interpretation within the categories of dramatic performance and musical composition.

[90] See *ep.* 138.5 (CSEL 44.130): 'qui [deus] multo magis quam homo nouit, quid cuique tempori accommodate adhibeatur, quid quando impertiat, addat, auferat, detrahat, augeat minuatue immutabilis mutabilium sicut creator ita moderator, donec uniuersi saeculi pulchritudo, cuius particulae sunt, quae suis quibusque temporibus apta sunt, uelut magnum carmen cuiusdam ineffabilis modulatoris excurrat atque inde transeant in aeternam contemplationem speciei, qui deum rite colunt, etiam cum tempus est fidei'.

of words, from which, he says, the soul gradually draws meaning.[91] He further considers the effects of musical rests and unequal time spans (*spatium temporale*) on the overall perception of the musical composition.[92] This discussion leads him into his well-known remarks on the 'poem of the universe' (*carmen uniuersitatis*).[93] In this passage, Augustine compares human delight as it shifts from lower to higher realities, from the changeable to the unchanging, from time to eternity, a perspectival shift which is signified in the apprehension of the alteration of day and night, of the seasons of the year. In each case, temporal and spatial change harmonize, in imitation of the eternal, unchanging realities beyond this life.[94]

Reading the scriptures with these principles in mind likewise enables readers to discern a divine intention behind the superficial contradictions of the text. Augustine illustrates his use of these interpretative principles when he turns to Volusianus' objection to Christian pacifism. He identifies several scriptural passages in which the theme of violence is handled differently from in the specific passages cited by the proconsul. When struck by a centurion, Christ does not 'turn the other cheek', but instead asks the guard, 'If I have said something wrong, then reproach me . . . if I have spoken well, why do you strike me?' (Jn 18:23). Similarly, when struck by a guard at the order of Ananias, Paul also fails to turn the other cheek, but instead mocks the chief priest, remarking, 'God will strike you, whitewashed wall! You are sitting to judge me according to the law, and yet you order me to be struck in contravention of the law' (Acts 23:2–3). When Roman soldiers ask John the Baptist how they should live out their baptism of repentance, he does not prohibit their continuing to serve as soldiers, but merely advises them to avoid gratuitous violence (Lk 3:3, 3:14).[95] Augustine concludes that scriptural examples, like those of Christ, Paul, and John the Baptist, temper the pacifism urged elsewhere in the New Testament, and permit Christians to exercise a 'kind harshness' (*asperitas benigna*) in defence of the Empire.[96]

By harmonizing the scriptural passages cited by Volusianus (Mt 5:39–41, 1 Thes 5:15, Rom 12:17) with other passages pertaining to the Christian response to violence (Jn 18:23, Lk 3:3, 3:14, Acts 23:3–5), Augustine seeks

---

[91] See *mus.* 6.21.   [92] See *mus.* 6.27–8 (PL 32.1178–9).

[93] R. O'Connell, *St. Augustine's Early Theory of Man, A.D. 386–391* (Cambridge, Mass., 1968), 170, finds Augustine's reference to be reminiscent of Plotinus, *Enneads* 4.3.12.12–16.

[94] See *mus.* 6.29 (PL 32.1179) along with further remarks by R. O'Connell, *Art and the Christian Intelligence in St. Augustine* (Oxford, 1978), 75.

[95] See *ep.* 138.13–14.

[96] See *ep.* 138.14 (CSEL 44.140): 'agenda sunt autem multa, etiam cum inuitis benigna quadam asperitate plectendis, quorum potius utilitati consulendum est quam uoluntati, quod in principe ciuitatis luculentissime illorum litterae laudauerunt'. For Augustine's allusion to a parallel application in Roman literature, see Cicero, *Pro Sulla* 8.25.

to arrive at a unified, coherent truth, which can make sense of all passages together. 'If the earthly commonwealth observes Christian precepts in this way, then even wars will be waged in a spirit of benevolence, with the aim of serving the defeated more easily by securing a peaceful society of justice and piety.'[97] By highlighting this apparent contradiction between precepts rejecting violence and those passages in which a literal interpretation of these same precepts is set aside, Augustine claims to show that the real import of individual passages of the scriptures lies not in the prescription of just conduct per se, but in the preparation of the heart (*praeparatio cordis*) of the believer who seeks to arrive at just judgments.[98]

EXERCITATIO MENTIS

Like *Ad inquisitiones*, Augustine's Letter 138 to Marcellinus warns of the risks of too literal an approach to the scriptures in seeking a clear definition of justice. *Ad inquisitiones* makes this point, in part, by demonstrating the superior understanding of the 'Sabbath' which comes from interpreting the concept figuratively. The experience of rest which this sacramental understanding elicits enables Christians to see the ultimate significance of their just deeds as extending beyond the realm of moral contingency toward a transcendental horizon. Augustine's letter to Marcellinus accomplishes a similar shift of perspective by pointing out the need to harmonize different scriptural passages into a whole, much as one 'works' passively at the enjoyment of music. When Augustine insists that the scriptural passages concerning just and unjust responses to violence are not intended to provide moral guidance for external acts but to train the heart, he refers, in effect, to this intellectual process of reconciling multiple interpretations of scriptural passages in order to produce a synthesis. Yet, even this intellectual effort does not guarantee that the resulting moral decision meets the divine standard of justice. Augustine will not allow that a correct apprehension

---

[97] See *ep.* 138.14 (CSEL 44.140): 'ac per hoc si terrena ista res publica praecepta Christiana custodiat, et ipsa bella sine beneuolentia non gerentur, ut ad pietatis iustitiaeque pacatam societatem uictis facilius consulatur'. Augustine intends his remarks as a criticism of the 'just-war' concept which Volusianus had invoked against the pacifism of the New Testament. Thus, at *ep.* 138.9–10, he argues the superiority of the scriptural precept not to return evil for evil (1 Thes 5:15, Rom 12:17) to traditional Roman understandings of the virtue of forgiveness offered by Sallust, *Bellum Catilinae* 9.5, and Cicero, *Pro Ligario* 12.35.

[98] See *ep.* 138.13 (CSEL 44.138): 'ista praecepta magis ad praeparationem cordis, quae intus est, pertinere quam ad opus, quod in aperto fit'. See also *ep.* 138.14 (CSEL 44.139–40): 'sunt ergo ista praecepta patientiae semper in cordis praeparatione retinenda'. Augustine reaches a similar conclusion almost a decade earlier while debating Faustus over the same question. See *c. Faust.* 22.76–7, in particular, 22.76 (CSEL 25/1.674): 'intellegant hanc praeparationem non esse in corpore, sed in corde; ibi est enim sanctum cubile uirtutis', in conjunction with Dodaro, 'Literary Decorum', 171–3.

of justice – even of the ideal of justice as far as it can be known by human reason – could ever be derived from scriptural interpretation without grace acting on the soul. Faith and grace can be understood as parallels for the rhetorical functions of teaching and moving the soul.[99] Both are key categories for his scriptural interpretation and his treatment of the transcendental nature of religious knowledge, and together they bring these concepts together. Examined in relation to rhetorical theory, Augustine's conceptions of faith and grace explain the connection between hearing the scriptures and the introspection through which the form of justice is apprehended in the mind as mystery.

His conception of the way the scriptures influence the perception of justice leads Augustine to adopt a rhetorical framework for the process of justification as well.[100] According to this framework, God exerts an irresistible attraction over human hearts, negatively in order to dissuade them from other influences, and positively in order to attract them into the love of himself as the highest good. The disjunction in oratory between wisdom and eloquence which both Cicero and Augustine regretted[101] is thus resolved by God, who heals ignorance and weakness in the mind of the hearer of his word by a 'sapiential eloquence'. Augustine outlines in *De trinitate* this graced enlightenment of the soul by means of which the implications of the scriptures for just judgments can be grasped.[102]

He begins this discussion by examining several Old Testament theophanies, because they illustrate how believers can come to know God in the tension between revelation and hiddenness that is present in mystery. In Books 2–3 of *De trinitate*, he proposes, in effect, that theophanies and other visions granted to Old Testament patriarchs and prophets be understood not simply as components of a *Heilsgeschichte* attesting a saving, divine intervention in history, but as signs pointing to the nature of all divine mysteries. Read in this way, Old Testament theophanies become figurative discourses or sacraments which outwardly dramatize the more profound, interior processes of revelation of which the incarnation, considered as mystery, is both symbol and cause. As a result, the designation of Abraham, Moses, and other recipients of theophanies as 'just men of ancient times'

---

[99] See my discussion of faith and grace at *trin.* 4.2 (below, p. 144 n. 120).

[100] See, for example, *gr. et pecc. or.* 1.14 (CSEL 42.136), where he likens grace to a teaching which God communicates to the soul 'with an ineffable sweetness': 'Haec gratia si doctrina dicenda est, certe sic dicatur, ut altius et interius eam deus cum ineffabile suauitate credatur infundere non solum per eos, qui plantant et rigant extrinsecus, sed etiam per se ipsum, qui incrementum suum ministrat occultus, ita ut non ostendat tantummodo ueritatem, uerum etiam inpertiat caritatem'.

[101] Cicero, *De oratore* 3.16.59–61; and 3.31.121. See also *conf.* 3.7, concerning which see the remarks of Marrou, *Saint Augustin*, 161–72, and Testard, *Saint Augustin*, 1:18–9, 22.

[102] I discuss these implications below, pp. 165–8.

(*iusti antiqui*) does not pertain exclusively, or even principally, to their role as moral examples understood narrowly as rhetorical figures who portray virtues. It is, rather, as pointers to the corrrect apprehension of divine mysteries that the patriarchs and prophets constitute important examples for Christians.[103]

Augustine best illustrates this figurative role of theophanies in his commentary on Exodus 33. Moses asks to see God, but is denied his request (Ex 33:13, 33:18).[104] Augustine interprets this narrative as a paradox: the desire on the part of the just to see God contrasts with the impossibility that human intelligence could ever grasp the divine essence.[105] Moses, as a type for all believers, is denied a direct perception of God.[106] Instead, he is told to peer through a cleft in the rock once God has passed, in order to see the divine majesty from behind.[107] Augustine understands the rock as a symbol of faith. Human beings, as it were, 'peer through' faith in order to perceive wisdom: both the human perception and the divine communication occur indirectly. The theophany thus constitutes a symbol or sacrament of God's indirect self-communication in mystery. In this context, faith again functions 'grammatically' by teaching the soul how to distinguish the signs which communicate true knowledge of God from those which seduce this desire away from its true path. Like any grammar, faith teaches how to read – in this case, how to read the mystery of God.[108]

---

[103] See *trin.* 4.2 (below, p. 144 n. 120). See also Augustine's treatment of Ps 73(74) at *ciu.* 10.25, where he links the psalmist's ability to act justly to his faith in the divine mystery.

[104] See *trin.* 2.27–8.

[105] See *trin.* 2.28 (CCL 50.118): 'ipsa est enim species cui contemplandae suspirat omnis qui affectat diligere deum ex toto corde et ex tota anima et ex tota mente; ad quam contemplandam etiam proximum quantum potest aedificat qui diligat et proximum sicut se ipsum, in quibus duobus praeceptis tota lex pendet et prophetae' (cf. Mt 22:39). To live justly is to fulfil these commandments. See above, p. 76 n. 13.

[106] See *trin.* 2.27 (CCL 50.116): 'quid est autem: *ostende mihi temetipsum manifeste ut uideam te* [Ex 33:13], nisi ostende mihi substantiam tuam?', 2.28 (CCL 50.118): 'siue quod etiam nunc in quantum dei sapientiam per quam facta sunt omnia [cf. 1 Cor 1:24.21] spiritaliter intellegimus, in tantum carnalibus affectibus morimur ut mortuum nobis hunc mundum deputantes nos quoque ipsi huic mundo moriamur'.

[107] See Ex 33:22. The Maurists read that Moses is positioned by God 'in specula petrae'. See *trin.* 2.27–8 (PL 42.863), which E. Hill, *Saint Augustine, The Trinity. The Works of Saint Augustine. A Translation for the 21st Century*, tr. E. Hill, ed. J. Rotelle (New York, 1991), 117, translates 'at a look-out in the rock'. CCL 50.117 reads 'in spelunca petrae', which Hill translates 'in a cave'. Hill (126 n. 53) supports the Maurist reading by pointing out other occurrences of *specula* at *trin.* 2.28 and 2.30. G. Beschin, ed., *Sant'Agostino, La Trinità* (Rome, 1973), 112, also reads 'specula', but is aware of 'in spelunca petrae' at *Gn. litt.* 12.55 (PL 34.477). Both readings offer an intriguing image of indirect communication.

[108] See *trin.* 8.6–7. God must be known to be loved, but in this mortal life we can only know God by means of faith (2 Cor 5:7) in corporeal realities (*corporalia*). Faith therefore has to distinguish between material signs which point to God and those which the human imagination invents. Thus Paul refers to 'an unfabricated faith' (1 Tim 1:5) which purifies the heart by preventing it from fabricating falsehoods, which Augustine takes to mean false material signs.

Understood in these 'grammatical' terms, faith imposes a discipline on reason, at once purifying desire of influences which distract it from the love of God and, equally importantly, purging desire from any tendency to seek to 'know' God reductively, as created beings are known.[109] Augustine recognizes this double role of faith when he examines Moses' encounter with God, and there compares the 'face' and 'back' of God to the 'form of God' (*forma dei*) and the 'form of a servant' (*forma serui*) in Christ. In saying this, Augustine invites his readers to understand the incarnation through the symbolism associated in Exodus with Moses' theophany. The biblical text provides Christians with a means of understanding the relevance of the relationship between Christ's human and divine natures for attaining wisdom. Broadly speaking, Christ's human nature, and more specifically his words and deeds, becomes a figurative discourse, a 'look-out point' or a 'peep hole' which Christians can 'peer through' as an indirect means of discerning the word and wisdom of God. The mystery of God incarnate confirms what theophanies dramatize: that the knowledge of God which Christ imparts through grace is simultaneously visible and hidden, and that it should be understood and accepted as such. God prescribes faith as a means of knowing what can only be 'seen' partially,[110] and as an impetus for seeking God until death creates the possibility for unfettered contemplation.[111] Properly interpreted, this narrative of Moses' vision dramatizes and symbolizes what for Christians must be an interior process of illumination, one which is mediated through divine sacraments.[112]

The Christian who attempts to unravel all the possible interpretations of biblical sacraments and reach the hidden (*secretum*) meaning of the text relives analogously the experience of the patriarch who is caught up in the tension of the theophany.[113] Augustine notes that in the case of such exegesis, it is the 'laborious troubles' (*difficultates laboriosae*) expended in the effort of interpreting the figurative language which lead to humility.

---

[109] For this reason, God can only be known through faith which interprets visible signs. See especially *trin.* 2.28 (CCL 50.119): 'illa est ergo species quae rapit omnem animam rationalem desiderio sui tanto ardentiorem quanto mundiorem et tanto mundiorem quanto ad spiritalia resurgentem, tanto autem ad spiritalia resurgentem quanto a carnalibus morientem. sed *dum peregrinamur a domino et per fidem ambulamus non per speciem* [2 Cor 5:6–7], posteriora Christi, hoc est carnem, per ipsam fidem uidere debemus'. See also *trin.* 4.24.

[110] See especially *trin.* 8.6–7, in connection with Acts 15:9.   [111] See *trin.* 2.28, 4.2.

[112] Note at *trin.* 2.35 the explicit reference to the content of theophanies as *sacramenta*. See my discussion of *trin.* 4.2 (below, p. 144 n. 120).

[113] See *trin.* 2.1 (CCL 50.80): 'cum homines deum quaerunt et ad intellegentiam trinitatis pro captu infirmitatis humanae animum intendunt, experti difficultates laboriosas siue in ipsa acie mentis conantis intueri *inaccessibilem lucem* [1 Tim 6:16] siue in ipsa multiplici et multimoda locutione litterarum sacrarum, ubi mihi non uidetur nisi atteri Adam ut Christi gratia glorificata dilucescat, cum ad aliquid certum discussa omni ambiguitate peruenerint, facillime debent ignoscere errantibus in tanti peruestigatione secreti'.

The primary effect of such effort is to reveal the underlying presumption (*praesumptio*) which obstructs religious understanding.[114] His description of this process as 'wearing down Adam' and thereby 'allowing Christ's grace to shine through'[115] delineates the boundary (*confinium*) between the 'old' and 'new' man (cf. Col 3:9), the equivalent on a moral plane to the boundary he sees at the cognitive level between the 'outer' and 'inner' man (cf. 2 Cor 4:16).[116] The grace by which the soul is enlightened in penetrating the scriptural text diminishes the moral presumption on account of which the mind believes itself to understand the hidden meaning of the text. For Augustine, this presumption is personified in Adam.[117]

Augustine assumes that similar encumbrances will be met in an attempt to penetrate the sacrament within any text, scriptural or liturgical. At the beginning of Book 4 of *De trinitate*, just prior to his explanation of the relationship between divine examples and sacraments, he summarizes his views concerning theophanies, and applies them to the investigation of eternal truths. He notes that all such visions granted to the Old Testament patriarchs and prophets function rhetorically by admonishing (*admonere*) their recipients to continue to seek eternal realities, while persuading (*persuadere*) them of God's love as an incentive to reach out to the saving truths which the visions disclose. However, the difficulties encountered during the struggle to perceive these lasting truths through visions make known (*ostendere*) to their recipients the extent to which their weakness poses an obstacle to understanding. They thus become aware that reliance upon their own moral strength and intelligence constitutes presumption. In effect, the patriarchs and prophets learn that the transcendent knowledge of eternal realities revealed by their visions differs from the contingent knowledge of earthly things to which their natural intelligence is well suited.[118] Only by abandoning reliance upon their own insights and virtue can they begin to interpret their visions correctly through faith. Faith, therefore, exercises a purifying effect on the soul by continuing to remind it that it cannot understand the realities disclosed by God by relying upon its own efforts. This self-knowledge, achieved in humility, draws the soul into a deeper love of God.

---

[114] See *trin.* 2.1 (CCL 50.80): 'sed duo sunt quae in errore hominum difficillime tolerantur: praesumptio priusquam ueritas pateat, et cum iam patuerit praesumptae defensio falsitatis. a quibus duobus uitiis nimis inimicis inuentioni ueritatis et tractationi diuinorum sanctorumque librorum'. See also *trin.* 4.2 (below, n. 120).

[115] See *trin.* 2.1 (above, n. 113).

[116] See *trin.* 12.1 (CCL 50.356): 'hominis exterioris interiorisque confinium'. Augustine pairs the expressions *homo uetus* and *homo nouus* with *homo exterior* and *homo interior* at *en. Ps.* 6.2 (below, p. 150 n. 13). See the discussion by Studer, 'Sacramentum', 127.

[117] See *trin.* 2.1 (above, n. 113).

[118] See *trin.* 4.1 (below, n. 119). A.-M. La Bonnardière, *Recherches de chronologie augustinienne* (Paris, 1965), 172, holds that *trin.* 2.13–35, 3.4–27, and 4.2 constitute a coherent 'block' of passages.

For Augustine, knowing the truth by means of faith is possible only in the humility of a love converted from self to God. Knowledge of eternal truths is, therefore, not possible for human beings unless they undergo a form of moral conversion. Only an experience of true self-knowledge, the perception of one's moral presumption, can allow grace to convert the soul to the love of God, and thereby enlighten the intellect regarding eternal truths.[119] To illustrate these principles, Augustine cites Paul's teachings that Christ 'has now justified us in his blood' (Rom 5:8) and that God gives us 'all things' with Christ (Rom 8:31), and concludes that these truths were already shown (*ostendere*) to the patriarchs and prophets of the Old Testament. However, this revelation could only have occurred as mystery because the effort which the patriarchs and prophets expended upon the difficult act of believing the material forms they saw weakened them and caused them to abandon presumption upon their own efforts to know and love God. Only when their self-reliance was diminished could they be perfected in faith and love, through which they attained an indirect form of the knowledge they desired.[120]

In this complex summary statement, Augustine stresses more clearly than in either *Ad inquisitiones* or Letter 138 the 'grammatical' role of faith in imparting a necessary self-knowledge to the human subject.[121] Faith is, therefore, joined with humility. The difficulties experienced from God's

---

[119] See *trin.* 4.1 (CCL 50.159): 'qui uero iam euigilauit in deum spiritus sancti calore excitatus atque in eius amore coram se uiluit ad eumque intrare uolens nec ualens eoque sibi lucente attendit in se inuenitque se suamque aegritudinem illius munditiae contemperari non posse cognouit, flere dulce habet et eum deprecari ut etiam atque etiam misereatur donec exuat totam miseriam, et precari cum fiducia iam gratuito pignore salutis accepto per eius unicum saluatorem hominis et inluminatorem – hunc ita egentem ac dolentem *scientia* non *inflat* quia *caritas aedificat* [1 Cor 8.1]'. On humility, true self-knowledge, and the knowledge of God, see also Schaffner, *Christliche Demut*, 185–206.

[120] See *trin.* 4.2 (CCL 50.161–2): 'ac primum nobis persuadendum fuit quantum nos diligeret deus ne desperatione non auderemus erigi in eum. quales autem dilexerit ostendi oportebat ne tamquam de meritis nostris superbientes magis ab eo resiliremus et in nostra fortitudine magis deficeremus, ac per hoc egit nobiscum ut per eius fortitudinem potius proficeremus atque ita in infirmitate humilitatis perficeretur uirtus caritatis [. . .] persuadendum ergo erat homini quantum nos dilexerit deus et quales dilexerit: quantum ne desperaremus, quales ne superbiremus [. . .] quod autem factum nobis annutiatur, hoc futurum ostendebatur et antiquis iustis, ut per eandem fidem etiam ipsi humilitati infirmarentur et infirmati perficerentur'.

[121] Augustine anticipates this point at the opening of Book 4 by emphasizing the superior quality of self-knowledge, along with the knowledge that leads to salvation, to the natural sciences. See *trin.* 4.1 (CCL 50:159): 'scientiam terrestrium caelestiumque rerum magni aestimare solet genus humanum. in quo profecto meliores sunt qui huic scientiae praeponunt nosse semetipsos, laudabiliorque est animus cui nota est uel infirmitas sua quam qui ea non respecta uias siderum scrutatur etiam cogniturus aut qui iam cognitas tenet ignorans ipse qua ingrediatur ad salutem ac firmitatem suam'. As a philosophical principle, the argument has parallels and antecedents. See, for example, Cicero, *De finibus* 2.12.37, *De officiis* 1.43.153, 2.2.5, *Libri tusculanorum disputationum* 4.26.57, 5.3.7, *De oratore* 1.49.212.

indirect communication with them allow Moses and other recipients of visions to see their own pride in the form of moral and intellectual presumption. Once they acknowledge th. ` pride, they are able to grow in humility, as a result of which knowledge changes into a form of non-possessive love, a transformation which Augustine later refers to as the passage from reason as it pertains to knowledge (*ratio scientiae*) to reason as it pertains to wisdom (*ratio sapientiae*).[122]

Augustine argues in *De trinitate* that God repeats this lesson in humility for the benefit of those who read accounts of theophanies or of other sacraments. The figurative quality of these narratives enables them to lead readers to the central, divine mystery in the scriptures, the incarnation. Christians who seek to work out the meanings behind Christ's words and deeds are thus urged to approach them with the same faith through which Moses and other recipients of theophanies struggled to appreciate the hidden meanings of their visions. Efforts to understand Christ's words and deeds without faith, for example by approaching them in too literal a fashion or by presuming to have grasped their meanings already, result in a failure to understand the indirection of the scriptural discourse. They therefore misapprehend the inexpressible, boundless nature of the truths which it communicates.

CONCLUSION

Augustine's conviction that the scriptures offer a divine discourse which communicates teaching concerning the nature of true justice is tempered by his awareness that justice is communicated only indirectly. Justice as a virtue can be defined; however, direct apprehension of its essential form and, hence, clear understanding of its requirements in the realm of moral judgments can be known by reason only as it approaches knowledge of God in and through mystery. This is not a negative, apophatic knowledge. Nevertheless, the understanding of justice through mystery requires scriptural exegesis that combines resistance to the lure of any literal, restrictive interpretation of individual precepts or examples with a respect for an intuitive understanding of justice. This latter sensibility offers a standard by which the quality of any synthesis constructed from multiple scriptural passages is to be judged. However, given ignorance and weakness as a result of original sin, any true understanding of justice acquired through an intellectual effort to pierce the symbolic surface of scriptural language requires a simultaneous

---

[122] See *trin.* 12.16–22, and my discussion below, pp. 165–71.

movement of the soul away from the presumption with which the mind pursues all knowledge. This conversion releases the soul, momentarily at least, into love of neighbour and God. This is why Augustine frequently invokes I Cor 8:1, 'knowledge puffs up, but love builds up'. Gradual understanding of justice in its ideal form, as outlined in the *De trinitate* account of Old Testament theophanies, requires self-knowledge in the form of a deepening moral conversion with respect to one's own conception of himself in relation to others and God. The mind itself, therefore, undergoes conversion as it calls into question its own certainties, and it relies more completely upon what Augustine terms 'faith'. To say that 'the just live by faith' (Rom 1:17, cf. Hab 2:4, Gal 3:11, Heb 10:38) in Augustinian terms is, therefore, to understand faith in part as the graced purification of the soul from self-reliance of intellect and will. Given their capacity to purify the soul of pretension, sacraments, as figurative discourses both in the scriptures and in the liturgy, characterize the encounter between knowledge and wisdom in a way that examples cannot.

Grace is the category in which Augustine explores this conversion leading to a deeper understanding of justice. It provides the key in his strenuous efforts to explain to a host of adversaries, especially Pelagius and his associates, what he considers to be the precise role of Christ in the construction of a just society. To do so, he returns after AD 411 to his earlier accounts of Christ's example of justice and related virtues and sets in greater relief a number of principles governing the relationship between reason and grace, as they pertain to scriptural interpretation and the gradual growth of the soul in its apprehension of justice. These themes are the topics of the following chapter.

CHAPTER 5

Wisdom's hidden reasons

Augustine's differences with Pelagius over human nature lead him to redefine the role of grace in mediating knowledge and love of justice within the soul. Against Pelagius and his associates, he insists that all intellectual activity which aims at understanding virtue depends upon Christ's union with the soul. In Chapter 3 we observed that Augustine's primary model for the just society makes use of the Pauline image of Christ as 'head of the body, which is the church' (Col 1:18, 1:24). Within this image of the body, Augustine was also seen to describe a dialogue between Christ and his members, through which he mediates virtue to the soul. Furthermore, we saw that this dialogue depends in Augustine's thought on the concept of unity 'in one person', through which he explains the union of Christ's divine and human natures. In this chapter, we shall see how Augustine draws upon this complex image of Christ's divine–human dialogue to explain the relationship he assumes between two sets of exegetical categories: examples and sacraments, and knowledge and wisdom. For Augustine, human knowledge (*scientia*) regarding what the scriptures reveal about virtues such as justice requires a transformation by divine wisdom (*sapientia*), which is analogous to the transformation of Christ's human nature through its union with his divine nature. It will be shown here that Augustine posits this same transformation between scriptural examples and sacraments. He suggests that through this transformation, the soul acquires a partial and indirect understanding of justice in the form of mystery (*sacramentum, mysterium*). Finally, it will be shown that Augustine uses these terms in such a way as to place greater distance than the Pelagians between Christ's direct perception of justice and the indirect understanding of it that is granted to human beings through their union with Christ.

SACRAMENTUM ET EXEMPLUM

In Book 11 of the *City of God*, Augustine refers almost in passing to 'a sense belonging to the inner man' by which reason is able to discriminate between justice and injustice. This occurs, he observes, because the mind is able to perceive the form of justice.[1] In *De trinitate*, he both expands upon and provides crucial qualifications to this assertion. In Book 4 he introduces the topic of Christ's death and resurrection, and indicates his intention to examine how these events, both as sacrament and example, communicate deeper understandings of eternal truths, such as justice, than are found in Old Testament theophanies. In doing so, his first and most crucial step is to pair his conceptions of sacraments and examples with what Paul terms the 'inner man' and 'outer man' (cf. 2 Cor 4:16).[2] Differentiating sacraments and examples in this way enables him to indicate more precisely the role that grace plays in interpreting the scriptures, as far as justice and other eternal truths are concerned.

In order to understand better the distinction which Augustine seeks to draw between examples and sacraments, some explanation of his use of the terms 'outer man' and 'inner man' is required. In general, Augustine differentiates the 'outer man' and the 'inner man' as he does the human body and the mind, observing frequently with Paul that 'while the outer man undergoes corruption, the inner man is being renewed day by day' (2 Cor 4:16).[3] Within the 'outer man' is the sphere of intellectual activity pertaining to those 'lower' intellectual operations, such as sensory perception and the basic functions of memory and imagination, that human beings share with animals. The 'inner man' by contrast represents the 'higher' capacities of reason and the potential for divine illumination that belong exclusively to the mind (*mens*).[4] Augustine's assignment of certain intellectual functions to the outer man preserves it from being dismissed as altogether irrelevant to reason. Thus, although its operations and objects are less significant than those of the inner man, they are nonetheless essential for reason. Augustine sees this point acknowledged in Paul's affirmation that 'faith comes by hearing' (Rom 10:17), since the first step in believing consists in

---

[1] See *ciu.* 11.27 (CCL 48.347): 'habemus enim alium interioris hominis sensum isto longe praestantiorem, quo iusta et iniusta sentimus, iusta per intelligibilem speciem, iniusta per eius priuationem'. On this passage in the context of divine illumination, see O'Daly, *Augustine's Philosophy*, 204–7 (along with more general studies indicated at 204 n. 115).

[2] See *trin.* 4.6 (CCL 50.167–9): 'ea sola nobis ad utrumque concinuit cum in ea fieret interioris hominis sacramentum, exterioris exemplum'.

[3] See *trin.* 13.2 (CCL 50A.382): 'homo cuius exteriorem partem, id est corpus . . . interiorem uero, id est animam', together with *trin.* 11.1, *diu. qu.* 51.1, 64.2, *c. Faust.* 24.1–2, *ciu.* 11.2, 13.24. See also *en. Ps.* 6.2 (below, n. 13).

[4] On these differences between the outer man/inner man, see *trin.* 11.1, 12.1–2, 12.13, along with *ciu.* 11.2, *diu. qu.* 51.1–3, *c. Faust.* 24.2. See also the discussions by G. Matthews, 'The Inner Man', *American Philosophical Quarterly* 4 (1967), 166–72, A. Solignac, 'Homme intérieur. Augustin', *Dictionnaire de spiritualité*, vol. 7:1, ed. A. Rayez et al. (Paris, 1969), 655–8, O'Daly, *Augustine's Philosophy*, 7 (on the parallel distinction between the irrational and rational soul), 175–6, and Hill, *Trinity*, 258–64.

hearing the divine word preached.[5] Augustine says that he is concerned with the boundary (*confinium*) between the outer and inner man, because it provides the key to understanding how the one influences the other.[6]

He distinguishes the operations of the outer and inner man according to the presence or absence of reason.[7] Mental activities pertaining to the outer man include attraction to and repulsion from material reality to which the soul is alerted by sensations or emotions, whether experienced at the time or recalled by memory, provided that reflection upon them does not involve some act of reason.[8] Much of what he says about the outer man and its preoccupation with 'lower', material reality reduces its moral and intellectual stature, in particular when compared with the realm of the inner man.[9] Yet Augustine also vigorously defends the outer man's functions and objects of interest on the grounds that all created reality is good, fashioned as it is in the likeness of the Creator, but also because in human beings, the outer man is governed by the inner man, enlightened in turn by wisdom.[10] Writing against the Manichean bishop Faustus, Augustine insists that Paul's reference to an outer and inner man does not imply two distinct human beings, only one of whom is created in the divine image. Although this image resides exclusively in the inner man, God created the human being as a unity. As a result, like the inner man, the outer man experiences a spiritual renewal when the body is transformed in the resurrection.[11] Consequently, Augustine understands the relationship between the outer and inner man in terms of a radical unity that retains their essential difference. He views this same principle at work in the relationship between flesh (*caro*) and spirit (*spiritus*), an analogous couplet which he applies to scriptural interpretation.[12]

---

[5] See *trin.* 13.4–5.

[6] See *trin.* 12.1 (CCL 50A.356): 'uideamus ubi sit quasi quoddam hominis exterioris interiorisque confinium', in the context of his discussion at 12.13, 12.25. See also *c. Faust.* 22.27.

[7] See *trin.* 12.13 (CCL 50A.368): 'unde incipit aliquid occurrere quod non sit nobis commune cum bestiis, inde incipit ratio, ubi iam homo interior possit agnosci'.

[8] See *trin.* 13.1–2, 11.1, 11.6. At *trin.* 11.7, Augustine includes the visual content of dreams and the emotions it engenders within the realm of the outer man. On the limited 'imitation knowledge' of which non-rational animals are capable, see O'Daly, *Augustine's Philosophy*, 98–9. See also M. Baltes and D. Lau, 'Animal', *Augustinus-Lexikon*, vol. 1, ed. C. Mayer (Basle, 1986–94), 356–74, at 358–60.

[9] See *trin.* 11.6, 11.8, and, especially, *diu. qu.* 64.2–3, in conjunction with 64.7–8.

[10] See *trin.* 11.8, *diu. qu.* 51.3.

[11] See *c. Faust.* 24.2 (citing Rom 8:10–11, 1 Cor 15:39–40), *ciu.* 13.16–18, 13.20, *en. Ps.* 140.16, *ep.* 118.14. See also M. Miles, *Augustine on the Body* (Missoula, 1979), 99–125, T. van Bavel, 'No One Ever Hated his own Flesh: Eph 5:29 in Augustine', *Augustiniana* 45 (1995), 45–93, C. W. Bynum, *The Resurrection of the Body in Western Christianity, 200–1336* (New York, 1995), 94–114, M. Miles, 'Corpus', *Augustinus-Lexikon*, vol. 2, ed. C. Mayer (Basle, 1996–2002), 6–20, especially 13–17.

[12] See *en. Ps.* 6.2 (below, n. 13), and C. Mayer, 'Caro-spiritus', *Augustinus-Lexikon*, vol. 1, ed. C. Mayer (Basle, 1986–94), 743–59, especially 746–8.

While Augustine is concerned primarily to pair examples with the outer man and sacraments with the inner man, he also acknowledges a relationship between sacraments and the outer man, as he does between examples and the inner man. Careful notice should be taken of this chiasm that Augustine sees in the relationship between the pairs sacrament/example and inner man/outer man. Its significance will become clearer further on in this discussion. In the case of sacraments, Augustine allows that the 'fleshly' perception of the sacrament's exterior features is the function of the sensory grasp of the outer man, while the sacrament's hidden, 'spiritual' meaning is revealed only to the inner man through grace.[13] He thus acknowledges in the term 'sacrament' an exterior and interior dimension, which he correlates with the functions both of the flesh and spirit, and of the outer and inner man.

He relates examples to the inner man for the first time in *De uera religione* (AD 390), where he identifies the inner man's seven stages of spiritual renewal and progress. He acknowledges that during the first of these stages, the inner man 'is taught by the rich stores of history that nourish by examples (*exempla*)'.[14] Augustine's description of the role of examples in relation to the inner man is consistent both with their literary and rhetorical structure and with his clear assignment of responsibility to the inner man for all intellectual operations which involve even minimal use of reason.[15] At the same time, he acknowledges that only during the higher, second stage does the soul turn its attention from human to divine matters.[16] Although he does not say so directly, by limiting the role of examples to the lowest rung of the seven-runged ladder of spiritual perfection, he implies what he will later state clearly in *De trinitate*, namely that examples of virtue could not

---

[13] See *en. Ps.* 6.2 (CCL 38.28): 'ab Adam enim usque ad Moysen genus humanum uixit ex corpore, id est secundum carnem; qui etiam exterior et uetus homo dicitur, et cui uetus testamentum datum est, ut quamuis religiosis, tamen carnalibus adhuc operationibus futura spiritalia praesignaret [. . .] quoniam *usque ad Moysen* [Rom 5:14] accipiendum est, quo usque legis opera, id est carnaliter obseruata illa sacramenta, etiam eos obstrictos tenuerunt certi mysterii gratia, qui uni deo subditi erant. ab aduentu autem domini, ex quo ad circumcisionem cordis a carnis circumcisione transitum est, facta uocatio est, ut secundum animam uiueretur, id est secundum interiorem hominem, qui etiam nouus homo propter regenerationem dicitur morumque spiritalium innouationem'.

[14] See *uera rel.* 49 (CCL 32.218): 'iste dicitur nouus homo et interior et caelestis habens et ipse proportione non annis, sed prouectibus distinctis quasdam spiritales aetates suas. primam in uberibus utilis historiae, quae nutrit exemplis. secundam iam obliuiscentem humana et ad diuina tendentem, in qua non auctoritatis humanae continetur sinu, sed ad summam et incommutabilem legem passibus rationis innititur'.

[15] On the general structure and function of the *exemplum* in Roman rhetoric, see the studies cited above, p. 35 n. 38, and p. 131 n. 63, in relation to Augustine.

[16] See *uera rel.* 49 (above, n. 14).

lead Christians toward the moral life without engagement of the higher reasoning functions of the inner man.[17]

Augustine further clarifies this point by explaining that Christ's death and resurrection, considered as both sacraments and examples, enable believers to understand and love justice. In order to comprehend the distinction between these categories as he applies them to Christ's death and resurrection, readers of Augustine must consider first how he joins the concept of 'sacrament' to that of 'mystery' (*mysterium*). For Augustine, the expression 'mystery of God' (*mysterium dei*), as at Col 2:3, refers in its strictest sense to God's trinitarian nature and to the incarnation, 'mysteries' through which God is most clearly revealed to believers. Augustine holds that the divine trinity and incarnation can only be understood by believers under the form of mystery. He explains that Christ imparts the understanding of mystery to the soul as grace.[18] When believers receive this grace, they are said to participate in the divine mystery. For Augustine, this participation means that they know God and his attributes (for example, love, justice) in a real way, but only partially, in the manner that Christ's divinity is known through his humanity. He frequently indicates what he thinks it means to know something as a 'mystery' by citing 1 Cor 13:12 ('For now we see in a glass darkly, but then we shall see face to face').[19] His discussion in *De trinitate* of the Old Testament theophanies describes the kind of knowing that he associates with the term 'mystery'. To know virtues such as love and justice through 'mystery' (*mysterium*) means to know them partially and dimly. Moreover, each of his various uses of the term *mysterium* refers back in some way to the core mysteries of the trinity and the incarnation, and to the real but partial way in which they are understood by believers. This is the point in his thinking at which the terms *mysterium* and *sacramentum* become most synonymous. Both terms as he uses them connote a tension, absent in examples, between God's secret purposes and his self-revelation.[20]

Thus, Augustine holds that, unlike examples, sacraments depend in part for their meaning upon a divine presence which exerts a therapeutic, non-verbal influence on the mind.[21] At the same time, he recognizes that, like examples, sacraments and mysteries employ linguistic and rhetorical

[17] See Geerlings, *Christus*, 151–3, 173–83, especially 177, on *exemplum* in relation to *ratio*.

[18] See my discussion of Col 2:3 at *trin.* 13.24 below, pp. 167–8 and n. 94.

[19] See, for example, *spir. et litt.* 64 (below, n. 100).

[20] See C. Couturier, 'Sacramentum et mysterium *dans l'œuvre de S. Augustin*', *Etudes augustiniennes* (Paris, 1953), 162–332, at 162–3, 173–274. Couturier's demonstration that, for Augustine, the concept of sacrament can never be entirely divorced from mystery has never been contested.

[21] See my discussion of *ep.* 140.62–4, below, pp. 160–4.

structures such as proper words, which as signs refer their recipients to certain meanings. He admits that in order for believers to be influenced by sacraments, they must therefore hear the divine word preached, whether in the scriptures or in liturgical rites such as baptism and eucharist.[22] Scholars detect in Augustine's use of both concepts, sacrament and mystery, a semantic fluidity which incorporates the categories of symbol and ritual.[23] But it seems just as important to remember that when, at the beginning of *Ad inquisitiones Ianuarii*, Augustine defines *sacramentum* as a 'sacred sign', he also states that it must be received 'in a holy manner'. In making this point, he does not mean to say only that the sign refers to something sacred, but that its interpretation must be met by a holy disposition in the believer.[24] This capacity of sacraments and mysteries to express events in the life of Christ in such a way as to lead the soul to an interior, spiritual renewal thus represents their primary function as rhetorical figures within a divine discourse. However, in *De trinitate* he is careful to observe that the power of sacraments and mysteries to induce an interior, spiritual renewal does not depend solely on their symbolic function. He explains that the terms 'sacrament' and 'mystery' denote an interaction between language and grace in the spiritual process by which the soul overcomes ignorance and weakness as it pursues a deeper understanding of eternal truths.[25] Augustine

---

[22] See especially *c. Faust.* 19.16 (CSEL 25/1.513), where Augustine refers to Old Testament sacraments as 'visible words' (*uerba uisibilia*) whose meaning is capable of changing over time. Sacramental actions, such as baptism, require language in order to communicate interior spiritual renewal. See *Io. eu. tr.* 80.3 (CCL 36.529): 'detrahe uerbum, et quid est aqua nisi aqua? accedit uerbum ad elementum, et fit sacramentum, etiam ipsum tamquam uisibile uerbum'. See also *Io. eu. tr.* 15.4, *bapt.* 3.19–20, 4.6, 4.24. See also H.-M. Féret, 'Sacramentum-res dans la langue théologique de saint Augustin', *Revue des sciences philosophiques et théologiques* 29 (1940), 218–43, at 222–3, on the exegetical sense of sacrament as 'sign' (*signum*).

[23] See C. Mohrmann, 'Sacramentum dans les plus anciens textes chrétiens', *Harvard Theological Review* 47 (1954), 141–52 = Mohrmann, *Etudes*, 233–44, T. Camelot, 'Le Christ, sacrement de Dieu', *L'Homme devant Dieu. Mélanges offerts au Henri de Lubac*, vol. 1: *Exégèse et patristique* (Paris, 1963), 355–63, Mayer, *Die Zeichen . . . in der Theologie des jungen Augustin*, 287–302, on the scriptural and early Christian sources of the term *sacramentum*. See also Mayer, *Die Zeichen . . . II: Die antimanichäische Epoche*, 398–415, on ritual and liturgical applications of the term. Couturier, 'Sacramentum', 177–8, claims that, for Augustine, sacraments and mysteries as Christian rites (1) symbolize events in the life of Christ, principally his death and resurrection; (2) symbolize the invisible, inaudible grace which they produce; and (3) draw their participants' attention to the reality of salvation and sanctification.

[24] See *ep.* 55.2 (CSEL 34/2.170): 'sacramentum est . . . ut aliquid etiam significare intellegatur quod sancte accipiendum est'. He is discussing the sacramental nature of a liturgical rite, such as that of Easter. In this regard, a *sacramentum* is a *signum sacrum* (see above, p. 117 n. 6).

[25] According to this logic, the 'incredible diversity of meaning' that J. de Ghellinck et al., *Pour l'histoire du mot 'sacramentum'*, vol. 1: *Les Anténicéens* (Louvain, 1924), 16, once claimed for Augustine's use of the term 'sacrament' need not denote the lack of a unifying theme in his use of it. Each of Augustine's multiple references to 'sacrament' and to its synonym 'mystery' points to a specific instance of Christ's salvific activity, as it extends from his death and resurrection to Christian baptism, the eucharist, and scriptural interpretation.

pairs the example of Christ's death and resurrection with the 'outer man', whereas he says that the sacrament of Christ's death and resurrection acts on the 'inner man'.[26] One concludes from these pairings that he distinguishes examples and sacraments principally by the fact that the interior, spiritual renewal of the believer can only come about through sacraments, and that examples do not exercise this function on their own.

To illustrate this principle, Augustine identifies Christ's words spoken on the cross, 'My God, my God, why have you forsaken me' (Ps 21[22]:1, Mk 15:34), as 'a sacrament for the inner man', which when received in faith counters the effects of sin on the soul. Significantly, he says that this sacrament includes the 'rigours of penance and continence' (*dolores poenitentiae et continentiae*).[27] When Augustine turns to the resurrection, he designates Christ's instruction to Mary, 'Do not touch me, for I have not yet ascended to my Father' (Jn 20:17), as a 'sacrament for the inner man' as well as a 'mystery'. Following the rules for interpreting metaphorical expressions which he elaborates elsewhere,[28] he pairs Jn 20:17 with Col 3:1 ('If you have risen with Christ, seek the things that are above, where Christ is seated at God's right hand; set your thoughts on the things that are above'), and concludes that Christ's instruction not to touch his body urges believers not to seek to know him in a 'fleshly' manner (*carnaliter sapere*).[29] In saying this, Augustine indicates that sacramental understandings of eternal truths impose an intellectual and moral asceticism upon believers, inasmuch as sacraments and mysteries, like all figurative language, do not reveal their deeper meanings to the mind directly.[30] It is in this context that he interprets Christ's instruction to Mary not to touch him as a 'mystery'. In his view, Christ's words call for an intellectual renunciation of the material concepts through which he is imagined, one that allows for a deeper understanding of his divine nature.

---

[26] See *trin.* 4.6 (CCL 50.167): 'neque enim fuit peccator aut impius et ei tamquam spiritu mortuo in interiore homine renouari opus esset et tamquam resipicendo ad uitam iustitiam reuocari, sed indutus carne mortali et sola moriens, sola resurgens, ea sola nobis ad utrumque concinuit cum in ea fieret interioris hominis sacramentum, exterioris exemplum'.

[27] See *trin.* 4.6 (CCL 50.167): 'interioris enim hominis nostri sacramento data est illa uox pertinens ad mortem animae nostrae significandam non solum in Psalmo uerum etiam in cruce: *deus meus, deus meus, ut quid me dereliquisti* [Ps 21[22]:1, Mt 27:46]? [. . .] crucifixio quippe interioris hominis poenitentiae dolores intelleguntur et continentiae quidam salubris cruciatus, per quam mortem mors impietatis perimitur in qua nos non relinquit deus'.

[28] See my discussion above, pp. 126–9.

[29] See *trin.* 4.6 (CCL 50.168): 'resurrectio uero corporis domini ad sacramentum interioris resurrectionis nostrae pertinere ostenditur ubi postquam resurrexit ait mulieri: *noli me tangere; nondum enim ascendi ad patrem meum* [Jn 20:17]. cui mysterio congruit apostolus dicens: *si autem resurrexistis cum Christo, quae sursum sunt quaerite ubi Christus est in dextera dei sedens; quae sursum sunt sapite* [Col 3:1–2]. hoc est enim Christum non tangere nisi cum ascenderit ad patrem, non de Christo carnaliter sapere'.

[30] I refer here to the 'poenitentiae dolores . . . et continentiae' mentioned at *trin.* 4.6 (above, n. 27).

Important as Augustine believes sacraments and mysteries to be for revealing eternal truths to the mind, they do not in his view negate the significance of Christ's examples. He insists that Christ's example, and not merely his help (*adiutorium*), understood as grace, is necessary for salvation.[31] However, considered in themselves, that is, apart from the grace which is proper to sacraments, examples only provide external models of virtue. As a consequence, they do not renew the inner man, as do sacraments. Examples may, therefore, present models of virtue to the mind, and even act rhetorically to incite a desire for virtuous living, but by themselves they do not bring about the spiritual transformation of the inner man that ultimately allows the believer to become virtuous.[32] Augustine holds that nothing about Christ's examples of hope and courage in the face of death enables the believer to imitate these virtues, or to overcome ignorance or weakness by applying the hope and courage that they illustrate. He reasons that in order for the soul to imitate examples, the inner man must also be spiritually renewed.

Viewed in this way, the relationship between examples and sacraments parallels the relationships both between the outer and inner man and between flesh and spirit. The chiasm suggested between these pairings is significant for Augustine, because it indicates that the principle governing the relationship between Christ's sacrament and example derives from the exchange of characteristics which occurs between his divinity and humanity. As we have seen, the unity of these natures in Christ's one 'person' implies for Augustine an interaction between the attributes proper to each of Christ's natures.[33] Christ's grace, acting through his sacrament, allows

---

[31] See *trin.* 4.17 (CCL 50.183): 'cui se ipse quoque tentandus praebuit, ut ad superandas etiam temptationes eius mediator esset, non solum per adiutorium, uerum etiam per exemplum'.

[32] In response to Julian of Eclanum's claim that Peter thought Christians capable of following the example of Christ in leading sinless lives (cf. 1 Pet 2:21), Augustine argues that Peter did not believe that Christians were born as Christ was, of the Holy Spirit and the Virgin Mary, and that he was no more likely to believe Christians capable of perfect imitation of Christ. According to Augustine, Christ's examples model the behaviour Christians ought to strive for; however, to accomplish this imitation, their natures must be regenerated. See *c. Iul. imp.* 4.86 (PL 45.1387): 'proinde ut imitemur Christum, uoluntas nostra formatur: ut autem liberemur ab originali malo, natura regeneratur'.

[33] See my discussion above, pp. 91–4. B. Studer, 'Zur Christologie Augustins', *Augustinianum* 19:3 (1979), 539–46, at 545–6 (citing *corrept.* 11.30 and *c. s. Arrian.* 7), criticizes Geerlings, *Christus*, 209–22, for failing to take sufficient account of the unity of Christ's natures as a model for the unity of his sacrament and example. Studer argues that Augustine emphasizes the unity of natures in Christ and parallels it with the unity of his sacraments and examples as a way of drawing attention to the essential interrelationship between Christ's person and work. Christ does as Christ is. I follow Studer on these points; however, in my view it is the interrelationship between the two natures in Christ, and not simply their unity in one 'person', that provides Augustine with an analogy for the relationship between Christ's sacraments and examples. See my discussion of *communicatio idiomatum* above, pp. 91–2.

believers to understand and love the virtue illustrated in his example in a manner parallel to the union through which his divine nature enables his human nature to be free of sin.[34] Augustine's point is that the interaction between Christ's sacraments and examples makes it possible for his example to teach and persuade the inner man to love virtue. At the same time, the sense of mystery that sacraments convey to the mind results in the believers recognizing that it is Christ's virtue, not their own, that acts in them. In this sense for Augustine, Christ's sacrament constitutes a bridge between his example and his grace, much as the inner man acts as a bridge between the outer man and Christ's grace. This understanding of the interrelationship of Christ's sacrament and example also allows Augustine to use the terms interchangeably in certain contexts.[35]

Some scholars have observed a close similarity between Augustine's discussion of sacraments, examples, and grace in Book 4 of *De trinitate* and his treatment of these themes in his anti-Pelagian writings, and have concluded that either the entire book, or a portion of it, was written after AD 411.[36] However, not all scholars accept this view.[37] Moreover, the arguments in favour of this date depend on a series of parallel themes, technical terms,

---

[34] On Christ's freedom from sin as a result of this union, see my discussion above, pp. 93–4.

[35] At *perf. ius.* 43 (CSEL 42.46), Augustine indicates that, along with sacraments, biblical examples and precepts help the soul to overcome temptation and sin: 'currimus ergo, cum proficimus, dum sanitas nostra in proficientibus currit (sicut etiam cicatrix currere dicitur, quando bene uulnus diligenterque curatur) ut omni ex parte perfecti sine ulla simus omnino infirmitate peccati, quod non solum uult deus, uerum etiam ut impleatur facit atque adiuuat. et hoc nobiscum agit *gratia dei per Iesum Christum dominum nostrum* [Rom 7:25] non solum praeceptis, sacramentis, exemplis, sed etiam spiritu sancto, per quem latenter *diffunditur caritas in cordibus nostris* [Rom 5:5]'.

[36] J. Plagnieux, 'Influence de la lutte antipélagienne sur le "De trinitate" ou: Christocentrisme de saint Augustin', *Augustinus Magister. Congrès international augustinien, Paris, 21–24 septembre 1954*, vol. 2 (Paris, 1954), 817–26, especially 821–2, suggests that the preface and some of the initial chapters of Book 4 were edited as late as AD 419, and that they betray echoes of Augustine's opposition to Pelagius' teaching on human nature. La Bonnardière, *Recherches*, 165–77, provides support for Plagnieux's position. A. Schindler, *Wort und Analogie in Augustins Trinitätslehre* (Tübingen, 1965), 10, dates Book 4 to some time between AD 399 and 405, although, with Plagnieux, he allows (9, 142 n. 166) that its prologue was composed at some time between AD 418 and 421. P.-M. Hombert, *Nouvelles recherches de chronologie augustinienne* (Paris, 2000), 66–80, concludes that Book 4 was written in its entirety between AD 411 and 415, most likely at the end of 414, or the beginning of 415.

[37] E. Hendrikx, 'La Date de composition du *De trinitate*', *Œuvres de saint Augustin*, vol. 15: *La Trinité (Livres I–VIII) 1. Le Mystère*, ed. M. Mellet and T. Camelot (Paris, 1955), 557–66, and L. van der Lof, 'L'Exégèse exacte et objective des théophanies de l'Ancien Testament dans le "De trinitate"', *Augustiniana* 14 (1964), 485–99, at 487, date Book 4 to AD 399–405. Although Hendrikx maintains that sections of *De trinitate* were revised in later years up to AD 419, he makes no mention of emendations to Book 4. E. TeSelle, *Augustine the Theologian* (New York, 1970), 223–4, dates Book 4 to within a few years after AD 401. F. Dolbeau (ed.), *Augustin d'Hippone. Vingt-six sermons au peuple d'Afrique. Retrouvés à Mayence* (Paris, 1996) 357 and n. 70, identifies the central themes of Book 4 with *s. Dolbeau* 26, and dates it together with the sermon to AD 404. Studer, 'Sacramentum', 127–33, takes no position on the dating of Book 4, but rejects Plagnieux's suggestions of anti-Pelagian intentions behind it.

and scriptural passages which are present both in Book 4 and in other Augustinian writings whose dates are assumed to be certain.[38] Despite the sophistication of these arguments, no convincing evidence for dating any part of Book 4 has yet been produced. Moreover, the absence in Book 4 of even one identifiably anti-Pelagian accusation or argument from Augustine, combined with the uncertainty over the nature, extent, and date of emendations to this book, tells against the possibility of demonstrating anti-Pelagian echoes in it with certainty.[39] However, despite these conclusions, a clear affinity exists between Book 4 and Augustine's anti-Pelagian writings as far as his discussion of sacraments and examples is concerned.[40] In his criticism of Pelagian views concerning the role of biblical examples in leading Christians to live virtuously, Augustine adheres to the paradigm describing the relationship between Christ's sacraments, examples, and grace that he elaborates most completely in Book 4 of *De trinitate*.

In Book 8 Augustine returns to this discussion of sacraments and examples as they relate specifically to justice. He cites Gal 4:4 ('God was born of a woman'), and indicates that the verse is both an example of humility and a sacrament. He implies that the faith necessary for imitating the example is also required for understanding the biblical verse as a 'sacrament of the incarnation'. Significantly, he affirms that faith in this sacrament heals the soul of pride and frees it from sin.[41] It is equally important to recognize that in these affirmations Augustine does not intend two discrete acts of faith,

---

[38] Hombert, *Nouvelles*, 71–80, bases his dating of Book 4 in a series of this kind of internal arguments. These arguments are often forceful; however, they do not prove, either singly or collectively, that Book 4 was written between AD 411 and 415.

[39] This is the position taken by Studer, '*Sacramentum*', 127–33.

[40] Studer, ibid., 94–7, 127, argues that the same general structure of the pair 'sacrament/example', as represented in Book 4 of *De trinitate*, can be found in Augustine's writings prior to his controversy with Pelagius (citing, for example, *c. Faust.* 16.29). In my view, however, the treatment accorded this pair in the texts cited by Studer fails to show the chiastic relationship between sacrament/example and inner man/outer man as this is elaborated in Book 4. Consequently, it is not possible to draw out of the parallel texts cited by Studer the same conclusions regarding Christ's sacrament in relation to his example that makes Augustine's argument in *De trinitate* so pertinent to his dispute with the Pelagians. I illustrate this point later in this chapter in my discussion of *ep.* 140. See also Augustine's discussion of 'sacrament' in relation to 'example' at *pecc. mer.* 3.21 and *ench.* 108. In a number of passages in his anti-Pelagian writings, Augustine indicates that without grace, the biblical example does not communicate true virtue to the mind. See, for example, *pecc. mer.* 1.19, *spir. et litt.* 9–11, *nat. et gr.* 47, *perf. ius.* 43 (above, n. 35), *gr. et pecc. or.* 1.38, 1.43, 1.45, *c. Iul.* 5.58, *c. Iul. imp.* 2.108, 2.146, 2.222.

[41] See *trin.* 8.7 (CCL 50.276): 'secundum hanc notitiam cogitatio nostra informatur cum credimus pro nobis deum hominem factum ad humilitatis exemplum ad demonstrandam erga nos dilectionem dei. hoc enim nobis prodest credere et firmum atque inconcussum corde retinere, humilitatem qua natus est deus ex femina [cf. Gal 4:4], et a mortalibus per tantas contumelias perductus ad mortem summum esse medicamentum quo superbiae nostrae sanaretur tumor et altum sacramentum quo peccati uinculum solueretur'.

one focused on the example of humility, the other on the mystery of the incarnation. He claims, instead, that Christians understand the humility exemplified by Christ's birth to the extent that they believe and hope in the incarnation as the mystery which frees them from sin. He implies that even without faith in this sacrament, the mind might still recognize Christ's birth as an example of divine humility, but this recognition would not heal the soul of the 'tumour of pride' or free it from the 'bond of sin'. For Augustine, understanding the incarnation as a sacrament represents something other than an act of faith in which the mind acknowledges Christ's miraculous birth. It implies that God extends his humility to the soul, as a result of which it overcomes the pride and sin which prevent it from comprehending the incarnation as a mystery.[42] In this illumination, God also enables the believer to imitate the humility exemplified in the incarnation. Once again we see Augustine affirming that insofar as it involves grace, the interaction between sacraments and examples is patterned on the interaction between the divine and human natures within Christ's unique 'person'.[43]

Augustine's discussion of the apostle Paul in Book 8 further illustrates the relationship between example and sacrament that he sets out in Book 4. He states that believers know Paul by 'reading or hearing' (*legere, audire*) what the apostle has written (*scribere*). By referring to Paul's epistles, Augustine indicates that the context for his remarks about Paul's justice is largely scriptural.[44] Augustine then asserts that what Christians love about the apostle Paul is his 'just soul'.[45] But how do they know, he asks, what 'just' is?[46] At first he examines the possibility that, as the believer reflects upon Paul's justice, he directly perceives the 'form of justice' (*forma iustitiae*) in

---

[42] See *trin.* 8.7. (above, n. 41). Augustine actually refers *tumor superbiae* to *medicamentum* in this passage. However, it is also clear that he aligns *medicamentum* with *sacramentum*, just as he parallels *exemplum* with *demonstratio*. Studer, 'Sacramentum', 105, especially n. 83, points out that *medicamentum* normally applies to *sacramentum* in conjunction with *exemplum*. In my view, this is true if the pair is understood in terms of the interrelationship between the two terms, whereby the effects proper to one term can rightly be said to apply to the other. Note the chiastic relationship between 'exempla-sacramenta' and 'medicamenta-fomenta' at *s. Denis* 20.1.

[43] At *trin* 8.7 Augustine suggests this unity and interaction through a juxtaposition of explicit references (on the human side) to Christ's birth, suffering and death, and (on the divine side) to the miraculous nature of his birth, his miraculous powers, his omnipotence, and his resurrection and ascension.

[44] It should be noted that this point is wholly neglected by scholars who examine Book 8. See *trin.* 8.7 (CCL 50.275–6): 'quis enim legentium uel audientium quae scripsit apostolus Paulus, uel quae de illo scripta sunt, non fingat animo et ipsius apostoli faciem, et omnium quorum ibi nomina commemorantur'. The statement should be read in the context of this section and in relation to what Augustine says about Paul at *trin.* 8.9–13.

[45] See *trin.* 8.9 (CCL 50.279): 'sed id quod in illo amamus, etiam nunc uiuere credimus; amamus enim animum iustum'.

[46] See *trin.* 8.9 (CCL 50.280): 'sed quid sit iustus, unde nouimus'?

his own mind.[47] In Platonic fashion, Augustine considers this 'form' or 'idea' to be the ultimate standard of justice, from which the mind measures all justice. In the human mind this form is a reflection of the form of justice as it inheres in the divine mind.[48] But Augustine immediately abandons the possibility that the attraction to Paul's justice can be explained by a direct perception of the form of justice, because, he says, not everyone is capable of contemplating this form as it appears in the mind.[49] Nevertheless, he insists, Christians know what justice is, and they love Paul's justice, to the extent that they love the form of justice which they recognize in Paul.[50] Because they love this form, he argues, their capacity to understand and love justice deepens over time, and they become just. Moreover, Augustine maintains that as their justice increases, their concept of what it is undergoes change. They no longer regard the virtue as obliging them to measure what they owe to one another according to the classical definition of justice, 'to render to each his due'. Instead, in the light of the scriptural precept, 'Let no one owe anything except to love one another' (Rom 13:8), they understand that justice obliges them to love their neighbour.[51] For Augustine, Christians who at first love the justice they recognize in Paul progress to loving love, and to loving God as love.[52]

---

[47] See *trin.* 8.9 (CCL 50.282–3): 'an illud quod uidet ueritas est interior praesens animo qui eam ualet intueri? neque omnes ualent; et qui intueri ualent, hoc etiam quod intuentur non omnes sunt, hoc est, non sunt etiam ipsi iusti animi, sicut possunt uidere ac dicere quid sit iustus animus'.

[48] See especially *diu. qu.* 46. O'Daly, *Augustine's Philosophy* 189–99, provides an informative summary of the question and literature. See also A. Solignac, 'Analyse et sources de la question "De ideis"', *Augustinus Magister. Congrès international augustinien, Paris, 21–24 septembre 1954*, vol. 1 (Paris, 1954), 307–15, R. Nash, *The Word of God and the Mind of Man: The Crisis of Revealed Truth in Contemporary Theology* (Grand Rapids, 1982), 79–90, and R. Williams, '*Sapientia* and the Trinity: Reflections on the *De trinitate*', *Collectanea Augustiniana. Mélanges T. van Bavel*, ed. B. Bruning et al. (Leuven, 1990) = *Augustiniana* 40: 1–4 (1990), 316–32.

[49] See *trin.* 8.9 (above, n. 47).

[50] See *trin.* 8.9 (CCL 50.283): 'cur ergo alium diligimus quem credimus iustum et non diligimus ipsam formam ubi uidemus quid sit iustus animus ut et nos iusti esse possimus? an uero nisi et istam diligeremus nullo modo eum diligeremus quem ex ista diligimus, sed dum iusti non sumus minus eam diligimus quam ut iusti esse ualeamus. homo ergo qui creditur iustus ex ea forma et ueritate diligitur quam cernit et intelligit apud se ille qui diligit; ipsa uero forma et ueritas non est quomodo aliunde diligatur'.

[51] See *trin.* 8.9 (CCL 50.283): 'quod unde esse poterunt nisi inhaerendo eidem ipsi formae quam intuentur, ut inde formentur et sint iusti animi; non tantum cernentes atque intuentur iustum esse animum qui scientia atque ratione in uita ac moribus *sua cuique distribuit*, sed etiam ut ipsi iuste uiuant iusteque morati sint, sua cuique distribuendo *ut nemini quidquam debeant nisi ut inuicem diligant* [cf. Rom 13:8]? et unde inhaereretur illi formae nisi amando?' See also the discussion by MacIntyre, *Whose Justice?*, 146–63. I consider the convergence in Augustine of justice and love above, 70 n. 189.

[52] See *trin.* 8.13 (CCL 50.290): 'ita et ipsorum uitam facit a nobis diligi formae illius dilectio, secundum quam uixisse creduntur, et illorum uita credita in eamdem formam flagratiorem excitat caritatem;

In describing this movement in the believer's soul, Augustine stresses the importance of the role played by the scriptures. Christians love Paul's justice, Augustine states, because they read those passages which outline his just deeds, and because they believe that he truly lived the just life portrayed in them.[53] Augustine says that as the faithful hear and read (*audire, legere*) about the beatings and imprisonment that Paul endured, the fasting and vigils he underwent, the chastity and unfeigned charity he practised (cf. 2 Cor 6:2–10), they burn with love of justice.[54] He insists, however, that these readers of Paul could not react this way to the biblical example unless they already loved justice, even to a limited extent.[55] He then makes the significant affirmation that the love both of justice and of God increases in the soul as the 'tumour of pride' is removed.[56] From what he says earlier in this book, we know that it is the function of the sacrament of the incarnation to remove the tumour of pride and to break the bond of sin.[57] Thus, it seems clear that according to Augustine it is only through faith in Christ's sacrament that the example of Paul's justice spurs the soul on to a deeper love of God, in whom the form of justice resides.

FIGURA CRUCIS

In a treatise titled *De gratia noui testamenti* (AD 412), Augustine illustrates, better than in any other work, the close interrelationship between Christ's sacrament and example that he outlines in Books 4 and 8 of *De trinitate*. He returns in this treatise to the exposition of Eph 3:18 which featured prominently in his earlier work *Ad inquisitiones Ianuarii* (AD 400), and to the image of Christ crucified as a symbol of the virtues associated with the just life.[58] *De gratia* shows that, at the time of its writing, Augustine's

---

ut quando flagrantius diligimus deum, tanto certius sereniusque uideamus, quia in deo conspicimus in commutabilem formam iustitiae, secundum quam hominem uiuere oportere iudicamus. ualet ergo fides ad cognitionem et ad dilectionem dei, non tamquam omnino incogniti, aut omnino non dilecti; sed quo cognoscantur manifestius, et quo firmius diligatur'.

53 See *trin.* 8.13 (CCL 50.289): 'quid enim est, quaeso, quod exardescimus, cum audimus et legimus?'. Here follows the text of 2 Cor 6:2–10, a description of Paul's sufferings for Christ. Augustine insists, 'quid est quod accendimur in dilectione Pauli apostoli cum ista legimus?'.

54 See *trin.* 8.13 (above, n. 53).

55 See *trin.* 8.13 (CCL 50.290): 'et nisi hanc formam quam semper stabilem atque incommutabilem cernimus praecipue diligeremus, non ideo diligeremus illum quia eius uitam cum in carne uiueret huic formae coaptatam et congruentem fuisse fide retinemus'.

56 See *trin.* 8.12 (CCL 50.287): 'quanto igitur saniores sumus a tumore superbiae tanto sumus dilectione pleniores. et qui nisi deo plenus est qui plenus est dilectione?'

57 See *trin.* 8.7 (above, n. 41).

58 On *Ad inquisitiones Ianuarii* (= *ep.* 54–5), see my discussion above, pp. 123–33. The treatise *De gratia noui testamenti* is better known as *ep.* 140 (CSEL 45.155–234). For a summary of its argument

attention was already absorbed by the relationship between nature and grace which is central to his controversy with the Pelagians.[59] He provides in this treatise yet another account of the relationship between the unity and interaction of Christ's two natures, and the analogous unity and interaction of his grace, sacraments, and examples. Only at the end of the treatise does the full significance of its title, *The Grace of the New Testament*, become clear, as Augustine turns his attention to the 'enemies of grace', whom he will later identify as 'Pelagians'. He accuses them of claiming for themselves the merit for their own virtuous deeds.[60] In taking this position, he argues, they refuse to acknowledge the hidden source of justice in the grace that comes from God. For this reason, Augustine specifies in *De gratia* the role of grace in the interpretation of biblical examples of justice to a further extent than he does in *Ad inquisitiones*. To do so, he illustrates the relationship between Christ's examples and sacraments.

In *De gratia* as in *Ad inquisitiones*, Augustine divides the cross into four parts, each of which he pairs with one of the four coordinates employed at Eph 3:18 to describe the height, breadth, length, and depth of Christ's love ('May you and all the saints be enabled to measure, in all its breadth and length and height and depth, the love of Christ, in order to know what surpasses knowledge'). Thus, the portion of the vertical beam extending upward from the crossbeam, against which Christ's head is positioned, recalls for Augustine the 'height' of Christ's love, and symbolizes his perseverance in hope as he faces death. The crossbeam represents the 'breadth' of his love and symbolizes his just deeds. The vertical beam represents the 'length' of his love and symbolizes his endurance of suffering and evil. As in his exposition of the cross in *Ad inquisitiones*, Augustine is clear in *De gratia* that these three parts of the cross illustrate examples which Christ offers to the faithful for their imitation.[61] He likens the ease with which these three

---

see G. Bonner, 'The Significance of Augustine's *De gratia novi testamenti*', *Collectanea Augustiniana. Mélanges T. van Bavel*, ed. B. Bruning et al. (Leuven, 1990) = *Augustiniana* 40:1–4 (1990), 531–59, at 532–5, where he dates this treatise to the early months of AD 412. Augustine's discussion of *figura crucis* is found at *ep.* 140.62–4. He first employs the symbolism of the cross to interpret Eph 3:18 in AD 397 at *doctr. chr.* 2.41. In addition to these two passages and the aforementioned passage at *ep.* 55.25 (AD 400), the symbolism of the cross is found in conjunction with Eph 3:18 at *en. Ps.* 103.1.14, *s.* 53.15, 165.2–5, and *ep.* 147.34, of which only the last can be dated with certainty (AD 413/14).

[59] Bonner, 'Significance', 555–8, emphasizes the work's anti-Pelagian elements, about which see also *retr.* 2.36.

[60] See *ep.* 140.83–5.

[61] See *ep.* 140.62 (CSEL 44.208): 'unde ipsa caritas nunc in bonis operibus dilectionis exercetur, qua se ad subueniendum, quaqua uersum potest, porrigit, et haec latitudo est; nunc longanimitate aduersa tolerat et in eo, quod ueraciter tenuit, perseuerat, et haec longitudo est; hoc autem totum propter adipiscendam uitam facit aeternam, quae illi promittitur in excelso, et haec altitudo est'. It is clear

segments of the cross are visible to any observer to the ease with which the reader of the scriptures is able to identify Christ's virtues exemplified in the Gospel accounts of his crucifixion.[62] Augustine then turns to the part of the vertical beam buried beneath the earth, which is not visible. He concludes that it represents the 'depth' of Christ's love, and that it symbolizes the hidden source of Christ's virtues. In *Ad inquisitiones*, Augustine had touched only briefly upon this portion of the cross, saying that it represents the 'hiddenness of the sacrament'.[63] Although vague, this reference to the sacrament in relation to the example of Christ's virtue is consistent with the later, fuller exposition in *De gratia*. There, confronted for the first time with presuppositions about the capacity of believers to understand Christ's example without grace, Augustine draws a starker contrast between the visible part of the cross representing examples of just conduct and the invisible part, buried beneath the earth, which he identifies variously as God's love, grace, and mercy. He thinks of this hidden part of the cross as a symbol of the difficulty involved in understanding the source of Christ's example, citing 1 Cor 13:12 ('now we see in a glass darkly, then we shall see face to face').[64] This contrast in symbolism between Christ's visible example and its invisible source represents the tension between the mind's surface perception of virtue in the biblical text and the more difficult but fuller understanding which the text offers as sacrament or mystery, and which the soul receives as grace. This tension is similar to that found in Augustine's explanation of the relationship between 'flesh' and 'spirit', and, as will be demonstrated, between knowledge (*scientia*) and wisdom (*sapientia*). Augustine highlights this tension by quoting Rom 11:33–4:

that Augustine intends the image of Christ crucified as a biblical example of his justice. See also *ep.* 140.64, 140.82. Other references to Christ's example concern the visible elements of his passion. See, for example, *ep.* 140.25, 140.27, 140.29. See my discussion of Augustine's parallel argument in *Ad inquisitiones* above, pp. 130–3.

[62] In addition to the references given above, n. 61, see *ep.* 140.66 (CSEL 44.213), where the term *exemplum* occurs in the context of 1 Pet 2:21, following the treatment of Eph 3:14–19 at *ep.* 140.62–4. See also *ep.* 140.68 (CSEL 44.215–16): 'haec quippe nos admonens, et exemplo suo exhortans in euangelio suo locutus est'.

[63] See *ep.* 55.25 (CSEL34/2.197): 'profundum autem, quod terrae infixum est, secretum sacramenti praefigurat'.

[64] See *ep.* 140.62 (CSEL 44.208): 'uita enim Christus est, qui habitat in cordibus eorum interim per fidem, post etiam per speciem. uident enim *nunc in aenigmate per speculum, tunc autem facie ad faciem* [. . .] existit uero ex occulto ista caritas, ubi *fundati* quodam modo et *radicati* sumus [Eph 3:17], ubi causae uoluntatis dei non uestigantur, cuius gratia sumus salui facti *non ex operibus iustitiae, quae nos fecimus, sed secundum eius misericordiam* [Tit 3:5]. *uoluntarie quippe genuit nos uerbo ueritatis* [Jas 1:18]. et haec uoluntas eius in abdito est. cuius secreti profunditatem quodam modo expauescens apostolus clamat: *o altitudo diuitiarum sapientiae et scientiae dei. quam inscrutabilia sunt iudicia eius et inuestigabiles uiae eius. quis enim cognouit sensum domini?*' [Rom 11:33–4].

O the depth (*altitudo*) of the riches and wisdom (*sapientia*) and knowledge (*scientia*) of God! How unsearchable are his judgments (*iudicia*) and how inscrutable his ways (*uiae*)! For who has known the mind of the Lord (*sensum domini*)?

Augustine pairs the references to 'depth' at Rom 11:33 (*altitudo*) and at Eph 3:18 (*profundum*). He interprets these scriptural verses together in order to affirm that the hidden nature of divine wisdom (*sapientia*) and knowledge (*scientia*) ultimately frustrates attempts to comprehend the full meaning (*sensus, uia*) of biblical examples of justice.[65]

Augustine argues that believers who desire to understand and practise true justice should seek to know and love God, and not an abstract concept of virtue. He accuses his adversaries of failing to grasp the hiddenness of divine grace and its role in enabling the soul to imitate Christ's virtues. He traces this error to their concept of God. Citing 1 Cor 8:2–3 ('If anyone thinks he knows anything, he does not yet know as he ought to know, but if anyone loves God, he knows God'), Augustine equates knowledge of God with love of God.[66] He insists that both knowledge and love of God are received by the soul as one and the same divine grace. God cannot be known in a true sense in any other way. Virtues are also known and loved through this same divine gift. Christians who take credit for their own just deeds, in effect, refuse God's gift of himself. Not knowing God as the source of justice, they do not know him in any true sense.[67] Not

---

[65] See *ep.* 140.62 (CSEL 44.207–9): 'existit uero ex occulto ista caritas, ubi *fundati* [Eph 3:17] quodam modo *et radicati* [Eph 3:17] sumus, ubi causae uoluntatis dei non uestigantur, cuius gratia sumus salui facti *non ex operibus iustitiae, quae nos fecimus, sed secundum eius misericordiam* [Tit 3:5]. *uoluntarie quippe genuit nos uerbo ueritatis* [Jas 1:18]. et haec uoluntas eius in abdito est. cuius secreti profunditatem quodam modo expauescens apostolus clamat: *o altitudo diuitiarum sapientiae et scientiae dei. quam inscrutabilia sunt iudicia eius et inuestigabiles uiae eius. quis enim cognouit sensum domini?* [Rom 11:33–4] et hoc est profundum. altitudo quippe commune nomen est excelso et profundo, sed, cum in excelso dicitur, sublimitatis eminentia commendatur, cum autem in profundo, difficultas inuestigationis et cognitionis. unde et illud deo dicitur: *quam magnificata sunt opera tua, domine. nimis profundae factae sunt cogitationes tuae* [Ps 91[92]:6]. et iterum: *iudicia tua uelut multa abyssus* [Ps 35[36]:7]. hinc igitur est illud apostoli, quod requirendum inter cetera posuisti: *huius rei gratia,* inquit, *flecto genua mea ad patrem domini nostri Iesu Christi, ex quo omnis paternitas in caelis et in terra nominatur, ut det uobis secundum diuitias gloriae suae uirtute corroborari per spiritum eius, in interiore homine habitare Christum per fidem in cordibus uestris, ut in caritate radicati et fundati praeualeatis comprehendere cum omnibus sanctis, quae sit latitudo et longitudo et altitudo et profundum, scire etiam supereminentem scientiam caritatis Christi, ut impleamini in omnem plenitudinem dei'* [Eph 3:14–19]. See also his concluding remarks at 140.82 (CSEL 44.231): 'intellegentes igitur peregrinationem nostram in hac uita mundo crucifigamur extendentes manus in latitudine bonorum operum et longanimitate usque in finem perseuerantes atque habentes cor sursum, *ubi Christus est in dextera dei sedens* [Col 3:1], totumque hoc non nobis sed illius misericordiae tribuentes, cuius profunda iudicia omnem scrutatorem fatigant'.

[66] See *ep.* 140.85.

[67] For references to Augustine's concept of God as *fons iustitiae*, see above, p. 13 n. 42.

knowing him, they also do not understand or love the justice of which he is the only source.[68]

Augustine's treatment of Eph 3:17–18 in *De gratia* suggests that 'mystery' provides the form under which God is known and loved in this life. He concludes that those Christians who reject grace as the source of their own justice also reject the role of mystery in deepening the understanding of justice. In his treatment of justice throughout *De gratia*, Augustine employs numerous scriptural passages, in addition to Rom 11:33–4 and 1 Cor 8:2–3, that underscore the incomplete nature of knowledge concerning eternal truths: 2 Cor 5:6–7 ('we walk by faith and not by sight'), Jn 1:18 ('no one has ever seen God'), Rom 1:17 ('the just man lives by faith'), 1 Cor 13:12 ('now we see through a glass darkly'), and Eph 3:19 ('the love of Christ surpasses all knowledge').[69] In this context, he also speaks of the eucharist as the sacrament by which the 'high things' (*alta*) that God has hidden from the wise and prudent are revealed to little ones (cf. Mt 11:25). Partaking of this 'bread come down from heaven' (Jn 6:50) implies clinging to Christ as the giver of grace by which alone one is enabled to observe the commandment to live justly.[70] Christ's admonition, 'unless you eat my flesh and drink my blood, you shall not have life in you' (Jn 6:54) means that the love by which Christians 'see now through a glass darkly' and by the light of which they practise just deeds lies hidden and beyond their grasp.[71] At the close of his discussion of the figure of Christ crucified, Augustine contrasts the partial, indirect character of knowledge in the present life with the direct, complete, and enduring understanding of truth in the life to come.[72] Concluding that his adversaries do not acknowledge that the virtues which proceed from God are known and practised only partially in this life, he likens them to the

---

[68] Augustine's frequent references to 'participation' and 'illumination' in this treatise are intended to strengthen his argument that Christians who believe themselves to be the source of their own justice reject the divine initiative through which such knowledge is made possible. See, for example, *ep.* 140.52 (CSEL 44.198): 'quia non fit anima iusta nisi participatione melioris, qui iustificat impium – quid enim habet, quod non accepit' (1 Cor 4:7). See also *ep.* 140.7, 140.10–12, 140.54–8, 140.66, 140.68–70, 140.74, 140.77, 140.80–2.

[69] See *ep.* 140.24, 140.45, 140.52, 140.62. This last section, in which Augustine quotes 1 Cor 13:12 and Eph 3:19, marks the beginning of his discussion of the figure of Christ crucified in relation to Eph 3:17–18. Other scriptural passages are cited in this section which also support his emphasis on mystery as the form that expresses reason's difficult grasp of eternal truths: Ps 91(92):6 ('your thoughts are exceedingly deep'), Ps 35(36):7 ('your judgments are a great abyss'). See *ep.* 140.62 (above, n. 65).

[70] See *ep.* 140.60–2 (CSEL 44.206–8).

[71] See *ep.* 140.62 (CSEL 44.207): 'uita enim Christus est, qui habitat in cordibus eorum, interim per fidem, post etiam per speciem. uident enim nunc in aenigmate per speculum, tunc autem facie ad faciem. unde ipsa caritas nunc in bonis operibus dilectionis exercetur, qua se ad subueniendum quaquauersum potest, porrigit'.

[72] See *ep.* 140.26.

foolish virgins of Mt 25:1–13. He says that he is aware of their reputation for leading upright Christian lives, but observes that they lack wisdom. As a consequence, he charges, although they outwardly resemble holy men and women, their virtues are only apparent.[73] Reminding his readers that wisdom is another name for love, and love is the light that illuminates human reason and judgment, he says in conclusion that Christians who believe themselves to be the source of their own justice despise the light of right judgment, God's love freely given. Wise Christians resemble the wise virgins of Mt 25 who recognize God as the depthless source of their own wisdom, love, and justice.[74]

Augustine's designation of the scriptural passage at Eph 3:17–18 as a 'mystery' (*mysterium*) not only reveals the limited capacities of reason to understand virtue, but also heightens the sense of ambiguity regarding justice as illustrated in the scriptures.[75] He notes that the buried part of the cross is hidden, yet it alone provides the foundation for the visible remainder of the cross.[76] Unseen as it is, this hidden portion of the cross 'shows' (*ostendere, exsurgere*) the figure of Christ crucified to the mind as an example of virtue. Augustine's point is that grace has a hidden dimension which ensures that the scriptural passage's complete meaning will elude human understanding. Paradoxically, it is this same hidden quality of grace that provides the basis for true understanding of the biblical text.[77] By his conclusion that 'the figure of the cross is shown in this mystery', Augustine means two things. First, that the scriptural passage in question (Eph 3:18) can be interpreted through the image of the cross as a divine instruction about the virtues illustrated by Christ's crucifixion. Second, that the deepest understanding of those virtues, and of their source, lies beyond the grasp of reason.[78]

---

[73] See *ep.* 140.83–4.   [74] See *ep.* 140.45, 140.54, 140.82.

[75] See *ep.* 140.64 (CSEL 44.211): 'in hoc mysterio figura crucis ostenditur [. . .] iam uero illud ex ligno, quod non apparet, quod fixum occultatur, unde totum illud exsurgit, profunditatem significat gratuitae gratiae; in quo multorum ingenia conteruntur id uestigare conantia, ut ad extremum eis dicatur: *o homo tu quis es, qui respondeas deo?* [Rom 9:20]. The parallel text of Eph 3:18–19 given at *ep.* 55.25 (CSEL 34/2.197) employs *sacramentum* in place of *mysterium*: 'profundum autem, quod terrae infixum est, secretum sacramenti praefigurat'.

[76] See *ep.* 140.64 (above, n. 75). See also a parallel statement of this principle at *s.* 165.3 (PL 38.904): 'habet et profundum, hoc est quod in terra figitur, et non uidetur. uidete magnum sacramentum. ab illo profundo quod non uides, surgit totum quod uides'.

[77] See *ep.* 140.63 (CSEL 44.208), where Augustine returns to a discussion of the four coordinates of Eph 3:18 and explains this double effect of grace upon the perception and understanding of the text: '*et profundum*, unde gratuita gratia dei secundum secretum et abditum uoluntatis eius existit, ibi enim *radicati*, ibi *fundati* sumus, radicati, propter agriculturam, fundati, propter aedificationem'.

[78] See *ep.* 140.62 (above. n. 65) with reference to *causa uoluntatis dei* and *sensus domini* (Rom 11:34). At *pecc. mer.* 1.29–30 and *s.* 165.5–7, Augustine argues on the basis of Eph 3:18 that human reason cannot

SAPIENTIA ET SCIENTIA

Augustine's discussion of Christ's example and sacrament in Books 4 and 8 of *De trinitate* is closely linked with his discussion in Books 12 and 13 of knowledge (*scientia*) in relation to divine wisdom (*sapientia*). These books contain Augustine's clearest theoretical discussion of the relationship between knowledge and wisdom as they pertain to moral reasoning. In Book 12 Augustine defines two different types of reasoning, *ratio scientiae* and *ratio sapientiae*. He applies the term *ratio scientiae* to reasoning about material reality, including the events and temporal goods that belong to the physical world.[79] He describes wisdom as 'the love of God by which we desire to see God, and believe and hope that we shall'.[80] It follows for him that *ratio sapientiae* consists in the faith, hope, and love through which the mind reflects on God and on those eternal things (*res aeternae*) that pertain to God, such as true virtue and happiness, as well as eternal rest.[81] Augustine calls *ratio sapientiae* 'contemplation', whereas he understands *ratio scientiae* as a form of moral action in which the mind 'makes good use of temporal things' and 'abstains from evil things'.[82] Augustine explains that these two forms of reason are distinct,[83] and he illustrates the difference between them by turning to their respective roles in biblical interpretation. He says that *ratio scientiae* reflects on the historical circumstances surrounding various scriptural accounts of Christ's words and deeds, as background to understanding his examples.[84] But Augustine insists that because Christ is the incarnate Word of God, every word and deed of his expresses an eternal truth, extending beyond the particular circumstances

---

    fathom the justice of God's decision to allow some young children to be saved through baptism, while denying that salvation to other young children who are not baptized.

[79] *Ratio scientiae* is defined at *trin.* 12.17 (CCL 50.371): 'cognitio rerum temporalium atque mutabilium nauandis uitae huius actionibus necessaria', and '[intentio] mentis quae in rebus temporalibus et corporalibus propter actionis officium ratiocinandi uiuacitate uersatur'. *Scientia* is defined in general terms at *util. cred.* 25 (CSEL 25/1.32) as something seen clearly in the mind: 'aliquid mentis certa ratione uideatur'.

[80] See *trin.* 12.22 (CCL 50.375): 'amor eius quo nunc desideramus eum uidere credimusque et speramus nos esse uisuros, et quantum proficimus *uidemus nunc per speculum in aenigmate, tunc autem* [1 Cor 13:12] in manifestatione'.

[81] See *trin.* 12.22.

[82] See *trin.* 12.22 (CCL 50.375): 'actio qua bene utimur temporalibus rebus [. . .] *Abstinere autem a malis* (Job 28:28), quam Iob scientiam dixit esse, rerum procul dubio temporalium est'. On action–contemplation in regard to knowledge–wisdom, see *trin.* 12.17, 12.19.

[83] See especially *trin.* 12.21–5. See also *trin.* 12.17 (CCL 50.371): 'nunc de illa parte rationis ad quam pertinet scientia, id est cognitio rerum temporalium atque mutabilium nauandis uitae huius actionibus necessaria [. . .] aeterna uero et incommutabilia spiritalia ratione sapientiae intelleguntur', along with the discussion by O'Daly, *Augustine's Philosophy*, 92–102.

[84] See *trin.* 12.22. Cf. *trin.* 14.11.

of his earthly life.[85] In making this point, he implies that by reflecting upon Christ's examples against the broader spiritual perspective provided by faith, hope, and love, *ratio sapientiae* leads to a fuller comprehension of these examples.[86] At the same time, he does not dismiss *ratio scientiae* because it is the subordinate form of reason.[87] 'Knowledge' as Augustine uses the term in this context refers to thought processes through which the mind makes judgments on the basis of temporal criteria, such as natural science and history. He acknowledges that its function in providing believers with an understanding of the world in which they live, including the store of knowledge passed on to them by books and formal instruction, is essential to moral decision-making. He insists that without this knowledge, no one could practise those civic virtues – prudence, fortitude, temperance, and justice – that are necessary for right living.[88] However, citing 1 Cor 8:1 ('knowledge puffs up, but love builds up'), Augustine warns that when it is not guided by wisdom, knowledge induces in the soul an inflated self-esteem (*praegrauatus animus*).[89] He thus identifies in human knowledge the same kind of presumption which he says occurs in the mind when it interprets Christ's example without the benefit of faith in his sacrament. In both cases, the soul relies on its own capacities to draw moral lessons from the scriptures. By doing so, it rejects the humility which grace introduces to the mind when it seeks to understand the scriptures by loving God.[90] Knowledge and wisdom are united only when the soul opens itself to the grace of humility, through repentance of sin, confession, and prayer for divine pardon.[91] In saying this, Augustine echoes a similar point which he

---

[85] See *trin.* 12.22.   [86] See *trin.* 13.24.

[87] At *trin.* 12.25, Augustine expressly declares the superiority of *ratio sapientiae* over *ratio scientiae*.

[88] See *trin.* 12.21 (CCL 50.374): 'sine scientia quippe nec uirtutes ipsae quibus recte uiuitur possunt haberi, per quas haec uita misera sic gubernetur, ut ad illam quae uere beata est, perueniatur aeternam', together with *trin.* 12.22 (CCL 50.376): 'quamobrem quidquid prudenter, fortiter, temperanter et iuste agimus, ad eam pertinet scientiam, siue disciplinam, qua in euitandis malis bonisque appetendis actio nostra uersatur'. At *trin.* 14.11 Augustine includes within the realm of knowledge the learning acquired from books and teaching.

[89] See, for example, *trin.* 12.16 (CCL 50.370): 'cum enim neglecta caritate sapientiae quae semper eodem modo manet. concupiscitur scientia ex mutabilium temporaliumque experimento, inflat non aedificat [cf. 1 Cor 8:1], ita praegrauatus animus quasi pondere suo a beatitudine expellitur'. See also *trin.* 12.21. I discuss 1 Cor 8:1 as it pertains to Augustine's scriptural exegesis above, pp. 127–8.

[90] See *trin.* 12.16.

[91] See *trin.* 12.16–19, 12.21–3. At *trin.* 12.16 (CCL 50.370–1), Augustine affirms, 'nec redire potest effusis ac perditis uiribus nisi gratia conditoris sui ad poenitentiam uocantis et peccata donantis. *quis enim infelicem animam liberabit a corpore mortis huius nisi gratia dei per Iesum Christum dominum nostrum?* (Rom 7:24–5). The argument continues at *trin.* 12.18 (CCL 50.372): 'et ideo de talibus quoque cogitationibus uenia petenda est pectusque percutiendum atque dicendum: *dimitte nobis debita nostra*, faciendumque quod sequitur atque in oratione iungendum: *sicut et nos dimittimus debitoribus nostris* [Mt 6:12]'.

made in Book 4 about the 'rigours of penance' (*dolores poenitentiae*) that are necessary for the soul's understanding of Christ's sacraments.[92]

Other parallels between the pairs sacrament–example and wisdom–knowledge become apparent when in Book 13 of *De trinitate* Augustine turns to Col 2:3, where Paul expresses the hope that believers 'recognize the mystery of God (*mysterium dei*) that is Christ Jesus, in whom are hidden all the treasures of wisdom and knowledge'.[93] Augustine interprets this passage to mean that the unity of Christ's divine and human natures in his unique 'person' entails the same kind of unity between the wisdom he possesses as the eternal Word and the human knowledge he acquires through the incarnation.[94] For Augustine, this form of unity requires that Christ's wisdom and knowledge not be understood as detached modes of reason, but as communicating with one another, without losing their distinctiveness. He deduces from Col 2:3 that Christ mediates his wisdom and knowledge to the soul in this unity, so that *ratio sapientiae* and *ratio scientiae* interact with each other in the human mind in a manner analogous to Christ's wisdom and knowledge.[95] Augustine concludes that what pertains in the reasoning process to knowledge therefore applies equally to wisdom, and vice versa, so that the terms can be employed interchangeably.[96] As a consequence, the grace by which the human mind loves God (*ratio sapientiae*) enlightens reason as it reflects on its acquired learning about the temporal world (*ratio scientiae*). Applying this principle to scriptural interpretation, Augustine determines that human wisdom and knowledge do not constitute two unconnected modes of reason, whereby the believer first reflects

---

[92] See above p. 153 n. 27.

[93] See *trin.* 13.24. For a parallel interpretation, also employing Col 2:1, see *ep.* 149.24.

[94] See *trin.* 13.24 (CCL 50A.415): 'haec autem omnia quae pro nobis *uerbum caro factum* [Jn 1:14] temporaliter et localiter fecit et pertulit secundum distinctionem quam demonstrare suscepimus ad scientiam pertinent non ad sapientiam. quod autem uerbum est sine tempore et sine loco, est patri coaeternum et ubique totum, de quo si quisquam potest quantum potest ueracem proferre sermonem, *sermo* erit ille *sapientiae* [1 Cor 12:8]; ac per hoc *uerbum caro factum* est Christus Iesus, et sapientiae thesauros habet et scientiae. nam scribens apostolus ad Colossenses: . . . *ad conoscendum mysterium dei, quod est Christus Iesus, in quo sunt omnes thesauri sapientiae et scientiae absconditi* [Col 2:3] [. . .] si inter se distant haec duo ut sapientia diuinis, scientia humanis attributa sit rebus, utrumque agnosco in Christo et mecum omnis eius fidelis. et cum lego: *uerbum caro factum est, et habitauit in nobis* [Jn 1:14], in uerbo intellego uerum dei filium. in carne agnosco uerum hominis filium, et utrumque simul in unam personam dei et hominis ineffabili gratiae largitate coniunctum'.

[95] See *trin.* 13.24 (CCL 50A.415): 'scientia ergo nostra Christus est, sapientia quoque nostra idem Christus est. ipse nobis fidem de rebus temporalibus inserit; ipse de sempiternis exhibet ueritatem. per ipsum pergimus ad ipsum, tendimus per scientiam ad sapientiam; ab uno tamen eodemque Christo non recedimus *in quo sunt omnes thesauri sapientiae et scientiae absconditi* [Col 2:3].

[96] See *trin.* 13.24 (CCL 50A.417): 'nec ista duo sic accipiamus quasi non liceat dicere uel istam sapientiam quae in rebus humanis est uel illam scientiam quae in diuinis. loquendi enim latiore consuetudine utraque sapientia utraque scientia dici potest'.

on Christ's deeds, and then confesses his sinfulness and prays to God for guidance. Instead, Christ's mediation cleanses the believer of his sinfulness and incapacity to understand clearly the revealed truths expressed in the scriptures. As a consequence, the mind reflects on the scriptures with faith, hope, and love of God, and understands eternal truths under the form of mystery.[97]

Nowhere in Augustine's writings can a clearer application of these discussions in *De trinitate* be found than in his writings against the Pelagians. We have already seen them applied in *De gratia noui testamenti*, in relation to the example and sacrament of Christ's death. In another early anti-Pelagian treatise, *De spiritu et littera*, Augustine clarifies further the nature of the interrelationship between knowledge and wisdom for the proper interpretation of scriptural passages concerning the just life. There, he takes up the argument advanced by some Christians (he does not yet call them 'Pelagians') that in the double commandment to love God and to love one's neighbour as oneself (Mt 22:37–9, Mk 12:30–1, Lk 10:27), Christ plainly summarizes the essential features of the just life. As a consequence, these Christians maintain that there is no excuse for ignorance about what constitutes just conduct.[98] Against this argument, Augustine alludes to Jas 3:2 ('we all sin in many ways'), and insists that even Christians who believe God's law to be clear and who intend to observe it always fail to do so in at

---

[97] See *trin.* 13.24 (CCL 50A.416): 'quod uero idem ipse est *unigenitus a patre plenus gratiae et ueritatis* [Jn 1:14], id actum est ut idem ipse sit in rebus pro nobis temporaliter gestis, cui per eamdem fidem mundamur, ut eum stabiliter contemplemur in rebus aeternis'. See Augustine's discussion just prior to this statement (above, n. 95), where the function of the term 'mystery' (*mysterium*) at Col 2:3 in relation to Christ and to his wisdom and knowledge is underscored by Paul's reference to 'hidden treasure' (*thesaurus absconditus*). Augustine's description of the 'ineffable abundance of grace' by which the two natures are conjoined in one 'person' likewise points to the mystery through which the incarnation is understood by believers. In his deservedly well-regarded study, R. Lorenz, 'Gnade und Erkenntnis bei Augustinus', *Zeitschrift für Kirchengeschichte* 75 (1964), 21–78, leads us into this relationship between knowledge and wisdom as between faith and love, but fails to explain the unity between faith and love as being derived from the interrelationship of Christ's two natures. Hence, his account of Augustine's view does not altogether succeed in avoiding the dualism of a knowledge situated beside love, without interaction between them. D. Hassel, 'Conversion, Theory and Scientia in *De trinitate*', *Recherches augustiniennes* 2 (1962), 383–401, at 393–4, similarly omits any reference to this interrelationship of natures in Christ's unique 'person' as the cause of what he refers to as Augustine's understanding of the 'dynamic union of wisdom with *scientia*'.

[98] See *spir. et litt.* 64 (CSEL 60.225): 'sed fortasse quispiam putauerit nihil nobis deesse ad cognitionem iustitiae, quod dominus uerbum consummans et breuians super terram dixit in duobus praeceptis totam legem prophetasque pendere nec ea tacuit, sed uerbis apertissimis prompsit. *diliges*, inquit, *dominum deum tuum ex toto corde tuo et ex tota anima tua et ex tota mente tua*, et: *diliges proximum tuum tamquam te ipsum* [Mt 22:37, 39]. quid uerius his inpletis inpleri omnino iustitiam?'. A clear example of this reasoning concerning Mt 22:37–39 can be found in Pelagius, *De uita christiana* 8 (PL 50.391–2). I accept the arguments of R. Evans, 'Pelagius, Fastidius, and the Pseudo-Augustinian *De vita christiana*', *Journal of Theological Studies* n. s. 13 (1962), 72–98, in favour of attributing this work to Pelagius. However, Frede, *Kirchenschriftsteller*, 304, questions the attribution, without offering arguments. Nuvolone and Solignac, 'Pélage', 2912–14, ascribe it to Fastidius.

least some minor respects. He holds that such failure is readily apparent to all observers, and that reason confirms it.[99] Even those who study the scriptures attentively attain only a partial understanding of God's law. For to derive moral law even from the clear language of the scriptures in anything more than a rudimentary fashion requires that one know God. Knowledge of the justice required by God's law is commensurate with knowledge of God. Augustine offers no further explanation of this principle, but cites 1 Cor 13:12 ('For now we see in a glass darkly, but then we shall see face to face') in support of his position that although knowledge of God is acquired gradually in this life, it is complete only after death.[100] Thus, both God and justice can only be fully known in the afterlife.

In this same argument, he suggests that one's knowledge of God is proportionate to his love of God. As a result, he argues, since knowledge of God and knowledge of justice are commensurate with each other, and knowledge and love of God are similarly interrelated, then knowledge of justice and love of God are likewise commensurate with each other.[101] In other words, believers are able to draw deeper understandings of what justice requires of them from scriptural precepts only insofar as their love of God also deepens. By way of illustration, he suggests, on the basis of Christ's testimony at Jn 15:13 ('no one has greater love than to lay down his life for his friends'), that the martyrs are a prime example of the interrelationship of knowledge and love of God. Christians are more willing to die for Christ the more they love him, and they love him more deeply as they know him better through faith. Knowing Christ as thoroughly as they do – as his 'friends' – they love him to the furthest extent possible in this life. By giving their lives in defence of Christ's name, martyrs are moved by love of God to understand and fulfil what Christ called the most extreme demand of justice.[102] Finally,

---

[99] See *spir. et litt.* 64 (CSEL 60.225): 'uerum tamen qui hoc adtendit, etiam illud adtendat, quam in multis offendamus omnes [cf. Jas 3:2], dum putamus deo quem diligimus placere uel non displicere quod facimus et postea per scripturam eius siue certa et perspicua ratione commoniti, cum didicerimus quod ei non placeat, paenitendo deprecamur, ut ignoscat. plena humana uita est documentis talibus'.

[100] See *spir. et litt.* 64 (CSEL 60.225): 'unde autem minus nouimus quid ei placeat, nisi quia et ipse minus notus est nobis? *uidemus enim nunc per speculum in enigmate, tunc autem facie ad faciem* (1 Cor 13:12). quis uero existimare audeat, cum eo uentum fuerit, quod ait: *ut cognoscam sicut et cognitus sum* [1 Cor. 13:12], tantam dei dilectionem fore contemplatoribus eius, quanta fidelibus nunc est, aut ullo modo hanc illi tamquam de proximo conparandam?'.

[101] See *spir. et litt.* 64 (CSEL 60.225): 'porro si quanto maior notitia tanto erit maior dilectio, profecto nunc quantum deest dilectioni tantum perficiendae iustitiae deesse credendum est. sciri enim aliquid uel credi et tamen non diligi potest; diligi autem quod neque scitur neque creditur non potest'.

[102] See *spir. et litt.* 64 (CSEL 60.225): 'at si credendo ad tantam dilectionem sancti peruenire potuerunt, qua certe maiorem in hac uita esse non posse dominus ipse testatus est, ut animam suam pro fide uel pro fratribus ponerent [cf. Jn 15:13]'.

Augustine reasons that, because God can be loved perfectly only in the life to come, the commandment to love him with one's 'whole heart and whole soul and whole mind' (Mt 22:37) must be understood as instructing believers to love him in faith and in the hope that they will attain perfection in the afterlife. Augustine counters the assurance with which his adversaries claim to understand fully the dictates of the moral law by suggesting that those, instead, who recognize how imperfect is their virtue have made great progress toward perfecting it.[103]

Turning his attention in *De natura et gratia* (AD 415) to Pelagius specifically, Augustine once again rejects the assumption that clearly expressed divine commands in the scriptures prove that God believes human beings naturally capable of understanding and fulfilling them. Commenting on Jas 3:8 ('No man can tame his own tongue'), Pelagius had concluded that the apostle was rebuking the faithful for their unwillingness to observe straightforward divine commandments. 'You can tame wild animals; can none of you tame your tongue?', Pelagius imagines James to be saying. In response, Augustine turns to the wider context of James's epistle in order to determine that the apostle, instead, is making a general observation about the moral limits inherent in the human condition.[104] He cites Jas 3:13–17, where the apostle contrasts 'earthly wisdom' (*sapientia terrena*) with 'the wisdom that comes down from above' (*sapientia desursum descendens*), and says about the latter that it 'does not derive from the human heart', meaning 'within the power of a human being'.[105] Augustine implies that the distinction which James draws between the two kinds of wisdom should alert Pelagius to his failure to acknowledge that the wisdom required for moral reasoning has God as its source and is communicated to believers only as grace. For this reason, Augustine says, although James urges believers to

---

[103] See *spir. et litt.* 64 (CSEL 60.225): 'cum ab hac peregrinatione, in qua per fidem nunc ambulatur, peruentum erit ad speciem, quam nondum uisam speramus et per patientiam expectamus, procul dubio et ipsa dilectio non solum supra quam hic habemus, sed longe supra quam petimus et intellegimus erit, nec ideo tamen plus esse poterit quam ex toto corde, ex tota anima, ex tota mente. neque enim restat in nobis aliquid quod addi possit ad totum, quia si restabit aliquid, illud non erit totum. proinde hoc primum praeceptum iustitiae, quo iubemur diligere deum ex toto corde et ex tota anima et ex tota mente, cui est de proximo diligendo alterum consequens [Mt 22:37], in illa uita inplebimus, cum uidebimus facie ad faciem [cf. 1 Cor 13:12]. sed ideo nobis hoc etiam nunc praeceptum est, ut admoneremur, quid fide exposcere, quo spem praemittere et obliuiscendo quae retro sunt in quae anteriora nos extendere debeamus [cf. Phil. 3:13]. ac per hoc, quantum mihi uidetur, in ea quae perficienda est iustitia multum in hac uita ille profecit, qui quam longe sit a perfectione iustitiae proficiendo cognouit'.

[104] See *nat. et gr.* 17.

[105] See *nat. et gr.* 17 (CSEL 60.244): '*non est ista sapientia desursum descendens, sed terrena, animalis, diabolica. ubi enim zelus et contentio, ibi inconstantia et omne opus prauum. quae autem desursum est sapientia* [Jas 3:15] [. . .] haec est sapientia, quae linguam domat, desursum descendens, non ab humano corde prosiliens. an et istam quisque abrogare audet gratiae dei et eam superbissima uanitate ponit in hominis potestate'.

pray to God to grant them wisdom, he also stresses the necessity of praying with faith (Jas 1:5–6). This emphasis on faith indicates to Augustine that wisdom is an attribute of God, and that human nature, afflicted by sin, is not able to understand fully how to observe God's precepts concerning justice, unless it is aided by divine intervention.[106]

Augustine further criticizes Pelagius' position in his response to his opponent's treatise *Pro libero arbitrio*. There Pelagius had explicitly acknowledged that divine wisdom reveals precisely what justice requires believers to do.[107] Augustine accuses Pelagius of divorcing the function of wisdom in revealing justice to the soul from its role in moving the soul to love justice. His criticism relies upon his understanding of the dynamic interrelationship of knowledge and wisdom. For Augustine, Pelagius' remark that God 'rouses the sluggish will to a desire for himself through revealing his wisdom', understood in its context, reduces divine wisdom to a kind of school lesson during which the instructor makes the pupils aware of the rewards that will later be granted to those who follow instructions.[108] Crucial for Augustine's criticism is that he regards Pelagius as restricting the effects of divine wisdom to the 'exterior' of human reason, to the 'letter' of the divine law. Such wisdom would involve the soul in nothing like the conversion from presumption so central to Augustine's understanding of the way the soul comprehends justice. From Augustine's perspective, Pelagius' concept of wisdom resembles the knowledge that, when separated from love, 'puffs up' the soul with self-reliance (1 Cor 13:4, cf. 1 Cor 8:1).[109]

---

[106] See *nat. et gr.* 17 (CSEL 60.244): 'cur ergo oratur ut accipiatur, si ab homine est ut habeatur? an et huic orationi contradicitur, ne fiat iniuria libero arbitrio, quod sibi sufficit possibilitate naturae ad inplenda omnia praecepta iustitiae? Contradicatur ergo eidem ipsi apostolo Iacobo ammonenti et dicenti: *si quis autem uestrum indiget sapientia, postulet a deo, qui dat omnibus affluenter et non inproperat, et dabitur ei; postulet autem in fide nihil haesitans*' (Jas 1:5–6). Augustine continues this argument at *nat. et gr.* 19 (CSEL 60.245): 'tractat etiam iste de peccatis ignorantiae et dicit hominem praeuigilare debere, ne ignoret, ideoque esse culpandam ignorantiam, quia id homo nescit neglegentia sua, quod adhibita diligentia scire debuisset, dum tamen omnia potius disputet quam ut oret et dicat: *da mihi intellectum ut discam mandata tua* [Ps 119[120]:73]. aliud est enim non curasse scire, quae neglegentiae peccata etiam per sacrificia quaedam legis uidebantur expiari, aliud intellegere uelle nec posse et facere contra legem non intellegendo quid fieri uelit. unde ammonemur petere a deo sapientiam, *qui dat omnibus affluenter* [Jas 1:5], utique his omnibus qui sic petunt et tantum petunt quomodo et quantum res tanta petenda est'.

[107] See Pelagius, *Pro libero arbitrio* 3 = Augustine, *gr. pecc. or.* 1.11 (CSEL 42.153): 'operatur in nobis uelle quod bonum est, uelle quod sanctum est, dum nos terrenis cupiditatibus deditos et mutorum more animalium tantummodo praesentia diligentes futurae gloriae magnitudine et praemiorum pollicitatione succendit; dum reuelatione sapientiae in desiderium dei stupentem suscitat uoluntatem'.

[108] N. Cipriani, 'La morale pelagiana e la retorica', *Augustinianum* 31 (1991) 309–27, offers a suggestive assessment of the foundational assumptions behind Pelagius' ethics in classical Roman rhetorical and pedagogical theory.

[109] See *gr. et pecc. or.* 1.12 (CSEL 42.135): 'quid autem dicam de reuelatione sapientiae? neque enim facile quisquam sperauerit in hac uita posse peruenire ad magnitudinem reuelationum apostoli Pauli et

OCCULTA SAPIENTIAE

Augustine's discussions concerning Christ's examples in relation to his sacraments, and knowledge in relation to wisdom, underscore the importance of humility for the Christian who seeks to learn from the scriptures how to lead a just life. As an antidote to moral self-reliance, humility produces in the believer an awareness of sinfulness and a recognition that virtue is a gift of God.[110] It is axiomatic for Augustine that this moral self-knowledge acquired from humility is contingent upon the believer's repentance and confession of sin.[111] Christ's response to the prayer of the publican, 'Lord, be merciful to me, a sinner' (Lk 18:13), provides Augustine with a scriptural basis linking repentance and confession with growth in virtue.[112] Confession, he says, constitutes the only human speech whose truthfulness can be known with certainty.[113] Understood in this way, confession characterizes the fundamental discourse of the just because it reveals to them the truth about themselves. As such, it also represents the paradigmatic dialogue between the soul and God.[114] Confession of sin is the only form of speech

utique in eis quid aliud credendum est ei reuelari solere, nisi quod ad sapientiam pertineret? et tamen dicit: *in magnitudine reuelationum mearum ne extollar, datus est mihi stimulus carnis meae, angelus satanae, qui me colaphizet. propter quod ter dominum rogaui, ut auferret eum a me, et dixit mihi: sufficit tibi gratia mea; nam uirtus in infirmitate perficitur* [2 Cor 12:7–9]. procul dubio si iam summa et cui nihil esset addendum caritas in apostolo tunc fuisset, quae omnino non posset inflari, numquid necessarius esset angelus satanae, quo colaphizante reprimeretur elatio, quae in magnitudine reuelationum posset existere? quid est autem aliud elatio quam inflatio? et utique de caritate uerissime dictum est: *caritas non aemulatur, non inflatur'* [1 Cor 13:4].

[110] See my references to *trin.* 12.16 and 12.18 (above, 166 n. 91), where Augustine indicates that wisdom produces contrition for sins and moves the soul to confession and prayer for pardon.

[111] See, for example, *en. Ps.* 103.4.13 (CCL 40.1532): 'inuenit se homo paenitens de peccato suo, quia non habebat uires ex se; et confitetur deo, dicens se esse terram et cinerem. o superbe, conuersus es in puluerem tuum, ablatus est spiritus tuus; iam non te iactas, non te extollis, non te iustificas'. See also *en. Ps.* 57.4 (CCL 39.712): 'quamdiu connectis, ligas peccatum peccato: te solue a peccatis. sed non possum, inquis. clama ad illum: *infelix ego homo. quis me liberabit de corpore mortis huius* [Rom 7:24]? ueniet enim gratia dei, ut delectet te iustitia, sicut delectabat iniquitas; et homo qui ex uinculis resolutus es, exclamabis ad deum: *disrupisti uincula mea'* [Ps 115[116]:16].

[112] See *en. Ps.* 84.14–15, especially 84.15 (CCL 39.1174): '*et iustitia de caelo prospexit* [Ps 84[85]:12], id est a domino deo data est iustificatio confitenti, ut ipse agnoscat impius pium se fieri non posse, nisi ille fecerit cui confitetur, credendo in eum qui iustificat impium'. In this regard, see also A. Fitzgerald, 'Ambrose and Augustine: *confessio* as *initium iustitiae'*, *Augustinianum* 40:1 (2000), 173–85.

[113] See *en. Ps.* 84.14 (CCL 39.1173), where Augustine comments upon Ps 85(86):12, 'Truth has sprung out of the earth': 'quomodo a te oritur ueritas, cum tu peccator sis, cum tu iniquus sis? confitere peccata tua, et orietur de te ueritas. si enim cum sis iniquus, dicis te iustum. quomodo a te ueritas orietur? si autem cum sis iniquus, dicis te iniquum'.

[114] See *en. Ps.* 103.4.18 (CCL 40.1534): 'quae est disputatio hominis ad deum nisi confessio peccatorum? confitere deo quod es, et disputasti cum illo. disputa cum illo, fac bona opera, et disputa [. . .] quid est disputare cum deo? te illi indica scienti, ut indicet se tibi nescienti'. Note, too, the subordination of good works to confession, which provides a check against pride.

capable of eluding ignorance and weakness, the only occasion in which the soul may overcome self-deception.

Perhaps nowhere in Augustine's writings is the importance of conversion of the individual for his recognition of justice, and the vital role of Christ in inducing this conversion, better illustrated than in his numerous treatments of Jn 8:3–11, the pericope of the woman caught in adultery.[115] In his commentary on John's Gospel, Augustine claims that Christ as the 'voice of justice' (*uox iustitiae*) challenges the Pharisees and scribes to 'let him who is without sin cast the first stone' (Jn 8:7).[116] For Augustine, these words are 'wisdom's response' (*responsio sapientiae*) to the question about the justice of punishing the adulteress.[117] Augustine sees in Christ's words a skilful revelation to the Pharisees and scribes of their hidden sinfulness, which prompts in them a conversion of heart. The self-awareness which they gain from Christ's intervention also subverts their conventional thinking about the requirements of justice, by freeing them from the grasp of too literal an interpretation of Dt 22:22–4 and Lv 20:10, in which God commands the stoning to death of adulterers. Augustine's commentary on Jn 8:3–11 illustrates the convergence of several principles found in his discussions in *De trinitate* and other works regarding the relationship between knowledge and wisdom in moral reasoning. For example, he suggests that in Christ's intervention against the Pharisees and scribes, human speech and divine grace interact with each other and prompt a moral conversion in his hearers based on seeing their sinfulness reflected in that of the accused woman. As a result of this conversion, they are moved to repentance, to a public acknowledgement of their sinfulness, and to a deeper understanding of the requirements of justice than their knowledge of the scriptures alone had produced in them. Finally, the repentance which Christ's words induced in them leads them to show clemency to the adulteress.

Other preaching on Jn 8:3–11 following the outbreak of the Pelagian controversy further demonstrates Augustine's application of these principles concerning the transformation of moral reasoning to situations involving public officials. In a sermon preached at Carthage in AD 418, Augustine offers a meditation on the importance of self-knowledge, repentance, and

---

[115] See, for example, *Io. eu. tr.* 33, *en. Ps.* 30.2.1.7, 50.8, 102.11, *ep.* 153.8–10, *s.* 13.4–8, 302.14, *s. Denis* 20.4–5, *s. Mai* 158.5, *adult. coniug.* 2.6.5, 2.7.6, 2.14.14. A thorough analysis of Augustine's treatment of this pericope and comparison with that of Ambrose, which served as a source for Augustine, is provided by E. Sánchez, 'El comentario de Ambrosio y Augustín sobre la perícopa de la adúltera (Jn 7, 55–8, 11). Parte primera: los materiales ambrosiano y agustiniano. Parte segunda: análisis comparativo', *Augustinus* 46 (2001), 291–344, 47 (2002), 155–84.

[116] *Io. eu. tr.* 33.5–6. At *Io. eu. tr.* 33.6 (CCL 36.309), Augustine refers to Christ as *lingua iustitiae*.

[117] *Io. eu. tr.* 33.5. Note the forensic setting in which Augustine depicts the encounter.

confession for judges faced with the administration of justice.[118] After bluntly stating that many, if not most, judges acquire their appointments with bribes, he asks them to judge themselves before judging the accused who stands before them. Through such self-interrogation, he says, judges may discover that they too have committed serious crimes and sins. Augustine asks them to recall how they judged themselves in those circumstances. Did they not find in these occasions opportunities for repentance and conversion rather than for self-destruction? Because they responded to their own moral defects with love – by persuading themselves to repent – they ought to love those accused of serious crimes in the same way.[119] Augustine puts the matter directly: public officials who fail to love those whom they are obliged to judge with the same love with which they loved themselves, and who would instead destroy convicted criminals through capital punishment, destroy justice itself.[120] Even in practical terms, therefore, justice is achieved through a love born in the compassion in which one recognizes oneself as a sinner, and through that recognition pardons other sinners. Augustine counsels magistrates to 'love and judge' with this principle in mind.[121]

On another occasion, Augustine makes use of the Johannine pericope to comment on Psalm 50(51), King David's prayer for divine mercy.[122] He associates this prayer with the king's repentance of his seduction of Bathsheba and his role in the death of Uriah, her husband. In the encounter between Nathan and David described at 2 Sam 12:2–14, the prophet confronts the king with his sinfulness by telling him the imaginary tale of a wealthy landowner who defrauds a poor man of his only lamb. Upon hearing Nathan's report, the king is angered by this injustice and immediately issues a death sentence against the accused. In response, Nathan turns David's words back upon him, forcing the king to recognize himself in the man he had just condemned, and to repent of his sins. Thanks to this repentance, God spares his life. Augustine refers to Nathan's use of this similitude as a tool (*ferramentum*) for 'lancing and healing' the king's

---

[118] See, especially, *s*. 13.7–9. I am persuaded by the arguments of A.-M. La Bonnardière, *Biblia augustiniana A. T. Le Livre de Jérémie* (Paris, 1972), 92, who locates and dates the sermon to Carthage, 27 May 418. For further discussion of the sermon in its context, see R. Dodaro and J. Szura, 'Augustine on *John* 8:3–11 and the Recourse to Violence', *Augustinian Heritage* 34:1 (1988), 35–62, at 49–51.

[119] See *s*. 13.7–8. Fundamental to Augustine's conception of self-love is its orientation to the love of God. See my discussion of *ciu*. 10.4–5, above, pp. 103–4. In this sense contrition and repentance can be understood as acts of self-love.

[120] See *s*. 13.8 (CCL 41.182): 'quid perdis non amando quem iudicas? quoniam iustitiam perdis, non amando quem iudicas'.

[121] See *s*. 13.9 (CCL 41.183): 'diligite et iudicate'.   [122] See *en. Ps*. 50.

heart, and compares it to Christ's similar use of figurative speech in telling the Pharisees and scribes that the one without sin should cast the first stone.[123]

This commentary was originally preached at Carthage on 15 July 413, during the city's annual celebration of its *dies natalis*, and in the wake of the defeat of a military revolt against the Emperor Honorius instigated earlier that year by the *comes Africae*, Heraclian.[124] Suzanne Poque reasons that Augustine chose this opportunity to appeal to high-ranking public officials in his congregation to grant clemency to rebels who had recently repented of their involvement in the uprising.[125] Crucial to Augustine's purposes in this commentary is the moral symmetry which both John 8 and 2 Sam 12 demonstrate between judges and those whom they condemn. Augustine's remarks reinforce this comparison by pointing out the fundamental difference between Christ and David in their abilities to judge justly. As a consequence, Augustine grounds his plea for clemency both in the similarity between the emperor and the usurper, Heraclian, and in the corresponding dissimilarity between the emperor and Christ.

For Augustine, Nathan's tale induces David to acknowledge a moral likeness between himself and the wealthy man he condemns, insofar as both are guilty of serious sin. The prophet's choice of a lamb as the object of the wealthy man's theft ironically underscores the proportionately graver nature of the injustice behind the king's deeds. Struck by this paradox, David is moved to confess, 'I have sinned' (2 Sam 12:13). A parallel irony can be detected in the account of the woman caught in adultery, inasmuch as the Pharisees and scribes, by seeking to trap Jesus into violating the law in order to put him to death for blasphemy, are guilty of a greater evil than

---

[123] See *en. Ps.* 50.8 (CCL 38.604): 'ad secandum et sanandum uulnus cordis eius, ferramentum fecit [Nathan] de lingua eius. hoc fecit dominus Iudaeis, quando ad eum adulteram mulierem adduxerant'. At *en. Ps.* 50.2 (CCL 38.600), Augustine indicates that Nathan acted as God's prophetic voice: 'missus est ad eum Nathan propheta, missus a domino, qui eum argureret de tanto commisso'.

[124] See S. Poque, 'L'Echo des événements de l'été 413 à Carthage dans la prédication de saint Augustin', *Homo spiritalis. Festgabe für Luc Verheijen zu seinem 70. Geburtstag*, ed. C. Mayer (Würzburg, 1987), 391–9, who confirms the tentative assignment of the commentary to this date by A.-M. La Bonnardière, 'Les Enarrationes in Psalmos prêchées par saint Augustin à l'occasion de fêtes de martyrs', *Recherches augustiniennes* 7 (1971), 73–104, at 80–1. O. Perler and J.-L. Maier, *Les Voyages de saint Augustin* (Paris, 1969), 294, 295 n. 2, cites earlier studies arguing for the summer of AD 411.

[125] See Poque, 'L'Echo'. Citing *en. Ps.* 50.8, Poque locates Augustine's plea within his argument that, should the emperor grant clemency, he could not be justly accused of acting in a manner contrary to his own laws, for such an accusation is contradicted by the example of Christ, who forgave the adulteress at John 8. In what follows I argue that the analogy between the emperor and David, and not the analogy that Poque sees between the emperor and Christ, constitutes Augustine's most powerful application of John 8 within the context of the events at Carthage which she otherwise so ably describes.

the adulteress.[126] Christ's intervention alerts them to their own clouded moral vision, and they depart without taking action against the woman, thus acknowledging their sinfulness. In retelling the story of Nathan and David, and suggesting parallels between it and Jn 8:3–11, Augustine suggests that the emperor and his agents ought both to acknowledge a moral similarity between themselves and those they are prepared to condemn and to recognize the greater injustices which they may have committed in the exercise of their offices. Clemency is thus warranted not simply on account of mercy, but also for the sake of justice.

However, in addition to the social unrest in Carthage due to the suppression of Heraclian's revolt, Carthaginian Christians at this time are also keenly aware of the controversy surrounding the claim by some among their number that it is possible for human beings to avoid sinning completely, because human nature was created good.[127] Against this view, Augustine argues in this commentary that Adam's sin and the penalty for it had been transmitted to all human beings, and that even infant children should be baptized. Some observers might conclude that the manner in which these echoes of the developing Pelagian controversy intrude into this commentary shows that Augustine had intentionally wandered off his principal topic, hoping to take advantage of his presence in Carthage to hammer home his doctrinal views.[128] Yet it becomes clear in the course of the commentary that Augustine works his anti-Pelagian arguments into his explanation of David's repentance. For example, he interprets the king's confession, 'Against you only have I sinned and done what is evil in your sight' (Ps 50[51]:4), as signifying David's recognition that Christ alone is sinless, and therefore that he alone is capable of judging justly and of administering justice with mercy.[129] Augustine thus argues the difference between the complete understanding and example of justice found exclusively in Christ and the partial justice of which human beings are capable.

---

[126] See *en. Ps.* 50.8 (CCL 38.604): 'tamquam bicipiti muscipula tentantes capere sapientiam dei, ut si iuberet occidi, perderet mansuetudinis famam; si autem iuberet dimitti, incurreret, tamquam reprehensor legis, calumniam'. See also *Io. eu. tr.* 33, where Augustine begins his treatment of Jn 8:3–11 with the concluding verses of John 7, indicating the treachery of the Pharisees and scribes against Christ.

[127] The position is often attributed to Celestius, a disciple of Pelagius, but see R. Dodaro, 'Note on the Carthaginian Debate over Sinlessness, AD 411–412 (Augustine, *pecc. mer.* 2.7.8–16.25)', *Augustinianum* 40:1 (2000), 187–202.

[128] See, for example, the anti-Pelagian content at *en. Ps.* 50.10–11.

[129] See *en. Ps.* 50.9 (CCL 38.605): 'quia tu solus sine peccato. ille iustus punitor, qui non habet quod in illo puniatur; ille iustus reprehensor, qui non habet quod in illo reprehendatur [. . .] uidet futurum iudicem iudicandum, iudicandum a peccatoribus iustum, et in eo uincentem, quia quod in illo iudicaretur non erat'. For parallel statements in Augustine's anti-Pelagian writings, see the references above, p. 92 n. 82.

Equally important to Augustine's argument in this commentary is his conclusion that only those who approach the incarnation through faith as a mystery perceive the enormous void between divine and human justice. He explains that David's prophetic admission that Christ would be the only just man ever to live was essential to his repentance, in that it provided him with an ultimate standard against which he was able to measure his own injustice. Crucial to this awareness, in Augustine's view, was David's understanding that Christ could be perfectly just only if he were the God-man.[130] David thus understood that Christ's virtue, unlike that of all other human beings, would result from the union between his divine and human natures. Augustine proposes that David reached this conclusion while praying, 'Against you alone have I sinned . . . Behold, I was conceived in iniquity' (Ps 50[51]:7). He reasons that in confessing that he was conceived in iniquity, David was speaking on behalf of all human beings. Moreover, in confessing that he had sinned against Christ alone, David acknowledged that Christ alone would be born of a virgin, and thus conceived without original sin.[131] Finally, David understands that because of Christ's complete and unique freedom from sin, his justice alone among human beings is perfect. As a consequence, David realizes, he can find no one better to judge him than the only judge in history who is without fault. For this reason, Augustine concludes, David's insight into the extent of his own sinfulness reflects a deeper insight into the mystery of God incarnate.[132]

Two further consequences follow for Augustine. The awareness that David gains about his sinfulness in relationship to others and to God comes through faith, and ultimately through grace. Augustine sees David's faith manifested in his acceptance of Christ as the only just human being, of the unity in Christ's unique person of divine and human natures, and of his

---

[130] See *en. Ps.* 50.9 (CCL 38.605): 'solus enim in hominibus uerum dicere potuit homo deus: si inuenistis in me peccatum, dicite' (cf. Jn 8:46).

[131] See *en. Ps.* 50.10 (CCL 38.606–7): 'suscepit personam generis humani Dauid, et adtendit omnium uincula, propaginem mortis considerauit, originem iniquitatis aduertit, et ait: *ecce enim in iniquitatibus conceptus sum* [Ps 50[51]:7] [. . .] praeter hoc uinculum concupiscentiae carnalis natus est Christus sine maculo, ex uirgine concipiente de spiritu sancto. non potest iste dici in iniquitate conceptus; non potest dici: in peccatis mater eius in utero eum aluit, cui dictum est: *spiritus sanctus superueniet in te, et uirtus altissimi obumbrabit tibi*' (Lk 1:35). See *ciu.* 10.24–5 (CCL 47.297–8), where Augustine explains that the just men of the Old Testament were able to discern the mystery (*sacramentum*) of the incarnation behind the figurative language (*mystice loqui*) of the scriptures.

[132] This is also the logic of Augustine's discussion at *gr. et pecc. or.* 2.28–33 concerning the faith in God incarnate by which saintly persons of the Old Testament have been justified. This work has an anti-Pelagian intention, as does *c. ep. Pel.* 3.6, where Augustine cites Ps 50(51):10 to argue that David was saved by his faith in Christ. In this connection, see also, *c. ep. Pel.* 3.11, 3.15.

own salvation through Christ's unjust death.[133] Moreover, his observation that once David confesses his sin, the 'uncertain and hidden secrets of God's wisdom are shown to him', added to his conclusion that Nathan speaks to the king on behalf of God, expresses his view that David's faith in the mystery of the incarnation is met by his reception of divine grace.[134] In this way, Augustine perceives a close relationship between David's faith in the incarnation and the humility with which he publicly confesses his injustice.

The anti-Pelagian character of Augustine's discussion also suggests that the difference between David's justice and Christ's is rooted not merely in the king's lack of a firm resolve to avoid sin, as Pelagius argues, but in the effects of ignorance and weakness on the soul, against which David was powerless.[135] As demonstrated earlier, Augustine does not believe that awareness of oneself as a sinner is easily achieved. He is certain that such insight into oneself is connected with one's faith in the incarnation, as his discussion in Book 8 of *De trinitate* of the healing effect of Christ's sacrament reveals.[136] Augustine makes a related point indirectly in this psalm commentary by observing that David knew that adultery and murder were sinful acts, so that he could not claim to have sinned out of ignorance of God's law. Yet if he had truly recognized what he did to Uriah and Bathsheba as sinful, Augustine argues, he might have found the compassion with which to pardon the man in Nathan's tale.[137] In Augustine's view, ignorance and weakness contribute to moral failure because they encourage presumption in its most insidious form, by impeding recognition of moral similarities between oneself and those whom one judges. Overcoming this presumption and the illusion of justice that it causes in the soul offers the key to a truer self-knowledge and, consequently, to the compassion with which others ought to be judged.

---

[133] No one except Christ can rightly claim innocence of all sin. By this logic, Christ would suffer death not as a just punishment for his own sin, but vicariously, on behalf of all men.

[134] See *en. Ps.* 50.11 (CCL 38.608): 'cum enim dixisset, stante et arguente se propheta: *peccaui*, statim audiuit a propheta, id est a spiritu dei qui erat in propheta: *dimissum est tibi peccatum tuum* [2 Sam 12:13]. incerta et occulta sapientiae suae manifestauit ei'. See Ambrose, *l.* 2 *ep.* 7 (= Maur. 37).29 (CSEL 82.x,1.57): 'quis igitur sapiens, nisi qui ad ipsa peruenit diuinitatis secreta et manifestata sibi cognouit occulta sapientiae?' (Ps 50[51]:8).

[135] For Pelagius' view that the roots of David's sin are in his lack of determination to obey God's law, see Pelagius, *Epistula ad Celantiam* 3 (CSEL 29.438), in the context of the letter's preceding sections.

[136] See above, p. 159 and n. 56.

[137] See *en. Ps.* 50.6 (CCL 38.603): 'iste Dauid non posset dicere: *ignorans feci* [1 Tm 1:13]. non enim ignorabat quantum mali esset contrectatio coniugis alienae, et quantum malum esset interfectio mariti nescientis', along with his comments at *en. Ps.* 50.8 (CCL 38.604): 'suam iniquitatem nondum agnoscebat, et ideo alienae non ignoscebat', in the full context of this section.

Such a rare and intellectually demanding understanding of Christ's supreme justice, complemented by so humble an act of public confession, brings about in David what he would otherwise have received through divine punishment, a fact acknowledged by Nathan's pronouncement, 'Your sin is far removed from you' (2 Sam 12:13).[138] Augustine accepts that divine justice involves both punishment and mercy; however, he suggests that, by bringing David to contrition and confession of his sins, God has reformed David, which was his true aim. In not condemning David to eternal damnation, God has treated him mercifully.[139] In keeping with his view, so often repeated in the course of the Pelagian controversy, that divine justice is never transparent to human scrutiny, Augustine contends that the reconciliation of truth and mercy according to divine justice is hidden from human reason by divine wisdom. He points out that if Nineveh had been judged according to the conventional understanding of justice, it would have deserved destruction. Instead, he said, God in his justice spared the city (cf. Jonah 3:10). Alluding once again to the impending imperial vengeance against Heraclian's Carthaginian co-conspirators, Augustine suggests that those listening to him might profitably remember Nineveh. If the ancient Ninevites could find pardon in a just God through their display of true repentance, would a Christian emperor and his officials deny mercy to penitent Carthaginians?[140]

CONCLUSION

Augustine's association in Book 4 of *De trinitate* of Christ's sacraments and examples to what he terms the 'inner man' and the 'outer man' resolves questions about his understanding of the relationship between these two exegetical categories. The relationship between sacraments and examples described here is all the more significant in view of Augustine's arguments against the Pelagian position that Christ's examples are sufficient in themselves for guiding Christians in the just life. How does Augustine see the

---

[138] See also *pecc. mer.* 2.56.
[139] See *en. Ps.* 50.7 (CCL 38.603): 'non, domine, non erit impunitum peccatum meum; noui iustitiam eius, cuius quaero misericordiam; non impunitum erit, sed ideo nolo ut tu me punias, quia ego peccatum meum punio; ideo peto ut ignoscas, quia ego agnosco'.
[140] See *en. Ps.* 50.11 (CCL 38.607–8): '*ecce enim ueritatem dilexisti; incerta et occulta sapientiae tuae manifestasti mihi* [Ps 50[51]:8]. quae *occulta*? quae *incerta*? quia deus ignoscit et talibus. nihil tam occultum, nihil tam incertum. ad hoc incertum Niniuitae paenitentiam egerunt [. . .] quis non diceret ciuitatem istam, in qua nunc sumus, feliciter euersam, si omnes illi insani, nugis suis desertis, ad ecclesiam compuncto corde concurrerent, dei misericordiam de suis factis praeteritis inuocarent?'.

process of understanding biblical examples of virtue to be aided by grace? It becomes clear in the course of his discussion in *De trinitate* that the interaction of Christ's examples and sacraments is analogous to the unity of sense perception (the 'outer man') and reason illuminated by grace (the 'inner man'), which is in turn analogous to the union between Christ's human and divine natures. Essential to Augustine's conception of this unity is the principle of an exchange in which the characteristics proper to one of Christ's natures are also proper to the other.[141] He applies this same principle to the relationship between Christ's examples and sacraments, as they are apprehended by believers through faith and humility.

For Augustine, 'sacraments' are like 'mysteries' in that they are visible images, whose surface relationships to religious truths are easily perceived by the mind, but whose deeper meanings are only partially knowable. Understanding and loving God and his attributes through sacraments or mysteries requires faith and humility, Augustine argues. He indicates that these virtues are ascetical dispositions in the soul: faith because it requires belief in the difficult, because unseen, aspects of mysteries such as the incarnation; humility because it requires renunciation of the pretence of one's own virtue. For Augustine, understanding the scriptural word, in which God communicates precepts and examples concerning the just life, requires this kind of asceticism. As a consequence of practising it, the believer who encounters God's scriptural word in the form of mystery also attains a degree of self-awareness as sinner.

In *De gratia noui testamenti* Augustine offers a parallel interpretation to that found in Books 4 and 8 of *De trinitate*, concerning the relationship between Christ's sacraments and examples. He does so explicitly in the context of his emerging opposition to positions which, slightly later, he attributes explicitly to Pelagius and his associates. Augustine dismisses their concept of moral reasoning as deficient, because they conceive divine wisdom as a rhetorical enticement to obey scriptural mandates whose full significance is assumed to be transparent to an autonomous moral reason. In *De gratia noui testamenti*, he suggests on the basis of Eph 3:17–18 that Christians who seek to interpret the scriptures without faith and humility are able to recognize only the outward form of the virtue being portrayed in Christ's example. Since their interpretation lacks acknowledgement of the hidden truths of Christ's sacrament, it does not heal them of the presumption which inhibits a fuller understanding of moral lessons contained in the example.

---

[141] See my explanation of this principle above, pp. 91–4.

In Books 12–13 of *De trinitate*, Augustine further develops this two-tiered concept of a moral reason, wherein the deeper meanings of biblical examples of virtue are apprehended to the extent that reason acts under the influence of grace. *Ratio scientiae* and *ratio sapientiae* are thus related to each other in a manner analogous to Christ's examples and sacraments and, more fundamentally, to Christ's two natures. Human knowledge, as it considers moral decisions, is transformed by the experience of grace. When knowledge is tempered by true wisdom, conceived as the love of God, it is cleansed of presumption. As a consequence, the believer renounces his claim to autonomy and acknowledges his dependence upon God. The soul experiences this divine love as pardon, and its newly transformed reason (*ratio sapientiae*) reaches truer moral judgments than when reason acts on knowledge without divine grace.

Augustine finds in the 1 Samuel 12 account of King David's repentance and of his pardon by God a scriptural example illustrating the penitential qualities necessary for the Christian statesman who desires to rule justly and mercifully. Augustine uses this scriptural narrative to insist against the Pelagians that no human being other than Christ can be perfectly just in this life, and that believers make progress in virtue only to the extent that they acknowledge their dependence upon divine grace for the virtue that they achieve. Augustine is also able to suggest through this narrative the essential connection he holds between insight into the hidden nature of divine justice and faith in the mystery of the incarnation. In the following chapter, we shall examine how Augustine applies this model of the ideal statesman to Christian statesmen of his own day.

CHAPTER 6

Eloquence and virtue in Augustine's statesman

In Chapter 1, we examined the development in Cicero's *De re publica* of his concept of the ideal statesman, whose just conduct and eloquence enabled him, in Cicero's view, to lead and sustain the just commonwealth. We noted as well that in his correspondence with public officials contemporaneous with his work on the *City of God*, Augustine referred to Roman statesmen and to Cicero's related discussion of the virtues of *optimi uiri*. Yet as we also observed in Chapter 2, Augustine did not endorse Cicero's concept of statesmanship, in particular the view that the statesman should be 'nourished on glory', nor did he accept Cicero's explanations of the model statesman's virtue, or the value of his example in oratory for fostering virtue within the commonwealth. Instead, as we observed, Augustine's true paradigm of the statesman (*rector rei publicae*) is found not in Cicero's *optimus uir*, but in Christ, who governs the city of God as the just society.

Yet, although Augustine is certain that Christian rulers will find in Christ the supreme model of civic virtue and eloquence, he also recognizes that neither Christ's virtue nor his eloquence can be fully imitated, because the source of his virtue, the unity between his divine and human natures, is unique to him. Moreover, Christ can never provide an example of contrition for sins or prayer for pardon. Instead, as we shall argue in this chapter, Augustine suggests that examples of this kind are given by the saints, whose struggle with the effects of original sin makes them fitting models of civic virtue in ways that Christ cannot be. Moreover, unlike Christ, they depend upon a divine justice that is only partially knowable to them, in the form of mystery. For these reasons, Augustine contends that many saints, both Old Testament figures such as Job and David and those who follow Christ, such as Peter and Paul, offer statesmen of his own day an alternative model of civic virtue to that of Cicero's *optimates*. This is also true with regard to the rhetorical differences between the two groups. As demonstrated in Chapter 2, Cicero argues that the achievements of model leaders such as Marcus Regulus, the Scipios, and the Decii, when recounted by skilled orators, can persuade Rome's elite to undertake noble service to the *patria*.[1] Cicero thus regards glory both as the source of personal motivation for Rome's 'best citizens' and as the key element in the political discourse which urges Romans to virtuous public service. Augustine, instead, holds that humility, not glory, is the foundation of statesmanship and political discourse in a truly just society. Augustine's preference for humility, as demonstrated in Chapter 3, is rooted in the example of Christ, the divine Word who assumed human nature in the incarnation. In Chapter 5, we saw that this divine humility is communicated to the saints through the same graced experience of conversion by which they come to know and love divine justice. In this chapter, it will be argued that the saints, in contrast to Roman *optimates*, acknowledge that their grasp of justice is partial and contingent. In Augustine's view, they openly confess their sins while also praising God for his forgiveness and for the strength to live in his virtue. For Augustine, they and not Cicero's *optimates* are the true exemplars of civic virtue, and their confessions of sin are a more authentically virtuous political discourse than he finds in any author of his day, pagan or Christian. Furthermore, we shall see in this chapter that Augustine's critique in the *City of God* of the Roman heroic ideal is supported by his growing preoccupation with Pelagian views on human nature and grace, and their implications for any heroic ideal, pagan or Christian. Finally, in a return to Augustine's letters to public officials discussed at the beginning of Chapter 1, we shall see that he urges imitation not of Christ's unreachable perfection, but of the pentitential qualities of the saints as best suited to a wise and just rule in the earthly city.

OPTIMUS ET FORTISSIMUS

In considering Augustine's concept of the ideal statesman as it emerges in the *City of God*, attention ought first to be paid to his criticism of the Roman ideal, as represented in Book 5. In the midst of his discussion of the Romans' love for praise, Augustine claims that this fault of theirs, while not producing saints, has at least produced less base individuals (*minus turpes*).[2] He means by this that the desire of Roman statesmen to

---

[1] See, for example, Cicero, *De inuentione* 2.176–7, where he delineates the topics attributes of epideictic speeches: office-holding, wealth, marriage-connections, pedigree, political allies, service to the homeland, influence, all of which, as MacKendrick, *Philosophical*, 30, and Achard, *Pratique*, 473, point out, pertain to the 'optimates'.

[2] See *ciu.* 5.13 (CCL 47.147): 'uerumtamen qui libidines turpiores fide pietatis inpetrato spiritu sancto et amore intellegibilis pulchritudinis non refrenant, melius saltem cupiditate humanae laudis et gloriae

safeguard their honour frequently restrained many of them from committing unjust deeds which would have tarnished their reputations. Numerous modern scholars cite this and similar claims as acknowledgement by Augustine of a legitimate paradigmatic force in Roman pagan *exempla*.[3] Augustine does at times express admiration for Roman heroes in the *City of God*, as when he praises Regulus for his courage (1.15).[4] Yet his statement about the positive consequences of the Romans' love of praise should not be understood as affirmation that theirs were 'true virtues'.[5] *Vir iustus* and *uir turpis* are not part of the same continuum for Augustine, but occupy two altogether different spectra. He believes that the absolute political value that Cicero and other Roman authors attach to the pursuit of glory deprives their model statesmen of any opportunity for true repentance or for open confession of wrongdoing, both of which are required in his view for true virtue, as he will demonstrate in the *City of God* in the case of Paul (14.9). Repentance and confession of moral failings, two prime aspects of moral conversion, represent for Augustine the fruit of a developed life of virtue.

---

non quidem iam sancti, sed minus turpes sunt'. See also *ciu.* 5.19 (CCL 47.156) 'eos tamen, qui ciues non sint ciuitatis aeternae, quae in sacris litteris nostris dicitur ciuitas dei, utiliores esse terrenae ciuitati, quando habent uirtutem uel ipsam, quam si nec ipsam'.

[3] Swift, 'Pagan', 522, can perhaps be taken as a representative of this position: 'Such a begrudging description cannot, however, hide the bishop's admiration for their heroic stature. If the *virtus* practiced by Rome's best citizens is not to be compared with that of Christian believers, and if their love of glory is sometimes characterized by the bishop as a *vitium* (v,13), they remain noble models for the Christians to emulate' (514). G. Combès, *La Doctrine politique de saint Augustin* (Paris, 1928), 37–8, V. Pöschl, 'Augustinus und die römische Geschichtsauffassung', *Augustinus Magister. Congrès international augustinien*, vol. 2 (Paris, 1954–5), 962–3, Kamlah, *Christentum*, 281–8, Hand, *Augustin*, 19, 22, K. Thraede, 'Das antike Rom in Augustins De Ciuitate Dei. Recht und Grenzen eines verjährten Themas', *Jahrbuch für Antike und Christentum* 20 (1977)', 142, Markus, *Saeculum*, 57–8, and Lettieri, *Il senso*, 302–4, offer, on the whole, similar interpretations. F. Maier, *Augustin und das antike Rom* (Stuttgart, 1955), 89–91, and Honstetter, *Exemplum*, 191–8, insist that Augustine was inclined toward this positive evaluation of pagan examples through his contact with the literature produced by Roman rhetorical schools and by Latin Christian apologists.

[4] Throughout this chapter, references to the *City of God* will be placed in parentheses within the text. See also above, p. 37 n. 42, where I explain my use of the term 'hero'.

[5] Augustine explicitly denies that pagan virtues are 'true virtues'. See, for example, *ciu.* 5.19 (CCL 48.156): 'dum illud constet inter omnes ueraciter pios, neminem sine uera pietate, id est ueri dei uero cultu, ueram posse habere uirtutem, nec eam ueram esse, quando gloriae seruit humanae', and *ciu.* 19.4 (below, above, pp. 55–7 and 111–12, in conjunction with *ciu.* 19.24–7. At *c. Iul.* 4.16–17, Augustine offers another condemnation of pagan virtues. Not all scholars suggest a positive reading of Augustine's position with regard to the virtues of the Romans. Maier, *Augustin*, 138–42, offers perhaps the most painstakingly nuanced assessment of them all. Yet in the end, he too detects approval, if highly qualified, behind Augustine's judgment: 'Die römischen Tugenden sind in einem strengen Sinn ohne Zweifel zu verurteilen, können aber teilweise wenigstens einen bedingten Wert besitzen, der sich jedoch nur negativ ausdrücken läst' (130). However, F. Paschoud, *Roma aeterna. Etudes sur le patriotisme romain dans l'occident latin à l'époque des grandes invasions* (Rome, 1967), 245–51, 254–5, cautions against interpretations which exaggerate Augustine's approval of the virtues of Roman pagans, and views as insignificant in this regard the statement at *ciu.* 5.15 that God rewarded the 'virtues' of the pagans by granting them an extensive empire. See also the discussion by Milbank, *Theology*, 408–11, and Hombert, *Gloria*, 226–33.

Speaking about Regulus, Augustine insists that 'greed for praise and glory' lay behind his intention to impose excessively harsh peace terms on the Carthaginians during the First Punic War.[6] Because of their pride and thirst for glory, Roman heroes like Regulus are impervious to this kind of moral self-knowledge and conversion. Christians ought therefore to view idealized accounts of the virtues of Roman pagan statesmen, such as Regulus, the Scipios, and Gaius Fabricius Luscinus, only as counter-examples. In Augustine's view, the fact that Regulus' courage outshines that of the Christian martyrs and that no Christian ascetic could match the voluntary poverty demonstrated by Gaius Fabricius should be a warning to Christians against boasting on behalf of the virtues of their martyrs.[7] Augustine's deeper point is that true virtue does not consist in the accomplishment of externally 'heroic' deeds. The fact that such feats can be accomplished by the will alone, without divine assistance, indicates that they are empty of virtue. In Augustine's view, the motivation behind such deeds derives either from the soul's desire for some temporal benefit such as peace, or from sin, as when the soul longs for glory. When the motivation behind the deed is other than love of God, it cannot be considered virtuous, either wholly or in part. Augustine's portrait of pagan statesmen like Marcus Regulus is therefore intentionally ironic, and is ultimately aimed at overturning pagan Rome's accepted heroic traditions.[8]

Augustine dedicates further discussion in the *City of God* to the role of human glory in undermining virtue. In Book 5 he uses the example of Paul to contrast Roman pagan understandings of glory with the Christian view. He says that Paul points out the way to true glory at 2 Cor 1:12 ('This is our glory; the testimony of our own conscience') and Gal 6:4 ('Let each individual test his own work; and thus he will have his glory in himself, not in another') (5.12). The glory of pagan Romans is false, Augustine concludes, because it ignores the testimony of conscience. His treatment of Sallust in the *City of God* provides an illustrative example of his argument. Regarding Sallust's praise of Marcus Porcius Cato 'the Younger' and Julius

---

[6] See *ciu.* 3.18, along with my remarks above, pp. 36–7, 41. Compare it with the less censorial portrait of Regulus offered by Orosius, *Historiarum aduersum paganos libri* 4.8–10. Swift, 'Pagan', 517 n. 33, refers to this passage as 'Augustine's only criticism of the hero', but offers no further explanation for its presence or meaning. Although Maier, *Augustin*, 88–9, accepts that it weakens the otherwise positive tone of Regulus' portrait, he discounts its significance by insisting that the Roman officer remains for Augustine an 'Ansporn für die Christen'.

[7] In general, see *ciu.* 5.18. On Regulus, see *ciu.* 1.15, 1.24 (as above, pp. 36–7 n. 42), 2.23, 2.29, 3.18, 3.20, 5.18. On the Scipios, see *ciu.* 1.30 (but see also above, p. 42 n. 67), 2.5, 2.29, 3.21. On the Fabricii, see *ciu.* 2.29, and for Gaius Fabricius, see *ciu.* 5.18. See also *ciu.* 5.16. See also Cicero, *De officiis* 1.15–17, and 1.20–33, on justice (*iustitia*). For general discussion, see Honstetter, *Exemplum*, 177–95.

[8] His strongest expression of this viewpoint is found at *c. Iul.* 4.17–26. See also my discussion of this point above, pp. 53–7.

Caesar as *magni et praeclari uiri*, Augustine notes Sallust's view that Cato was not driven by desire for glory (*cupido gloriae*). Sallust exalts Cato's moral stature in particular, noting, 'The less he sought glory, the more it pursued him' (5.12). Augustine agrees, yet ultimately finds the distinction between Cato and other Roman statesmen to be trifling. His rejection of Sallust's portrayal of Cato follows from his conviction that the source of this so-called glory is public opinion reinforced by rhetorical persuasion, and not the 'testimony of conscience', which Paul says true glory requires. When Augustine cites Cato's discourse approvingly, he does so on the strength of its open admission of Roman injustices and the collective self-criticism that it offers.[9] Cato's speech therefore adheres to the pattern of just discourse that Augustine finds most exemplified in Paul, although it does so only externally.

Augustine's criticism of human glory as a political motivation in Book 5 also parallels concerns raised at this time in his debate with the Pelagians, specifically, his opposition to the Pelagian views (1) that human beings can be sinless; (2) that they can act virtuously without grace; (3) that virtue can be perfected in this life; and (4) that fear of death can be completely overcome.[10] Augustine argues that because the Pelagians hold these positions, they glorify individuals whom they judge to be virtuous with the glory that should be reserved for God alone. By the time Augustine has completed Book 5 of the *City of God* (AD 415), he has also produced a series of writings against the Pelagians in which he criticizes them for glorifying human beings on account of their virtuous deeds. In *De peccatorum meritis et remissione* (AD 411/12), for example, he frames his objections to the Pelagian viewpoint on human merit and virtue by citing 1 Cor 4:7 ('What do you have that you have not received? But if you have received, why do you boast as if you had not received?') and 1 Cor 1:31 ('Let him who boasts, boast in the Lord').[11] Meanwhile, as we have seen, in *De gratia noui testamenti* (AD 412) he holds that Christians who credit themselves for their virtue, and who believe that virtue can be perfected in this life, do not

---

[9] See *ciu.* 5.12, citing Sallust, *Bellum Catilinae* 52.19–20. See also Honstetter, *Exemplum*, 177–8.

[10] J. Wang Tch'ang Tche, *Saint Augustin et les vertus des païens* (Paris, 1938), 106–20, especially 117–20, appreciates this point in general terms. However, he also interprets Augustine's remarks at *ciu.* 5.18 as positive with respect to pagan *exempla*, and credits Augustine with regarding them as 'stimulants pour les chrétiens eux-mêmes' (118). Maier, *Augustin*, 141–2, mentions the controversy briefly in connection with Roman pagan virtues. However, Hombert, *Gloria*, 217–18, asserts that the *De ciuitate dei* gives 'almost no' evidence of any theological controversy contemporary with its composition, although he also thinks it 'incontestable' that *ciu.* 17.4 reflects anti-Pelagian concerns (248–9).

[11] See *pecc. mer.* 2.28, 2.30, 2.31. In general, see Hombert, *Gloria*, 160–71.

practise true virtue, even if their deeds seem to be virtuous.[12] In the treatise *De perfectione iustitiae hominis*, Augustine rebuts arguments from the *Liber definitionum*, a brief work associated with the Pelagian movement, which cites biblical examples of outstanding virtue in order to affirm that all human beings are obliged to live without ever sinning.[13] Augustine argues instead that no example can be found in scripture of anyone completely free from sin except Christ, and that Christian progress in virtue is made gradually in this life and is never complete before death. Similar arguments are advanced in *De natura et gratia* (AD 415), where he argues that without the grace of Christ to assist it, human nature is incapable of avoiding sin or of acting virtuously.

Two letters which Augustine and Alypius, his lifelong friend and fellow bishop, wrote in the years immediately following the composition of Book 5 of the *City of God* also indicate in clear terms his opposition to any attribution of merit to human beings for their virtuous deeds. In a letter written in AD 417 to Paulinus, the bishop of Nola in southern Italy, the two African bishops seek to recruit Paulinus in their fight against the Pelagians, in part because they believe Nola to be a city where Pelagius has numerous adherents.[14] One sign that Pelagius' notion of grace is false, Augustine and Alypius tell Paulinus, is his assumption that grace is identical to human nature, and thus the same for pagans and Christians alike.[15] As a result, they conclude, Pelagius wants to destroy any belief in the grace bestowed on the human race through Christ, the one mediator of God and man (cf. 1 Tim 2:5).[16] At the heart of this ambiguity, they argue, lurks the danger of believers reasoning that they themselves, and not God, are ultimately responsible for their virtue and for the good they accomplish.[17] Augustine and Alypius stress to Paulinus that human beings should not glory in their own works, but only in the Lord.[18] They criticize those who, like the Pelagians, expect 'a reward for their merits as if it were due to them', and thus

---

[12] See *ep.* 140.83–4, and my discussion above, pp. 163–4. See also Hombert, *Gloria*, 172–81.

[13] The work, which is only known through Augustine's *De perfectione iustitiae hominis*, is commonly ascribed to Celestius, but the attribution is not secure. See Dodaro, 'Note'. The dating of Augustine's work is not certain. It is generally assigned to AD 414/15, but may have been completed already in AD 412. See *spir. et litt.* 1.

[14] See *ep.* 186.29. At *ep.* 186.1 Augustine indicates awareness that Paulinus once regarded Pelagius warmly. On this relationship, see D. Trout, *Paulinus of Nola: Life, Letters, and Poems* (Berkeley, 1999), 229–35.

[15] See *ep.* 186.1 (CSEL 57.46): 'quae paganis atque christianis . . . communis est'. See also *gr. et lib. arb.* 25.

[16] See *ep.* 186.1.

[17] See *ep.* 186.1 (CSEL 57.46): 'cum possibilitate uolendi atque operandi, sine qua nihil boni uelle atque agere ualeremus'.

[18] See *ep.* 186.4, with allusions to 1 Cor 4:7 and 1 Cor 1:31.

seek their heavenly reward not by faith, but by works.[19] Finally, toward the conclusion of their letter, the bishops acknowledge that they do not find these heretical views in Paulinus' letters, but instead see him standing out as 'an intimate lover and defender of grace'.[20]

As evidence for this claim, they quote from a letter of Paulinus to his friend Sulpicius Severus. Severus had written to Paulinus, asking him to send a portrait of himself so that he could display it in a church he was building at Primuliacum in Gaul.[21] In a letter that was later read by Augustine and Alypius, Paulinus wrote back to Severus in AD 402, refusing the request and the honour it implied. Augustine and Alypius tell Paulinus that they find in his letter the 'truest kind of confession' (*ueracissima confessio*) when he declares to Severus that he is poor and sorrowful on account of his own sinfulness.[22] Employing symbolic imagery, Paulinus describes himself as 'still caked with the filth of an earthly image', because his bodily senses and worldly actions force him to see in himself 'more of the first Adam than of the second'.[23] He then adds, in a clear allusion to Rom 7:15, 'I blush to paint myself as I am, I do not dare to paint myself as I am not. I hate myself as I am, and am not what I long to be . . . I prefer to do what I hate, and idly neglect the attempt at doing what I love.'[24] Augustine and Alypius continue to quote Paulinus telling Severus that he is distraught by the conflict with himself, which he likens to the 'inner war' between the 'spirit' and the 'flesh', in which the 'law of the mind' is pitted against the 'law of sin'.[25] Finally, he complains to Severus, 'How wretched I am, for even the wood of the cross has not helped me to dissolve the poisonous taste of that hostile tree'.[26] Augustine and Alypius tell Paulinus that they see

---

[19] See *ep.* 186.8 (CSEL 57.51): 'hi uero, qui suis meritis praemia tamquam debita expectant'.

[20] See *ep.* 186.39. It is at this point in the letter that Augustine and Alypius ask Paulinus to aid them in their campaign against the Pelagians by denouncing Pelagian teachings publicly. See T. Piscitelli Carpino, *Paolino di Nola: Epistole ad Agostino* (Naples, 1989), 70–9.

[21] See Paulinus of Nola, *Epistula* 30. See also M. G. Bianco, 'Ritratti e versi per le basiliche di Sulpicio Severo e Paolino Nolano (Paul. Nol. *Epp.* 30–32)', *Romanobarbarica* 12 (1993), 291–310, at 292–4. On Paulinus and Sulpicius Severus, see S. Mratschek, *Der Briefwechsel des Paulinus von Nola. Kommunikation und soziale Kontakte zwischen christlichen Intellektuellen* (Göttingen, 2002), 456–64.

[22] See *ep.* 186.40 (CSEL 57.78–9): 'Pauper ego et dolens', quoting Ps 68(69):30. Cf. Paulinus of Nola, *Epistula* 30.2.

[23] See *ep.* 186.40 (CSEL 57.79): 'qui adhuc terrenae imaginis squalore concretus sum et plus de primo quam de secundo Adam carnis sensibus et terrenis actibus refero'. See C. Conybeare, *Paulinus Noster. Self and Symbols in the Letters of Paulinus of Nola* (Oxford, 2000), 102–5.

[24] See *ep.* 186.40 (CSEL 57.79): 'erubesco pingere, quod non sum; odi, quod sum, et non sum, quod amo [. . .] cum id potius agam, quod odi, nec elaborem piger id potius agere, quod amo', citing Paulinus of Nola, *Epistula* 30.2.

[25] See *ep.* 186.40, alluding to Rom 7:23.

[26] See *ep.* 186.40 (CSEL 57.79): 'infelix ego, qui uenenatum inimicae arboris gustum nec crucis ligno digessi. durat enim mihi illud per Adam uirus paternum, quo uniuersitatem generis multa contexis ingemiscendo expectans redemptionem corporis tui et nondum re sed spe saluum te esse cognoscens', citing Paulinus of Nola, *Epistula* 30.2.

in his letter an endorsement of the Pauline mandate to 'await the grace of Christ' (Rom 7:25), a grace that is always experienced as a liberation from without and not from within one's own natural capacities. They conclude by acknowledging that throughout his letter and in all of his writings, they see Paulinus consistently emphasizing the need for Christians to acknowledge that divine assistance is necessary in order to make progress in living justly, an attitude reflected in the Lord's prayer, 'Lead us not into temptation.'[27]

The second letter written by Augustine and Alypius in AD 418 concerns Demetrias, the daughter of Anicia Juliana and the Roman consul Anicius Hermogenianus Olybrius, and grand-daughter of Anicia Faltonia Proba.[28] Although her family was probably the wealthiest of the Roman aristocracy of her day, Demetrias voluntarily renounced material riches and marriage and committed herself to virginity in AD 413. Her decision attracted wide attention among western Christians, and Augustine wrote to Proba and Juliana, congratulating them on Demetrias' decision.[29] Sometime before AD 415, Pelagius sent to the young virgin his *Epistula ad Demetriadem*, intended as an instruction in the ascetical life.[30] In this letter, he contrasts the material wealth which she had acquired through her family connections, and which she renounced, with the 'spiritual riches' that, he says, she must acquire for herself, adding crucially that these riches 'come from herself'.[31] Pelagius insists that Demetrias clearly deserves to be praised (*laudanda esse*) and 'set above others' (*praeponi*) on account of her virtue. Augustine and Alypius quote these passages from the *Epistula ad Demetriadem* in their letter to Juliana.[32] They do so in order to express their fear that she may

---

[27] See *ep.* 186.41 (CSEL 57.80): 'de orando autem, et gemitibus flagitando proficiendi ac recte uiuendi adiutorio quae tua non feruet epistola? quid est tui quantumcumque sermonis, ubi non sit sparsum gemibunda pietate quod in oratione dominica dicimus: *ne nos inferas in tentationem*' (Mk 6:13, Lk 11:4). Paulinus composed a panegyric in honour of Theodosius I which was widely known after its publication (AD 395), but is no longer extant. Y.-M. Duval, 'L'Eloge de Théodose dans la Cité de Dieu (v, 26, 1), sa place, son sens et ses sources', *Recherches augustiniennes* 4 (1966), 169 n. 123, suggests the possibility ('l'hypothèse') that Augustine knew the work.

[28] See *Prosopographie chrétienne du bas-empire*, vol. 2: *Italie (313–604)*, part 1: *A–K*, ed. C. Pietri et al. (Rome, 1999), 544–7, s.v. 'Demetrias Amnia'. See also K. Krabbe, *Epistula ad Demetriadem De vera humilitate: A Critical Text and Translation with Introduction and Commentary* (Washington, 1965), P. Brown, 'Pelagius and his Supporters: Aims and Environment', *Journal of Theological Studies* n. s. 19 (1968), 93–114 = P. Brown, *Religion and Society in the Age of Saint Augustine* (New York, 1972), 183–207, B. Rees, *The Letters of Pelagius and his Followers* (Woodbridge, Suffolk, 1991), 29–70, and O. Wermelinger, 'Demetrias', *Augustinus-Lexikon*, vol. 2, ed. C. Mayer (Basle, 1996–2002), 289–91, who dates the letter to AD 418.

[29] See *ep.* 150.   [30] CPL 737. See PL 30.15–46, PL 33.1099–1120.

[31] See Pelagius, *Epistula ad Demetriadem* 11 (PL 33.1107): 'habes ergo et hic, inquit, per quae merito praeponaris aliis; immo hinc magis; nam corporalis nobilitas atque opulentia tuorum intellegentur esse non tua; spiritales uero diuitias nullus tibi praeter te conferre poterit. in his ergo iure laudanda, in his merito ceteris praeferenda es, quae nisi ex te et in te esse non possunt'.

[32] See *ep.* 188.4 (CSEL 57.122), quoting Pelagius, *Epistula ad Demetriadem* 11 (above, n. 31).

be underestimating the extent to which her household is influenced by Pelagius' teaching 'that we possess from ourselves whatever justice, continence, piety, and chastity there is in us'. Pelagius and other heretics with him, Augustine and Alypius claim, 'define human nature and teaching as the only form of grace and help given to us by God'.[33] The bishops express concern about the possible negative influence on Demetrias and others who will read Pelagius' letter. Will they not conclude that her holiness is a product of her efforts alone? Worse yet, is such an attitude not likely to render Demetrias herself ungrateful to God?[34] Augustine and Alypius insist instead that her virginal continence 'is not from herself but is a gift of God'.[35] Turning to the difference between human and divine glory, the bishops declare that Demetrias ought to glory in herself only when 'God who is in her is himself her glory.'[36]

Much of what Augustine and Alypius write to Juliana about the importance of recognizing that virtue is a gift of God to the soul and not a product of human nature can already be found in Augustine's treatise *De sancta uirginitate*, a document which precedes the Pelagian controversy.[37] Written against the teaching of the Roman monk Jovinian that matrimony represented a state of life equal in merit to virginity and clerical celibacy, Augustine's treatise nonetheless emphasizes the necessity of humility as the foundational virtue for chastity and virginity.[38] *De sancta uirginitate* shows that many of the arguments on the subject of virtue which Augustine will advance against the Pelagians are already evident in his writings before his initial contact with them. In *De sancta uirginitate*, for example, he argues that a virgin requires humility in order to see that her virtue is a result of God's 'splendid gift', and not something of her own doing.[39] Christians should realize, he maintains, that they cannot keep God's commandments

---

[33] See *ep.* 188.3 (CSEL 57.121): 'nec sane paruus est error illorum, qui putant ex nobis ipsis nos habere, si quid iustitiae, continentiae, pietatis, castitatis in nobis est eo quod ita nos condiderit deus, ut ultra, praeter quod nobis reuelat scientiam, nihil nos adiuuet, ut ea, quae facienda discendo nouimus, etiam diligendo faciamus, naturam scilicet atque doctrinam definientes tantum modo esse dei gratiam et adiutorium, ut iuste recteque uiuamus'.

[34] See *ep.* 188.4 (CSEL 57.122): 'in quo libro, si fas est, legat uirgo Christi, unde credat uirginalem suam sanctitatem omnesque spiritales diuitias non nisi ex seipsa sibi esse, atque ita, priusquam sit plenissime beata, discat deo esse – quod absit! – ingrata'. See also *ep.* 188.7 (CSEL 57.125), where, commenting once again on the passage cited from Pelagius, Augustine and Alypius insist: 'nolumus prorsus ita glorietur, quasi non acceperit'.

[35] See *ep.* 188.6 (CSEL 57.123): 'non sibi sit ex seipsa, sed sit dei donum', citing 1 Cor 7:7.

[36] See *ep.* 188.9 (CSEL 57.127): 'cum deus qui in illa est, ipse est gloria eius'. See also *ep.* 188.5.

[37] The precise date of this work is in question. It is usually dated to AD 401.

[38] See *uirg.* 31.

[39] See *uirg.* 42 (CSEL 41.285): 'prima sit induendae humilitatis cogitatio, ne a se sibi putet esse dei uirgo, quod talis est, ac non potius hoc donum optimum desuper descendere a patre luminum'.

without the help of God's grace.[40] As an antidote to self-glorification, Augustine counsels virgins to recognize that they are pardoned sinners. With this same end in view, he cautions them to be careful not to overestimate their strength in acting virtuously, but to confess their sins and pray that they may avoid giving in to temptation.[41]

Given the similarity between his arguments in *De sancta uirginitate* on the relationship of virtue to grace and those he expresses in his early anti-Pelagian writings and in Letter 188 to Anicia Juliana, it is not surprising that Augustine sends a copy of the *De sancta uirginitate* to Juliana in AD 414, asking her to pass it on to Demetrias.[42] In Augustine's view, Pelagius had dangerously raised to the level of Christian doctrine a set of assumptions about the human capacity to act virtuously which the bishop saw as previously lacking any authoritative status in the church. For Augustine, Christians who aspire to a more virtuous life could now find in this 'Christian' teaching the basis for what he regarded as none other than presumption and self-congratulation, the very attitudes he views as the foundation of sin and the prime threat to virtue.

It is therefore equally unsurprising that in Book 5 of the *City of God* Augustine approaches the theme of Roman glory with these anti-Pelagian concerns in mind. It becomes clear in the course of this book that he intends to offer in the *City of God* a portrait of the ideal statesman in opposition to that proposed by Cicero. Augustine's longstanding insistence that human virtue depends upon divine mediation in Christ will in the course of his work on the *City of God* be joined to his more recent opposition to the attempt by the Pelagians to assert as Christian orthodoxy their viewpoint that virtue derives from human nature and that it is perfectible in this life. For this reason, he is all the more compelled to emphasize humility as the trait which most characterizes Christian statesmen. For example, in a discussion of virtues and vices in Chapter 19, he surmises that a truly virtuous ruler will develop a natural suspicion of *laudatio*, the praise offered by skilful panegyrists who normally surround them at the imperial court. An awareness both of their own susceptibility to flattery and of their subjects' tendency to deception would lead such rulers to renounce or at least to restrain imperial propaganda.[43] For Augustine, only when statesmen would

---

[40] See *uirg.* 42 (CSEL 41.286): 'quibus ostenditur ea ipsa quae praecipiuntur a deo, non fieri nisi dante atque adiuuante qui praecepit. mendaciter enim petuntur, si ea non adiuuante eius gratia facere possemus'.

[41] See *uirg.* 53.   [42] See *b. uid.* 29.

[43] See this passage from *ciu.* 5.19 (CCL 47.155) in the context of the entire chapter: 'in laudatoribus autem suis, quamuis paruipendat quod eum laudant, non tamen paruipendit, quod amant, nec eos uult fallere laudantes, ne decipiat diligentes; ideoque instat ardenter, ut potius ille laudetur, a quo habet homo quidquid in eo iure laudatur'.

prefer to see God praised rather than themselves are they able to act in the true public interest. He concludes that *gloria dei* – rendering glory to God – is in every sense a political discourse. Augustine cautions that earthly rulers ought, in imitation of Paul, to develop a conception of themselves as repentant sinners. The desire for glory (*cupiditas gloriae*), he says, can only be overcome in the soul when God is duly praised for pardoning one's sins. He claims that this is how the saints give glory to God concretely: they offer to God a *gratiarum actio* that includes confession of sins and prayer for pardon.[44] In Chapter 19, he extends this discussion into his treatment of the 'art of governing' (*scientia regendi*), with the result that the remainder of Book 5 is concerned chiefly with political ethics (5.19–26). In a significant statement in this chapter, he affirms that model rulers are characterized by true piety (*uera pietas*) and upright living. However, he insists that they should also attribute their virtuous deeds to grace, thus recognizing 'how far they fall short of the perfection of justice'.[45] The latter statement directly attacks the Pelagian view that human beings can perfect their justice in this life through their own efforts. It also closely parallels an affirmation in his anti-Pelagian treatise *De spiritu et littera*.[46]

Augustine's opposition to Pelagian presuppositions about virtue and human nature offers a key to interpreting his better-known yet generally misunderstood portrait of the Emperor Theodosius I at the conclusion of the book (5.26).[47] Augustine's primary focus in Chapter 26 is Theodosius' repentance for his role in the massacre at Thessalonica in AD 390. Traditional accounts of this event do not resolve the uncertainties surrounding it. Theodosius is represented as having played a significant role in unleashing an attack on the residents of the city by imperial troops stationed there. To atone for the massacre, he subsequently submitted to public penance

---

[44] See *ciu.* 5.20 (CCL 47.157): 'nec illi se ab ista foeditate defenderint, qui, cum aliena spernant iudicia uelut gloriae contemptores, sibi sapientes uidentur et sibi placent. nam eorum uirtus, si tamen ulla est, alio modo quodam humanae subditur laudi; neque enim ipse, qui sibi placet, homo non est. qui autem uera pietate in deum, quem diligit, credit et sperat, plus intendit in ea, in quibus sibi displicet, quam in ea, si qua in illo sunt, quae non tam ipsi quam ueritati placent; neque id tribuit, unde iam potest placere, nisi eius misericordiae, cui metuit displicere; de his sanatis gratias agens, de illis sanandis preces fundens'.

[45] See *ciu.* 5.19 (CCL 47.156): 'tales autem homines uirtutes suas, quantascumque in hac uita possunt habere, non tribuunt nisi gratiae dei, quod eas uolentibus credentibus petentibus dederit, simulque intellegunt, quantum sibi desit ad perfectionem iustitiae'.

[46] See *spir. et litt.* 64 (CSEL 60.225): 'quantum mihi uidetur, in ea quae perficienda est iustitia multum in hac uita ille profecit, qui quam longe sit a perfectione iustitiae proficiendo cognouit'.

[47] Guy, *Unité*, 47, believes that the chapter is out of place in the first five books. Both Markus, *Saeculum*, 57 n. 1, and Swift, 'Pagan', 520 n. 41, agree with P. Brown, 'Saint Augustine', *Trends in Medieval Political Thought*, ed. B. Smalley (Oxford, 1965), 8, that *ciu.* 5.24–6 represents 'some of the most shoddy passages of the *City of God*.'

in Milan under the bishop Ambrose.[48] Augustine asserts that the penance demonstrates the emperor's religious humility (*humilitas religiosa*), and he singles it out as more wondrous (*mirabilius*) than any other deed of his reign.[49] By incorporating the massacre and the emperor's public penance for it into his portrait of the emperor, Augustine is able to highlight some of the public signs of repentance and confession that are proper to his Christian ideal. In view of the wider context surrounding his treatment of Theodosius' public penance suggested in Chapters 19–20, the purpose of his discussion of the emperor in Chapter 26 is clearly political. Augustine is not interested in extolling private virtue.[50] Although he follows Ambrose's depiction of Theodosius' penance closely in many respects, what is most significant about the repentance, in his view, is its wholly public character. Such an interpretation is further supported when one compares Augustine's sketch of Theodosius with that of the model emperors (*imperatores felices*) of Chapter 24. In these accounts Augustine makes the following points: (1) both Theodosius and the *imperator felix* are not puffed up with pride, but remember that they are only men; (2) they use their power (*potestas*) to extend the worship of the true God throughout their realms; (3) they are slow to punish and ready to pardon, making use of vengeance only to protect the commonwealth; (4) they pardon not out of a desire to see wrongdoing go unpunished, but for the purpose of reforming the criminal; (5) they combine severity with mercy and generosity; (6) they practise temperance; (7) they offer to God humility, compassion, and prayer (*humilitas, miseratio, oratio*) as a sacrifice for their sins and an antidote to *ardor gloriae*.[51]

In this respect, Paul is the only Christian Augustine refers to in the *City of God* as an *optimus uir*. As his alternative to Rome's 'best citizens',

---

[48] See Rufinus, *Historia ecclesiastica* 11.18, Sozomen, *Historia ecclesiastica* 7.25, Theodoret, *Historia ecclesiastica* 5.17–18, Paulinus of Milan, *Vita Ambrosii* 24. Scholarly assessments of the events include F. Kolb, 'Der Bussakt von Mailand. Zum Verhaltnis von Staat und Kirche in der Spätantike', *Geschichte und Gegenwart. Festschrift für K. D. Erdmann*, ed. H. Boockmann et al. (Neumünster, 1980), 41–74, and P. Brown, *Power and Persuasion in Late Antiquity: Towards a Christian Empire* (Madison, 1992), 109–13. But see especially N. McLynn, *Ambrose of Milan: Church and Court in a Christian Capital* (Berkeley, 1994), 315–30.

[49] See *ciu.* 5.26 (CSEL 47.162): 'quid autem fuit eius religiosa humilitate mirabilius, quando in Thessalonicensium grauissimum scelus, cui iam episcopis intercedentibus promiserat indulgentiam, tumultu quorundam, qui ei cohaerebant, uindicare compulsus est et ecclesiastica cohercitus disciplina sic egit paenitentiam, ut imperatoriam celsitudinem pro illo populus orans magis fleret uidendo prostratam, quam peccando timeret iratam?'.

[50] R. Williams, 'Politics and the Soul: A Reading of the *City of God*', *Milltown Studies* 19/20 (1987), 55–72, at 64–5, argues strongly in favour of the public character of Theodosius' virtue.

[51] See *ciu.* 5.24 (CCL 47.160). Duval, 'L'Eloge', 135–79, at 142–3, suggests that Augustine has Theodosius in mind in this description.

Augustine presents Paul in Book 14, Chapter 9 as a man who combines good works exhibiting virtues like faithfulness and truthfulness with occasions of sorrowful confession of sins.[52] This penitential emphasis is central to Augustine's revision of the heroic ideal, as his argument in *City of God* makes clear. Paul's boast that his weakness is his strength (2 Cor 12:5, 9–10) represents for Augustine an alternative approach to the political discourse described in Cicero's portraits of ideal statesmen. The apostle's example shows that the confession of moral weakness, the antithesis of the Stoic and Roman ideals, is in fact a precondition of the just life. However, in Augustine's view, 'weakness' triumphs over 'strength' only when the insight into the particulars of one's sinfulness are combined, as in Paul's case, with an openness to conversion and healing through divine grace. In order to convey this aspect of his alternative heroic ideal, Augustine inserts his discussion of Paul into his treatment of *apatheia*, the courageous resignation which the Stoics exalt as the ideal guide for virtuous action (14.8–9).

Augustine begins his assault on the Stoic ideal by stating that when citizens of the city of God possess a correct love (*amor rectus*) they desire what is right for them to desire, and they feel emotions which reinforce their just desires (14.9). He then contrasts this paradigmatic form of love with what he earlier refers to as Stoic *apatheia* (14.8). He asserts that while citizens loyal to the earthly city cultivate the appearance of control over their emotions, Christ's subjects are encouraged by Christ's example, by the scriptures, and by sound church teaching to experience a range of emotions, such as the fear of eternal punishment and the desire for eternal life (14.9). Christian life, Augustine says, is characterized in the words of Paul by an 'inward groaning' for the resurrection of the body (Rom 8:23) and by sorrow for sins. Among biblical examples that he mentions in this context, Augustine cites Peter weeping for his sins (Mt 26:75). He claims that Paul's statement, 'Death has been swallowed up in victory' (1 Cor 15:54) was intended to help Christians to feel hopeful. Through Paul, the scriptures also command Christians to feel a cheerfulness in giving (2 Cor 9:8) (14.9).

---

[52] See *ciu.* 14.9 (CCL 48.426): 'illum quippe optimum et fortissimum uirum, qui in suis infirmitatibus gloriatur [cf. 2 Cor 12:5, 9–10], ut eum potissimum commemoremus, qui in ecclesiam Christi ex gentibus uenimus, doctorem gentium in fide et ueritate, qui et plus omnibus suis coapostolis laborauit et pluribus epistulis populos dei, non eos tantum, qui praesentes ab illo uidebantur, uerum etiam illos, qui futuri praeuidebantur, instruxit'. This is the only occasion of Augustine's use of the term apart from references to Roman pagan heroes. However, Christ is referred to as *optimus rex* at *ciu.* 17.16 (CCL 48.581).

Augustine treats the Stoic attitude of *apatheia* as the moral equivalent of claiming to be without sin.[53] His concern in making this claim is to point out what he understands as the symbiotic nature of the relationship between the expectation that one can live without sinning and the suppression of emotions. Pride (*superbia*), in the strict sense in which he speaks of it here, numbs a sensitivity for the suffering or, more accurately, for the moral failure of others. For Augustine, compassion for others is linked with the recognition of one's own continual sinfulness and need for divine pardon. He therefore denies that those who expect themselves and others to be able to live without sinning will be able to feel any real sympathy for other sinners, and more broadly, for those who suffer.[54] Augustine says that if others wish to call these emotions and feelings 'faults' or 'disordered passions', then perhaps Christians ought to regard such faults as 'virtues'.[55]

Paul, by contrast to Roman statesmen, does feel this sympathy, which allows him the compassion to be a just statesman. Augustine points out that he grieves with those who grieve, and rejoices with those who rejoice (Rom 12:15). He also feels enormous sympathy for those who fail, for the Jews who 'prefer their own justice to the justice of God' (Rom 10:3), or for those Christians who, by sinning, have injured the wider community (2 Cor 12:21).[56] Hence even Paul, whose love is properly ordered, understands that he lives as a pardoned sinner, subject to the continuing influence of ignorance and weakness. The Roman optimate ideal, with the 'pride' it conveys in an illusory peace of mind, lacks an experiential basis from which to generate sympathy for others.[57] But Paul knows how to apply this awareness of his weakened condition in order to sympathize with the failure of others.

---

[53] See *ciu.* 14.9 (CCL 48.428): 'tunc itaque *apatheia* ista erit, quando peccatum in homine nullum erit'. Clearly, Augustine draws too tight a connection here between *impassibilitas* and *impeccantia*. J. Valero, 'El estoicismo de Pelagio', *Estudios eclesiasticos* 57 (1982), 39–63, argues that Pelagius' ethics were founded along Stoic lines; however, his argument is unconvincing. A more promising line of inquiry into the sources of Pelagian ethics is offered by Cipriani, 'La morale', who suggests looking at the principles of classical *paideia* commonly found in rhetorical works of Cicero and Quintilian.

[54] See *ciu.* 14.9 (CCL 48.426): 'non solum autem propter se ipsos his mouentur affectibus, uerum etiam propter eos, quos liberari cupiunt et ne pereant metuunt, et dolent si pereunt et gaudent si liberantur'.

[55] See *ciu.* 14.9 (CCL 48.427): 'hi motus, hi affectus de amore boni et de sancta caritate uenientes si uitia uocanda sunt, sinamus, ut ea, quae uere uitia sunt, uirtutes uocentur'.

[56] See *ciu.* 14.2, 20.17.

[57] Note, too, Augustine's dismissal at *ciu.* 19.27 of the possibility that any human being could experience perfect interior peace. See above, pp. 111–12.

VERA PIETAS

In his correspondence with Christian public officials, Augustine describes a model statesman consistently with his depiction of the apostles, martyrs, and emperors in Book 5 of the *City of God*, and with his representation of Paul in Book 14. At the heart of this ideal is a concept of 'true piety' (*uera pietas*), whose fundamental feature is humility. This humility disregards personal glory and recognizes God, not reason or the soul, as the source of virtue. It encourages the statesman to cultivate a sense of himself as a sinner who resolves to extend the pardon he discovers in God to others, as far as his ability to reconcile justice and mercy allows. As required by this ideal, the Christian statesman recognizes that his justice will inevitably fall short of God's own justice, and he seeks to know and love that divine justice even as he longs to know and love God.

Augustine's correspondence with Nectarius exhibits features of this ideal statesman. When, following the anti-Christian violence at Calama in AD 408, Nectarius appeals to Augustine to intercede with imperial officials so that pagans found guilty of participation in the disorder will not be severely punished, the bishop replies that he will certainly seek to persuade officials not to employ capital punishment or torture against the accused. However, he does not agree with Nectarius that the guilty pagans should not be heavily fined.[58] Nectarius challenges the justice of Augustine's position that whereas Christians who joined in the violence could be allowed to substitute ecclesiastical penance for civil penalities, pagans ought not to be allowed similarly to avoid fines by making a public confession. In his defence, Augustine replies that, whereas a long period of church-sponsored penance is likely to force Christians to reflect upon their behaviour and repent of it, the perfunctory judicial exercise suggested by Nectarius for pagans would produce no change in attitude or behaviour, nor would it deter further anti-Christian violence. Nectarius' choice, says Augustine, is therefore between piety and licence.[59]

Nectarius opens his appeal to Augustine in Letter 90 on the grounds of 'love for one's home town' (*caritas patriae*), a virtue which Cicero had acknowledged as the only affection to take precedence over love of one's

---

[58] For the correspondence and background to the incident, see above, pp. 6–7. For Augustine's opposition to excessive punishments, see *ep.* 91.6, 91.9–10, 104.2–6, 104.16–17.

[59] See *ep.* 91.2 (CSEL 34/2.428): 'compara nunc, utrum malis florere patriam tuam pietate an impunitate, correctis moribus an securis ausibus'. See also *ep.* 104.9, where Augustine argues the merits of ecclesiastical penance for producing repentance.

parents.[60] Nectarius implicitly accuses Christian imperial legislation of provoking the riots at Calama and of seeking to destroy the traditional religious foundation for his city's welfare, which depended upon observance of rituals in honour of the gods.[61] His sentiment thus expresses a fondness for those classical religious traditions, such as festivals and processions in honour of the gods, concerned with preserving the sacred character of the city. To care for the city in terms of these traditions is to embrace the concept of a bonding between citizens and local deities as a guarantee of honour and security. Augustine tells Nectarius in Letter 91 that he recognizes his allusion to Ciceronian patriotism, *caritas patriae*, but replies that, for Cicero, love for one's home town was rooted in civic virtues, such as simplicity (*frugalitas*), restraint (*continentia*), and faithfulness (*fides*) in the marriage bond.[62] Augustine reminds Nectarius that Cicero found such virtues wanting in the gods, like Jupiter, who were often depicted in pagan literature as committing adultery. Instead, Augustine continues, Cicero saw these civic virtues exemplified in political leaders, such as Gaius Laelius 'Sapiens', Quintus Aelius Tubero, and Quintus Mucius Scaevola Augur.[63] Augustine's point is ironic; Nectarius cannot appeal to Cicero against Augustine in arguing that pagan religious festivals which honour gods such as Jupiter enhance the security of cities like Calama by encouraging civic virtues among their citizens. Furthermore, Augustine asserts, because Cicero recognized that civic virtues are exemplified not by gods, but by statesmen (*uiri optimi*), if Nectarius wishes to compare Christianity with traditional Roman religion in order to determine which of them promotes those virtues that guarantee the welfare of Calama, he ought to compare Christian statesmen with Roman pagan statesmen.

Nectarius' reply in Letter 103 shows that he understands Augustine's strategy. Continuing Augustine's discussion of Cicero's *De re publica*, he

---

[60] See *ep.* 90 (Nectarius to Augustine) (CSEL 34.426): 'quanta sit caritas patriae, quoniam nosti, praetereo. sola est enim, quae parentum iure uincat affectum. cui si ullus esset consulendi modus aut finis bonis, digne iam ab eius muneribus meruimus excusari'. Cf. Cicero, *De re publica* 6.16.16: 'magna in parentibus . . . in patria maxima'. See also Cicero, *De officiis* 1.57, *De partitione oratoriae* 25.8.

[61] The imperial legislation at issue is found at *C. Th.* 16.5.43 and *C. Th.* 16.10.9 = *C. Sirm.* 12, dated 15 November 407. See the discussion by Lepelley, *Les Cités*, 1:293–2, 1:357–8, 2:97–101. For a different view, see Atkins, 'Old Philosophy', who argues that in his correspondence with Augustine, Nectarius cares little for religious or philosophical argument, but is concerned almost exclusively with enlisting the bishop's help in protecting leading citizens of Calama from facing almost certain punishment for failing to prevent the riots.

[62] See *ep.* 91.3 (CSEL 34/2.429).

[63] See *ep.* 91.3–4. Augustine refers to Cicero, *De re publica* 4.7.7 (the passage exists only in fragmentary condition). He repeats this point to Nectarius at *ep.* 104.6. See also his discussion of these Roman leaders at *ciu.* 2.9 and 2.14, and my discussion above, pp. 53–63.

expands Cicero's conception in Book 6 of a heavenly homeland, pointing
out that it provides a destiny for those political leaders who, during their
lives, care best for their home town.[64] He suggests that Augustine, by failing
to urge imperial officials to show clemency to non-Christians, misses an
opportunity to contribute to social reconciliation and thus to the welfare
of Calama. Augustine, in turn, defends himself against this charge in Letter
104, his second response to Nectarius, once again inviting him to consider
the vast gulf that separates pagan and Christian civic traditions. He argues
in this letter that the imperial officials to whom Nectarius would have him
appeal for clemency identify as their civic ideals statesmen such as Marcus
Aurelius, Seneca, and Cicero, each of whom was influenced by an eclectic
combination of Stoic ethical traditions and Roman patriotism, and military heroes such as Marcus Atilius Regulus, Mucius Scaevola, and Marcus
Curtius, whose lives exemplified the courage that these ancient traditions
promoted. He adds that, although Cicero said of Caesar, 'None of your
virtues are more admirable or more welcome than your mercy', Christians
prefer Christ to the emperor as an exemplar of mercy.[65] Augustine's point
is that the administration of justice that Calama fears, and against which
Nectarius implores him to intercede, consists in an insensitive, Stoic justice,
as practised by existing imperial officials, and not in the more compassion-
ate, Christian justice that he would like to instil in them.[66] Mindful of the
emphasis that Stoic philosophers place upon love and friendship between
neighbours as the core values behind civic harmony, he nonetheless insists to
Nectarius that the Stoics characteristically disparage mercy as a vice because
it stems from an undisciplined, sentimental reflex in the soul and not from
a dispassionate act of reason.[67] In effect, Augustine replaces Nectarius' Stoic
view that pardon should be extended to everyone who sins because all *sins*
are equal with his own Christian view that human beings ought to pardon
each other because all are equally *sinners*. True social reconciliation thus
arises when people recognize a similarity between themselves and their

---

[64] See *ep.* 103.2 (Nectarius to Augustine). Cf. Cicero, *De re publica* 6.26.29: 'Sunt autem optimae curae de salute patriae.'

[65] See *ep.* 104.16 (CSEL 34/2.593): 'melius itaque tibi occurreret, de tuo Cicerone quod diceres, qui Caesarem laudans: *nulla*, inquit, *de uirtutibus tuis admirabilior uel gratior misericordia est* [Cicero, *Pro Ligario* 37]. quanto magis debet ea in ecclesiis praeualere, quando eum sequuntur, qui dixit: *ego sum uia* [Jn 14.6], et legunt: *uniuersae uiae domini misericordia et ueritas* [Ps 24[25]:10].

[66] See *ep.* 104.15–16.

[67] See *ep.* 104.16 (CSEL 34/2.594): 'apud nos pro ciuibus tuis agis ingerendo nobis misericordiam christianorum non duritiam Stoicorum, quae causae a te susceptae non modo nihil suffragatur, uerum etiam multum aduersatur. nam ipsam misericordiam, quam si non habeamus, nulla tua petitione, nullis illorum precibus flecti poterimus, in uitio Stoici ponunt eamque a sapientis animo penitus expellunt, quem prorsus ferreum et inflexibilem uolunt'. See also Seneca, *De clementia* 2.5, Cicero, *Libri tusculanarum disputationum* 3.9.20, and my discussion of *ciu.* 9.5 above, pp. 59–60.

enemies as sinners, an identification that is impossible unless it emerges from a searching self-examination and confession, as well as a recognition that moral failure cannot be overcome in this life. In Augustine's view, Stoic mercy stems from a form of *apatheia* which suppresses self-doubt and anxiety and therefore ruthlessly severs in the soul any continuity between one's present behaviour and the moral failures committed in the past.[68] In taking this position against Nectarius, Augustine anticipates his portrait of the apostle Paul in Book 14 of the *City of God*.

Augustine rejects Nectarius' argument that there are 'different ways' (*uiae diuersae*) for good citizens who practise civic virtues to arrive at the heavenly city.[69] He reminds Nectarius that in the scriptures, Christ refers to himself as '*the* way' (Jn 14:6), and that mercy and truth are said there to be found in him (Ps 24[25]:10).[70] He describes piety as the pinnacle of all civic virtues, which, he says, are taught to people in churches in every city. Yet acquiring virtue is not simply a matter of receiving correct instruction. Augustine insists that God 'not only commands us to seek, but also enables us to acquire' these virtues.[71] This insistence that the true God is the only source of virtue, and that human beings cannot gain it from alternative sources (least of all from themselves), justifies Christian leaders in suppressing other religious cults.[72] Elaborating upon this conviction, he adds that to please God is difficult in this life, and impossible to accomplish perfectly, that is, without sin. For this reason, all civic leaders must take refuge in God's grace.[73] In short, Christianity is more able than rival forms of worship to promote social reconciliation because, unlike other religions, it accepts that

---

[68] For further discussion of this point in relation to Augustine's correspondence with Nectarius, see Dodaro, 'Secular City', especially 243–8.

[69] See *ep.* 104.12 (CSEL 34/2.590): 'sed quia dixisti, quod omnes eam leges diuersis uiis et tramitibus appetant, uereor, ne forte, cum putas etiam illam uiam, in qua nunc constitutus es, eo tendere, pigrior sis ad eam tenendam, quae illuc sola perducit'. For Nectarius' argument, see *ep.* 103.2 (Nectarius to Augustine) (CSEL 34/2.579): 'Non enim illam mihi ciuitatem dicere uidebare, quam muralis aliquis gyrus coercet, nec illam quam philosophorum tractatus mundanam memorans communem omnibus profitetur; sed quam magnus deus, et bene meritae de eo animae habitant atque incolunt, quam omnes leges diuersis uiis et tramitibus appetunt, quam loquendo exprimere non possumus, cogitando forsitan inuenire possemus.'

[70] Augustine cites Jn 14.6 at *ep.* 104.13. References to Ps 24(25):10 occur at *ep.* 104.12 and 104.16.

[71] See *ep.* 91.3 (CSEL 34/2.429): 'autem mores in ecclesiis toto orbe crescentibus tamquam in sanctis auditoriis populorum docentur atque discuntur et maxime pietas, qua uerus et uerax colatur deus, qui haec omnia, quibus animus humanus diuinae societati ad inhabitandam aeternam caelestemque ciuitatem instruitur et aptatur, non solum iubet adgredienda, uerum etiam donat implenda'. The end of the passage is reminiscent of Augustine's well-known prayer at *conf.* 10.40 (CCL 27.126): 'da quod iubes et iube quod uis'.

[72] See *ep.* 91.3 (CSEL 34/2.429): 'inde est, quod deorum multorum falsorumque simulacra et praedixit euersum iri et praecepit euerti. nihil enim homines tam insociabiles reddit uitae peruersitate quam illorum deorum imitatio, quales describuntur et commendantur litteris eorum'.

[73] See *ep.* 104.11 (CSEL 34/2.590): 'nullum enim tempus est, quo non deceat et oporteat agere, unde deo placere possimus; quod in hac uita usque ad eam perfectionem impleri, ut nullum omnino peccatum

in return to God for the pardon that they receive from him as sinners, all human beings are obliged to forgive one another.

This same emphasis on the relationship between true piety and forgiveness of sins returns in Augustine's Letter 185, a treatise entitled *De correctione Donatistarum*, which he addressed c. AD 417 to the military tribune Boniface. Here Augustine justifies the Catholic church's strenuous efforts, including recourse to the emperor, to force the Donatists to submit to its authority.[74] In this treatise, Augustine argues that true piety resides only in the Catholic church, because it alone offers believers the means of attaining true reconciliation with one another and with God. At the root of the Donatist error, he explains, lies the presumption that the church itself, in the person of its ministers, reconciles human beings to God through baptism. Augustine repeats his earlier accusation that Donatists usurp the mediatorial role of Christ, and regard their bishops as mediators worthy of veneration, contrary to the biblical affirmation that God alone is 'just and justifying' (Rom 8.33).[75] By losing sight of God as the source of justice, they come to conceive human virtue neither as mediated by Christ nor as wanting in comparison with divine virtue. They therefore mistake virtue as contained in their church, where it is produced and safeguarded in a pure and complete form by their bishops. Augustine accuses the Donatists, like the Pelagians, of the same error that Paul observes among the Jews: 'not recognizing the justice of God and wanting to establish their own, they were not subject to the justice of God'.[76] He continues in this vein by accusing the Donatists of concluding that, with regard to the members of their church, to be 'just' means to be 'sinless', an inference derived from their use of Eph 5:27 to describe their church as 'without stain or wrinkle'.[77] Given the absoluteness with which the Donatist church assesses its

---

insit in homine, aut non potest aut forte difficillimum est. inde praecisis omnibus dilationibus ad illius gratiam confugiendum est, cui uerissime dici potest'.

[74] On Boniface in general, see Mandouze, *Prosopographie*, 152–5, s.v. Bonifatius 13, R. Markus, 'Bonifatius comes Africae', *Augustinus-Lexikon*, vol. 1, ed. C. Mayer (Basle, 1986–94), 653–5.

[75] See *ep*. 185.37 (CSEL 57.33): 'scimus quidem illos tantam sibi adrogare iustitiam, ut eam se iactent non solum habere sed etiam aliis hominibus dare. a se quippe dicunt iustificari eum, quem baptizauerint, ubi nihil eis restat nisi dicere illi, qui baptizatur ab eis, ut in baptizatorem suum credat. cur enim non faciat, quando apostolus dicit: *credenti in eum, qui iustificat impium, deputatur fides eius ad iustitiam* [Rom 4:5]? in ipsum ergo credat, si eum ipse iustificat, ut deputetur fides eius ad iustitiam. sed puto, quod etiam ipsi se ipsos horrent, si tamen ista uel cogitare dignantur. iustus enim et iustificans non est nisi deus. See my discussion of this point above, pp. 97–102.

[76] Rom 10:3. See *ep*. 185.37 (CSEL 57.33): 'potest autem et de istis dici, quod dixit apostolus de Iudaeis, quia *ignorantes dei iustitiam et suam iustitiam uolentes constituere iustitiae dei non sunt subiecti*' [Rom 10:3].

[77] See *ep*. 185.38 (CSEL 57.34): 'absit autem, ut quisquam nostrum ita se iustum dicat, ut aut suam iustitiam uelit constituere, id est quasi a se ipso sibi datam, cum dicatur ei: *quid enim habes, quod*

possession of justice, it is incapable of practising true penitence and reconciliation. Hence it cannot pray, 'Forgive us our sins as we forgive those
who sin against us' (Mt 6:12): even if it pronounces the words, it cannot act
upon their meaning.[78] Not recognizing that all of its members sin and that
God offers forgiveness for sins, the Donatist church can never become a
community that actively promotes forgiveness and reconciliation. Augustine invites Boniface to contemplate the difficult paradox that, in spite of
its hostility to the Donatists' cause and its appeals to the emperors against
them, only the Catholic church can heal the strife between the two churches,
because it alone believes that the universal extension of sinfulness implied at
1 Jn 1:8–9 includes all the members of the church, including its bishops,
and it alone accepts the real, God-given possibility of forgiveness after baptism.[79] To understand fully that Christ alone is just and that he alone makes
the members of his body virtuous is to acknowledge that no one within the
church can be just except in Christ.[80] Augustine, it should be remembered,
holds that the Donatists make their bishops rivals to Christ, by believing
them to be sinless mediators of divine forgiveness for lay members of their

---

non accepisti (1 Cor 4:7)? aut sine peccato se esse iactare audeat in hac uita, sicut ipsi in nostra
conlatione dixerunt in ea se esse ecclesia, quae iam non habet *maculam aut rugam aut aliquid eius
modi* [Eph 5:27], nescientes hoc in eis modo compleri, qui uel post baptismum continuo uel dimissis
debitis, quae dimittenda in oratione poscuntur [cf. Mt 6:12], de hoc exeunt corpore, in tota uero
ecclesia tunc futurum, ut sit omnino non habens *maculam aut rugam aut aliquid eius modi,* quando
dicendum erit: *ubi est, mors, uictoria tua? ubi est, mors, aculeus tuus? aculeus enim mortis est peccatum*'
(1 Cor 15:55–6). Further examples of his use of stock anti-Pelagian arguments can be found at *ep.*
185.40, where he insists that Christ is 'just and justifying', and where he cites 1 Jn 1:8 ('If we say we
have no sin, we deceive ourselves') to offset 1 Jn 3:9 ('anyone who is born of God does not sin'), a
stratagem that one first finds him employing at *pecc. mer.* 2.8–10.

[78] See *ep.* 185.39 (CSEL 57.35): 'in hac autem uita, ubi *corpus, quod corrumpitur, adgrauat animam* [Wis
9:15], si ecclesia eorum iam talis est, non ergo dicant deo, quod dominus orare nos docuit: *dimitte
nobis debita nostra* [Mt 6:12]. cum enim in baptismo cuncta dimissa sint, ut quid hoc poscit ecclesia,
si iam etiam in hac uita non habet *maculam aut rugam aut aliquid eius modi* [Eph 5:27]? contemnant
et apostolum Iohannem clamantem in epistula sua: *si dixerimus, quia peccatum non habemus, nos
ipsos decipimus et ueritas in nobis non est. si autem confessi fuerimus peccata nostra, fidelis est et iustus,
qui dimittat nobis peccata et mundet nos ab omni iniquitate*' [1 Jn 1:8–9]. See also *ep.* 185.38 (above,
n. 77).

[79] See *ep.* 185.39–40 (CSEL 57.34–5): 'propter hanc spem dicit uniuersa ecclesia: *dimitte nobis debita
nostra* [Mt 6:12], ut non superbientes sed confitentes *mundet ab omni iniquitate* [1 Jn 1:9] atque
ita sibi exhibeat dominus Christus in illa die *gloriosam ecclesiam non habentem maculam aut rugam
aut aliquid eius modi* [Eph 5:27], quam modo mundat *lauacro aquae in uerbo* [Eph 5:26] [. . .]
et, quicquid ab eis, qui post acceptum baptismum hic uiuunt, humana infirmitate contrahitur
quarumque culparum, propter ipsum lauacrum dimittitur [. . .] modo mundat ecclesiam suam
lauacro aquae in uerbo, ut tunc eam sibi exhibeat *non habentem maculam aut rugam aut aliquid
eius modi,* totam scilicet pulchram atque perfectam, quando absorbebitur *mors in uictoriam*' [1 Cor
15:54]. Augustine cites the full text of 1 Jn 1:8–9 at *ep.* 185.39 (see above, n. 78). At *ep.* 185.47, he
recalls instances wherein the Catholic church extended forgiveness to heretics and schismatics, even
at the risk of causing scandal within its own ranks.

[80] See *ep.* 185.40, 185.42.

church.[81] It follows, for Augustine, that only those leaders whose church encourages them to acknowledge their sins and to seek pardon from God can hope to avoid the desire to dominate (*dominare*) others.[82] By implication, Augustine argues that those responsible for correcting the behaviour of others forfeit their moral authority when they lose sight of their own need for repentance and conversion. But should they fall into this or other sins, bishops find within the truly pious church the possibility of repenting and once again being healed.[83] Both King David and the apostle Peter are examples of religious leaders who, after sinning gravely, performed acts of penance while continuing to hold their respective offices.[84] With biblical examples such as these to guide them, Donatists must recognize that the authority of bishops to govern is not impeded by their sins, because the holiness of the church is rooted in Christ alone. Although it concerns the virtues of bishops, and not public officials, Augustine's letter to Boniface offers another instance of the link he wants to establish between the humble acknowledgement of sinfulness and virtuous leadership.

Late in AD 411 or early in AD 412, the pagan proconsul of Africa Rufius Volusianus writes to Augustine expressing doubts about the incarnation. How can God, 'the lord of the universe', still govern the world while physically confined in the body of Jesus Christ?, Volusianus asks. He also charges that the miracles performed by Christ – casting out demons, healing the sick, and raising the dead to life – are insignificant for a man said to be God, especially when compared with miracles performed by other men.[85] When, following his reply to Volusianus, Augustine receives a letter from Marcellinus and learns from him that Volusianus and his associates have

---

[81] See my discussion of this point above, pp. 98–9.

[82] This theme is prominent in Book 10 of Augustine's *Confessions*. See especially *conf.* 10.39–66, where he discusses his own failures as a bishop to overcome those sins, such as love of flattery (*conf.* 10.59), which he recognizes as impeding a virtuous rule over his flock.

[83] See *ep.* 185.42 (CSEL 57.37): 'huius ergo compagem corporis ueniant et labores suos non dominandi cupiditate sed bene utendi pietate possideant. nos autem uoluntatem nostram, ut iam dictum est, ab huius cupiditatis sordibus quolibet inimico iudicante purgamus, quando eos ipsos, quorum labores dicuntur, ut nobiscum et illis et nostris in societate catholica utantur, quantum ualemus, inquirimus'.

[84] See *ep.* 185.45 (CSEL 57.39): 'nam et sanctus Dauid de criminibus mortiferis egit paenitentiam et tamen in honore suo perstitit et beatum Petrum, quando amarissimas lacrimas fudit, utique dominum negasse paenituit et tamen apostolus mansit'. See also *ep.* 185.46. Augustine employs these examples in an effort to explain to Boniface the reasonableness of the agreement between Catholic bishops and Marcellinus just prior to the Conference of Carthage (AD 411) that Donatist bishops who submit to Catholic authority would be permitted to continue to hold their offices even though they would also be required to undergo penance. See also *ep.* 128.2–3, 142.

[85] See *ep.* 135.2 (Volusianus to Augustine) (CSEL 44.92): 'nec ullis competentibus signis clarescunt tantae maiestatis indicia, quoniam larualis illa purgatio, debilium curae, reddita uita defunctis, haec, si et alios cogites, deo parua sunt'.

Apollonius of Tyana and Apuleius in mind as rival miracle-workers to Christ, he recognizes more clearly that Volusianus' questions about Christ have serious political consequences.[86]

Significantly, Augustine opens his response to Volusianus in Letter 137 by affirming the difficulties inherent in understanding mysteries, first those which involve metaphorical language in the scriptures, then those which concern the incarnation directly. He acknowledges that the fundamental scriptural truths which are necessary for salvation are readily apparent, such as the command to love God and one's neighbour. However, in order to understand how to live piously and justly (*pie recteque*), the believer must also apprehend truths that are 'shrouded in the darkness of mystery' and within 'a depth of wisdom that lies hidden' from reason. This truth is veiled from the inquiring mind not only as a result of the language used to communicate it, but on account of the nature of the subject matter.[87] He then considers Volusianus' questions concerning Christ. By employing this theme of the impenetrability of divine truths in his argument, Augustine seems to suggest that the difficulties in understanding morality are linked with those in understanding the incarnation.[88] His treatment of the incarnation in this letter to Volusianus culminates in a brief discussion of the unity of Christ's divine and human natures 'in one person', the first occasion on which he employs the specific formula *una persona* in order to describe this unity.[89] Augustine's point is that Christ's mediation to human beings of his salvific grace and of his divine wisdom and knowledge (Col 2:3), as well as of his teaching (*magisterium*), assistance (*adiutorium*), and example

---

[86] See *ep.* 136.1. See my discussion above, p. 95, of pagan efforts in Roman Africa at the beginning of the fifth century to reintroduce this Porphyrian teaching concerning Christ as thaumaturge.

[87] See *ep.* 137.3 (CSEL 44.100): 'tanta est enim christianarum profunditas litterarum, ut in eis cotidie proficerem, si eas solas ab ineunte pueritia usque ad decrepitam senectutem maximo otio, summo studio, meliore ingenio conarer addiscere, non quo ad ea, quae necessaria sunt saluti, tanta in eis peruveniatur difficultate, sed, cum quisque ibi fidem tenuerit, sine qua pie recteque non uiuitur, tam multa tamque multiplicibus mysteriorum umbraculis opacata intellegenda proficientibus restant tantaque non solum in uerbis, quibus ita dicta sunt, uerum etiam in rebus, quae intellegendae sunt, latet altitudo sapientiae, ut annosissimis, acutissimis, flagrantissimis cupiditate discendi hoc contingat, quod eadem scriptura quodam loco habet: *cum consummauerit homo, tunc incipit*' (Eccl 18:6). Augustine repeats these points with additional emphasis at *ep.* 137.18. See also my discussion above, pp. 135–9, concerning Augustine's reply to Volusianus (*ep.* 138 to Marcellinus).

[88] At *ep.* 137.4–5 (CSEL 44.101), Augustine exclaims, in relation to the understanding of spiritual substances, such as the divine nature or the human soul: 'longe aliud est animae natura quam corporis; quanto magis dei, qui creator est et animae et corporis. non sic deus implere dicitur mundum uelut aqua, uelut aer, uelut ipsa lux, ut minore sui parte minorem mundi partem impleat et maiore maiorem. nouit ubique totus esse et nullo contineri loco; nouit uenire non recedendo, ubi erat; nouit abire non deserendo, quo uenerat. miratur hoc mens humana et, quia non capit, fortasse nec credit'.

[89] See *ep.* 137.9–11 (CSEL 44.108–10). See Drobner, *Person-Exegese*, 169, and my discussion above, pp. 91–4.

(*exemplum*) regarding the just life, occurs as a consequence of the unity of his divine and human natures.[90] In replying with this doctrinal explanation to Volusianus' view that Christ may be no more 'divine' than Apollonius of Tyana and other celebrated human miracle-workers and sages, Augustine anticipates his arguments in Books 8–10 of the *City of God* concerning the role of Christ as the sole mediator of virtue in human beings, as well as those in Book 19 regarding the necessity of true piety to achieve true virtues, the core of his argument against Cicero's assumption that Rome had ever been a commonwealth.[91] Turning to Christian examples that inspire true virtues, he points to Abraham's piety in the creation of a strong people,[92] as well as the humility of the apostles and martyrs, who preached the way of piety and salvation.[93]

Shortly after sending Letter 137 to Volusianus with these comments, he writes Letter 138 to Marcellinus with Volusianus' objections in mind. Augustine observes that Cicero praises Julius Caesar for the mercy he showed to subjugated peoples, and concludes that the ideal of a civil governor (*princeps ciuitatis*) who pardons offences is not absent in Roman literature or ethics.[94] Yet, he argues, if Christ's commands concerning civic virtues such as forbearance with one's enemies were adopted by all ranks of society, from military officers to simple soldiers, from tax collectors to taxpayers, the Empire would enjoy greater growth and security than under early 'ideal'

---

[90] See *ep.* 137.9 (CSEL 44.108): 'factum est et tamen quidam haeretici peruerse mirando eius laudandoque uirtutem naturam humanam in eo prorsus agnoscere noluerunt, ubi est omnis gratiae commendatio, qua saluos facit credentes in se profundos thesauros sapientiae et scientiae continens [cf. Col 2:3] et fide inbuens mentes, quas ad aeternam contemplationem ueritatis incommutabilis peruehat [. . .] uero ita inter deum et homines mediator apparuit, ut in unitate personae copulans utramque naturam et solita sublimaret insolitis et insolita solitis temperaret'. On Christ as *magisterium, adiutorium,* and *exemplum,* see *ep.* 137.12. Note, too, that Augustine emphasizes in this section the relationship between Christ's teaching/example and his grace. For clarification of Augustine's thinking in this regard, see my discussion above, pp. 151–64.

[91] See, for example, *ciu.* 19.4 (CCL 48.668): 'si enim uerae uirtutes sunt, quae nisi in eis, quibus uera inest pietas, esse non possunt, non se profitentur hoc posse, ut nullas miserias patiantur homines, in quibus sunt – neque enim mendaces sunt uerae uirtutes [. . .] unde et apostolus Paulus non de hominibus inprudentibus inpatientibus, intemperantibus et iniquis, sed de his, qui secundum ueram pietatem uiuerent et ideo uirtutes, quas haberent, ueras haberent, ait: *spe enim salui facti sumus*' (Rom 8:24). See also *ciu.* 19.25.

[92] See *ep.* 137.15.   [93] See *ep.* 137.16.

[94] See *ep.* 138.9 (CSEL 44.134): 'opus est, ut diutius laboremus ac non ipsos potius percontemur, quo modo poterant gubernare atque augere rem publicam, quam ex parua et inopi magnam opulentamque fecerunt, qui *accepta iniuria ignoscere quam persequi malebant* [Sallust, *Bellum Catlinae* 9.5]? quo modo Caesari, utique administratori rei publicae, mores eius extollens Cicero dicebat, quod nihil obliuisci soleret nisi iniurias [Cicero, *Pro Ligario* 12.35]? dicebat enim hoc tam magnus laudator aut tam magnus adulator; sed si laudator, talem Caesarem nouerat, si autem adulator, talem esse debere ostendebat principem ciuitatis, qualem illum fallaciter praedicabat. Quid est autem non reddere malum pro malo nisi abhorrere ab ulciscendi libidine, quod est accepta iniuria ignoscere malle quam persequi et nihil nisi iniurias obliuisci'.

leaders, such as Romulus, Numa, and Brutus.[95] He grounds this claim in the New Testament principle (which he says is unmatched outside Christian teaching) that examples of goodness toward evildoers can move them to repentance and conversion.[96] Drawing his discussion of the ideal statesman back to Volusianus' misunderstanding of the incarnation, Augustine suggests that Christ offers a greater example of this virtue than Caesar or any other Roman leader, because he does not resist those who put him to death, and moreover he prays God to forgive them.[97] Here Augustine once again implies that the unrivalled character of Christ's virtue is rooted in his unique freedom from fear of death. This freedom marks for Augustine the vast difference between Christ's virtue and that of even the most virtuous human beings. For this reason, Augustine asserts, Christian teachers are right to insist upon the greater suitability of a biblical ethics for the welfare of the Empire than that inspired by Rome's heroic traditions. He notes, for example, that the scriptures identify both King David's sins and his worthy deeds as instruction for believers on the way to avoid sin and to atone for those they commit.[98] Christian emperors and other officials can certainly be found who fail to live up to these biblical standards, he acknowledges. However, he argues, such moral failures only implicate the men in question, not the doctrine they profess.[99] That the Christian understanding of civic virtue is superior to the pagan understanding is due to the fact that true piety unites the virtues practised by Christians in the earthly city with those found in the heavenly city.[100]

---

[95] See *ep.* 138.10 (CSEL 44.135): 'cum uero legitur praecipiente auctoritate diuina non reddendum malum pro malo, cum haec tam salubris admonitio congregationibus populorum tamquam publicis utriusque sexus atque omnium aetatum et dignitatum scholis de superiore loco personat, accusatur religio tamquam inimica rei publicae. quae si, ut dignum est, audiretur, longe melius Romulo, Numa, Bruto ceterisque illis Romanae gentis praeclaris uiris constitueret, consecraret, firmaret augeretque rem publicam'. See also *ep.* 138.15, *ciu.* 2.19.

[96] See *ep.* 138.11–12. At *s.* 302.10, Augustine urges a parallel reason on townspeople who beat to death a customs official accused of extortion, by insisting that they might have converted the unjust official through their good example. See my discussion of this sermon above, p. 118. But see also *ep.* 138.13–14, and my discussion of this letter above, pp. 135–9, where it becomes clear that Augustine does not intend this argument as an endorsement of pacifism.

[97] See *ep.* 138.13.

[98] See *ep.* 138.19 (CSEL 44.147): 'uideant Dauid nostrum sine ullis talibus artibus ex pastore ouium peruenisse ad regiam dignitatem, cuius et peccata et merita fidelis scriptura non tacuit, ut sciremus, et quibus modis non offenderetur deus et quibus modis placaretur offensus'.

[99] See *ep.* 138.16.

[100] See *ep.* 138.17 (CSEL 44.144–5): 'ista enim conluuie morum pessimorum et ueteris perditae disciplinae maxime uenire ac subuenire debuit caelestis auctoritas, quae uoluntariam paupertatem, quae continentiam, beniuolentiam, iustitiam atque concordiam ueramque pietatem persuaderet ceterasque uitae luminosas ualidasque uirtutes non tantum propter istam uitam honestissime gerendam nec tantum propter ciuitatis terrenae concordissimam societatem uerum etiam propter

Augustine's correspondence in AD 413/14 with Macedonius, the vicar of Africa, culminates in an even fuller discussion of the relation of piety to civic virtues in the Christian statesman. This exchange of letters begins with a request by Augustine to Macedonius for clemency on behalf of an individual facing the death penalty. In his initial reply, Macedonius, who is a Christian, expresses puzzlement that bishops in general consider it a religious duty to intercede for clemency on behalf of persons facing the death penalty.[101] In the course of two letters in response, Augustine characterizes at length the piety of the Christian statesman. As will be shown, he suggests that the conception of the civic virtues which they practise in the earthly city should undergo change as a result of their anticipation of the fulfilment of these same virtues in the heavenly city. Thus, he develops a line of argument already evident in his correspondence with Nectarius and Volusianus.

Augustine begins by asserting that by comparing their virtues with God's supreme mercy, blessedness, and justice, earthly judges can see that they are not sinless, despite the praise lavished upon them. They ought therefore to fear God's judgment, seek his pardon, and try to show mercy in imitation of Christ, an act which is emphatically not a failure to perform their duty.[102] This last point is a direct contradiction of Macedonius' principal objection to clemency, as expressed in his previous letter to Augustine, that mercy can be easily mistaken for leniency, thereby compromising justice.[103] Augustine readily admits the difficulties involved in balancing mercy and justice in cases involving punishment of criminals.[104] He acknowledges the existence in the scriptures of two arguments concerning capital punishment: the first, expressed at Rom 13:3–5, claims that the civil authority 'is a minister of God and avenger of his anger on the wrongdoer', and that 'he therefore does not wield the sword pointlessly'. This passage indicates to Augustine that

---

adipiscendam sempiternam salutem et sempiterni cuiusdam populi caelestem diuinamque rem publicam, cui nos ciues adsciscit fides, spes, caritas, ut, quam diu inde peregrinamur, feramus eos, si corrigere non ualemus, qui uitiis inpunitis uolunt stare rem publicam, quam primi Romani constituerunt auxeruntque uirtutibus etsi non habentes ueram pietatem erga deum uerum, quae illos etiam in aeternam ciuitatem posset salubri religione perducere, custodientes tamen quandam sui generis probitatem, quae posset terrenae ciuitati constituendae, augendae conseruandaeque sufficere'. For a parallel text, see *ciu.* 5.20. Augustine offers a more developed version of this argument at *ep.* 155. See my discussion below, pp. 208–12.

[101] See *ep.* 153.1 (CSEL 44.396), citing *ep.* 152.2 (Macedonius to Augustine). Augustine's initial letter is not extant, but see *ep.* 152.1 (Macedonius to Augustine) (CSEL 44.393): 'itaque sine mora quod, optabat, obtinuit. uerum quoniam extitit occasio, hoc ipsum, quantulumcumque est, quod admonitus indulsi, nolo sine mercede remanere'. In a later letter, Macedonius again refers to the favour. See *ep.* 154.1 (Macedonius to Augustine) (CSEL 44.428): 'miro modo afficior sapientia tua et in illis, quae edidisti, et in his, quae interueniens pro sollicitis mittere non grauaris [. . .] proinde statim commendatis effectum desiderii tribui; nam sperandi uiam ante patefeceram'. See also Possidius, *Vita Augustini* 20.

[102] See *ep.* 153.8.   [103] See *ep.* 152.2–3 (Macedonius to Augustine).   [104] See *ep.* 153.17–18.

capital punishment may in certain cases be justified. However, the second argument, at Jn 8:7 ('let the one without sin cast the first stone'), suggests that only Christ could justly apply the death penalty.[105] Augustine frames his discussion of capital punishment between these two scriptural passages because they indicate the dilemma faced by the magistrate who desires to observe both justice (Rom 13:3–5) and mercy (Jn 8:3–11) in capital cases. He then proposes to explain these two competing logics in a way similar to his response to Volusianus' concern over Christian non-violence.[106] He does so, once again, without collapsing one mode of reason into the other, by using Jn 8:3–11 to resolve the tension between approbation for capital punishment as found in the Old Testament and in the Epistle to the Romans, and general precepts in the New Testament in favour of forgiveness and love of enemies.[107] Christian rulers might, indeed, cite passages from the scriptures in support of their decision to impose the death penalty, he says. In doing so, however, they should bear in mind that the scribes and Pharisees who brought the adulteress to Christ for condemnation also supported their arguments with the scriptures.[108] Augustine thus draws Macedonius' attention to Christ's function at Jn 8:3–11 in clarifying the spiritual attitudes that are necessary in order to interpret scriptural precepts correctly. He points out that, although they are unambiguous, the scriptural passages which the scribes and Pharisees have in mind concerning the punishment for adultery do not prevent Christ from showing mercy to the woman. At the same time, in pardoning the adulteress, Christ cannot be said to contradict or abrogate the divine law.[109] Christ illustrates how ethical precepts contained in the scriptures are to be interpreted in the light of the divine wisdom which he personifies.[110] By implication, statesmen who seek to resolve the apparent disharmony between justice and mercy in deciding

---

[105] Augustine cites Rom 13 at *ep.* 153.19; however, he anticipates the passage already at *ep.* 153.16. He introduces discussion of Jn 8:3–11 at *ep.* 153.9.

[106] See my discussion of *ep.* 138 above, pp. 135–9.

[107] See especially *ep.* 153.15–16. See R. Dodaro, 'Augustine of Hippo between the Secular City and the City of God', *Augustinus Afer. Saint Augustin: africanité et universalité. Actes du colloque international, Alger-Annaba, 1–7 avril 2001*, ed. P.-Y. Fux et al. (Fribourg, 2003), 287–305.

[108] See *ep.* 153.9, where Augustine makes this point in a reference to the obligation of the judges at Jn 8:3–11 to 'serve the law'. Both Dt 22:22–4 and Lv 20:10 oblige death by stoning as punishment for adultery.

[109] See *ep.* 153.9 (CSEL 44.405): 'ita nec legem inprobauit, quae huius modi reas iussit occidi'. See also *s.* 13.4, *Io. eu. tr.* 33.5 (CCL 36.308): 'Non dixit: Non lapidetur! ne contra legem dicere uideretur.' The argument also recurs at *en. Ps.* 50.8.

[110] Augustine makes this point more clearly elsewhere in texts where he comments on Jn 8:3–11. See, for example, *Io. eu. tr.* 33.5 (CCL 36.308): 'Quid ergo respondit dominus Iesus? quid respondit ueritas? quid respondit sapientia? quid respondit ipsa cui calumnia parabatur iustitia?'. See also *s.* 13.5 (CCL 41.180): 'remansit peccatrix et saluator. Remansit misera et misericordia [. . .] quia ille ei iudex remanserat qui erat sine peccato [. . .] Illos a uindicta repressit conscientia, me ad subueniendum inclinat misericordia.'

whether to impose capital punishment can do so only by seeking that same divine wisdom.

Augustine repeats this last point in Letter 155, his final letter to Macedonius. Here he moves beyond the specific concerns regarding capital punishment that he had previously discussed in Letter 153, by exploring the personal, interior manner in which judges must seek divine wisdom in order to balance justice and mercy. He states that to do this, they should fix their attention on the love of God as it is exists in the heavenly city.[111] By introducing the topic of the 'heavenly city' with the implied difference between it and the 'earthly city', Augustine sets up a series of oppositions important to his discussion of the statesman's virtues.[112] First, the heavenly city consists in the afterlife in which those human beings granted eternal life with God live in complete happiness. Now totally free of the consequences of original sin, they know and love God as completely as possible for human beings who have attained salvation. In the heavenly city, human life is characterized by true happiness and true peace, a condition sustained by the complete absence of evil. This absence of evil is guaranteed to the saints by their possession of God, who is the supreme good. Thus, life in the heavenly city differs from life in the earthly city, where evil results in different kinds of suffering, temptations, and the necessity of toil, all of which are epitomized for Augustine in death. Augustine believes that on account of the absence of evil in the heavenly city, human virtue differs in the afterlife from virtue in this world. He illustrates this point to Macedonius by comparing fortitude and justice as they are conceived in the two cities.

Before making this comparison, however, he explains how the virtues of faith and hope transform the way in which civic virtues like fortitude and justice are understood in the earthly city, by harmonizing them with the way they are understood in the heavenly city. He describes in detail how this transformation occurs through hope. First, he defines hope as the virtue which sustains Christians in their endurance of the trials associated with this temporal life, such as illness, poverty, and war. Hope, he says, aids believers together with faith by teaching them that the happiness they seek for themselves cannot be found in this life, but must be longed for in the

---

[111] See *ep.* 155.1 (CSEL 44.430): 'quod animum tuum caritate aeternitatis et ueritatis atque ipsius caritatis affectum diuinae illi caelestique rei publicae, cuius regnator est Christus et in qua sola semper beataque uiuendum est, si recte hic pieque uiuatur, agnosco inhiantem, uideo propinquantem eiusque potiundae amplector ardentem'.

[112] See van Oort, *Jerusalem*, 115–18.

life to come, on the basis of trust in God's promises.[113] This last point is important to Augustine's general argument. He leads up to it by observing that in the past, philosophers have failed to find happiness in this life.[114] He insists that the Christian statesman must govern prudently and justly while recognizing what the virtue of hope teaches: that he not conceive of his primary aim to foster happiness in this earthly life as an end it itself. Were he to do so, he would risk elevating the pursuit of temporal benefits, such as health, wealth, and liberty above the pursuit of eternal goods, such as happiness and life in God, which transcend death.[115] Hope therefore redirects the aim of civic virtues away from an exclusive concern with acquiring prosperity and security in the earthly city to the pursuit of the happiness that belongs to the heavenly city. To demonstrate that the path to 'true virtue' (*uera uirtus*) encompasses faith, hope, and love, Augustine pairs Ps 17(18):1 ('I will *love* you, Lord, my virtue') with Ps 39(40):4 ('Blessed is the man whose *hope* is in the name of the Lord'), and states that believers should 'hold these words *faithfully* in [their] hearts.' Christians who seek true virtue must have God as the object of their faith, hope, and love, and they should pray to God to increase these virtues in them.[116]

In Augustine's view, without the transformation of civic virtues through faith, hope, and love, the statesman will pursue a form of peace and prosperity for the earthly city which does not have the love of God as the supreme good. Augustine holds that the statesman invariably corrupts civic virtues when he fails to consider their aims in the heavenly city. He illustrates this point by comparing these virtues from a secular perspective with the same virtues when they are transformed by faith, hope, and love. Considered solely by the standards of the earthly city, he says, fortitude is understood as 'the courage with which fear of enemies is overcome', temperance as 'the avoidance of excess', and justice as the 'rendering to each of his due'.[117] He

---

[113] See *ep.* 155.4 (CSEL 44.434): 'hoc piorum praemium est, cuius adipiscendi spe uitam istam temporalem atque mortalem, non tam delectabiliter quam tolerabiliter ducimus, et mala eius tunc bono consilio et diuino munere fortiter ferimus, cum bonorum aeternorum fideli dei promissione et fideli nostra exspectatione gaudeamus'. Note the expression 'fideli nostra exspectatione' ('in our faithful hope'), by which Augustine connects faith and hope. For further discussion of the relationship of faith and hope, see M. Jackson, 'Faith, Hope and Charity and Prayer in St. Augustine', *Studia Patristica: Papers Presented to the Tenth International Conference on Patristic Studies held in Oxford 1987*, vol. 22, ed. E. Livingstone (Leuven, 1989), 265–70.

[114] See *ep.* 155.2–3.   [115] See my discussion above, pp. 33–5.

[116] See *ep.* 155.6 (CSEL 44.436): 'Si ergo nos uirtus uera delectat, ei dicamus, quod in eius sacris litteris legimus: *diligam te, domine, uirtus mea* [Ps 17[18]:1]; et si uere beati esse uolumus – quod nolle non possumus – id quod in eisdem litteris didicimus, fido corde teneamus: *beatus uir cuius est nomen domini spex eius, et non respexit in uanitates et insanias mendaces*' (Ps 39[40]:4).

[117] See *ep.* 155.10 (CSEL 44.440): 'itaque si omnis prudentia tua, qua consulere conaris rebus humanis; si omnis fortitudo, qua nullius iniquitate aduersante terreris, si omnis temperantia, qua in tanta

observes that these definitions arise from the fact that in the earthly city, virtue must struggle against evil. For example, justice seeks equity among social classes, as when wealth is redistributed from the rich to the poor. But in the heavenly city, he argues, human beings feel no need or desire other than for God. So in the heavenly city, justice ensures that nothing deprives its citizens of adhering to God.[118] This understanding of justice represents its 'true' nature, for Augustine. Virtues, he says, are called 'true' (*uerae uirtutes*) insofar as they lead the soul to adhere to God, the source of happiness, because only those individuals who adhere to God overcome the consequences of sin – suffering, temptation, toil, and death.[119] The statesman who wishes to rule the earthly city in a truly just manner should therefore seek to harmonize secular virtue with true virtue, understood as a life of happiness in God, and not merely as freedom from need or want.[120]

By objecting to secular understandings of civic virtues, Augustine does not wish statesmen to neglect the pursuit of temporal social benefits for their subjects. Instead, he proposes that their expectations about the substance of justice and peace should change. For this reason, Augustine subordinates true virtues in the earthly city to true piety, by which he means the love through which the soul adheres to God. In Augustine's view, the Christian statesman's primary objective in governing piously should be to assist his subjects to love God in the truest way possible. This fundamental aim

labe nequissimae consuetudinis hominum te a corruptionibus abstines, si omnis iustitia, qua recte iudicando sua cuique distribuis . . .'. These conventional definitions of the civic virtues can be found in Stoic authors. See references to ancient works and modern studies above, pp. 9–10, n. 21.

[118] See *ep.* 155.12 (CSEL 44.442–3): 'si enim uirtutes, quas accepisti, a quo acceperis, sentiens eique gratias agens eas ad ipsius cultum etiam in tuis istis saecularibus honoribus conferas tuaeque potestati subditos homines ad eum colendum et exemplo religiosae tuae uitae et ipso studio consulendi seu fouendo seu terrendo erigas et adducas nihilque aliud in eo, quod per te securius uiuunt, uelis, nisi ut hinc illum promereantur, apud quem beate uiuent, ut uerae illae uirtutes erunt et illius opitulatione, cuius largitate donatae sunt, ita crescent et perficientur, ut te ad uitam uere beatam, quae non nisi aeterna est, sine ulla dubitatione perducant, ubi iam nec prudenter discernantur a bonis mala, quae non erunt, nec fortiter tolerentur aduersa, quia non ibi erit, nisi quod amemus, non etiam, quod toleremus, nec temperanter libido frenetur, ubi nulla eius incitamenta sentiemus, nec iuste subueniatur ope indigentibus, ubi inopem atque indignum non habebimus. una ibi uirtus erit et id ipsum erit uirtus praemiumque uirtutis, quod dicit in sanctis eloquiis homo, qui hoc amat: *mihi autem adhaerere deo bonum est* [Ps 72[73]:28]. haec ibi erit plena et sempiterna sapientia eademque uita ueraciter iam beata; peruentio quippe est ad aeternum ac summum bonum, cui adhaerere in aeternum est finis nostri boni. dicatur haec et prudentia, quia prospectissime adhaerebit bono, quod non amittatur, et fortitudo, quia firmissime adhaerebit bono, unde non auellatur, et temperantia, quia castissime adhaerebit bono, ubi non corrumpatur, et iustitia, quia rectissime adhaerebit bono, cui merito subiciatur'.

[119] See *ep.* 155.12 (above, n. 118). See also C. Mayer, '"Pietas" und "vera pietas quae caritas est". Zwei Kernfragen der Auseinandersetzung Augustins mit der heidnischen Antike', *Augustiniana Traiectina. Communications présentées au Colloque International d'Utrecht 13–14 novembre 1986*, ed. J. den Boeft and J. van Oort (Paris, 1987), 119–36.

[120] See *ep.* 155.10.

should guide all of his endeavours to advance the temporal welfare of his subjects, whether he seeks to assist those in material need or to discipline those who undermine public security.[121]

Finally, Augustine argues that all virtues are united in the heavenly city.[122] He is aware that statesmen sometimes have difficulty conceiving of virtues as a unity, as in cases involving punishment, when justice seems to conflict with mercy. But in the heavenly city, all virtues are simply aspects of the love of God. Prudence, for example, chooses God as the supreme good among other goods; fortitude suffers any hardship in order not to lose God; temperance allows no temptation to divert the soul from God; justice prevents pride from leading the soul to serve anything other than God.[123] For Augustine, the civic virtues are united in the proper love of God through which the soul adheres to God as its only good.[124] He also insists that by loving God in this manner, the statesman fulfils the divine commandment to love his neighbour as himself (cf. Mt 22:37–40, Mk 12:30–1, Lk 10:27). Augustine explains that by loving God, the statesman also loves himself, because he can choose no greater good for himself than God. Moreover, the statesman's love of God obliges him to assist his subjects in loving God. Thus, by loving God properly he also loves his neighbour, because he can seek no greater good for his neighbour than God. These two loves, of self and neighbour, are united in the love of God. Finally, Augustine emphasizes that the commandment to love one's neighbour obliges the statesman to love all human beings without discrimination.[125]

Letter 155 thus clarifies Augustine's view that as a consequence of sin, the statesman's rule of the earthly city will never be perfectly virtuous. He will therefore never completely overcome the difficulties in harmonizing justice and mercy, as when he is faced with the need to punish criminals. Nevertheless, Augustine is confident that as long as the statesman's desire to govern with true piety leads him to understand the aims of civic virtues in harmony with the love of God, and provided that he receives with humility the grace that Christ bestows on him, his virtues gradually increase in strength while

---

[121] See *ep.* 155.12 (above, n. 118).   [122] See *ep.* 155.12 (above, n. 118).

[123] See *ep.* 155.12 (above, n. 118).

[124] See *ep.* 155.13 (CSEL 44.443): 'quamquam et in hac uita, uirtus non est nisi diligere, quod diligendum est; id eligere, prudentia est, nullius inde auerti molestiis fortitudo est, nullis inlecebris, temperantia est, nulla superbia iustitia est'.

[125] See *ep.* 155.14 (CSEL 44.444): 'ad illum ergo quanta opera possumus, etiam illi ut peruenant agamus, quos tamquam nosmetipsos diligimus, si nosmetipsos diligere, illum diligendo iam nouimus. Christus namque, id est ueritas, dicit in duobus praeceptis totam legem prophetasque pendere, ut diligamus deum ex toto corde, ex tota anima, ex tota mente, et diligamus proximos tamquam nosmetipsos [cf. Mt 22:37–40, Mk 12:30–1, Lk 10:27, Dt 6:5, Lv 19:18]. proximus sane hoc loco, non sanguinis propinquitate, sed rationis societate pensandus est, in qua socii sunt omnes homines'.

they also converge in the love of God. Augustine counsels Macedonius to compare God's perfect virtue with his own moral shortcomings. By making this effort, the imperial vicar will realize that he lives under a divine pardon. If he subsequently governs the earthly city with his attention fixed upon the love of God, he will deepen this awareness of himself.[126] He will also love himself and his neighbour with a love that reflects the pardon which God has granted to all human beings.[127] Finally, in this state of humility, he will begin to experience the happiness that belongs ultimately only to those who dwell in the heavenly city.[128] Augustine's description of Macedonius in this letter thus corresponds to his description of the *imperator felix* in Book 5 of the *City of God*.[129] In this final letter to Macedonius, Augustine says of Macedonius that even though he wears the belt of an earthly judge, he has his mind largely fixed on the heavenly commonwealth.[130] He expresses his conviction that the governor already 'approaches near to God's heavenly commonwealth' and that he 'burns with a desire for it', insofar as he is also 'inspired with a love for eternity, for truth and for love'.[131]

CONCLUSION

Augustine's effort to reform the Roman heroic ideal as found in Cicero's accounts of *optimi uiri* may not appear particularly systematic, but its core elements can be detected especially after AD 411 in his preaching and writing on martyrs such as Peter and Paul, in his letters to public officials, and in his representation in the *City of God* of the public penance of the Emperor Theodosius I. At the beginning of his controversy with the Pelagians, Augustine recognizes general characteristics of his adversaries' conception of the workings of virtue that he has already encountered in Stoic, Manichean, Platonist, and Donatist thought, and throughout ancient and contemporary political culture. In Augustine's view, all these philosophies hold that,

---

[126] See *ep.* 155.6.   [127] See *ep.* 155.14–15.   [128] See *ep.* 155.1.

[129] See my discussion of *ciu.* 5.24 above, p. 193.

[130] See *ep.* 155.17 (CSEL 44.447): 'pietas igitur, id est uerus ueri dei cultus ad omnia prodest, et quae molestias huius uitae auertat aut leniat et quae ad illam uitam salutemque perducat, ubi nec aliquid iam mali patiamur et bono summo sempiternoque perfruamur. ad hanc te perfectius assequendam et perseuerantissime retinendam exhortor ut me ipsum. cuius nisi iam particeps esses tuosque istos honores temporales ei seruire opotere iudicares [. . .] ut te appareat in terreni iudices cingulo non parua ex parte caelestem rem publicam cogitare'.

[131] See *ep.* 155.1 (CSEL 44.430): 'quod animum tuum caritate aeternitatis et ueritatis atque ipsius caritatis affectum diuinae illi caelestique rei publicae, cuius regnator est Christus et in qua sola semper beataque uiuendum est, si recte hic pieque uiuatur, agnosco inhiantem, uideo propinquantem eiusque potiundae amplector ardentem'.

in principle, the human soul is able to know what is required for the just life, even without divine assistance, and it can completely suppress those passions, including fear of death, which impede moral action. Although he already opposes these premises before his encounter with Pelagian thought, it is on account of the latter that his own, alternative concept of the heroic emerges in his writings. The heart of this ideal is the apostle Paul, the only Christian referred to in the *City of God* as *optimus uir*.

Augustine presents Paul in this light both in the *City of God* and in *De trinitate* for a number of reasons. First, the story of the apostle's early persecution of Christians, his conversion, and his sufferings on behalf of his new faith is confirmed by divine authority, being contained within the New Testament. Second, according to Augustine, Paul articulates in his epistles the key principles of Augustine's alternative ideal. For Augustine, Paul contradicts the heroic ideal commonly accepted by contemporary pagans and Christians. Although the apostle exhibits strong moral character in the traditional sense, he is also aware of his own moral weakness, which he publicly confesses. Moreover, in Augustine's view, this awareness of personal weakness shapes Paul's compassion for other human beings, susceptible as they are to moral failure. The apostle's fear of death is readily attested in the scriptures (2 Cor 5:4), and this and his frequent acknowledgement of total dependence on the mediation and grace of Christ for whatever good he accomplishes during his ministry (Rom 7:15–25) are vital features of Augustine's conception of 'heroic' human virtue, as distinct from the Pelagian view.

Augustine's revised model of heroic virtue also incorporates Old Testament figures such as Abraham and David, early Christian martyrs such as Lawrence, and even contemporaries such as the Emperor Theodosius I, or those holy men yet 'on pilgrimage' such as Paulinus of Nola and Macedonius. Common to each of these Augustinian 'heroes' is an admission that his virtue is not his own, either at its source or in its deeds, and that the most noble political accomplishment is to thank God for the gift of pardon and to show mercy to others. Augustine's correspondence with public officials during the Pelagian controversy and his composition of the *City of God* reveal something of the role that he hopes this penitential consciousness will play in the statesman's administration of justice. Augustine is convinced that, without neglecting their duty to safeguard order, public officials should employ the least violent means at their disposal to promote the moral reform of wrongdoers – which they will achieve only by recalling that they too are sinners. As in all interior movements of the soul, however, such a realization also depends on divine initiative and grace; all that the statesman can do to further this spiritual process is to nurture faith, hope, and love through daily prayer and penance, thereby asking God to give him the grace necessary to act justly. Cultivation of these attitudes requires that he avoid self-glorification, as it impedes the humility necessary for repentance and moral conversion.

General conclusion

Just two years after the sack of Rome by Alaric, at the time when Augustine begins work on the *City of God*, Flavius Marcellinus informs him of a complaint by the pagan proconsul of Africa, Rufius Volusianus, that the non-violence preached by Christ diminishes Christianity's capacity to defend the Roman Empire, and that Christian emperors have in fact harmed it. At the same time, Volusianus writes to Augustine about his objections over the incarnation. How can God be present in Jesus, the proconsul asks, and why, if Christ is God, are his miracles so less impressive than those of other wise and holy miracle-workers in history? Augustine's letters to Marcellinus and Volusianus (Letters 138, 137) reveal how seriously he views these challenges to the political significance of the Christian faith. Both in his letters to public officials and in the *City of God* he takes as his point of departure what Cicero says in *De re publica* concerning the statesman and the virtues through which Rome's leading citizens had earlier maintained the justice and security of the *res publica*. At the heart of Augustine's denial in Books 2 and 19 of the *City of God* that Rome was ever a true commonwealth is his conviction that it never practised true justice. His response to those in his own day who challenge the suitability of the Christian religion for the security of the Roman Empire is, therefore, to demonstrate the falsehood of Rome's widely held conceptions of virtuous leadership, and the defective virtues of its heroes. To do this, Augustine redefines civic virtues, summarized in justice, by asserting that they are only real virtues when they are based in true piety. In taking this position, however, Augustine's principal aim is less to disparage Rome's pagan statesmen than to establish a new Christian understanding of virtue and heroism.

Piety is the traditional Roman virtue that promotes traditional devotion to the gods, the key to maintaining the security of the commonwealth in the view of the ancients. Augustine distinguishes it from 'true piety', which he defines as the knowledge and love of the true God. Only by loving God, and one's neighbour and self in God, Augustine declares, can human beings achieve eternal happiness, which is their deepest longing. He holds that the human soul is prevented from knowing and loving God as its highest good by the twin consequences of original sin, ignorance and weakness. In Augustine's view, these defects, which are only partially overcome in the soul as a result of baptism, continue to deter it from knowing and loving the moral good – and therefore God. He insists that ignorance and weakness are epitomized in fear of death, which, following the beginning of his dispute with the Pelagians c. AD 411, he ascribes to all human beings throughout their lives, regardless of their individual progress in virtue. In taking this latter position, which differentiates his view on fear of death from that of all other Christian and pagan philosophers, Augustine expresses one of the cardinal principles of his revision of the heroic ideal which is so central to Ciceronian and other Roman political thought.

Augustine develops his thinking about the continuing effects of original sin in individuals outstanding in virtue, such as Paul, in conjunction with a parallel development in his understanding of the unity of Christ's divine and human natures 'in one person'. Beginning in AD 411, Augustine sharpens his criticism of Pelagius and his associates for asserting that human virtue can be perfected in this life, and that for human beings to act virtuously they do not require a divine intervention in the soul. At the same time, he begins to insist that Christ is uniquely free from sin and fear of death, and that his virtue alone among human beings is perfect. Augustine argues against the Pelagians that Christ's uniquely virtuous status is entirely due to the manner in which his human nature is united to his divine nature. He suggests that an exchange occurs between Christ's natures so that, in effect, the immortality and blessedness which pertain to his divine nature can also be said to pertain to his human nature, and the mortality that belongs to his human nature can be ascribed as well to his divine nature. This exchange between Christ's natures provides Augustine with a key concept for explaining Christ's mediation of virtue to the human soul. To do this, he pairs his explanation of Christ's unity 'in one person' with the Pauline image of Christ as the head of a body which is composed of the faithful (cf. Col 1:18, 1:24). Augustine suggests that, as a consequence of the exchange of characteristics between his natures, Christ vicariously experiences the darkness and pain of human sinfulness, while he also communicates to human beings the virtue which is proper to him as a sinless human being. Key to Augustine's representation of Christ's mediation of virtue is the image of a dialogue between Christ, the head, and his 'members'. Against those religious and philosophical accounts of virtue which emphasize the autonomy of human reason as the seat of virtue, Augustine contrasts the image of Christ mediating virtue to his members by uniting his 'voice' with theirs. This mediated virtue is 'true virtue', as Augustine conceives it. It can only be achieved by those individuals who renounce the presumption that they can produce their own virtue, and who faithfully and humbly seek it in God's grace through Christ.

Augustine thus insists that faith and humility are the initial virtues required by human beings who desire to live justly. They are necessary, he believes, first in order to accept the incarnation, and second, to renounce reliance upon one's own strength in living virtuously. In his view, these acts of faith and humility are related to each other and are repeated in the interpretation of the scriptures. Augustine parallels the scriptures as God's 'oratory' to the role that Cicero assigns to the statesman's oratory in promoting justice in the commonwealth. Christians who seek to know how to live justly discover in the scriptures divine teachings that reveal the nature of true virtue. However, Augustine insists, the true meaning of the scriptural word is often hidden from the surface of the text, just as Christ's divine nature was unseen beneath his human nature. The incarnation, considered as 'mystery' or 'sacrament', becomes for Augustine the model for understanding how the believer should approach the virtue hidden in scriptural precepts and examples. Augustine concludes that to know God and his attributes (for example love, justice) as 'mystery' means to know them in a real way, but only partially, in the manner that Christ's divinity is known through his humanity. Thus, in order to understand the virtues illustrated in biblical examples, such as Christ's, believers must be purified of intellectual and moral presumption by their faith in biblical sacraments and mysteries. Augustine's repeated appeal to 1 Cor 8:1, 'Knowledge puffs up, but love builds up', expresses the importance he attaches to the transformation of moral judgments drawn entirely from human reason to judgments which reflect the believer's recognition of his own sinfulness and of God's pardon. This latter insight results from divine wisdom which the soul receives as a grace.

Although Augustine explains most clearly in *De trinitate* the process by which biblical examples of virtue are united with sacraments, and human knowledge drawn from the scriptures is transformed by divine wisdom, he applies these principles to his concept of the ideal Christian statesman in the *City of God* and in letters to public officials written contemporaneously with it. Exemplars of heroic virtue, such as King David and the apostles Peter and Paul, offer Christian statesmen, in Augustine's view, examples of a 'virtue' which, though considerably less than perfect, can be identified as 'true' because it expresses the spiritual strength that Augustine believes is gained from awareness of sinfulness, of repentance, and of dependence upon divine grace. Augustine tells Volusianus that the difficulties in understanding morality are linked with those in understanding the incarnation. Understanding how to live piously and justly, he insists, requires the believer to apprehend truths that are shrouded in the darkness of mystery and within a depth of wisdom that lies hidden from reason. He maintains that Christ's mediation to human beings of divine wisdom and knowledge, as well as of his teaching, assistance, and example regarding the just life, occurs as a consequence of the unity of his divine and human natures. Meanwhile, Augustine assures Macedonius that Christian statesmen can govern the earthly city justly provided their attention is fixed on the heavenly city, to which they draw nearer.

True love for one's city requires, as Augustine reminds Nectarius, a shared understanding of the nature of reconciliation among individuals who accept that the spiritual arts of penitence – self-examination, confession, prayer for pardon, and forgiveness of others, especially of enemies – constitute the essence of civic virtue, of piety, and thus the heart of patriotism. Moreover, such penitence will only be efficacious for the just rule of the city when it draws its subjects away from concern with the illusory achievement of moral and spiritual autonomy and perfection, and toward the freedom to live interiorly as citizens in God's 'city'.

Select bibliography

WORKS BY AUGUSTINE

Acad. = *De Academicis*: CCL 29.3–61.

c. Adim. = *Contra Adimantum Manicheum discipulum*: CSEL 25/1.115–90.

adn. Iob = *Adnotationes in Iob*: CSEL 28/2.509–628.

adult. coniug. = *De adulterinis coniugiis*: PL 40.451–86, CSEL 41.347–410.

agon. = *De agone christiano*: PL 40.289–310, CSEL 41.101–38.

an. et or. = *De anima et eius origine*: PL 44.475–548, CSEL 60.303–419.

an. quant. = *De animae quantitate*: PL 32.1035–80, CSEL 89.131–231.

bapt. = *De baptismo*: CSEL 51.145–375.

b. coniug. = *De bono coniugali*: CSEL 41.187–231.

cat. rud. = *De catecizandis rudibus*: PL 40.309–48, CCL 46.121–78.

ciu. = *De ciuitate Dei*: PL 41.13–804, CSEL 40/1.3–660, 40/2.1–670, CCL 47.1–314, 48.321–866.

conf. = *Confessiones*: PL 32.659–868, CSEL 33.1–388, CCL 27.1–273.

cons. eu. = *De consensu euangelistarum*: PL 34.1041–1230, CSEL 43.1–418.

corrept. = *De correptione et gratia*: CSEL 92.219–80.

Cresc. = *Ad Cresconium grammaticum*: CSEL 52.325–582.

diu. qu. = *De diuersis quaestionibus octoginta tribus*: PL 40.11–100, CCL 44A.11–249.

doctr. chr. = *De doctrina christiana*: PL 34.15–122, CSEL 80.3–169, CCL 32.1–167.

duab. an. = *De duabus animabus*: CSEL 25/1.51–80.

ench. = *De fide spe et caritate*: PL 40.231–90, CCL 46.49–114.

en. Ps. = *Enarratio(nes) in Psalmos*: PL 36.67–1028, 37.1033–1966, CCL 38.1–616, 39.623–1417, 40.1425–2196.

ep. Io. tr. = *In epistulam Iohannis ad Parthos tractatus X*: PL 35.1977–2062.

c. ep. Parm. = *Contra epistulam Parmeniani*: CSEL 51.19–141.

c. ep. Pel. = *Contra duas epistulas Pelagianorum*: PL 44.549–638, CSEL 60.423–570.

ep. = *Epistula(e)*: PL 33.61–1094, CSEL 34/1.1–125, 34/2.1–746, 44.1–736, 57.1–656, 58.xciii, 88.3–138.

exc. urb. = *De excidio urbis Romae*: PL 40.715–24, CCL 46.249–62.

exp. Gal. = *Expositio epistulae ad Galatas*: CSEL 84.55–141.

exp. prop. Rm. = *Expositio quarundam propositionum ex apostoli ad Romanos*: CSEL 54.

f. et symb. = *De fide et symbolo*: CSEL 41.3–32.

c. Faust. = *Contra Fortunatum Manicheum*: PL 42.207–518, CSEL 25/1.251–797.

c. Fort. = *Contra Faustum Manicheum*: CSEL 25/1.83–112.

gest. Pel. = *De gestis Pelagii*: PL 44.319–60, CSEL 42.51–122.

Gn. adu. Man. = *De Genesi aduersus Manicheos*: PL 37.173–220.

Gn. litt. = *De Genesi ad litteram*: PL 34.245–468, CSEL 28/1.3–435.

gr. et lib. arb. = *De gratia et libero arbitrio*: PL 44.881–912.

gr. et pecc. or. = *De gratia Christi et de peccato originali*: PL 44.359–410, CSEL 42.125–206.

Io. eu. tr. = *In Iohannis euangelium tractatus CXXIV*: PL 35.1379–1976, CCL 36.1–688.

c. Iul. = *Contra Iulianum*: PL 44.641–874.

c. Iul. imp. = *Contra Iulianum opus imperfectum*: PL 45.1049–1608, CSEL 85/1.3–506.

lib. arb. = *De libero arbitrio*: PL 32.1221–1310, CSEL 74.3–154, CCL 29.211–321.

c. litt. Pet. = *Contra litteras Petiliani*: CSEL 52.3–227.

mag. = *De magistro*: PL 32.1193–1220, CSEL 77/1.3–55, CCL 29.157–203.

c. Max. = *Contra Maximinum Arrianum*: PL 42.743–814.

mend. = *De mendacio*: PL 40.487–518, CSEL 41.413–66.

c. mend. = *Contra mendacium*: PL 40.517–48, CSEL 41.469–528.

mor. = *De moribus ecclesiae catholicae et de moribus Manicheorum*: PL 32.1309–78.

mus. = *De musica*: PL 32.1081–1194.

nat. et gr. = *De natura et gratia*: PL 44.247–90, CSEL 60.233–99.

op. mon. = *De opere monachorum*: CSEL 41.531–96.

ord. = *De ordine*: PL 32.977–1020, CSEL 63.121–85, CCL 29.89–137.

pat. = *De patientia*: CSEL 41.663–91.

pecc. mer. = *De peccatorum meritis et remissione et de baptismo paruulorum ad Marcellinum*: PL 44.109–200, CSEL 41.663–91.

perf. ius. = *De perfectione iustitiae hominis*: PL 44.291–318, CSEL 60.3–151.

perseu. = *De dono perseuerantiae*: PL 45.993–1034.

praed. sanc. = *De praedestinatione sanctorum*: PL 44.959–92.

retr. = *Retractationes*: PL 32.583–656, CSEL 36.(1-)7–204, CCL 57.(1-)5–143.

rhet. = *De rhetorica*: PL 32.1439–48, R. Giomini, 'A. Augustinus, "De rhetorica"'. *Studi latini e italiani* 4 (1990), 35–76.

s. = *Sermo(nes)*: PL 38.23–1484, PL 39.1493–1638, 1650–2, 1655–7, 1657–9, 1663–9, 1671–84, 1695–7, 1701–6, 1710–15, 1716–18, 1719–36, CCL 41.3–633 (= *s.* 1–50).

c. s. Arrian. = *Contra sermonem Arrianorum*: PL 42.683–708.

s. Casin. 2, 76 = *Sermo in bibliotheca Casinensi editi*: MA 1.413–15.

s. Denis = *Sermo(nes) a M. Denis editi*: MA 1.11–164.

s. Dolbeau = *Sermo(nes) a F. Dolbeau editi*: Augustin d'Hippone, *Vingt-six sermons au peuple d'Afrique. Retrouvés à Mayence*, ed. F. Dolbeau. Paris, 1996.

s. Guelf. = *Sermo(nes) Moriniani ex collectione Guelferbytana*: MA 1.450–585.

s. Lambot 2 = *Sermo a C. Lambot editus*: PLS 2.750–5.

s. Mai = *Sermo(nes) ab A. Mai editi*: MA 1.285–386.

spec. = *Speculum de scriptura sacra*: CSEL 12/3.3–285.
spir. et litt. = *De spiritu et littera ad Marcellinum*: PL 44.201–46, CSEL 60.155–229.
trin. = *De trinitate*: PL 42.819–1098, CCL 50.(3-)25–380, 50A.381–535.
util. cred. = *De utilitate credendi*: CSEL 25/1.3–48.
uera rel. = *De uera religione*: PL 34.121–72, CSEL 77/2.3–81, CCL 32.187–260.
uirg. = *De sancta uirginitate*: CSEL 41.235–302.

WORKS BY OTHER ANCIENT AUTHORS

Ambrose. *De bono mortis*: CSEL 32/1.
  De fuga saeculi: CSEL 32/2.
  De Nabuthe historia: Sant'Ambrogio. *De Nabuthe*. ed. D. Minotta. Florence, 1998.
  De uirginibus: Ambrosio de Milán. *Sobre las vírgenes, Sobre las viduas*. ed. D. Ramos Lissón. Madrid, 1999.
Apuleius. *De deo Socratis*: Apuleio, *Sul dio di Socrate*. ed. R. Del Re. Rome, 1966.
Aristotle. *Art of Rhetoric*: Aristotle, *The 'Art' of Rhetoric*. ed. J. Freese. Cambridge, Mass., 1982.
  Nicomachean Ethics: Aristotle. *The Nicomachean Ethics*. ed. H. Rackham. Cambridge, Mass., 1990.
  Poetics: *Aristotelis De arte poetica liber*. ed. R. Kassel. Oxford, 1965.
Cicero. *Pro Archia*: Cicéron, *Pour le poète Archias*. ed. F. Gaffiot. Paris, 1959.
  Brutus: Cicero. *Brutus, Orator*. ed. H. Hubbell. Cambridge, Mass., 1939.
  In Catilinam: Cicero. *In Catilinam, Pro Murena, Pro Sulla, Pro Flacco*. ed. C. Macdonald. London, 1977.
  De finibus bonorum et malorum: Cicero. *De finibus bonorum et malorum*. ed. H. Rackham. Cambridge, Mass., 1961.
  De inuentione: Cicero. *De inventione, De optimo genere oratorum, Topica*. ed. H. Hubbell. Cambridge, Mass., 1976.
  De legibus: Cicero. *De re publica, De legibus*. ed. C. Keyes. London, 1928.
  De natura deorum: Cicero. *De natura deorum, Academica*. ed. H. Rackham. London, 1933.
  De officiis: Cicero. *De officiis*. ed. W. Miller. Cambridge, Mass., 1968.
  Orator: Cicero. *Brutus, Orator*. ed. H. Hubbell. Cambridge, Mass., 1939.
  De oratore: Cicero. *De oratore I–II*. ed. E. Stitton and H. Rackham. Cambridge, Mass., 1942.
  De oratore III, De fato, Paradoxa Stoicorum, De partitione oratoria. ed. H. Rackham. London, 1942.
  De partitione oratoria: Cicero. *De oratore III, De fato, Paradoxa Stoicorum, De partitione oratoria*. ed. H. Rackham. London, 1942.
  De re publica: Cicéron. *La République*. ed. E. Bréguet. Paris, 1980.
  Pro Sestio: Cicero. *The Speeches Pro Sestio and In Vatinium*. ed. R. Gardner. Cambridge, Mass., 1966.
  Topica: Cicero. *De inventione, De optimo genere oratorum, Topica*. ed. H. Hubbell. Cambridge, Mass., 1976.

Libri tusculanarum disputationum: Cicéron. Tusculanes. ed. G. Fohlen. 2nd edn. Paris, 1960.

Cyprian. *De mortalitate*: CSEL 3/1.297–314.

    De opere et eleemosynis: SC 440.

Gellius, Aulus. *A. Gellii Noctes atticae.* ed. P. Marshall. Oxford, 1990.

Jerome. *Dialogus adversus Pelagianos*: PL 23.495–590.

Lactantius. *Diuinae institutiones*: CSEL 19.1–672.

    Epitome divinarum institutionum: CSEL 19.675–761.

Livy. *Ab urbe condita: Livy. Ab urbe condita.* ed. B. Foster et al. Cambridge, Mass., 1948–59.

Origen. *Commentarium in Iohannem*: SC 120.

    Contra Celsum: SC 132, 136, 147, 150, 227.

    De principiis: SC 252, 253, 268, 269, 312.

Orosius. *Historiarum aduersum paganos libri I–VII: Orose, Histoires.* ed. M.-P. Arnaud-Lindet. Paris, 1990.

Paulinus of Milan. *Vita Ambrosii*: PL 14, 28–50.

Paulinus of Nola. *Carmina*: CSEL 30.

    Epistulae: CSEL 29–30.

Pelagius. *Epistula ad Celantiam*: CSEL 29.

    Epistula ad sacram Christi uirginem Demetriadem: PL 30, 15–45; PL 33, 1099–1120.

    Expositiones XIII epistularum Pauli: Pelagius's Expositions of Thirteen Epistles of St. Paul. ed. A. Souter. Cambridge, 1922.

Plato. *Apology: Plato in Twelve Volumes with an English Translation.* vol. 1. ed. H. Fowler. London, 1914.

    Gorgias: Platon. Gorgias, Ménon. ed. A. Croiset. Paris, 1949.

    Phaedrus: Platon. Phèdre. ed. L. Robin. Paris, 1954.

    The Republic: Plato in Twelve Volumes with an English Translation. vols. 5, 6. ed. P. Shorey. London, 1963.

    The Statesman: Plato in Twelve Volumes with an English Translation. vol. 8. ed. W. Lamb. London, 1952.

    Timaeus: Plato in Twelve Volumes with an English Translation. vol. 9. ed. R. Bury. London, 1952.

Plotinus. *Enneads: Plotinus.* ed. A. Armstrong. Cambridge, Mass., 1989–.

Porphyry. *De abstinentia: Porphyre. De l'abstinence.* ed. J. Bouffartigue and M. Patillon. Paris, 1977–.

    Ad Marcellam: Porphyry, the Philosopher to Marcella: Text and translation With Introduction and Notes. ed. K. O'Brien Wicker. Atlanta, 1987.

Possidius. *Vita Augustini: Vita di Cipriano, Vita di Ambrogio, Vita di Agostino.* ed. A. Bastiaensen. Milan, 1975.

Quintilian. *Institutio oratoria: Quintilian.* ed. H. Butler. London, 1921.

Rufinus the Syrian. *Liber de fide: Rufini Presbyteri 'Liber de fide'.* ed. M. Miller. Washington, 1964.

Sallust. *Bellum Catilinae: Sallust.* ed. J. Rolfe. Cambridge, 1985.

Seneca. *Epistulae morales: Sénèque. Lettres à Lucilius.* ed. F. Préchac. 2nd edn. Paris, 1956.

Stoicorum veterum fragmenta. ed. H. von Arnim. Stuttgart, 1968.
Tertullian. *De carne Christi*: CCL 1/2, 873–917.
   'Ad martyras': CCL 1/1, 3–8.
Tractatus de diuitiis: A. Kessler, *Reichtumskritik und Pelagianismus. Die pelagianische Diatribe de duitiis: Situierung, Lesetext, Übersetzung, Kommentar*. Freiburg, 1999.
Varro, *Antiquitates rerum diuinarum*: M. *Terenti Varronis Antiquitates rerum diuinarum librorum I–II, fragmenta*. ed. G. Condemi. Bologna, 1965.

WORKS BY MODERN AUTHORS

Achard, G. *Pratique, rhétorique et idéologie politique dans les discours* optimates *de Cicéron*. Leiden, 1981.
Alfeche, M. 'The Basis of Hope in the Resurrection of the Body'. *Augustiniana* 36 (1986), 240–96.
Alflatt, M. 'The Responsibility for Involuntary Sin in Saint Augustine'. *Revue des études augustiniennes* 10 (1975), 171–86.
Alonso Del Real, C. '*De ciuitate Dei V: exempla maiorum, virtus, gloria*'. *L'etica cristiana nei secoli III e IV: eredità e confronti*. Rome, 1996, 423–30.
Arendt, H. *Der Liebesbegriff bei Augustin. Versuch einer philosophischen Interpretation*. Berlin, 1929.
Arnold, J. 'Begriff und heilsökonomische Bedeutung der göttingen Sendungen in Augustinus De trinitate'. *Recherches augustiniennes* 25 (1991), 3–69.
Atkins, E. M. '"Domina et regina virtutum": Justice and *Societas* in *De officiis*'. *Phronesis* 35 (1990), 258–89.
   'Old Philosophy and New Power: Cicero in Fifth-Century North Africa'. *Philosophy and Power in the Graeco-Roman World: Essays in Honour of Miriam Griffin*. ed. G. Clark and T. Rajak. Oxford, 2002, 251–69.
Atkins, E. M. and R. Dodaro. eds. *Augustine: Political Writings*. Cambridge, 2001.
Aubert, J.-M. 'Justice'. *Dictionnaire de spiritualité*. vol. 8, ed. A. Rayez et al. (Paris, 1974), 1622–40.
Auerbach, E. *Literary Language and its Public in Late Latin Antiquity and in the Middle Ages*. tr. R. Manheim. New York, 1965.
Babcock, W. *The Christ of the Exchange: A Study of Augustine's* Enarrationes in Psalmos. Ann Arbor, 1972.
   'Augustine's Interpretation of Romans (A.D. 394–396)'. *Augustinian Studies* 10 (1979), 55–74.
   'The Human and the Angelic Fall: Will and Moral Agency in Augustine's *City of God*'. *Augustine: From Rhetor to Theologian*. ed. J. McWilliam. Waterloo, 1992, 133–49.
Baltes, M. and D. Lau. 'Animal'. *Augustinus-Lexikon*. vol. 1. ed. C. Mayer. Basle, 1986–94, 356–74.
Bardenhewer, O. 'Augustinus über Röm. 7.14ff.'. *Miscellanea agostiniana*. vol. 2. Rome, 1931, 879–83.

Bardy, G. 'Introduction générale à *La Cité de* Dieu'. *Œuvres de saint Augustin*. vol. 33: *La Cité de Dieu, Livres I–V: Impuissance sociale du paganisme*. ed. G. Bardy and G. Combés. Paris, 1959, 7–163.

'L'Euhémérisme'. *Œuvres de saint Augustin*. vol. 33: *La Cité de Dieu, Livres I–V: Impuissance sociale du paganisme*. ed. G. Bardy and G. Combés. Paris, 1959, 785.

'Les Jeux séculaires'. *Œuvres de saint Augustin*. vol. 33: *La Cité de Dieu, Livres I–V: Impuissance sociale du paganisme*. ed. G. Bardy and G. Combés. Paris, 1959, 797–8.

'Les Passions chez Aristote et chez les stoïciens'. *Œuvres de saint Augustin*. vol. 34: *La Cité de Dieu, Livres VI–X: Impuissance spirituelle du paganisme*. Paris, 1959, 608–9.

Barker, E. *Saint Augustine, The City of God*. London, 1945.

Barwick, K. 'Augustins Schrift *De rhetorica* und Hermagoras von Temnos'. *Philologus* 105 (1961), 97–110.

Bastiaensen, A. 'Augustin et ses prédécesseurs latins chrétiens'. *Augustiniana traiectina, Communications au Colloque International d'Utrecht 1986*. ed. J. den Boeft and J. van Oort, Paris, 1987, 25–57.

Bathory, P. *Political Theory as Public Confession*. New Brunswick, 1981.

Bavel, T. van. *Recherches sur la christologie de saint Augustin. L'humain et le divin dans le Christ d'après saint Augustin*. Fribourg, 1954.

'No One Ever Hated his own Flesh: Eph 5:29 in Augustine'. *Augustiniana* 45 (1995), 45–93.

Bavel, T. van and B. Bruning. 'Die Einheit des "Totus Christus" bei Augustinus'. *Scientia augustiniana. Studien über Augustinus, den Augustinismus und den Augustinerorden. Festschrift A. Zumkeller OSA zum 60. Geburtstag*. ed. C. Mayer. Würzburg, 1975, 43–75.

Beard, M. and J. North, *Pagan Priests: Religion and Power in the Ancient World*. London, 1990.

Beard, M., J. North, and S. Price, *Religions of Rome*. vol. 1: *A History*. Cambridge, 1998.

Beare, W. *The Roman Stage*. 3rd edn. London, 1964.

Becker, C. 'Cicero'. *Reallexikon für Antike und Christentum*. vol. 3. ed. T. Klauser et al. Stuttgart, 1957, 86–127.

Beierwaltes, W. 'Zu Augustins Metaphysik der Sprache'. *Augustinian Studies* 2 (1971), 179–95.

Bernard, R. '*In figura:* Terminology pertaining to Figurative Exegesis in the Works of Augustine of Hippo'. unpublished dissertation, Princeton University, 1984.

Berrouard, M.-F. 'Le Christ, patrie et voie'. *Œuvres de Saint Augustin*. vol. 71: *Homélies I–XIV sur l'Evangile de Saint Jean*. ed. M.-F. Berrouard. Paris, 1969, 848–50.

'L'Exégèse augustinienne de Rom., 7, 7–25 entre 396 et 418 avec des remarques sur les deux premières périodes de la crise pélagienne'. *Recherches augustiniennes* 16 (1981), 101–96.

'La Seconde Mort'. *Œuvres de saint Augustin*. vol. 73A: *Homélies sur l'Evangile de saint Jean XXXIV–XLIII*. ed. M.-F. Berrouard. Paris, 1988, 523–5.

'Saint Augustin et le mystère du Christ chemin, vérité et vie. La médiation théologique du Tractatus 69 in Iohannis Euangelium sur Io. 14, 6a'. *Augustiniana* 41 (1991), 431–49.

Beyenka, M. *Consolation in Saint Augustine*. Washington, 1950.

Bianco, M. G. 'Ritratti e versi per le basiliche di Sulpicio Severo e Paolino Nolano (Paul. Nol. *Epp*. 30–32)'. *Romanobarbarica* 12 (1993), 291–310.

Bloch, H. 'The Pagan Revival in the West at the End of the Fourth Century'. *The Conflict between Paganism and Christianity in the Fourth Century*. ed. A. Momigliano. Oxford, 1963, 193–218.

Blümer, W. 'Eloquentia'. *Augustinus-Lexikon*. vol. 2. ed. C. Mayer. Basle, 1996–2002, 775–97.

Bochet, I. *Saint Augustin et le désir de Dieu*, Paris, 1982.

Boeft, J. den. 'Daemon(es)'. *Augustinus-Lexikon*. vol. 2. ed. C. Mayer. Basle, 1996–2002, 213–22.

Bögel, T. 'Definio'. *Thesaurus linguae latinae*. vol. 5:1. ed. M. Leumann et al. Leipzig, 1909–34, 342–50.

Bok, S. *Lying, Moral Choice in Public and Private Life*. New York, 1978.

Bonner, G. *Augustine and Modern Research on Pelagianism*. Villanova, 1972.

'Adam'. *Augustinus-Lexikon*. vol. 1. ed. C. Mayer. Basle, 1986–94, 63–87.

'Concupiscentia'. *Augustinus-Lexikon*. vol. 1. ed. C. Mayer (Basle, 1986–94), 1113–22.

'*Christus sacerdos*: The Roots of Augustine's Anti-Donatist Polemic'. *Signum pietatis. Festgabe für Cornelius P. Mayer OSA zum 60. Geburtstag*. ed. A. Zumkeller. Würzburg, 1989, 325–39.

'The Significance of Augustine's *De gratia novi testamenti*'. *Collectanea augustiniana. Mélanges T. van Bavel*. ed. B. Bruning et al. [= *Augustiniana* 40:1–4]. Leuven, 1990, 531–59.

Borgomeo, P. *L'Eglise de ce Temps dans la prédication de saint Augustin*. Paris, 1972, 211–18.

Brabant, O. *Le Christ: centre et source de la vie morale chez s. Augustin*. Gembloux, 1971.

Brachtendorf, J. 'Cicero and Augustine on the Passions'. *Revue des études augustiniennes* 43 (1997), 289–308.

Brown, P. 'Saint Augustine'. *Trends in Medieval Political Thought*. ed. B. Smalley. Oxford, 1965, 1–21.

Augustine of Hippo: A Biography. London, 1967.

'Pelagius and his Supporters: Aims and Environment'. *Journal of Theological Studies* n. s. 19 (1968), 93–114.

'Political Society'. *Augustine: A Collection of Critical Essays*. ed. R. Markus. Garden City, 1972, 311–35.

Religion and Society in the Age of Saint Augustine. London, 1972.

Power and Persuasion in Late Antiquity: Towards a Christian Empire. Madison, 1992.

Buchheit, V. 'Goldene Zeit und Paradies auf Erden (Lakt., inst. 5, 5–8)'. *Würzburger Jahrbücher für die Altertumswissenschaft* 4 (1978), 161–85.

'Der Zeitbezug in der Weltalterlehre des Laktanz (Inst. 5, 5–6)'. *Historia* 28 (1979), 472–86.

'Die Definition der Gerechtigkeit bei Laktanz und seinen Vorgängern'. *Vigiliae christianae* 33 (1979), 356–74.

'Juppiter als Gewalttäter (Inst. 5, 6, 6)'. *Rheinisches Museum* 125 (1982), 338–42.

Büchner, K. 'Die beste Verfassung. Eine philologische Untersuchung zu den ersten drei Büchern von Ciceros Staat'. *Studi italiani di filologia classica* 26 (1952), 37–140.

Ciceros Bestand und Wandel seiner geistigen Welt. Heidelberg, 1964.

M. Tullius Cicero. De re publica. Heidelberg, 1984.

Burnaby, J. *Amor Dei: A Study of the Religion of St. Augustine*. London, 1938.

Burns, J. P. *The Development of Augustine's Doctrine of Operative Grace*. Paris, 1980.

Bynum, C. W. *The Resurrection of the Body in Western Christianity, 200–1336*. New York, 1995.

Camelot, T. 'Le Christ, sacrement de Dieu'. *L'Homme devant Dieu. Mélanges offerts à Henri de Lubac*. vol. 1: *Exégèse et patristique*. Paris, 1963, 355–63.

Cameron, A. *The Later Roman Empire, AD 284–430*. Cambridge, Mass., 1993.

Cameron, M. *Augustine's Construction of Figurative Exegesis against the Donatists in the 'Enarrationes in Psalmos'*. Ann Arbor, 1996.

Cancelli, F. '*Iuris consensu* nella definizione ciceroniana di *res publica*'. *Rivista di cultura classica e medioevale* 14 (1972), 247–67.

'La giustizia tra i popoli nell'opera e nel pensiero di Cicerone'. *La giustizia tra i popoli nell'opera e nel pensiero di Cicerone. Convegno organizzato dall'Accademia Ciceroniana, Arpino, 11–12 ottobre 1991*. ed. F. Cancelli et al. Rome, 1993, 25–51.

Canning, R. *The Unity of Love for God and Neighbour in St. Augustine*. Heverlee-Leuven, 1993.

Carcaterra, A. *Iustitia nelle fonti e nella storia del diritto romano*. Bari, 1949.

Carlson, C. 'The Natural Order and Historical Explanation in St. Augustine's "City of God"'. *Augustiniana* 21 (1971), 417–47.

Carola, J. '*Solvitis et uos*. The Laity and their Exercise of the Power of the Keys according to Saint Augustine of Hippo', unpublished dissertation, Institutum Patristicum Augustinianum, Rome, 2001.

Chastagnol, A. 'Le Sénateur Volusien et la conversion d'une famille de l'aristocratie romaine au Bas-Empire'. *Revue des études anciennes* 58 (1956), 241–53.

Chéné, J. 'L'Ignorance et la difficulté, état naturel et primitif de l'homme'. *Œuvres de saint Augustin*. vol. 24: *Aux moines d'Adrumète et de Provence*. ed. J. Chéné and J. Pintard, Paris, 1962, 829–31.

'Le Péché d'ignorance selon saint Augustin'. *Œuvres de saint Augustin*. vol. 24: *Aux moines d'Adrumète et de Provence*. ed. J. Chéné and J. Pintard. Paris, 1962, 769–71.

Christes, J. 'Christliche und heidnische-römische Gerechtigkeit in Augustins Werk *De ciuitate dei*'. *Rheinisches Museum* 126 (1980), 163–77.

Ciarlantini, P. 'Mediator: Paganismo y cristianismo en *De civitate dei*, VIII, 12–XI, 2 de san Augustín'. *Revista augustiniana de espiritualidad* 24:73–4 (1983), 9–62.

'Mediator: Paganismo y cristianismo en *De civitate dei*, VIII, 12–XI, 2 de san Augustín (III)'. *Revista augustiniana de espiritualidad* 25:76–7 (1984), 5–69.

'Mediator: Paganismo y cristianismo en *De civitate dei*, VIII, 12–XI, 2 de san Augustín'. *Revista augustiniana de espiritualidad* 25:78 (1984), 325–401.

'Mediator (V): Cristo, mediador entre dios y los hombres'. *Revista augustiniana de espiritualidad* 26:79–80 (1985), 5–47.

Cipriani, N. 'La morale pelagiana e la retorica'. *Augustinianum* 31 (1991), 309–27.

Clerc, J.-B. '*Theurgica legibus prohibita*: à propos de l'interdiction de la théurgie (Augustin, *La Cité de Dieu* 10, 9, 1.16, 2; *Code théodosien* 9, 16, 4)'. *Revue des études augustiniennes* 42 (1996), 57–64.

Cochrane, C. N. *Christianity and Classical Culture: A Study of Thought and Action from Augustus to Augustine*. rev. edn. London, 1944.

Colish, M. *The Stoic Tradition from Antiquity to the Early Middle Ages*. vol. 1: *Stoicism in Classical Latin Literature*. vol. 2: *Stoicism in Christian Latin Thought through the Sixth Century*. Leiden, 1985.

Combès, G. *La Doctrine politique de saint Augustin*. Paris, 1928.

Consolino, F. 'Modelli di santità femminile nelle più antiche Passioni romane'. *Augustinianum* 24 (1984), 83–113.

Conybeare, C. *Paulinus noster. Self and Symbols in the Letters of Paulinus of Nola*. Oxford, 2000.

Courcelle, P. *Les Lettres grecques en Occident. De Macrobe à Cassiodore*, Paris, 1948. 'Propos anti-chrétiens rapportés par saint Augustin'. *Recherches Augustiniennes* 1 (1958), 149–86.

Late Latin Writers and their Greek Sources. tr. H. E. Wedeck. Cambridge, Mass., 1969.

Couturier, C. 'Sacramentum et mysterium *dans l'œuvre de S. Augustin*'. *Etudes augustiniennes*. Paris, 1953, 162–332.

Cranz, F. '*De ciuitate dei* xv, 2, and Augustine's Idea of the Christian Society'. *Speculum* 25 (1950), 215–25.

'*De civitate dei* xv, 2 et l'idée augustinienne de la société chrétienne'. *Revue des études augustiniennes* 3 (1957), 15–27.

Crespin, R. *Ministère et sainteté. Pastorale du clergé et solution de la crise donatiste dans la vie de Saint Augustin*. Paris, 1965.

Crouse, R. '*Paucis mutatis verbis*: St Augustine's Platonism'. *Augustine and his Critics*. ed. R. Dodaro and G. Lawless. London, 1999, 37–50.

Cutrone, E. 'Sacraments'. *Augustine through the Ages: An Encyclopedia*. ed. A. Fitzgerald et al. Grand Rapids, 1999, 741–7.

Davids, A. 'Het begrip gerechtigheid in de oude kerk'. *Tidjschrift voor theologie* 17 (1977), 145–70.

Deane, H. *The Political and Social Ideas of St. Augustine*. New York, 1963.

Decret, F. *Aspects du Manichéisme dans l'Afrique romaine. Les Controverses de Fortunatus, Faustus et Félix avec saint Augustin*. Paris, 1970.

Delaroche, B. *Saint Augustin lecteur et interprète de saint Paul dans le* De peccatorum meritis et remissione (*hiver 411–412*). Paris, 1996.

Des Places, E. *La Religion grecque*. Paris, 1969.

Descamps, A. *Les Justes et la justice dans les évangiles et le christianisme primitif: hormis la doctrine proprement paulinienne*. Louvain, 1950.

Dewart, J. 'The Christology of the Pelagian Controversy'. *Studia patristica*. vol. 17. ed. E. Livingstone. Oxford, 1982, 1221–44.

DeWitt, H. '*Quo virtus*: The Concept of Propriety in Ancient Literary Criticism', unpublished dissertation, Oxford University, 1987.

Dideberg, D. *Saint Augustin et la première épître de saint Jean. Une théologie de l'agapè*. Paris, 1975.

Dieter, O. and Kurth, W. 'The *De rhetorica* of Aurelius Augustine'. *Speech Monographs* 35 (1968), 90–108.

Dihle, A. 'Gerechtigkeit'. *Reallexikon für Antike und Christentum*. vol. 10. ed. T. Klauser et al. Stuttgart, 1978, 233–360.

The Theory of Will in Classical Antiquity. Berkeley, 1982.

Dodaro, R. '*Christus iustus* and Fear of Death in Augustine's Dispute with Pelagius'. *Signum pietatis. Festgabe für Cornelius P. Mayer OSA zum 60. Geburtstag*. ed. A. Zumkeller. Würzburg, 1989, 341–61.

'*Christus sacerdos*: Augustine's Polemic against Roman Pagan Priesthoods in *De ciuitate Dei*'. *Augustinianum* 33:1–2 (1993), 101–35.

'Eloquent Lies, Just Wars and the Politics of Persuasion: Reading Augustine's City of God in a "Postmodern" World'. *Augustinian Studies* 25 (1994), 77–138.

'Il *timor mortis* e la questione degli *exempla virtutum*: Agostino, *De civitate Dei* 1–x'. *Il mistero del male e la libertà possibile (III): Lettura del* De civitate Dei *di Agostino. Atti del VII Seminario del Centro Studi Agostiniani di Perugia*. ed. L. Alici et al. Rome, 1996, 7–47.

'*Christus sacerdos*: Augustine's Preaching against Pagan Priests in the Light of S. Dolbeau 26 and 23'. *Augustin prédicateur (395–411), Actes du Colloque International de Chantilly (5–7 septembre 1996)*. ed. G. Madec. Paris, 1998, 377–93.

'Augustine's Secular City'. *Augustine and his Critics*. ed. R. Dodaro and G. Lawless. London, 1999.

'Justice'. *Augustine through the Ages: An Encyclopedia*. ed. A. Fitzgerald et al. Grand Rapids, 1999, 481–3.

'Literary Decorum in Scriptural Exegesis: Augustine of Hippo, *Epistula* 138'. *L'esegesi dei padri latini. Dalle origini à Gregorio Magno. Atti del XXVIII Incontro di studiosi dell'antichità cristiana, Roma, 6–8 maggio 1999*. vol. 1: *Paste generale-Oriente, Africa*. Rome, 2000, 159–74.

'Note on the Carthaginian Debate over Sinlessness, AD 411–412 (Augustine, *pecc. mer.* 2.7.8–16.25)'. *Augustinianum* 40:1 (2000), 187–202.

'*Quid deceat uidere* (Cicero, *Orator* 70): Literary Propriety and Doctrinal Orthodoxy in Augustine of Hippo'. *Orthodoxie, christianisme, histoire = Orthodoxy, Christianity, History: travaux du groupe de recherches 'Définir, maintenir et remettre en cause l'"orthodoxie" dans l'histoire du christianisme'*. ed. S. Elm et al. Rome, 2000, 57–81.

'The Theologian as Grammarian: Literary Propriety in Augustine's Defense of Orthodox Doctrine', *Studia patristica: Papers Presented at the Thirteenth International Conference on Patristic Studies, Oxford University, 16–21 August 1999*, vol. 38, Leiden, 2001, 70–83.

'Augustine of Hippo between the Secular City and the City of God'. *Augustinus Afer. Saint Augustin: africanité et universalité. Actes du colloque international, Alger-Annaba, 1–7 avril 2001.* ed. P.-Y. Fux et al. Fribourg, 2003, 287–305.

Dodaro, R. and Szura, J. 'Augustine on *John* 8:3–11 and the Recourse to Violence'. *Augustinian Heritage* 34:1 (1988), 35–62.

Dodds, E. 'Theurgy and its Relationship to Neoplatonism'. *Journal of Roman Studies* 37 (1947), 55–69.

The Greeks and the Irrational. Berkeley, 1956.

Doignon, J. 'Le Retentissement d'un exemple de la survie de Lactance: un texte des *Institutions divines* inspiré de Cicéron dans la Lettre 104 d'Augustin'. *Lactance et son temps. Recherches actuelles. Actes du IVe colloque d'études historiques et patristiques, Chantilly, 21–23 septembre 1976.* ed. J. Fontaine and M. Perrin. Paris, 1978, 297–306.

'Souvenirs cicéroniens (Hortensius, consolation) et virgiliens dans l'exposé d'Augustin sur l'état humain d'"ignorance et de difficulté" (Aug., *lib. arb.* 3, 51–54)'. *Vigiliae christianae* 47 (1993), 131–9.

Dolbeau, F. ed. *Augustin d'Hippone, Vingt-six sermons au peuple d'Afrique. Retrouvés à Mayence.* Paris, 1996.

Donaldson, I. *The Rapes of Lucretia: A Myth and its Transformation.* Oxford, 1982.

Donatuti, G. 'Iustus, iuste, iustitia nel linguaggio dei giuristi classici'. *Annali della facoltà di giurisprudenza dell'Università di Perugia* 33 (1922), 377–436.

Donnelly, D. ed. *The City of God: A Collection of Critical Essays.* New York, 1995.

Dreyer, O. *Untersuchungen zum Begriff des Gottgeziemenden in der Antike: mit besonderer berücksichtigkeit Philons von Alexandrien.* Hildesheim, 1970.

Drobner, H. *Person-Exegese und Christologie bei Augustinus. Zur Herkunft der Formel Una Persona.* Leiden, 1986.

'Grammatical Exegesis and Christology in St. Augustine'. *Studia patristica: Papers of the 1983 Oxford Patristic Conference.* vol. 18:4. ed. E. Livingstone. Kalamazoo, 1990, 49–63.

'The Chronology of St. Augustine's *Sermones ad populum*'. *Augustinian Studies* 31:2 (2000), 211–18.

'The Chronology of St. Augustine's *Sermones ad populum* II: Sermons 5 to 8'. *Augustinian Studies* 34:1 (2003), 49–66.

Droge, A. and J. Tabor. *A Noble Death: Suicide and Martyrdom among Christians and Jews in Antiquity.* San Francisco, 1992.

Du Roy, O. *L'Intelligence de la foi en la Trinité selon saint Augustin.* Paris, 1966.

Duchrow, U. 'Der Aufbau von Augustins Schriften *Confessiones* und *De trinitate*'. *Zeitschrift für Theologie und Kirche* 62 (1965), 338–67.

Sprachverständnis und biblisches Hören bei Augustin. Tübingen, 1965.

Christenheit und Weltverantwortung, Traditionsgeschichte und systematische Struktur der Zweireichenlehre. Stuttgart, 1970.

Dulaey, M. 'Recherches sur les sources exégètiques d'Augustin dans les trente-deux premières *Enarrationes in Psalmos*'. *L'esegesi dei padri latini. Dalle origini a Gregorio Magno. Atti del XXVIII Incontro di studiosi dell'antichità cristiana, Roma, 6–8 maggio 1999.* vol. 1: *Parte Generale – Oriente, Africa.* Rome, 2000, 253–92.

Düll, R. 'Rechtsprobleme im Bereich des römischen Sakralrechts'. *Aufstieg und Niedergang der römischen Welt.* vol. 1:2. ed. H. Temporini. Berlin, 1972, 283–94.

Dumézil, G. 'Augur'. *Revue des études latines* 35 (1957), 126–51.

Idées romaines. Paris, 1969.

Duval, Y.-M. 'L'Eloge de Théodose dans la *Cité de Dieu* (v, 26, 1), sa place, son sens et ses sources'. *Recherches augustiniennes* 4 (1966), 135–79.

'Consolatio'. *Augustinus-Lexikon.* vol. 1. ed. C. Mayer. Basle, 1986–94, 1244–7.

Evans, G. R. *Augustine on Evil.* Cambridge, 1982.

Evans, R. 'Pelagius, Fastidius, and the Pseudo-Augustinian *De vita christiana*'. *Journal of Theological Studies* n. s. 13 (1962), 72–98.

Four Letters of Pelagius. New York, 1968.

Fears, J. R. 'The Cult of Virtues and Roman Imperial Ideology'. *Aufstieg und Niedergang der römischen Welt.* vol. 2.17.2. ed. W. Haase. Berlin, 1981, 827–948.

Féret, H.-M. 'Sacramentum-res dans la langue théologique de saint Augustin'. *Revue des sciences philosophiques et théologiques* 29 (1940), 218–43.

Fiedrowicz, M. *Psalmus vox totius Christi. Studien zu Augustins 'Enarrationes in Psalmos'.* Freiburg, 1997.

'General Introduction'. *The Works of Saint Augustine: A Translation for the 21st Century.* Part III. vol. 15: *Expositions of the Psalms, 1–32.* tr. M. Boulding. ed. J. Rotelle. New York, 2000, 13–66.

Figgis, J. *The Political Aspects of St. Augustine's City of God.* London, 1921.

Finaert, J. *Saint Augustin rhéteur.* Paris, 1939.

Fitzgerald, A. 'Ambrose and Augustine: *confessio* as *initium iustitiae*'. *Augustinianum* 40:1 (2000), 173–85.

Fleteren, F. Van 'Per speculum et in aenigmate: The Use of 1 Corinthians 13:12 in the Writings of Augustine'. *Augustinian Studies* 23 (1992), 69–102.

Fontaine, J. and M. Perrin. eds. *Lactance et son temps. Recherches actuelles. Actes du IVe colloque d'études historiques et patristiques, Chantilly, 21–23 septembre 1976,* Paris, 1978.

Fortin, E. *Political Idealism and Christianity in the Thought of St. Augustine.* Villanova, 1972.

'Saint Augustine and the Problem of Christian Rhetoric'. *Augustinian Studies* 5 (1974), 85–100.

'Augustine and Roman Civil Religion: Some Critical Reflections'. *Revue des études augustiniennes* 26 (1980), 238–56.

Franz, E. 'Totus Christus. Studien über Christus und die Kirche bei Augustin', unpublished dissertation, Evangelisch-Theologische Fakultät der Rheinischen Friedrich-Wilhelms-Universität, Bonn, 1956.

Frede, H.-J. *Kirchenschriftsteller. Verzeichnis und Sigel.* Freiburg, 1981.

Fredriksen, P. 'Beyond the Body/Soul Dichotomy: Augustine on Paul against the Manichees and the Pelagians'. *Recherches augustiniennes* 23 (1988), 87–114.

'*Exaecati occulta iustitia dei*: Augustine on Jews and Judaism'. *Journal of Early Christian Studies* 3 (1995), 299–324.

'Augustine and Israel: Interpretatio ad litteram, Jews, and Judaism in Augustine's Theology of History'. *Studia patristica: Papers Presented to the Thirteenth International Conference on Patristic Studies held at Oxford, 1999.* vol. 38. ed. M. Wiles and E. Yarnold. Leuven, 2001, 119–35.

Gaillard, J. 'Regulus selon Cicéron. Autopsie d'un mythe'. *Revue des études latines* 50 (1972), 46–9.

'"Auctoritas exempli": pratique rhétorique et idéologique au Ier s. av. J.-C.'. *Revue des études latines* 56 (1978), 30–4.

Galati, L. *Cristo la via nel pensiero di S. Agostino.* Rome, 1956.

Geerlings, W. *Christus exemplum. Studien zur Christologie und Christusverkündigung Augustins.* Mainz, 1978.

Ghellinck, J. de, et al. *Pour l'histoire du mot 'sacramentum'.* vol. 1: *Les Anténicéens.* Louvain, 1924.

Gilson, E. *Introduction à l'étude de saint Augustin.* 4th edn. Paris, 1969.

Girard, J.-M. *La Mort chez saint Augustin: grandes lignes de l'évolution de sa pensée.* Fribourg, 1992.

Girard, R. *Violence and the Sacred.* tr. P. Gregory. Baltimore, 1977.

Guy, J.-C. *Unité et structure logique de la Cité de Dieu de saint Augustin.* Paris, 1961.

Hadot, I. 'Citations de Porphyre chez Augustin (A propos d'un ouvrage récent)'. *Revue des études augustinennes* 6 (1960), 205–44.

Arts libéraux dans la pensée antique. Paris, 1984.

Hagendahl, H. *Augustine and the Latin Classics.* 2 vols. Göteborg, 1967.

Hamblenne, P. 'L'*exemplum* formel chez Jérome'. *Augustinianum* 36 (1996), 94–145.

Hand, V. *Augustin und das klassisch-römische Selbstverständnis. Eine Untersuchung über die Begriffe Gloria, Virtus, Iustitia und Res Publica in De Civitate Dei.* Hamburg, 1970.

Hardy, G. *Le* De civitate dei *source principale du Discours sur l'histoire universelle.* Paris, 1913.

Hassel, D. 'Conversion, Theory and Scientia in *De trinitate*'. *Recherches augustiniennes* 2 (1962), 383–401.

Haury, A. 'Cicéron et la gloire, une pédagogie de la vertu'. *Mélanges de philosophie, de littérature et d'histoire ancienne offerts à Pierre Boyancé.* Rome, 1974, 401–17.

Hawkins, P. 'Polemical Counterpoint in *De civitate dei*'. *Augustinian Studies* 6 (1975), 97–106.

Heather, P. *Goths and Romans 332–489.* Oxford, 1991.

Heck, E. *Die Bezeugung von Ciceros Schrift De re publica.* Hildesheim/New York, 1966.

'Iustitia civilis – iustitia naturalis'. *Lactance et son temps. Recherches actuelles. Actes du IVe colloque d'études historiques et patristiques, Chantilly, 21–23 septembre 1976.* ed. J. Fontaine and M. Perrin. Paris, 1978, 171–84.

Heinze, R. 'Ciceros "Staat" als politische Tendenzschrift'. *Hermes* 59 (1924), 73–4.
Vom Geist der Römertums. 3rd edn. Stuttgart, 1960.

Hellegouarc'h, J. *Vocabulaire latin des relations et des partis politiques*. 2nd edn. Paris, 1972.

Hendrikx, E. 'La Date de composition du *De trinitate* de saint Augustin'. *L'Année théologique augustinienne* 12 (1952), 305–16.
'La Date de composition du *De trinitate*'. *Œuvres de saint Augustin*. vol. 15: *La Trinité (Livres I–VII) 1. Le Mystère*, ed. M. Mellet and T. Camelot. Paris, 1955, 557–66.

Hill, E. *Saint Augustine, The Trinity. The Works of Saint Augustine: A Translation for the 21st Century*. ed. J. Rotelle New York, 1991.

Holte, R. *Béatitude et sagesse. S. Augustin et le problème de la fin de l'homme dans la philosophie ancienne*. Paris, 1962.

Hombert, P.-M. *Gloria gratiae. Se glorifier en Dieu, principe et fin de la théologie augustinienne de la grâce*. Paris, 1996.
Nouvelles recherches de chronologie augustinienne. Paris, 2000.

Honstetter, R. *Exemplum zwischen Rhetorik und Literatur. Zur gattungsgeschichtlichen Sonderstellung von Valerius Maximus und Augustinus*. Konstanz, 1981.

Horn, C. ed. *Augustinus. De civitate dei*. Berlin, 1997.

Huisman, H. *Augustinus Briefwisseling met Nectarius. Inleiding, tekst, vertalung, commentar*. Amsterdam, 1956.

Ijsseling, S. *Rhetoric and Philosophy in Conflict: An Historical Survey*. tr. P. Dunphy. The Hague, 1976.

Inge, W. *The Philosophy of Plotinus*. 3rd edn. London, 1929.

Inglebert, H. 'Les Héros romains, Les martyrs et les ascètes: les *uirtutes* et les préférences politiques chez les auteurs chrétiens latins du IIIe au Ve siècle'. *Revue des études augustiniennes* 40 (1994), 305–25.

Jackson, M. 'Faith, Hope and Charity and Prayer in St. Augustine'. *Studia Patristica. Papers Presented to the Tenth International Conference on Patristic Studies held in Oxford 1987*. vol. 22. ed. E. Livingstone. Leuven, 1989, 265–70.

Jaeger, W. *Paideia: The Ideals of Greek Culture*. 3 vols. tr. G. Highet. New York, 1943.

Jeremias, G. *Der Lehrer der Gerechtigkeit*. Göttingen, 1963.

Kamlah, W. *Christentum und Geschichtlichkeit. Untersuchungen zur Entstehung des Christentums und zu Augustins Bürgerschaft Gottes*. 2nd rev. edn. Cologne, 1951.

Kapp, I. and G. Meyer. 'Exemplum'. *Thesaurus linguae latinae* 5:2. ed. G. Dittmann et al. Leipzig, 1931–53, 1326–50.

Käsemann, E. 'Gottesgerechtigkeit bei Paulus'. *Zeitschrift für Theologie und Kirche* 58 (1961), 367–78.

Katayanagi, E. 'The Last Congruous Vocation'. *Collectanea augustiniana. Mélanges T. J. van Bavel*. vol. 2. ed. B. Bruning et al. Leuven, 1991.

Kaufmann-Bühler, D. 'Eusebia'. *Reallexikon für Antike und Christentum*. vol. 6. ed. T. Klauser et al. Stuttgart, 1966, 985–1052.

Kennedy, G. *Classical Rhetoric and its Christian and Secular Tradition from Ancient to Modern Times*. Chapel Hill, 1980.

Kessler, A. 'Exemplum'. *Augustinus-Lexikon*. vol. 2. ed. C. Mayer. Basle, 1996–2002, 1174–82.

Reichtumskritik und Pelagianismus. Die pelagianische Diatribe de duitiis: Situierung, Lesetext, Übersetzung, Kommentar. Freiburg, 1999.

Kirwan, C. *Augustine*. London/New York, 1989.

Klesczewski, R. 'Wandlungen des Lucretia-Bildes im lateinischen Mittelalter und in der lateinischen Literatur der Renaissance'. *Livius. Werk und Rezeption. Festschrift für Erich Burck zum 80. Geburtstag*. ed. E. Lefevre and E. Olshausen. Munich, 1983, 313–35.

Klima, U. *Untersuchungen zu dem Begriff sapientia. Von der republikanischen Zeit bis Tacitus*. Bonn, 1971.

Knoche, U. 'Gloria'. *Thesaurus linguae latinae*. vol. 6:2. ed. G. Dittmann et al. Leipzig, 1912–26, 2061–86.

Kohns, H. P. 'Consensus iuris – communio utilitatis (zu Cic. De re publica. I 39)'. *Gymnasium* 81 (1974), 485–98.

Kolb, F. 'Der Bussakt von Mailand. Zum Verhaltnis von Staat und Kirche in der Spätantike'. *Geschichte und Gegenwart. Festschrift für K. D. Erdmann*. ed. H. Boockmann et al. Neumünster, 1980, 41–74.

Krabbe, K. *Epistula ad Demetriadem De vera humilitate: A Critical Text and Translation with Introduction and Commentary*. Washington, 1965.

Krarup, P. *Rector rei publicae. Bidrag til fortokningen af Ciceros De re publica*. Copenhagen, 1956.

Kunzelmann, A. *Die Chronologie der Sermones des hl. Augustinus*. Rome, 1931.

Kursawe, B. *Docere – delectare – movere: Die officia oratoris bei Augustinus in Rhetorik und Gnadenlehre*. Paderborn, 2000.

La Bonnardière, A.-M. *Recherches de chronologie augustinienne*. Paris, 1965.
'Les Enarrationes in Psalmos prêchées par saint Augustin à l'occasion de fêtes de martyrs'. *Recherches augustiniennes* 7 (1971), 73–104.
Biblia augustiniana A. T. Le Livre de Jérémie. Paris, 1972.

La Croix, B. 'La Date du xie livre du De civitate dei'. *Vigiliae christianae* 5 (1975), 121–2.

Labriolle, P. *La Réaction païenne. Etude sur la polémique antichrétienne du Ie au VIe siècle*. Paris, 1948.

Lackenbacher, I. 'Disputo'. *Thesaurus linguae latinae*. vol. 5:1. ed. M. Leumann et al. Leipzig, 1909–34, 1443–50.

Laks, A. and M. Schofield. eds. *Justice and Generosity: Studies in Hellenistic Social and Political Philosophy. Proceedings of the Sixth Symposium Hellenisticum*. Cambridge, 1995.

Lamirande, E. *L'Eglise céleste selon saint Augustin*. Paris, 1963.

Latte, K. *Römische Religionsgeschichte*. Munich, 1960.

Lausberg, H. *Handbuch der literarischen Rhetorik. Eine Grundlegung der Literaturwissenschaft*. 2nd edn. Munich, 1973.

Lendon, J. E. *Empire of Honour: The Art of Government in the Roman World.* Oxford, 1997.

Lepelley, C. *Les Cités de l'Afrique romaine au bas-empire.* vol. 1: *La Permanence d'une civilisation municipale.* vol. 2: *Notices d'histoire municipale.* Paris, 1979, 1981.

'Spes saecvli: Le Milieu social d'Augustin et ses ambitions séculières avant sa conversion'. *Atti del congresso internazionale su s. Agostino nel XVI centenario della conversione.* vol. 1. Rome, 1987, 99–117.

Lepore, E. *Il princeps ciceroniano e gli ideali politici della tarda repubblica.* Naples, 1954.

Lettieri, G. *Il senso della storia in Agostino d'Ippona. Il* saeculum *e la gloria nel* De civitate dei. Rome, 1988.

Lewy, H. *Chaldean Oracles and Theurgy: Mysticism, Magic and Platonism in the Later Roman Empire.* rev. edn., ed. M. Tardieu. Paris, 1978.

Lilla, S. 'Theurgy'. *Encyclopedia of Early Christianity.* vol. 2. ed. A. Di Berardino. tr. A. Walford. Cambridge, 1992, 835–6.

Linderski, J. 'The Augural Law'. *Aufstieg und Niedergang der römischen Welt.* vol. 2.16.3. ed. W. Haase. Berlin, 1986, 2190–225.

Litchfield, H. 'National *exempla virtutis* in Roman Literature'. *Harvard Studies in Classical Philology* 25 (1914), 1–71.

Lof, L. van der. 'L'Exégèse exacte et objective des théophanies de l'Ancien Testament dans le De "Trinitate"'. *Augustiniana* 14 (1964), 485–99.

Loi, V. 'I valori etici e politici della romanità negli scritti di Lattanzio. Opposti atteggiamenti di polemica e di adesione'. *Salesianum* 27 (1965), 65–133.

'Il concetto di "iustitia" e i fattori culturali dell'etica di Lattanzio'. *Salesianum* 28 (1966), 583–625.

'La funzione sociale della iustitia nella polemica anti-pagana di Lattanzio'. *Letterature comparate. Problemi e metodo. Studi in onore di E. Paratore.* Bologna, 1981, 843–52.

Long, A. A. 'Cicero's Politics in *De officiis*'. *Justice and Generosity: Studies in Hellenistic Social and Political Philosophy. Proceedings of the Sixth Symposium Hellenisticum.* ed. A. Laks and M. Schofield. Cambridge, 1995, 213–40.

Lorenz, R. 'Die Wissenschaftslehre Augustins'. *Zeitschrift für Kirchengeschichte* 67 (1956), 213–51.

'Gnade und Erkenntnis bei Augustinus'. *Zeitschrift für Kirchengeschichte* 75 (1964), 21–78.

Lössl, J. *Intellectus gratiae. Die erkenntnis-theoretische und hermeneutische Dimension der Gnadenlehre Augustins von Hippo.* Leiden, 1997.

Luis Vizcaíno, P. de, *Los hechos de Jesús en la predicación de san Agustín. La retórica clásica al servicio de la exégesis patrística.* Rome, 1983.

MacBain, B. *Prodigy and Expiation: A Study in Religion and Politics in Republican Rome.* Brussels, 1982.

McCallin, J. 'The Christological Unity of St. Augustine's *De civitate dei*'. *Revue des études augustiniennes* 12 (1966), 85–109.

MacCormack, S. *The Shadows of Poetry: Vergil in the Mind of Augustine.* Berkeley, 1998.

McGrath, A. 'Divine Justice and Divine Equity in the Controversy between Augustine and Julian of Eclanum'. *Downside Review* 101 (1983), 312–19.

Iustitia dei. A History of the Christian Doctrine of Justification: The Beginnings to the Reformation. Cambridge, 1986.

MacIntyre, A. *After Virtue.* 2nd edn. Notre Dame, 1984.

Whose Justice? Which Rationality? Notre Dame, 1988.

MacKendrick, P. *The Philosophical Books of Cicero.* London, 1989.

McLynn, N. *Ambrose of Milan: Church and Court in a Christian Capital.* Berkeley, 1994.

'Augustine's Roman Empire'. *History, Apocalypse and the Secular Imagination: New Essays on Augustine's* City of God. ed. M. Vessey et al. Bowling Green, 1999.

McNew, L. 'The Relation of Cicero's Rhetoric to Augustine'. *Research Studies of the State College of Washington* 25:1 (1957), 5–13.

Madec, G. 'Christus, scientia et sapientia nostra. Le principe de cohérence de la doctrine augustinienne'. *Recherches augustiniennes* 10 (1975), 77–85.

La Patrie et la voie. Le Christ dans la vie et la pensée de saint Augustin. Paris, 1989.

'Le Christ des païens d'après le *De consensu euangelistarum* de saint Augustin'. *Recherches augustiniennes* 26 (1992), 3–67.

Introduction aux 'Révisions' et à la lecture des œuvres de saint Augustin. Paris, 1996.

Maier, F. *Augustin und das antike Rom.* Stuttgart, 1955.

Maier, J.-L. ed. *Le Dossier du donatisme.* 2 vols. Berlin, 1987, 1989.

Mainberger, G. *Rhetorica I. Reden mit Vernunft, Aristoteles, Cicero, Augustinus.* Stuttgart, 1987.

Mandouze, A. 'Saint Augustin et la religion romaine'. *Recherches augustiniennes* 1 (1958), 187–223.

'A propos de *sacramentum* chez saint Augustin. Polyvalence lexicologique et foisonnement théologique'. *Mélanges offerts à Mademoiselle Christine Mohrmann.* ed. L. Engles et al. Utrecht, 1963, 222–32.

Mandouze, A. ed. *Prosopographie chrétienne du Bas-Empire.* vol. 1: *Prosopographie de l'Afrique chrétienne (303–533).* Paris, 1982.

Markus, R. 'Bonifatius comes Africae'. *Augustinus-Lexikon.* vol. 1. ed. C. Mayer. Basle, 1986–94, 653–5.

Saeculum: History and Society in the Theology of St Augustine. 2nd edn. Cambridge, 1989.

The End of Ancient Christianity. Cambridge, 1990.

'Augustine on Magic: A Neglected Semiotic Theory'. *Revue des études augustiniennes* 40 (1994), 375–88.

Markus, R. ed. *Augustine: A Collection of Critical Essays.* New York, 1972.

Marrou, H.-I. 'La Théologie de l'histoire'. *Augustinus Magister. Congrès International Augustinien.* vol. 3. Paris, 1954, 193–204.

'Civitas Dei, civitas terrena, num tertium quid?' *Studia Patristica. Papers presented to the Second International Conference in Patristic Studies held at Christ Church, Oxford.* vol. 2. ed. K. Aland and F. L. Cross. Berlin, 1957, 342–50.

Saint Augustin et la fin de la culture antique. 4th edn. Paris, 1958.

Marrou, H.-I. and La Bonnardière A.-M. 'Le Dogme de la résurrection des corps et la théologie des valeurs humaines selon l'enseignement de saint Augustin'. *Revue des études augustiniennes* 12 (1966), 111–36.

Martain, P. 'Une conversion au Ve s.: Volusien'. *Revue augustinienne* 10 (1907), 145–72.

Martin, J. *Antike Rhetorik. Technik und Methode*. Munich, 1974.

Martindale, J. R. *A Prosopography of the Later Roman Empire*. vol. 2: *A.D. 395–527*. Cambridge, 1980.

Mason, J. *Philosophical Rhetoric: The Function of Indirection in Philosophical Writing*. London, 1989.

Mastandrea, P. 'll "dossier Longiniano" nell'epistolario di sant'Agostino (epist. 233–235)'. *Studia patavina* 25 (1978), 523–40.

Matthews, G. 'The Inner Man'. *American Philosophical Quarterly* 4 (1967), 166–72.

Matthews, J. *Western Aristocracies and Imperial Court: A.D. 364–425*. Oxford, 1975.

Mausbach, J. *Die Ethik des heiligen Augustinus*. 2 vols. 2nd edn. Freiburg, 1929.

Mayer, C. *Die Zeichen in der geistigen Entwicklung und in der Theologie des jungen Augustinus*. Würzburg, 1969.

Die Zeichen in der geistigen Entwicklung und in der Theologie Augustins II: Die antimanichäische Epoche. Würzburg, 1974.

'Allegoria'. *Augustinus-Lexikon*. vol. 1. ed. C. Mayer. Basle, 1986–94, 233–9.

'Caro-spiritus'. *Augustinus-Lexikon*. vol. 1. ed. C. Mayer. Basle, 1986–94, 743–59.

'Congruentia testamentorum'. *Augustinus-Lexikon*. vol. 1. ed. C. Mayer. Basle, 1986–94, 1195–1201.

'"Pietas" und "vera pietas quae caritas est"'. Zwei Kernfragen der Auseinandersetzung Augustins mit der heidnischen Antike'. *Augustiniana Traiectina. Communications présentées au Colloque International d'Utrecht 13–14 novembre 1986*. ed. J. den Boeft and J. van Oort. Paris, 1987, 119–36.

Merkel, H. 'Gerechtigkeit. IV'. *Theologische Realenzyklopädie*. vol. 12. ed. G. Krause and G. Müller. Berlin, 1984, 420–4.

Michel, A. *Rhétorique et philosophie chez Cicéron. Essai sur les fondements philosophiques de l'art de persuader*. Paris, 1960.

'A propos de l'art du dialogue dans le *de republica*: l'idéal et la réalité chez Cicéron'. *Revue des études latines* 43 (1965), 237–261.

Milbank, J. *Theology and Social Theory: Beyond Secular Reason*. Oxford, 1990.

Miles, M. *Augustine on the Body*. Missoula, 1979.

'Corpus'. *Augustinus-Lexikon*. vol. 2. ed. C. Mayer. Basle, 1996–2002, 6–20.

Miotti, M. '*De beata vita* di Agostino. Rapporto con il V libro delle *Tusculanae Disputationes* di Cicerone'. *Scritti offerti a R. Iacoangeli*. ed. S. Felici. Rome, 1992, 203–25.

Mohrmann, C. 'Sacramentum dans les plus anciens textes chrétiens'. *Harvard Theological Review* 47 (1954), 141–52.

Etudes sur le latin des chrétiens. 2nd edn. Rome, 1962.

Montcheuil, Y. de. 'L'Hypothèse de l'état originel d'ignorance et de difficulté d'après le *De libero arbitrio* de saint Augustin'. *Bulletin de littérature ecclésiastique* 23 (1933), 197–221.

Moreau, M. 'Le Dossier Marcellinus dans la correspondance d'Augustin'. *Recherches augustiniennes* 9 (1973), 5–181.

Morgenstern, F. *Die Briefpartner des Augustinus von Hippo. Prosopographische, sozial- und ideologie-geschichtliche Untersuchungen.* Bochum, 1993.

Mratschek, S. *Der Briefwechsel des Paulinus von Nola. Kommunikation und soziale Kontakte zwischen christlichen Intellektuellen.* Göttingen, 2002.

Müller, C. *Geschichtsbewußtsein bei Augustinus. Ontologische, anthropologische und universalgeschichtlich/heilsgeschichtliche Elemente einer augustinischen 'Geschichtstheorie'.* Würzburg, 1993.

Nash, R. *The Word of God and the Mind of Man: The Crisis of Revealed Truth in Contemporary Theology.* Grand Rapids, 1982.

Niebuhr, R. *Christian Realism and Political Problems.* New York, 1953.

North, H. 'Canons and Hierarchies of the Cardinal Virtues in Greek and Latin Literature'. *The Classical Tradition: Literary and Historical Studies in Honor of Harry Caplan.* ed. L. Wallach. Ithaca, 1966, 165–83.

Nuvolone, F. and A. Solignac, 'Pélage et pélagianisme'. *Dictionnaire de spiritualité.* vol. 12:2. ed. A. Rayez et al. Paris, 1986, 2889–942.

O'Connell, R. *St. Augustine's Early Theory of Man, A.D. 386–391.* Cambridge, Mass., 1968.

Art and the Christian Intelligence in St. Augustine. Oxford, 1978.

O'Daly, G. P. *Augustine's Philosophy of Mind.* London, 1987.

Augustine's City of God: *A Reader's Guide.* Oxford, 1999.

'Thinking through History: Augustine's Method in the *City of God* and its Ciceronian Dimension'. *History, Apocalypse and the Secular Imagination: New Essays on Augustine's* City of God. ed. M. Vessey et al. Bowling Green, 1999, 45–57.

O'Donovan, O. *The Problem of Self-Love in St. Augustine.* New Haven, 1980.

'Augustine's *City of God* xix and Western Political Thought'. *Dionysius* 11 (1987), 89–110.

O'Meara, J. *Porphyry's Philosophy from Oracles in Augustine.* Paris, 1959.

Charter of Christendom: The Significance of the City of God. New York, 1961.

Oort, J. van. *Jerusalem and Babylon: A Study into Augustine's* City of God *and the Sources of his Doctrine of the Two Cities.* Leiden, 1991.

Oroz Reta, J. *San Agustín y la cultura clásica.* Salamanca, 1963.

Paschoud, F. *Roma aeterna. Etudes sur le patriotisme romain dans l'occident latin à l'époque des grandes invasions.* Rome, 1967.

Pépin, J. 'Saint Augustin et la fonction protreptique de l'allégorie'. *Recherches augustiniennes* 1 (1958), 243–86.

Mythe et allégorie: Les Origines grecques et les contestations judéo-chrétiennes. 2nd edn. Paris, 1976.

'Influences païennes sur l'angelologie et la démonologie de saint Augustin'. *'Ex Platonicorum persona'. Etudes sur les lectures philosophiques de saint Augustin.* Amsterdam, 1977, 29–37.

Perler, O. and J.-L. Maier, *Les Voyages de saint Augustin.* Paris, 1969.

Pétrè, H. *Caritas. Etude sur le vocabulaire latin de la charité chétienne.* Louvain, 1948.

Philips, G. 'L'Influence du Christ Chef sur son corps mystique, suivant Saint Augustin'. *Augustinus Magister. Congrès international augustinien.* vol. 2. Paris, 1954–5, 805–15.

Piccaluga, G. *Elementi spettacolari nei rituali festivi romani.* Rome, 1965.

'Fides nella religione romana di età imperiale'. *Aufstieg und Niedergang der römischen Welt.* vol. 2.17.2. ed. W. Haase. Berlin, 1981, 703–35.

'*Ius* e *vera iustitia* (Lact. *div. inst.* VI 9,7). Rielaborazione cristiana di un valore assoluto della religione romana arcaica'. *L'etica cristiana nei secoli III e IV: Eredità e confronti. Atti del XXIV Incontro di studiosi dell'antichità cristiana, Roma, 4–6 maggio 1995.* Rome, 1996, 257–69.

Pietri, C. et al. eds. *Prosopographie chrétienne du bas-empire.* vol. 2: *Italie (313–604).* Part 1: *A–K.* Rome, 1999.

Piscitelli Carpino, T. *Paolino di Nola: Epistole ad Agostino.* Naples, 1989.

Pizzolato, L. *Capitoli di retorica agostiniana.* Rome, 1994.

Plagnieux, J. 'Influence de la lutte antipélagienne sur le "De trinitate" ou: Christocentrisme de saint Augustin'. *Augustinus Magister. Congrès international augustinien, Paris, 21–24 septembre 1954,* vol. 2 (Paris, 1954), 817–26.

'Le Binome *iustitia-potentia* dans la Sotériologie augustinienne et anselmienne'. *Spicilegium beccense* 1 (1959), 141–54.

Plumpe, J. 'Mors secunda'. *Mélanges De Ghellinck.* vol. 1: *Antiquité.* Gembloux, 1951, 387–403.

Pollmann, K. *Doctrina christiana. Untersuchungen zu den Anfängen der christlichen Hermeneutik unter besonderer Berücksichtigung von Augustinus, De doctrina christiana.* Fribourg, 1996.

'Augustins Transformation der traditionellen römischen Staats- und Geschichtsauffassung (Buch I–V)'. *Augustinus. De civitate dei.* ed. C. Horn. Berlin, 1997, 25–40.

Pontet, M. *L'Exégèse de saint Augustin prédicateur.* Paris, 1945.

Poque, S. 'L'Echo des événements de l'été 413 à Carthage dans la prédication de saint Augustin'. *Homo spiritalis. Festgabe für Luc Verheijen zu seinem 70. Geburtstag.* ed. C. Mayer. Würzburg, 1987, 391–9.

Porro, P. 'La morte, il tempo, il linguaggio: in margine al XIII libro del *De civitate dei*'. *Interiorità e intentionalità nel* De civitate dei *di Sant'Agostino.* ed. R. Piccolomini. Rome, 1991, 121–31.

Pöschl, V. 'Augustinus und die römische Geschichtsauffassung'. *Augustinus Magister. Congrès international augustinien.* vol. 2. Paris, 1954–5, 957–63.

Prete, B. 'I principi esegetici di s. Agostino'. *Sapienza* 8 (1966), 552–94.

Primmer, A. 'The Function of the genera dicendi in De doctrina christiana 4'. *De Doctrina Christiana: A Classic of Western Culture.* ed. D. W. H. Arnold and P. Bright. Notre Dame, 1995, 68–86.

Przybylski, B. *Righteousness in Matthew and his World of Thought.* Cambridge, 1980.

Quinot, B. 'L'Influence de l'Epître aux Hébreux dans la notion augustinienne du vrai sacrifice'. *Revue des études augustiniennes* 8 (1962), 129–68.

Rahner, H. *Griechische Mythen in christlicher Deutung.* 3rd edn. Zurich, 1966.

Ramsey, B. 'Two Traditions on Lying and Deception in the Ancient Church'. *The Thomist* 49 (1985), 504–33.

Raveau, T. 'Adversus Iudaeos. Antisemitismus bei Augustinus?' *Signum pietatis. Festgabe für Cornelius P. Mayer OSA, zum 60 Geburtstag.* ed. A. Zumkeller. Würzburg, 1989, 37–51.

Rebillard, E. *In hora mortis. Evolution de la pastorale chrétienne de la mort aux IVe et Ve siècles.* Rome, 1994.

'Augustin et le rituel épistolaire de l'élite sociale et culturelle de son temps. Eléments pour une analyse processuelle des relations de l'évêque et de la cité dans l'antiquité tardive'. *L'Evêque dans la cité du IVe au Ve siècle. Image et autorité,* ed. E. Rebillard and C. Sotinel. Rome, 1998, 127–52.

'Sociologie de la déviance et orthodoxie. Le cas de la controverse pélagienne sur la grâce'. *Orthodoxie, christianisme, histoire / Orthodoxy, Christianity, History: travaux du groupe de recherches 'Définir, maintenir et remettre en cause l'"orthodoxie" dans l'histoire du christianisme'.* ed. S. Elm et al. Rome, 2000, 221–40.

Rees, B. *The Letters of Pelagius and his Followers.* Woodbridge, Suffolk, 1991.

Refoulé, F. 'Datation du premier concile de Carthage contre les Pélagiens et du *Libellus fidei* de Rufin'. *Revue des Etudes augustiniennes* 9 (1963), 41–9.

Remy, G. *Le Christ médiateur dans l'œuvre de saint Augustin.* 2 vols. Lille, 1979.

Reveillaud, M. 'Le Christ-Homme, tête de l'Eglise. Etudes d'ecclésiologie selon les *Enarrationes in Psalmos* d'Augustin'. *Recherches augustiniennes* 5 (1968), 67–94.

Reynolds, L. D. ed. *Texts and Transmission: A Survey of the Latin Classics.* Oxford, 1983.

Richards, I. A. *The Philosophy of Rhetoric.* Oxford, 1964.

Ricoeur, P. *The Conflict of Interpretations: Essays in Hermeneutics.* ed. D. Ihde, Evanston, 1974.

Rist, J. *Augustine: Ancient Thought Baptized.* 2nd edn. Cambridge, 1995.

Rivera de Ventosa, E. 'El factor ético en la visión agustiniana de la historia de Roma'. *La Ciudad de Dios* 186 (1973), 333–54.

Rives, J. *Religion and Authority in Roman Carthage from Augustus to Constantine.* Oxford, 1995.

Rivière, J. 'Hétérodoxie des Pélagiens en fait de rédemption?' *Revue d'histoire ecclésiastique* 41 (1946), 5–43.

Rordorf, W. *Der Sonntag. Geschichte des Ruhe- und Gottesdiensttages im ältesten Christentum.* Zurich, 1962.

'Die theologische Bedeutung des Sonntags bei Augustin. Tradition und Erneuerung'. *Der Sonntag. Ansprung – Wirklichkeit – Gestalt. Festschrift Jacob Baumgartner.* ed. A. Altermatt and T. Schnitker. Würzburg, 1986, 30–43.

Ruokanen, M. *Theology of Social Life in Augustine's De civitate dei.* Göttingen, 1993.

'Augustine's Theological Criticism of Politics'. *Studia Patristica. Papers presented at the Twelfth International Conference of Patristic Studies held in Oxford 1995.*

vol. 33:16: *Augustine and his Opponents*. ed. E. Livingstone. Leuven, 1997, 236–8.

Ruppert, L. *Jesus als der leidende Gerechte? Der Weg Jesu im Lichte eines alt- und zwischentestamentlichen Motivs*. Stuttgart, 1972.

Rutherford, I. 'Decorum 1. Rhetorik'. *Historisches Wörterbuch der Rhetorik*. vol. 2. ed. G. Veding et al. Darmstadt, 1994, 423–34.

Sánchez, E. 'El comentario de Ambrosio y Augustín sobre la perícopa de la adúltera (Jn 7, 55–8, 11). Parte primera: los materiales ambrosiano y agustiniano. Parte segunda: análisis comparativo'. *Augustinus* 46 (2001), 291–344, 47 (2002), 155–84.

Schaffner, O. *Christliche Demut. Des hl. Augustinus Lehre von der Humilitas*. Würzburg, 1959.

Scheid, J. *Religion et piété à Rome*. Paris, 1985.

'The Priest'. *The Romans*. ed. A. Giardina. Chicago, 1993, 55–84.

Schindler, A. *Wort und Analogie in Augustins Trinitätslehre*. Tübingen, 1965.

Schmidt, P. 'Cicero *De re publica*: Die Forschung der letzten fünf Dezennien'. *Aufstieg und Niedergang der römischen Welt*. vol. 1:4. ed. H. Temporini. Berlin, 1973, 262–333.

Schofield, M. 'Cicero's Definition of *Res Publica*'. *Cicero the Philosopher*. ed. J. G. F. Powell. Oxford, 1995, 63–83.

'Two Stoic Approaches to Justice'. *Justice and Generosity: Studies in Hellenistic Social and Political Philosophy. Proceedings of the Sixth Symposium Hellenisticum*. ed. A. Laks and M. Schofield. Cambridge, 1995, 191–212.

Schumacher, L. 'Die vier hohen römischen Priesterkollegien unter den Flaviern, den Antoninen, und den Severern (69–235 n. Chr.)'. *Aufstieg und Niedergang der römischen Welt*. vol. 2:16.1. ed. W. Haase. Berlin, 1978, 655–819.

Sheridan, M. '*Digne deo*: A Traditional Greek Principle of Interpretation in Latin Dress'. *L'esegesi dei padri latini. Dalle origini a Gregorio Magno. Atti del XXVIII Incontro di studiosi dell'antichità cristiana, Roma, 6–8 maggio 1999*. vol. 1: *Parte generale – Oriente, Africa*. Rome, 2000, 23–40.

Sider, R. *Ancient Rhetoric and the Art of Tertullian*. Oxford, 1971.

Siniscalco, P. 'Christum narrare et dilectionem monere'. *Augustinianum* 14 (1974), 605–23.

Smith, A. *Porphyry's Place in the Neoplatonic Tradition*. The Hague, 1974.

'Porphyrian Studies since 1913'. *Aufstieg und Niedergang der römischen Welt*. vol. 2.36.2. ed. W. Haase. Berlin, 1987, 717–73.

Solignac, A. 'Analyse et sources de la question "De ideis"'. *Augustinus Magister. Congrès international augustinien, Paris, 21–24 septembre 1954*. vol. 1. Paris, 1954, 307–15.

'Homme intérieur. Augustin'. *Dictionnaire de spiritualité*. vol. 7:1. ed. A. Rayez et al. Paris, 1969, 655–8.

'Passions et vie spirituelle'. *Dictionnaire de spiritualité*. vol. 12. ed. A. Rayez and C. Baumgartner. Paris, 1983, 345–7.

Souter, A. ed. *Pelagius's Expositions of Thirteen Epistles of St Paul*. Cambridge, 1922.

Stahl, W. H. *Macrobius: Commentary on the Dream of Scipio*. New York, 1952.

Stark, R. 'Ciceros Staatsdefinition'. *Das Staatsdenken der Römer*. ed. R. Klein. Darmstadt, 1980.

Stierle, K. 'Geschichte als exemplum – exemplum als Geschichte. Zur Pragmatik und Poetik narratives Text'. *Geschichte, Ereignis und Erzählung*. ed. R. Koselleck and W. D. Stempel. Munich, 1973, 347–75.

Strasburger, H. 'Optimates'. *Paulys Real-Encyclopädie der klassischen Altertumswissenschaft*. vol. 18:1. Stuttgart, 1939, 773–98.

Strauss, G. *Schriftgebrauch, Schriftauslegung und Schriftbeweis bei Augustin*. Tübingen, 1959.

Straw, C. '*Timor mortis*'. *Augustine through the Ages: An Encyclopedia*. ed. A. Fitzgerald et al. Grand Rapids, 1999, 838–42.

Studer, B. '*Sacramentum et exemplum* chez saint Augustin'. *Recherches augustiniennes* 10 (1975), 87–141.

'Zur Christologie Augustins'. *Augustinianum* 19:3 (1979), 539–46.

'Das Opfer Christi nach Augustins *De civitate dei* x, 5–6'. *Lex orandi – lex credendi. Miscellanea P. Vagaggini*. Ed. G. Békés and G. Farnedi. Rome, 1980, 93–107.

'Le Christ, notre justice, selon saint Augustin'. *Recherches augustiniennes* 15 (1980), 99–143.

'*Delectare et prodesse*. Zu einem Schlüsselwort der patristischen Exegese'. *Mémorial J. Gribomont*. Rome, 1988, 555–81.

'*Delectare et prodesse*, ein exegetisch-homiletisches Prinzip bei Augustinus'. *Signum pietatis. Festgabe für Cornelius Petrus Mayer zum 60. Geburtstag*. ed. A. Zumkeller. Würzburg, 1989, 497–513.

'La *cognitio historialis* di Porfirio nel *De ciuitate dei* di Agostino (*ciu.* 10, 32)'. *La narrativa cristiana antica. Atti del XXIII Incontro di studiosi dell'antichità cristiana, Roma 5–7 maggio 1994*. Rome, 1995, 520–53.

The Grace of Christ and the Grace of God in Augustine of Hippo: Christocentrism or Theocentricism, tr. M. J. O'Connell. Collegeville, 1997.

Suerbaum, W. *Vom antiken zum frühmittelalterlichen Staatsbegriff. Über Verwendung und Bedeutung von res publica, regnum, imperium und status von Cicero bis Jordanis*. 3rd edn. Münster, 1977.

'Studienbibliographie zu Ciceros De re publica'. *Gymnasium* 85 (1978), 59–88.

Swift, L. 'Lactantius and the Golden Age'. *American Journal of Philology* 89 (1968), 144–56.

'Defining "Gloria" in Augustine's *City of God*'. *Diakonia: Studies in Honor of R. T. Meyer*. ed. T. Halton. Washington, 1986, 133–44.

'Pagan and Christian Heroes in Augustine's *City of God*'. *Augustinianum* 27:3 (1987), 509–22.

Szemler, G. *The Priests of the Roman Republic: A Study of Interactions between Priesthoods and Magistracies*. Brussels, 1972.

'Priesthoods and Priestly Careers in Ancient Rome'. *Aufstieg und Niedergang der römischen Welt*. vol. 2:16.3. ed. W. Haase, Berlin, 1986, 2314–31.

TeSelle, E. *Augustine the Theologian*. New York, 1970.

'Rufinus the Syrian, Caelestius, Pelagius: Explorations in the Prehistory of the Pelagian Controversy'. *Augustinian Studies* 3 (1972), 61–95.

'Credere'. *Augustinus-Lexikon*. vol. 2. ed. C. Mayer. Basle, 1996–2002, 119–31.

'Fides'. *Augustinus-Lexikon*. vol. 2. ed. C. Mayer. Basle, 1996–2002, 1333–40.

Testard, M. *Saint Augustin et Cicéron*. vol. 1: *Cicéron dans la formation et dans l'œuvre de saint* Augustin. vol. 2: *Répertoire des textes*. Paris, 1958.

Thonnard, F.-J. 'Justice de Dieu et justice humaine selon s. Augustin'. *Augustinus* 12 (1967), 387–402.

'Le Don d'intégrité et l'état de justice originelle'. *Œuvres de saint Augustin*. vol. 23: *Premières polémiques contre Julien*. ed. F.-J. Thonnard et al. Paris, 1974, 717–21.

Thraede, K. 'Euhemerismus'. *Reallexikon für Antike und Christentum*. vol. 6. ed. T. Klauser. Stuttgart, 1966, 877–90.

'Das antike Rom in Augustins De ciuitate dei. Recht und Grenzen eines verjährten Themas'. *Jahrbuch für Antike und Christentum* 20 (1977), 90–145.

Tilley, M. 'Sustaining Donatist Self-Identity: From the Church of the Martyrs to the *Collecta* of the Desert'. *Journal of Early Christian Studies* 5:1 (1997), 21–35.

Trapè, A. and G. Beschin. eds. *Sant'Agostino. La Trinità*. Rome, 1973.

Trout, D. 'Re-Textualizing Lucretia: Cultural Subversion in the *City of God*'. *Journal of Early Christian Studies* 2:1 (1994), 53–70.

Paulinus of Nola: Life, Letters, and Poems. Berkeley, 1999.

Ulrich, T. *Pietas (pius) als politischer Begriff im römischen Staate bis zum Tode des Kaisers Commodus*. Breslau, 1930.

Valenti, M. *L'Ethique stoïcienne chez Cicéron*. Paris, 1956.

Valero, J. *Las bases antropológicas de Pelagio en su tratado de las* Expositiones. Madrid, 1980.

'El estoicismo de Pelagio'. *Estudios eclesiasticos* 57 (1982), 39–63.

Velasquez, J. '*Gloriosissimam civitatem dei*. Algunas consideraciones en torno a *gloria*'. *Augustinus* 31 (1986), 285–9.

Vermeulen, A. *The Semantic Development of Gloria in Early-Christian Latin*. Nijmegen, 1956.

Verwilghen, A. *Christologie et spiritualité selon saint Augustin. L'Hymne aux Philippiens*. Paris, 1985.

Vessey, M. et al. eds. *History, Apocalypse and the Secular Imagination: New Essay on Augustine's* City of God. Bowling Green, 1999.

Wallraff, M. *Christus verus sol. Sonnenverehrung und Christentum in der Spätantike*. Münster, 2001.

Wang Tch'ang Tche, J. *Saint Augustin et les vertus des païens*. Paris, 1938.

Wardman, A. *Religion and Statecraft among the Romans*. London, 1982.

Waszink, J. 'Varro, Livy and Tertullian on the History of Roman Dramatic Art'. *Vigiliae christianae* 2 (1948), 224–42.

Weismann, W. *Kirche und Schauspiele. Die Schauspiele im Urteil der lateinischen Kirchenväter unter besonderer Berücksichtigung von Augustin*. Würzburg, 1972.

Wermelinger, O. *Rom und Pelagius. Die theologische Position der römischen Bischöfe im pelagianischen Streit in den Jahren 411–432.* Stuttgart, 1975.

'Le Canon des Latins au temps de Jérôme et d'Augustin'. *Le Canon de l'Ancien Testament. Sa formation et son histoire.* ed. J.-D. Kästli and O. Wermelinger. Geneva, 1984, 153–210.

'Neuere Forschungskontroversen um Augustinus und Pelagius'. *Internationales Symposium über den Stand der Augustinus-Forschung.* ed. C. Mayer and K. H. Chelius. Würzburg, 1989, 189–217.

'Demetrias'. *Augustinus-Lexikon.* vol. 2. ed. C. Mayer. Basle, 1996–2002, 289–91.

Wetzel, J. *Augustine and the Limits of Virtue.* Cambridge, 1992.

'Pelagius Anticipated: Grace and Election in Augustine's *Ad Simplicianum*'. *Augustine from Rhetor to Theologian.* ed. J. McWilliam. Waterloo, 1992, 121–32.

Wickert, L. 'Neue Forschung zum römischen Prinzipat'. *Aufstieg und Niedergang der römischen Welt.* vol. 2:1. ed. H. Temporini. Berlin/New York, 1974, 3–76.

Williams, R. 'Politics and the Soul: A Reading of the *City of God*'. *Milltown Studies* 19/20 (1987), 55–72.

'*Sapientia* and the Trinity: Reflections on the *De trinitate*'. *Collectanea augustiniana. Mélanges T. van Bavel.* ed. B. Bruning et al. Leuven, 1990, 316–32.

Wissowa, G. *Religion und Kultus der Römer.* 2nd edn. Munich, 1912.

Wood, N. *Cicero's Social and Political Thought.* Berkeley, 1988.

Young, F. *The Art of Performance: Towards a Theology of Holy Scriptures.* London, 1990.

Zetzel, J. E. G. *Cicero. De re publica: Selections.* Cambridge, 1995.

Ziesler, J. *The Meaning of Righteousness in Paul.* Cambridge, 1972.

Index of references to Augustine's works

Index of persons and subjects

DATE DUE